P9-DIW-996

BLACK'S NEW TESTAMENT COMMENTARIES

General Editor: Henry Chadwick, DD, FBA

THE SECOND EPISTLE TO THE CORINTHIANS

BLACK'S NEW TESTAMENT COMMENTARY

THE SECOND EPISTLE TO THE CORINTHIANS

C. K. BARRETT

HENDRICKSON PUBLISHERS
PEABODY, MASSACHUSETTS 01961-3473

First published 1973

A & C Black (Publishers) Limited, London

Hendrickson Publishers, Inc. Edition

ISBN 1-56563-021-1

Reprinted by arrangement with A & C Black (Publishers) Limited.

The mosaic fretwork on the cover comes from the Galla Placidia Mausoleum in Ravenna and is used courtesy of ITALCARDS, Bologna, Italy.

CONTENTS

PREFACE	*page* vi
ABBREVIATIONS	ix
INTRODUCTION	1
I Corinth	1
II Corinth after 1 Corinthians	5
III Special problems	21
IV Theology at Corinth	36
ANALYSIS OF THE EPISTLE	51
TRANSLATION AND COMMENTARY	53
INDEX OF NAMES AND SUBJECTS	347
INDEX OF GREEK WORDS AND PHRASES	353
INDEX OF ANCIENT SOURCES	355

PREFACE

With this book I complete my contribution to A. & C. Black's *New Testament Commentaries—Romans* (1957), *1 Corinthians* (1968), and now *2 Corinthians*. The writing of these commentaries has occupied what I suppose I must consider most of the best years of my life as a student of the New Testament; and I do not regret a minute of it—though I should like to be able to go back and write *Romans* again now. From the discipline of exegesis I have learnt method; and from Paul himself, I hope, to understand the Christian faith. Like most people, I sometimes wonder if Christianity is true; but I think I never doubt that, if it is true, it is truest in the form it took with Paul, and, after him, with such interpreters of his as Augustine, Luther, Calvin, Barth. And, as I read them, and especially Paul himself, conviction returns, and, though problems may abound, grace abounds much more.

In the commentary on this (in more senses than one) highly controversial epistle I have quoted other writers fairly freely; even so there are books I have found helpful which have not made their way into the text. I think, for example, of Karl Prümm's huge book *Diakonia Pneumatos* (1960, 1962); of small and practical (but not superficial) books like those of Walter Lüthi (*Der Apostel*; no date, based on sermons preached between 16 October 1958 and 24 July 1960) and Gerhard Friedrich (*Amt und Lebensführung*; 1963); of A. Q. Morton and J. McLeman, *St Paul, the Man and the Myth* (1966), and E. Dinkler's article in the third edition of *Die Religion in Geschichte und Gegenwart* (iv. 17-23); of W. Bousset's commentary in *Die Schriften des Neuen Testaments* (third edition, 1917). Two books which appeared too late to be noticed as they deserve call for special mention here: H. D. Betz, *Der Apostel Paulus und die sokratische Tradition* (1972), and J. F. Collange, *Énigmes de la deuxième Épître de Paul aux Corinthiens* (1972). Dr Betz's book, which deals mainly with the later part of the epistle, I have been able to quote fairly frequently on particular points, though I have not been able to state or discuss its theme as I should wish. A few references to Dr Collange's book, which deals with ii. 14–vii. 4, have been inserted, but their paucity must not be taken as representing my estimate of its worth. To the authors whom I do quote, to not a few whom I do not quote, and by no means least to those I disagree with, I am under deep obligation, and hope that they will accept my thanks—and forgive me, if I have misunderstood and so misrepresented them.

Paul's Christian agony, more perceptible in 2 Corinthians than in any other epistle, had more causes than one. He was obliged to view the corruption and seduction of the church that he had betrothed as a pure virgin to Christ. It was not simply that in practice and in doctrine they committed errors; their criteria for distinguishing between right and wrong, truth and falsehood, good and evil, were twisted. He was obliged to recognize that the point of origin from which Christianity was disseminated into the world had come to be a source of perversion. Satan, disguised as an angel of light, was sending out his servants in the guise of ministers of righteousness, of Christ. The church of Christ, so far from being an indefectible witness to truth, bore a lie at its heart. More than that, and most grievous of all, he found himself in these circumstances obliged in the interests of wisdom to play the fool, in the interests of good to do what was evil. He, first of all Christians, experienced the perpetual dilemma of the church: 'Sin stands in the midst of the Kingdom of Christ, and wherever the Kingdom is, there is sin; for Christ has set sin in the House of David'.[1] Confronted by a church convinced of its own rectitude and dominance he had to use weapons he would not have chosen and arguments that did not satisfy him, and, unlike the Corinthians, he knew what he was doing: 'as deceivers, yet true men'. Writing 2 Corinthians must have come near to breaking Paul, and (as I hinted in the Preface to *1 Corinthians*) a church that is prepared to read it with him, and understand it, may find itself broken too. Yet an earthenware vessel that contains such treasure need not fear breaking; it is the apostolic vocation to carry about the killing

[1] Luther, quoted by K. Barth, *The Epistle to the Romans* (E.T., 1933), p. 263.

of Jesus, and those who accept it are apt to find the funeral transformed into a triumph, as they learn to trust not in themselves but in him who raises the dead. 'Alles Vergängliche ist nur ein Gleichnis'; the forms of the church and of Christian existence belong to the world of the visible and transient, not the invisible and eternal. Yet it is well that they should be a true parable rather than a false, that tribulation should be real tribulation, and comfort real comfort.

C. K. BARRETT

Durham

ABBREVIATIONS

Adam	C. K. Barrett, *From First Adam to Last*, 1962.
Allo	E. B. Allo, *Saint Paul: Seconde Épître aux Corinthiens* (*Études Bibliques*), 1956.
Bachmann	P. Bachmann, *Der zweite Brief des Paulus an die Korinther*, third edition, 1918.
Background	C. K. Barrett (ed.), *The New Testament Background: Selected Documents*, 1956.
Barth, *C.D.*	K. Barth, *Church Dogmatics*, 1936–1969.
Bauer[1]	W. Bauer, *Griechisch-Deutsches Wörterbuch zu den Schriften des Neuen Testaments und der übrigen urchristlichen Literatur*, 1952.
B.D.[2]	F. Blass, *Grammatik des neutestamentlichen Griechisch*, revised by A. Debrunner, 1949.
Beginnings V	*The Beginnings of Christianity, Part I*, edited by F. J. F. Jackson and K. Lake; Volume V, edited by K. Lake and H. J. Cadbury, 1933.
Bengel	J. A. Bengel, *Gnomon Novi Testamenti*, 1862.
Benoit, I, II	P. Benoit, *Exégèse et Théologie*, two volumes, 1961.
Betz	H. D. Betz, *Der Apostel Paulus und die sokratische Tradition*, 1972.
Betz, *Lukian*	H. D. Betz, *Lukian von Samosata* (*Texte und Untersuchungen*, 76), 1961.
Beyer	K. Beyer, *Semitische Syntax im Neuen Testament I 1*, 1962.
Black, *Scrolls*	M. Black, *The Scrolls and Christian Origins*, 1961.
Bonsirven, *Ex.*	J. Bonsirven, *Exégèse rabbinique et Exégèse paulinienne*, 1939.
Bornkamm ii	G. Bornkamm, *Studien zu Antike und Urchristentum, Gesammelte Aufsätze II*, 1959.
Bornkamm, 'Vorgeschichte'	G. Bornkamm, 'Die Vorgeschichte des sogenannten Zweiten Korintherbriefes', in *Sitzungsberichte der Heidelberger Akademie der Wissenschaften, Phil.-hist. Klasse*, 1961: 2.[3]
Bousset-Gressmann	W. Bousset, *Die Religion des Judentums im*

[1] See also the English edition by W. F. Arndt and F. W. Gingrich (1957).

[2] The same paragraph references apply to the English edition by R. W. Funk (1961).

[3] There is a shorter English version of this paper in *N.T.S.* viii. 258–64.

	späthellenistischen Zeitalter, third edition by H. Gressmann, 1926.
Braun	H. Braun, 'Qumran und das Neue Testament', in *Theologische Rundschau* N.F. 29.3 (1963), reprinted separately, 1966.
Bultmann, *Exeg.*	R. Bultmann, *Exegetica*, edited by E. Dinkler, 1967.
Bultmann, *E. & F.*	R. Bultmann, *Existence and Faith*, edited by S. M. Ogden, 1961 (paperback, 1964).
Bultmann, *Probleme*	R. Bultmann, *Exegetische Probleme des zweiten Korintherbriefes* (*Symbolae Biblicae Upsalienses, 9*), 1947.
Bultmann, *Theol.*	R. Bultmann, *Theologie des Neuen Testaments*, 1948–1953; E. T.: *Theology of the New Testament*, 1965.
Calvin	J. Calvin, *The Second Epistle of Paul the Apostle to the Corinthians and the Epistles to Timothy, Titus and Philemon*, translated by T. A. Smail, 1964.
C.A.H.	*The Cambridge Ancient History.*
'Cephas and Corinth'	C. K. Barrett, 'Cephas and Corinth', in *Abraham unser Vater, Festschrift für Otto Michel* (ed. O. Betz, M. Hengel, P. Schmidt), 1963, pp. 1–12.
Cerfaux, *Christ*	L. Cerfaux, *Le Christ dans la Théologie de Saint Paul*, 1951; E.T.: *Christ in the Theology of Saint Paul*, 1959.
'Christianity at Corinth'	C. K. Barrett, 'Christianity at Corinth', in *Bulletin of the John Rylands Library* xlvi (1964), pp. 269–97.
Collange	J. F. Collange, *Énigmes de la deuxième Épître aux Corinthiens*, 1972.
Conzelmann, *Theologie*	H. Conzelmann, *Grundriss der Theologie des Neuen Testaments*, 1967.
1 Corinthians	C. K. Barrett, *A Commentary on the First Epistle to the Corinthians* (Black's New Testament Commentaries), 1968.
W. D. Davies	W. D. Davies, *Paul and Rabbinic Judaism*, 1948.
W. D. Davies, *C.O.J.*	W. D. Davies, *Christian Origins and Judaism*, 1962.
Denney	J. Denney, *The Second Epistle to the Corinthians* (Expositor's Bible), 1894.
Dibelius	M. Dibelius, *Paulus*, completed by W. G. Kümmel, 1951.
Dinkler	E. Dinkler, *Signum Crucis*, 1967.
Dodd, *A.S.*	C. H. Dodd, *According to the Scriptures*, 1952.

Dodd, *B.G.*	C. H. Dodd, *The Bible and the Greeks*, 1935.
Dodd, *Studies*	C. H. Dodd, *New Testament Studies*, 1953.
E.T.	English Translation.
'False Apostles'	C. K. Barrett, '*ΨΕΥΔΑΠΟΣΤΟΛΟΙ* (2 Cor. 11.13)', in *Mélanges Bibliques en hommage au R. P. Béda Rigaux* (ed. A. Descamps and A. de Halleux), 1970.
Friedrich, 'Gegner'	G. Friedrich, 'Die Gegner des Paulus im 2. Korintherbrief', in *Abraham unser Vater* (see above), pp. 181–215.
Georgi, *Gegner*	D. Georgi, *Die Gegner des Paulus im 2. Korintherbrief*, 1964.
Georgi, *Kollekte*	D. Georgi, *Die Geschichte der Kollekte des Paulus für Jerusalem*, 1965.
Goppelt	L. Goppelt, *Christentum und Judentum im ersten und zweiten Jahrhundert*, 1954.
Goudge	H. L. Goudge, *The Second Epistle to the Corinthians* (Westminster Commentaries), 1927.
Güttgemans	E. Güttgemans, *Der leidende Apostel und sein Herr*, 1966.
Hatch, *Essays*	E. Hatch, *Essays in Biblical Greek*, 1889.
Héring	J. Héring, *La Seconde Épître de Saint Paul aux Corinthiens* (Commentaire du Nouveau Testament VIII), 1958; E.T.: 1967.
Hughes	P. E. Hughes, *Paul's Second Epistle to the Corinthians*, 1962.
J.T.S.	*Journal of Theological Studies.*
Käsemann I	E. Käsemann, *Exegetische Versuche und Besinnungen*, Erster Band, 1960; E.T.: *Essays on New Testament Themes*, 1964.
Käsemann II	E. Käsemann, *Exegetische Versuche und Besinnungen*, Zweiter Band, 1964; E.T.: *New Testament Questions of Today*, 1969.
Käsemann, *Freiheit*	E. Käsemann, *Der Ruf der Freiheit*, 1972 (Endgültige Fassung); E.T.: *Jesus means Freedom*, 1969.
Käsemann, 'Legitimität'	E. Käsemann, 'Die Legitimität des Apostels', in *Z.N.T.W.* xli (1942), pp. 33–71; reprinted as a separate work, 1956.
Kasting	H. Kasting, *Die Anfänge der urchristlichen Mission*, 1969.
Knox, *H.E.*	W. L. Knox, *Some Hellenistic Elements in Primitive Christianity* (Schweich Lectures, 1942), 1944.
Knox, *P.G.*	W. L. Knox, *St Paul and the Church of the Gentiles*, 1939.
Kümmel	See Lietzmann.

Kümmel, *Introduction*	W. G. Kümmel, *Introduction to the New Testament*, 1966.
Kümmel, *Theologie*	W. G. Kümmel, *Die Theologie des Neuen Testaments*, 1969.
L.S.	H. G. Liddell and R. Scott, *A Greek–English Lexicon*, new edition by H. S. Jones and R. McKenzie, n.d.
Lietzmann	H. Lietzmann, *An die Korinther I, II* (Handbuch zum Neuen Testament 9), fifth edition with supplements by W. G. Kümmel, 1969.
Lindars	B. Lindars, *New Testament Apologetic*, 1961.
T. W. Manson, *P. & J.*	T. W. Manson, *On Paul and John*, 1963.
Moule, *Birth*	C. F. D. Moule, *The Birth of the New Testament*, 1962.
Moule, *Idiom*	C. F. D. Moule, *An Idiom Book of New Testament Greek*, 1953.
M. i	J. H. Moulton, *A Grammar of New Testament Greek*, Volume I, Prolegomena, 1908.
M. ii	The Same: Volume II, Accidence and Word-Formation, by J. H. Moulton and W. F. Howard, 1929.
M. iii	The Same: Volume III, Syntax, by N. Turner, 1963.
M.M.	J. H. Moulton and G. Milligan, *The Vocabulary of the Greek Testament*, 1914–1929.
Munck, *Paulus*	J. Munck, *Paulus und die Heilsgeschichte*, 1954; E.T.: *Paul and the Salvation of Mankind*, 1959.
New Testament Essays	C. K. Barrett, *New Testament Essays*, 1972.
N.T.S.	*New Testament Studies.*
Nickle, *Collection*	K. F. Nickle, *The Collection*, 1966.
Nov. T.	*Novum Testamentum.*
O.G.I.S.	W. Dittenberger, *Orientis Graeci Inscriptiones Selectae*, 1903, 1905.
P. & Q.	J. Murphy-O'Connor (ed.), *Paul and Qumran*, 1968.
'Paul's Opponents'	C. K. Barrett, 'Paul's Opponents in II Corinthians', in *N.T.S.* xvii (1971), pp. 233–54.
Plummer	A. Plummer, *A Critical and Exegetical Commentary on the Second Epistle of Saint Paul to the Corinthians* (International Critical Commentary), 1915.
Radermacher	L. Radermacher, *Neutestamentliche Grammatik* (Handbuch zum Neuen Testament 1), 1911.

Reicke, *Diakonie*	B. Reicke, *Diakonie, Festfreude und Zelos*, 1951.
Richardson, *Theology*	A. Richardson, *An Introduction to the Theology of the New Testament*, 1958.
Rissi	M. Rissi, *Studien zum zweiten Korintherbrief*, 1969.
Robertson	A. T. Robertson, *A Grammar of the Greek New Testament in the Light of Historical Research*, 1919.
Romans	C. K. Barrett, *A Commentary on the Epistle to the Romans* (Black's New Testament Commentaries), 1962.
Schlatter	A. Schlatter, *Paulus der Bote Jesu*, 1962.
Schmithals	W. Schmithals, *Die Gnosis in Korinth*, 1956.
Schoeps, *Paulus*	H. J. Schoeps, *Paulus*, 1959; E.T.: *Paul*, 1961.
Schoeps, *T.G.J.*	H. J. Schoeps, *Theologie und Geschichte des Judenchristentums*, 1949.
Schürer	E. Schürer, *The Jewish People in the Time of Jesus Christ*, 1885–1896.
Schweizer, *Beiträge*	E. Schweizer, *Beiträge zur Theologie des Neuen Testaments*, 1970.
Schweizer, *C.O.N.T.*	E. Schweizer, *Church Order in the New Testament*, 1961.
S.J.T.	*Scottish Journal of Theology*.
Sevenster, *Seneca*	J. N. Sevenster, *Paul and Seneca*, 1961.
Signs	C. K. Barrett, *The Signs of an Apostle*, 1970.
Singer	S. Singer (tr.), *The Authorised Daily Prayer Book of the United Hebrew Congregations of the British Empire*, 1912.
Stauffer, *Theol.*	E. Stauffer, *Die Theologie des Neuen Testaments*, 1945; E.T.: *New Testament Theology*, 1955.
Strachan	R. H. Strachan, *The Second Epistle of Paul to the Corinthians* (Moffatt New Testament Commentary), 1946.
S.B.	H. L. Strack and P. Billerbeck, *Kommentar zum Neuen Testament aus Talmud und Midrasch*, 1922–1961.
Studia Paulina	*Studia Paulina in honorem J. de Zwaan* (ed. J. N. Sevenster and W. C. van Unnik), 1953.
St. Th.	*Studia Theologica*.
Stuhlmacher, *Gerechtigkeit*	P. Stuhlmacher, *Gerechtigkeit Gottes bei Paulus*, 1965.
Syll.	W. Dittenberger, *Sylloge Inscriptionum Graecarum*, 1915, 1917, 1920, 1924.
'The Injury'	C. K. Barrett, ''*Ο 'ΑΔΙΚΗΣΑΣ* (2 Cor. 7.12)', in *Verborum Veritas: Festschrift für*

	Gustav Stählin (ed. O. Böcher and K. Haacker), 1970, pp. 149–57.
T.W.N.T.	*Theologisches Wörterbuch zum Neuen Testament*, ed. by G. Kittel and G. Friedrich, 1933– .[1]
Thrall	M. E. Thrall, *Greek Particles in the New Testament*, 1962.
'Titus'	C. K. Barrett, 'Titus', in *Neotestamentica et Semitica: Studies in Honour of Matthew Black* (ed. E. E. Ellis and M. Wilcox), pp. 1–14.
Turner, *Insights*	N. Turner, *Grammatical Insights into the New Testament*, 1965.
J. Weiss, *History*	J. Weiss, *The History of Primitive Christianity* (completed by R. Knopf), 1937.
Wendland	H. D. Wendland, *Die Briefe an die Korinther* (Das Neue Testament Deutsch 7), 1946.
Wilckens, *Weisheit*	U. Wilckens, *Weisheit und Torheit*, 1959.
Windisch	H. Windisch, *Der Zweite Korintherbrief* (Kritisch-exegetischer Kommentar über das Neue Testament—Meyer), 1924.
Z.N.T.W.	*Zeitschrift für die neutestamentliche Wissenschaft und die Kunde der älteren Kirche.*

Note: The usual sigla are employed for New Testament manuscripts and versions. They are explained in all good editions of the Greek New Testament.

[1] An English translation is in progress (Grand Rapids, Michigan: Eerdmans).

INTRODUCTION

I. Corinth[1]

Corinth was situated at the south-western extremity of the isthmus that connects the mainland of Greece with the Peloponnese. It was part of a complex that included, one and a half miles to the north, Lechaeum on the Gulf of Corinth, and, seven and a quarter miles to the east, Cenchreae on the Saronic Gulf (Rom. xvi. 1). The region was not fertile, but its economic advantages were great. It controlled the land route between north and south, and also acted as a land link, indispensable until the cutting of the Corinth Canal (begun but given up by Nero, and only completed in 1893), in the sea route between east and west. From time to time this control of the portage of ships had military significance;[2] it must constantly have been important in commerce, and as early as Homer the phrase 'wealthy Corinth' occurs (*Iliad*, ii. 570; cf. xiii. 664). The plain in which Corinth is situated is dominated by the hill which served as acropolis to the city, Acrocorinth, rising to 1857 feet. Economic and military advantages combined in favour of Corinth,[3] and it is not surprising that it reached a position of eminence in the ancient world; it is perhaps surprising that it never achieved preeminence.

In 146 B.C. a sharp line is drawn through the history of Corinth, when Rome brought the Achaean League to an end. After the decisive engagement at Leucopetra, on the Isthmus, the consul Lucius Mummius was able to occupy Corinth without a blow. The citizens were killed, or sold into slavery; the city itself was levelled

[1] This section is based on, and to a great extent reproduces, *1 Corinthians*, pp. 1–5.

[2] See e.g. Thucydides viii. 7: The Spartans sent off three full citizens (*Spartiatae*) to Corinth in order that when they had brought the boats over the Isthmus as quickly as possible from the other sea to that by Athens they might order them all to sail to Chios.

[3] See e.g. Plutarch, *Aratus* XVI, XVII (1034): . . . Acrocorinth, a very high mountain, rising up out of the midst of Greece [that is, between the Peloponnese and the Epirus], when garrisoned, stands in the way and cuts off all the land within the Isthmus from commerce and passage and military campaigning, and prevents traffic both by land and by sea, and makes him who rules and holds the place with a garrison master. . . . The place has always been fought for by all, by kings and rulers . . . .

with the ground, and rebuilding was forbidden. The territory became public land of Rome, except part that was given to the neighbouring state of Sicyon, on the understanding that henceforward Sicyon, in place of Corinth, would maintain the Isthmian Games. After 100 years of desolation Corinth was refounded by Julius Caesar as a Roman colony.

New Corinth naturally possessed the topographical characteristics of the old city; otherwise it bore little relation to its predecessor. Today, the traveller can see little of the Greek city but half a dozen columns of the temple of Apollo; the Roman foundation is much better represented. But this was already substantially true in the time of Pausanias,[1] whose account contrasts the old with the new. For example, '... yearly sacrifices were instituted in their honour, and a figure of Terror (δεῖμα) erected. The latter still remains to our day ... But since the destruction of Corinth by the Romans and the disappearance of the ancient Corinthians the sacrifices are no longer performed by the colonists, nor do the children cut their hair or wear black clothes' (Pausanias, II iii. 7). The new settlers, to whom the traditions of Corinth meant little, were drawn from various parts of the Empire; many would be discharged soldiers. No doubt there were Greeks among them, but it is impossible to think of the Corinth of Paul's day as in any way distinctively Greek. That there were Jews in Corinth is shown by an inscription[2] consisting of the broken words '[Syn]agogue of the Hebr[ews]' (... ΑΓΩΓΗ ΕΒΡ ...), and probably part of the lintel of the door of the synagogue. The date of this inscription cannot be narrowly determined, but it gives sufficient confirmation to Acts xviii. 4 (he discoursed in the synagogue every Sabbath). New Corinth was thus a cosmopolitan city. The immoral reputation of old Corinth (words derived from the name Corinth seem to have been used in the Old Comedy with the meanings *to practise fornication*, *whoremonger*, and the like) may not be simply carried across a century; it cannot however be said that the new foundation went out of its way to redeem the past. In Paul's day, Corinth was probably little better and little worse than any other great sea port and commercial centre of the age.

It was probably not a lurid reputation that put Paul in terror when he first visited Corinth (1 Cor. ii. 3), but the sense of his

[1] G. Roux, *Pausanias en Corinthe* (1958), p. 29, gives 155 ± –170 ± as the date of Pausanias's second book, in which he describes Corinth.

[2] See *Background*, p. 50.

vocation and responsibility. He had nothing to preach but Christ crucified (1 Cor. ii. 2), and he had resolved to make no use of human arts in setting forth this theme (1 Cor. i. 17; ii. 1). Notwithstanding this (or perhaps, as Paul himself would have said, because of this) his preaching effected the conversion of many in Corinth. Paul had laid the only conceivable foundation for a Christian church—Jesus Christ himself (1 Cor. iii. 10 f.); others were to build upon this foundation, and the superstructure, as both epistles attest, turned out to be less satisfactory than the base on which it rested. This may have been due in part to the number and variety of the builders. Apollos undoubtedly worked in Corinth (1 Cor. iii. 6). It is probable but not quite certain that Peter did also.[1] As a result of this, and no doubt because of their own imperfectly Christianized contentiousness too, the church membership early showed a tendency to break down into groups, each appealing to the name of a Christian leader (1 Cor. i. 11 f.). Other blemishes had already marred Corinthian church life by the time 1 Corinthians was written. There were abuses of the Lord's Supper (1 Cor. xi. 18-22), a notorious case of immorality (1 Cor. v. 1-5), public litigation among the members (vi. 1-8), disputes over the legitimacy of eating food that had been sacrificed to idols (1 Cor. viii. 1-13; x. 14–xi. 1), and disagreements about the propriety of marriage (1 Cor. vii. 1-40) and the admissibility of sexual relations outside marriage (1 Cor. vi. 12-20). The Christian doctrine of resurrection appeared to have been denied (1 Cor. xv. 12), and Paul's apostleship questioned (1 Cor. iv. 3, 15; ix. 1 f.).

Meanwhile Paul had left Corinth, but had not been without contact with the church there. He had been informed of the existence of parties in the church by members of Chloe's household (1 Cor. i. 11). Stephanas, Fortunatus, and Achaicus had visited Paul, apparently as representatives of the church (1 Cor. xvi. 17 f.), and may have delivered the letter referred to in 1 Cor. vii. 1 (see the notes). 1 Cor. v. 9 (see the notes) shows that Paul had written a letter to Corinth. This 'Previous Letter', as it is often called, may have been entirely lost. For the view that some part or parts of it are to be found in 1 Corinthians, see *1 Corinthians*, pp. 12–17; for the view that part of it is contained in 2 Cor. vi. 14–vii. 1, see below, pp. 11 f., 14, 23 ff., 193 ff.

The story of Paul's dealings with Corinth up to the writing of

[1] See 1 Cor. ix. 5; also 'Cephas and Corinth'.

the First Epistle can thus be sketched on the basis of Paul's own certainly genuine writings alone. This forms an indispensable foundation. The story as told in Acts is, however, consistent with the sketch. According to Acts, Paul reached Corinth after his visit to Athens (Acts xviii. 1). He encountered Aquila and Priscilla (Acts xviii. 2 f.; cf. 1 Cor. xvi. 19, where the lady's name is Prisca), and made use of the synagogue, with greater freedom when Silas and Timothy joined him (Acts xviii. 4 f.). Difficulties with the Jews led to a mission directed more specifically to Gentiles (especially perhaps God-fearers, who stood between the synagogue and the Gentile world—cf. Acts xviii. 7, which shows Paul at work in the house of Titius Justus, a God-fearer), but the synagogue-ruler Crispus (cf. 1 Cor. i. 14) was converted (Acts xviii. 6 ff.). With divine encouragement, Paul continued his ministry for eighteen months. At this point (xviii. 12-17), Acts narrates the appearance of Paul before Gallio,[1] who was proconsul in charge of Achaea probably from summer A.D. 51. It is reasonable to infer (though the dates may be a year or so out) that Paul reached Corinth in about March 50, and stayed there till about September 51.

In due course Paul left Corinth for Syria (Acts xviii. 18), touched at Ephesus, with a promise to return (xviii. 19 ff.), and brought his so-called second journey to a close (xviii. 22 f.). Here Acts mentions Apollos, his instruction by Priscilla and Aquila, and his journey to Achaea, which almost certainly included a visit to Corinth (xviii. 24-8; also xix. 1). In Acts xix Paul is back in Ephesus, and his ministry there occupies Acts xix. 1–xx. 1, and lasted two years and three months (xix. 8, 10; xx. 31, *three years*, is not inconsistent with this). In the course of it Paul is said to have sent Timothy and Erastus into Macedonia (Acts xix. 22), while himself making plans for such a journey (xix. 21). These journeys may reasonably be taken to correspond with those mentioned in 1 Cor. xvi. 5, 10; if so, and as far as the chronology of Acts may be trusted, we have a fairly precise means of dating the First Epistle. Allowing for some time in Antioch, and for the journey through the 'upper region' (Acts xix. 1), Paul will have reached Ephesus again in the late summer of 52; the Pentecost he was anxious to spend in Jerusalem (xx. 16) will have been that of 55; the Pentecost of 1 Cor. xvi. 8 that of 53, or more probably 54. The most probable date for

[1] The dates of Gallio's proconsulship are given by an inscription found at Delphi; see *Background*, pp. 48 f., and *Romans*, pp. 4 f.

1 Corinthians is therefore in the early months of 54, or possibly towards the end of 53.

This argument for the dating of 1 Corinthians assumes the integrity of the epistle. If it is regarded as a composite document, made up of parts of two or more letters from Paul to Corinth, dating becomes a more complicated problem. The present volume is not the place for a discussion of the composition of 1 Corinthians, except in so far as this is involved in the analysis of 2 Corinthians. It is argued in *1 Corinthians* (especially pp. 12–17; also 116, 188 f., 199 f.) that the First Epistle is a unity, and this conclusion will be assumed here. We shall proceed to the discussion of the problems raised by 2 Corinthians on the assumption (which is indeed not certain, and must not be maintained dogmatically, but is in fact very probable), that Paul was in Corinth from spring 50 to autumn 51; that he wrote the Previous Letter not long afterwards (we may guess, in 52 or 53); and that he wrote 1 Corinthians, in substantially the form in which we read it today, at the end of 53, or more probably early in 54.

II. Corinth after 1 Corinthians

(a) What happened in Corinth after the writing of 1 Corinthians, and how Paul responded to it, what visits Paul and his colleagues made and what letters he wrote, what other visitors made their way to Corinth and what Paul thought of them, can be deduced only from 2 Corinthians itself. Acts, even if we could use it with unquestioning confidence in its historical trustworthiness, fails almost completely as a source of information. 2 Corinthians, moreover, our only source, presents us with a number of literary problems of great difficulty, and there is serious danger of arguing in a circle—from historical reconstruction to literary hypothesis, and from literary hypothesis back to historical reconstruction. The field is one in which theories are more numerous than facts, and clear distinctions between the two are not always made. It will, I hope, make for clarity in this as well as in other respects if I first set out the view of events, and of literary relationships, to which the writing of this commentary has led me, and then set out the facts in detail, mention other views (as far as space permits), and finally attempt to justify, in the light of the data and of alternative opinions, my own reconstruction. It must be clearly understood that the next few lines claim no authority beyond what inner consistency they may possess, and that any appearance of dogmatism is due solely to the attempt to achieve brevity and clarity. No one who has made a serious attempt to study the Corinthian situation is likely to feel convinced that he has a monopoly of truth.

Paul, then, wrote 1 Corinthians in the early months of A.D. 54, and presumably hoped that he had thereby settled the Corinthian problem, at least for the present. He was indeed not completely convinced of this; there was still a possibility that he might have to visit Corinth with a stick in his hand (1 Cor. iv. 21); but he was looking forward to a fairly long stay in Corinth (1 Cor. xvi. 5-9), during which he hoped to complete the collection for the poor saints in Jerusalem (1 Cor. xvi. 1-4). At the end of it, he might himself travel to Jerusalem with the Corinthian delegates.

This first epistle 'was not a successful document';[1] at least it was not wholly successful. Some points were perhaps disposed of. We hear of no more disputation about the resurrection, or the eating of food sacrificed to idols; references to *gnosis* and to wisdom become in 2 Corinthians much less common, and it may be that the gnostic threat[2] declined. But if Paul hoped to have no more trouble from the Corinthian church he was to be grievously disappointed, though it is fair to remark that the cause of the new troubles seems to have entered Corinth from without.

Very soon after 1 Corinthians had been written—possibly indeed before—Corinth was entered by a group of persons who gave themselves out to be, and were accepted as, Christian apostles, preeminent servants of Christ. In support of their claim they carried letters of commendation from the church of Jerusalem. Whether these documents were authorized by the 'Pillars' (Gal. ii. 9) we cannot be sure, but even if they were not it must have been easy for their bearers to claim that anything issuing from Jerusalem must have behind it the authority of the earliest group of apostles, who had known Jesus 'after the flesh'. These 'apostles' were not missionaries in the sense of men who penetrated the non-Christian world with the intention of winning to faith in Christ those who hitherto had not known him; they were apostles in the normal sense of the Hebrew word *shaliaḥ*, that is, they were agents of those who commissioned them; they were representatives of the church of Jerusalem, charged with the task of bringing into con-

[1] *1 Corinthians*, p. 5.

[2] See *1 Corinthians*, pp. 54 ff., and Index, s.vv. Gnostics, gnosticism, knowledge, γνῶσις.

nection (perhaps even, into obedience) to Jerusalem the churches that were springing up in the Gentile world. In this sense at least they were Judaizers; whether, like the Judaizers of Galatia, they demanded circumcision as well as a general respect for the law we cannot be sure; probably, since Paul does not mention the matter, they did not. It is more likely that they took their stand on some such summary of the law as the so-called Decree of Acts xv. 20, 29, or possibly on the Noachian Precepts.[1] They did not accept Paul's apostolic status; he carried no letter of commendation, and his Gospel of justification by faith only apart from works of the law was suspect. Perhaps not at first, but probably later, they described him as a false apostle (his own use of this term, in xi. 13, would then be a counterblast), lacking in qualification and authority. In contrast with him, they left the authority they claimed in no doubt, and behaved in an aggressive and authoritarian manner.

These men were already in occupation of the church in Corinth when Paul paid the visit he had announced in 1 Cor. xvi. 5 (cf. iv. 19 ff.). In this verse he expresses the intention of visiting Corinth when he passes through Macedonia on a preaching tour. That is, he proposed to go from Ephesus to Macedonia, to pass through, and so come to Corinth. It seems that he changed his plan, intending to give the Corinthians the pleasure of a double visit: he would go to Achaea first, proceed to Macedonia, and then return to Ephesus by way of Achaea. On this double visit he would (as announced in 1 Cor. xvi. 1-4) deal with the matter of the collection. These plans were upset by the unpleasant surprise Paul found awaiting him in Corinth. There was no happy reunion between father and children (iv. 14 f.); it was impossible to deal with the collection. How many 'pseudo-apostles' (the word Paul uses at xi. 13) were present we do not know; eventually there was a group of them. On this occasion one in particular took the lead in attacking and insulting Paul. The Corinthians, many of them probably quite sincerely puzzled by the quarrel, hardly knew what to do; at all events, they did not come to Paul's support as he would have liked them to do, though neither did they come out clearly on his assailant's side. The situation was, at least for the present, intolerable, and Paul set out for Macedonia and Ephesus, abandoning his plan to return through Corinth. A second visit at this time would have done (he supposed) no good, and would have

[1] See S.B. iii. 37 f.; also *Adam*, pp. 23–6.

led to recrimination and angry talk. It would be better to spare the Corinthians the rebuke he would have had to administer.

The situation was painful, but it was by no means hopeless, though the decision not to return through Achaea had proved to be mistaken in that it provided the occasion for the charge that Paul's behaviour was marked by fickleness; he did not keep his promises, but changed his plans at his own whim. It was necessary to rebuke the Corinthians for their disloyalty; but this could be done by letter. It was necessary also to carry out the plan for the collection; but this Titus, a trusted lieutenant, could do as well as Paul. Accordingly Paul wrote a letter to Corinth, and entrusted it to Titus. The letter cost him many tears; it was not easy to rebuke his own children. But they must grow up; they must learn how to appraise their servants, the apostles. Titus, who had not previously visited Corinth, accepted the commission. This must have been in about midsummer of 54. We have no reason to think that Paul did not adhere to his plan of staying in Ephesus until Pentecost (1 Cor. xvi. 8), or to suppose that he stayed much longer—indeed, he cannot have done so. It would not take many days to cross the Aegean, and the flare-up in Corinth may well have happened in early June.

Titus set off for Corinth, bearing a letter which has not survived, and Paul was left in a state of considerable anxiety. He was not greatly troubled about the Corinthians—they would come to their senses; but he was concerned about Titus, partly because he would have to deal with the intruding 'apostles', and partly because, if all went well, he would be carrying back to Paul a large sum of money, and none knew better than Paul the perils from robbers that beset, notwithstanding the *pax romana*, the traveller on ancient roads. He could not wait in Ephesus (where in any case there were troubles enough) but set out to meet Titus at Troas. His aim was not simply to meet Titus but also to evangelize in Troas, and a favourable evangelistic opportunity developed, which in other circumstances he would have been delighted to pursue; but he could have no peace till he had found Titus, and pushed on (whether by land or sea we do not know) into Macedonia. Here the two met, and Paul was cheered by the news Titus had to give. The Corinthians were entirely on Paul's side. His letter had hurt them, as he thought it would, but it had stung them to repentance, and they were now eager to show that they had always been loyal to him, though they had not shown it as effectively as they should have done. This they regretted. Moreover, they (or at least a majority of them) had resolved to punish the ringleader who had attacked Paul. It is true that the collection had not been completed, but a good beginning had been made, which Paul, in conversation with the Macedonians, perhaps exaggerated. But the main thing was that the Corinthians had come out on the right side, as Paul had boasted to Titus that they would.

Happy in the new situation Paul wrote a further letter to Corinth—his fourth. This is contained in 2 Corinthians i–ix. Like the severe letter, though in a different vein, it combined two purposes. The collection still had to be finished; Titus, assisted by two brothers, would complete the work he had begun. This was a matter that required careful handling, for Paul, who now used the example of the Macedonians to spur on the Corinthians, had previously used the example of the Corinthians to encourage the Macedonians, and was anxious lest Macedonians arriving in Corinth should find the work less advanced than they expected. There was also the general question of apostleship. The Corinthians were enthusiastic (so Titus had told him) on his behalf, and were set upon punishing the offender too severely; Paul restrained them. In a general atmosphere of penitence mutual love must be the key-word. Notwithstanding their enthusiasm and his confidence in their good intentions Paul, it seems, did not really trust the theological judgement of the Corinthians with regard to apostleship and the Gospel. Apostles were indeed their servants, and as Christians they had the responsibility of judging where the truth lay, but they needed (so we may deduce from 2 Cor. i–vii) a good deal of instruction in the criteria proper to apply to the question before them.

Titus and his two colleagues departed with the letter. Either through their discomfited return, or by some other means, Paul learned that Titus had misjudged and misrepresented the situation in Corinth—unless indeed it had radically altered as soon as he left the city. Not Paul but the intruding false apostles were in control. Their leader was now freely insulting the absent Paul, and the group claimed the Achaean mission field for the Jerusalem jurisdiction. The Corinthians had evolved their own criteria for testing the validity of apostolic claims, and these criteria the false apostles had been able to satisfy. Not only did they use their letters of commendation and behave with the utmost arrogance, they professed to enjoy visions and revelations, to possess knowledge, and to utter inspired speech. As for Paul, he might be able to write letters, but he was no speaker, his bodily presence was feeble and unimpressive, he did not exercise and therefore cannot have possessed the right to be supported by the church, and made up for this by stealing the money he professed to be collecting for the poor. In short, he counted for nothing; he had never known Christ, and Christ did not speak in him.

It is worth noting in passing that this situation brought into being a new kind of Christian Jew, originating in Jerusalem and attached to the law, but accommodating himself to the Hellenistic or gnosticizing criteria employed by Gentile Christians in Corinth. This development marks an important stage in the growth of Christian gnosticism.

Paul saw that the situation could be retrieved only by drastic action. He first wrote a letter, contained (wholly or in part) in 2 Cor. x–xiii. It is marked by an unflinching defence of his apostolic status and a further explanation of what he understood by apostleship, and by bitter ironical attacks upon the false apostles. It was a difficult letter to write, for Paul had three groups of persons to bear in mind: the false apostles, whom he was prepared to fight tooth and nail; the Jerusalem apostles, with whom he had no quarrel, though he was unimpressed by them, knew that he was their equal, and doubtless wished that they would plainly dissociate themselves from the false apostles; and the Corinthians, whom he saw to be in danger of being seduced from their loyalty not only to him but to Christ, but still loved as his extremely wayward children. In the letter he promised a third visit to Corinth; and this time he would not spare. However painful it might be to him or to others he would take the necessary action.

The letter was delivered (for it found its way into the Corinthian archives), and the visit took place. If we may accept the statement of Acts xx. 1 f., Paul travelled once more through Macedonia; he may have sent the letter across the Aegean by sea, so that it should arrive ahead of him. After the Macedonian journey Paul spent three months in Greece (Acts xx. 3), early in 55. What happened neither Acts nor Paul tells us, except that we learn from Rom. xv. 26 that Achaea contributed to the collection. From this we may infer that Paul succeeded in dealing with as difficult and dangerous a situation as he had ever faced.

One further note may be made here. Less than twelve months cover the writing of 1 Corinthians and both parts of 2 Corinthians; it is unlikely that any notable development in Paul's thought took place in this short space.[1]

(b) The above account of the events between the writing of 1 Corinthians and Paul's third visit to Corinth passes by a number of notorious literary and historical problems, and in stating one view of the events in question omits all reference to others, some of which are widely held. I shall first take up literary problems and theories.

2 Corinthians contains a number of passages where the reader cannot fail to be struck by a measure of discontinuity or awkwardness in the text. The most important are the following.

(1) ii. 13, 14; vii. 4, 5. Each pair of verses makes a hard transition, but ii. 13 and vii. 5 would connect well. In ii. 12 f. Paul describes his anxious wait for Titus and the news he hoped he would bring from Corinth. He would not wait in Ephesus, but moved on to Troas. There was a good opportunity for evangelism in Troas, but Paul could not bring himself to take it up, but continued his journey to Macedonia. At this point he breaks off the narrative of his anxious movements, and breaks out in praise to God: But thanks be to God, who goes always at our head in a triumphal progress in Christ. In vii. 2 f. Paul pleads with the Corinthians to make a friendly response to him, but in verse 5 he takes up his journey in Macedonia; even there he had no relief from his anxiety until God comforted him by the coming of Titus. In the light of these facts it is natural to suggest that ii. 14–vii. 4 was interpolated into a document which originally ran on from ii. 13 to vii. 5, and described without interruption or digression Paul's anxiety as he hoped for Titus's return.

(2) vi. 13, 14; vii, 1, 2. Again a pair of discontinuities may seem to conceal a broken connection. In vi. 11 ff. Paul begs the Corinthians to respond to his affection for them; in vii. 2 f. he repeats his plea. But at vi. 14, and in the following verses up to vii. 1, he warns them sharply of the necessity of a clean break with the world. It is natural to suggest that vi. 14–vii. 1 is an interpolation (an interpolation within an interpolation, if the view of ii. 14–vii. 4 just mentioned is accepted).

[1] The dates suggested here are close to those adopted in the recent discussion of Pauline chronology by S. Dockx, in *Nov.T.* xiii, pp. 261–304.

(3) Chapters viii and ix. In chapter viii Paul begins abruptly to speak about the collection he had undertaken for the poor Christians in Jerusalem. There is nothing odd in this abruptness; the matter had to be introduced at some stage. In this chapter, however, Paul not only exhorts the Corinthians to generosity by the example of their brethren in Macedonia and the theological motivation provided by the grace of our Lord Jesus Christ (viii. 9) but also communicates detailed plans, including a mission by Titus and two brothers; he then continues (ix. 1), Concerning the service to the saints it is superfluous for me to write to you, and provides a new scriptural argument in favour of generous contributions (ix. 7, 9 f.). 'It is easy to see that the collection is introduced in ix. 1 as if there had been no previous mention of it. Chapter viii, therefore, cannot have preceded it; chapter ix must be attached to chapter vii, and chapter viii is an entirely independent document with its conclusion cut off. It is a letter of commendation for Titus and two unnamed brethren to the church at Corinth. It must have been composed before the dispute between Paul and the church. For in viii. 7 he praises the church's wealth in faith and utterance and all earnestness and in love to Paul in a more unconstrained way than would have been at all possible during the quarrel or even after its settlement.'[1]

(4) Chapters x–xiii. No reader of 2 Corinthians can fail to observe the sharp break between ix. 15 (Thanks be to God for his unspeakable gift!) and the opening words of chapter x, in which Paul, alluding to unfavourable opinions of him current in Corinth, warns his readers of the confident boldness he will show in correcting them. That there is an abrupt change of mood and temper is denied by no one; and not a few take the view that chapters i–ix and chapters x–xiii must be drawn from two (or more) different letters.

So much for the data. Hypotheses based upon them, and differing from that set out in II (a) above, have already been hinted at, and may now be described more fully.

The simplest form of a very common reconstruction of Paul's correspondence simply reverses the order of chapters i–ix, and x–xiii. It is certain that Paul wrote to Corinth a painful, or severe, letter, which cost him many tears (2 Cor. ii. 4; vii. 8-12). Few students today find this letter in 1 Corinthians, which hardly fits

[1] J. Weiss, *History*, i. 353.

the description Paul himself gives; the view under consideration finds it, or part of it, in chapters x–xiii. These chapters cannot have been easy to write, and may well have caused pain to their readers. It was after sending this letter that Paul received good news from Titus; he then wrote chapters i–ix, expressing his gladness and relief. This hypothesis is supported by pairs of passages, in which the later letter (i–ix) is thought to refer back, in a different tone, to passages in the earlier (x–xiii). Such are—

x. 2: . . . that confident boldness (πεποίθησις) which I think I shall dare to use . . .	viii. 22: . . . great confidence (πεποίθησις) in you.
x. 6: . . . ready to punish every disobedience when your own obedience (ὑπακοή) is perfect.	ii. 9: I wrote to you to find out how you would stand the test, whether you were obedient (ὑπήκοοι) in all things.
xii. 1-5: Paul was caught up to heaven.	v. 13: If we are beside ourselves . . .
xii. 16: Confidence trickster (πανοῦργος) as I was I caught you by craftiness.	iv. 2: We do not practise knavery (πανουργία).
xii. 17: Did I defraud (πλεονεκτεῖν) you?	vii. 2: We defrauded (πλεονεκτεῖν) no one.
xiii. 2: If I come for another visit I shall not spare (φείδεσθαι) them.	i. 23: It was with the intention of sparing (φείδεσθαι) you that I did not come again.
xiii. 10: The reason why, in my absence from you, I am writing these things is that I may not, when present, exercise severity.	ii. 3: I wrote to just this effect, that I might not come and be caused sorrow.

To these may be added what are said to be plain contradictions on the view that they belong to the same letter:

xiii. 5: Examine yourselves, to see whether you are in the faith.	i. 24: It is by faith that you stand.
xii. 20 f.: I am afraid lest, when I come, I should find you not such men as I desire, . . . and I should mourn for many . . .	vii. 16: I am glad that I have every confidence in you.

This simple hypothesis, which reverses the order of chapters i–ix and x–xiii, and finds in the latter section the 'Severe Letter' (or part of it), has been given two further degrees of complication.

In the first of these it is recognized that vi. 14–vii. 1 interrupts Paul's appeal, and it is taken to be an interpolation. Most of those who have held this view have believed the interpolated passage to have been part of the 'Previous Letter'.[1] According to 1 Cor. v. 9 f. Paul had written a letter to Corinth which the Corinthians had misunderstood, supposing Paul to have meant that they must have no contact whatever with any immoral person—in Corinth, an impossible requirement. 2 Cor. vi. 14–vii. 1 does in fact call for separation between the church and the world, though in truth it is scarcely open to the kind of misinterpretation which the 'Previous Letter' received. More recently, parallels have been pointed out[2] between vi. 14–vii. 1 and the Qumran literature, and it has been suggested that this paragraph is a stray piece of Qumran material which has been incorporated in Paul's text.

The second stage of development in the analysis of 2 Corinthians is based on the awkward connections at ii. 13, 14; vii. 4, 5, and the apparent link between ii. 13 and vii. 5. It is suggested that ii. 14–vii. 4 is an interpolation—or rather, that ii. 14–vi. 13; vii. 2-4 is an interpolation, vi. 14–vii. 1 being a further interpolation within the interpolation. The main interpolation is usually combined with x–xiii as the 'Severe Letter'.

At this point the separation of chapters viii and ix, mentioned above, should be recalled. As we have seen, J. Weiss regarded viii as an interpolation, and believed that chapter ix should be connected with vii; others think both viii and ix to have been originally separate notes, not connected with any of the major parts of 2 Corinthians.

Finally, it should be noted that the unity and integrity of 2 Corinthians have not been without defenders. See especially W. G. Kümmel, quoted below (pp. 17 f.); also Hughes (especially pp. xxi–xxxv), and W. H. Bates, 'The Integrity of II Corinthians', *N.T.S.* xii, pp. 56–69.

(c) Corresponding to, and partly overlapping with, the literary

[1] See *1 Corinthians*, pp. 4, 130, and Index s.v.

[2] See J. Gnilka, '2 Cor. vi. 14–vii. 1 in the light of the Qumran texts and the Testaments of the Twelve Patriarchs', in *P. and Q.*, pp. 48–68; J. A. Fitzmyer, 'Qumran and the interpolated paragraph in 2 Cor. vi. 14–vii. 1', in *Essays on the Semitic Background of the New Testament* (1971), pp. 205–17.

problems and theories that have now been sketched is a set of historical problems and theories. The main historical notices in the epistle will now be collected, and a few theories alternative to that outlined above (II (a)) will be sketched. The questions raised by the verses referred to are, in most cases, brought out more fully in the commentary.

i. 8: it is interesting to ask what troubles befell Paul in Asia, but the question is not strictly relevant to the unravelling of Paul's relations with Corinth.

i. 15 f.: Paul had intended to pay a double visit to Corinth, calling there on his way to Macedonia, and again on his way back.

i. 23: in fact he forbore to pay the second visit, in order to spare the Corinthians.

ii. 1-4: he did not visit Corinth because he did not wish to hurt the Corinthians, but instead wrote a letter, shedding many tears.

ii. 5-11: there is someone who has caused pain, not to Paul only but in some measure to the whole church. The majority of the Corinthians have resolved on censure for this man, but he should now be forgiven. If the Corinthians forgive him, so does Paul.

ii. 12 f.: Paul came to Troas to preach the Gospel, but was anxious because he did not find Titus there, and set off to Macedonia to meet him.

ii. 17: there are many who adulterate the word of God.

iii. 1: unlike others, Paul does not need commendatory letters.

vii. 5 ff.: eventually, in Macedonia, Paul did meet Titus, and was comforted not only by his presence but by the good news he brought of the Corinthian attitude to their apostle.

vii. 8-12: this was the result of the letter Paul had written. It had hurt the Corinthians, but to good effect; they now defended themselves, and showed that they were innocent. Paul had not written, he explains, on behalf either of the man who committed injury or the man who received it, but precisely in order to give the Corinthians an opportunity of manifesting this attitude.

vii. 13-16: Paul had boasted to Titus about the Corinthians, and their response had vindicated his boasting.

viii. 1–24: Paul sends Titus and two brothers to complete the collection. Titus had already made a beginning, and the Corinthians had shown willingness 'last year'.

ix. 1-15: further appeal for the collection.

x. 1–11: Paul has been vigorously attacked, as cowardly, unspiritual, and ineffectual—except on paper. He threatens a visit, which will prove the contrary.

x. 12: there are others, who boast in themselves.

xi. 1-4: the Corinthians are in danger of being perverted by a false Gospel, preached by some who came to Corinth from elsewhere.

xi. 5: Paul refers to 'super-apostles', to whom he is not inferior.

xi. 7-11: Paul has offended the Corinthians by preaching the Gospel for nothing, yet accepting support from other churches.

xi. 12-15: the church at Corinth has been invaded by false apostles, who, though disguised, are in fact servants of Satan.

xi. 20: the Corinthians put up with 'apostles' who bully them.

xi. 23-33: Paul's earlier adventures, including the escape from Damascus, are not relevant to the reconstruction of events in and relating to Corinth.

xii. 2-10: nor are his rapture to the third heaven, and his prayer for the removal of the thorn in his flesh.

xii. 13: cf. xi. 7-11.

xii. 14: Paul is now ready to come a third time to Corinth.

xii. 16 ff.: Paul was accused of having robbed the Corinthians under cover of his collection.

xii. 20 f.: Paul fears that on his next visit he will find the Corinthians not what he would wish, and that they too may be surprised to find him other than they supposed.

xiii. 1: Paul is coming a third time to Corinth.

Perhaps the most common reconstruction of the events alluded to in these passages is the following. It is given in the words of J. Weiss,[1] which continue the quotation in *1 Corinthians*, pp. 13 f.

(7) Timothy brings bad news from Corinth.

(8) Paul goes to Corinth, the 'intermediate journey', with disastrous result.

(9) A hasty departure—perhaps through Macedonia to Troas—with the promise to return.

(10) Instead, the vehement 'intervening letter' (C): 2 Cor. ii. 14–vi. 13; viii. 2 ff.; chapters x–xiii.

(11) After the arrival of the 'intervening letter', the coming

[1] *History*, i. 357.

of Titus in person, who had in the interval been in Macedonia. He received the commission to substantiate the success of the letter at Corinth and to announce this to Paul at Troas.

(12) Paul hastens to join him in Macedonia, meets him there, and writes the last letter (D): 2 Cor. i. 1.–ii. 13; vii. 5-16; ix.

(13) Paul travels with the 'Macedonians' to Corinth (Acts xx. 2).

This reconstruction of events is bound up with the analysis of the letter described above (pp. 11–14), and the literary and historical hypotheses stand or fall together. Some features of the historical reconstruction are indeed so plainly based upon texts in the epistle that they are hardly open to doubt. Paul must have paid a second ('intermediate') visit to Corinth; he did send Titus; there were unfortunate events in Corinth, culminating in an injury, probably to Paul himself. Much still remains open, however, to speculation.

A somewhat different view, depending on the belief that 2 Corinthians is a unity, is given by W. G. Kümmel, and again it will be best to quote:[1]

> The sending of Timothy to Corinth (1 Cor. iv. 17; xvi. 10) seems to have had no complete success; rather, Timothy probably brought with him bad reports out of Corinth. Even 1 Corinthians had not lastingly established Paul's authority. Then Paul, perhaps soon after 1 Corinthians, crossed over from Ephesus to Corinth, in order to create order. But he experienced a great disappointment. The visit to the church, which was close to open revolt against him, caused him deep sorrow, especially an injustice which a Corinthian inflicted upon him, and which the church permitted to happen. He did not succeed in becoming master of the situation. In displeasure and sadness he broke off the visit and returned to Ephesus, but promised to come again to Corinth soon. Whereas he abstained from this new visit out of consideration for the Corinthians, he won Titus to the task of restoring order to the church, and gave to him a stern epistle, the 'Epistle of Tears'. Under the eyes of Titus a sudden change took place in Corinth. The majority of the congregation submitted and repented of their insubordinate behavior. Paul, full of unrest, traveled to meet Titus and joined him in

[1] *Introduction*, p. 210.

> Macedonia. The good success of the mission filled him with joy and contentment. Immediately he sent Titus once again to Corinth, in order energetically to bring the business of the collection to its end before his own arrival in Corinth. . . . Paul gave to Titus 2 Corinthians as a harbinger of his own coming (2 Cor. xii. 20; xiii. 2).

There is naturally much that is common to this reconstruction and to Weiss's, common also to that which was sketched in II (a). Some of the most important points of difference will now be discussed in II (d).

(d) All attempts to analyse 2 Corinthians and to trace out the record of Paul's dealings with the church stand or fall by the exegesis of the relevant parts of the epistle. So far as space permits these are fully discussed in the body of the commentary, and it would be wrong to reproduce all this exegesis in the Introduction. The following discussion will take up some of the crucial points; for detail reference must be made to the commentary, and to some of the special notes in the Introduction (III (b) (c) (d)).

The initial problem that confronts the student who would reconstruct the events that lie behind 2 Corinthians is that the literary and historical questions cannot be separated from each other. If one could be settled first, the solution of the other would be greatly facilitated; but this cannot be done. Grant certain literary hypotheses, and historical conclusions follow almost if not quite of necessity; assume a certain sequence of events, and one is more or less committed to a corresponding view of the literary phenomena. For this reason, the only satisfactory way to approach the problem of 2 Corinthians is to fasten upon particular questions and view them from both sides, the literary and the historical, in as great detail as possible. In this Introduction it is possible only to refer to a few articles in which this has been attempted;[1] to go into the same detail here would unduly expand this Introduction, reproduce the articles, and also reduplicate a quantity of material which is better placed in the commentary on the text. It will be better to concentrate on the role of Titus, a vital issue in all attempts to reconstruct the Corinthian history.

It can be safely assumed, and is very seldom disputed, that after writing 1 Corinthians Paul paid a sorrowful visit to Corinth, and

[1] See 'Christianity at Corinth'; 'Cephas and Corinth'; 'Titus'; 'False Apostles'; 'The Injury'.

wrote a sorrowful letter. It is equally clear that Titus, who is not referred to in 1 Corinthians, was later brought into the arrangements, and had something to do with the organizing and carrying out of the collection (III (b)). But what exactly was Titus's function?

The view of Weiss is that Titus was first sent to Corinth to observe and report on the effect of the Severe, or Sorrowful, Letter. A variant of this view is that Titus himself conveyed the letter, but according to Weiss this 'seems to be excluded by 2 Cor. vii. 15, for the insubordinate church cannot have felt "fear and trembling" in the presence of the bearer of a letter even before they had read the letter' (op. cit. p. 345). It was with the news he had been commissioned to bring, and with the inquiry whether Paul was now satisfied by the punishment already inflicted on the offender, that Titus travelled to meet Paul. 'In the greatest suspense, Paul waited for him in Asia, and travelled as far as Troas to meet him (2 Cor. ii. 12 f.). Then, when he found that he had not yet arrived there, he went on further to Macedonia (vii. 5), until finally Titus arrived with good news' (ibid.). It was after this that Paul wrote the final, peaceful letter (consisting, according to Weiss, of i. 1–ii. 13; vii. 5-16; ix). 2 Cor. viii belonged to an earlier occasion, and commended Titus and two unnamed brothers to Corinth before the dispute between Paul and the church. This occasion Weiss puts very early indeed. 'The sending of Titus must have taken place before the return of Timothy with bad news, presumably also even before the arrival of the household of Chloe (1 Cor. i. 11) with the information about the party disputes' (op. cit. p. 353). It was the spontaneous enthusiasm of the Macedonians that 'prompted [Paul] to press the matter with renewed zeal in Corinth. . . . [The Corinthians] had already a year ago, earlier than the Macedonians, made a beginning not only to "will", but also to "do" (viii. 10). They should now carry out their program to completion (viii. 11)' (op. cit. p. 355). In this way Weiss seeks to avoid the difficulty created by xii. 17 f. on the view that x–xiii is part of the Severe Letter. Here 'Paul refers to the sending, either contemporary or past, of Titus and of the brother on the business of the collection for the saints, that is, to the incident of chapter viii where this mission has just been despatched' (op. cit. p. 353).

This is a very ingenious combination of literary and historical hypotheses, but it is not wholly convincing. It is not possible to put Titus's first collection-making visit before 1 Cor. xvi. 1–4, for there not only is he not mentioned, Paul seems to be giving the first instructions in response to a Corinthian inquiry (see *1 Corinthians*, p. 385). This observation explains another problem that Weiss glosses over. In 2 Cor. viii. 10 Paul does not say that the Corinthians made a beginning not only to 'will' but also to 'do'; he says, surprisingly, that they made a beginning not only to 'do' but also to 'will'. For the explanation of this, see the notes; it underlines the fact that the original Corinthian participation had been spontaneous. The first sending of Titus on collection business was after Paul's sorrowful visit, and quite probably as bearer of the sorrowful letter (see below, and 'Titus', pp. 9–13). Only on this view do the various notices of Titus's work fit together; and it has important consequences. It means that the sorrowful visit was not as sorrowful as is sometimes thought; the Corinthians had failed to come out in support of Paul as they should have done, but they had not yet abandoned him in favour of the false apostles. Paul had not lost confidence in them, or he would not have sent Titus to make a collection, and would certainly not have boasted to his colleague about them (vii. 14). It makes sense of Paul's account of his journey to Troas and of his meeting with Titus in Macedonia. It is not correct to describe Paul as consumed with anxiety about his standing with the Corinthian church, unable to wait for news in Ephesus, moving on to Troas to hear the sooner about Corinthian reactions, and finally pressing on to Macedonia for the same reason. Paul went to Troas to proclaim the Gospel of Christ (ii. 12), that is, in the execution of his evangelistic work. Only he had hoped to see Titus at Troas and was worried because he did not find him there; but it was primarily Titus that he was worried about—partly because he hoped that Titus would be carrying with him a quantity of money that would make him a prey to robbers. Correspondingly he was comforted by the arrival of Titus (vii. 6); also, indeed, additionally, by the comfort Titus had enjoyed 'among you' (vii. 7). This was an extra, though Paul was delighted to learn that his boasting about the good Corinthians had proved true (vii. 14). Paul must have said to Titus something like: The Corinthians are fundamentally sound, and are really on my side. They have been temporarily deceived by the man (not a Corinthian) who attacked me, but this letter (which I ask you to deliver to them) will give them an opportunity of showing how keen they are to support me. And the message that Titus eventually brought back was: You are right; they support you enthusiastically, and regret only that they did not do so publicly when you were attacked. Most of them now wish to punish the offender severely.

This was when Titus made a beginning (viii. 6) with the collection. He had not completed it because he was in a hurry to report to Paul the Corinthians' enthusiastic support (and perhaps because the Corinthians were better at talk than action). When Paul received the report he sent Titus back to finish the task he had begun. It was now that the trouble flared up and became severe (see above, pp. 9 f.); hearing of it, Paul wrote x–xiii, and paid a third visit. Not the least advantage of the view set forth in this commentary is that it does not require us to suppose that a situation Paul could not control was finally reduced to order by Titus. Titus was doubtless a good man, but he had not fully understood the mood of the Corinthians, and it was Paul who in the end established discipline and order, and obtained a gift for Jerusalem (Rom. xv. 26).

This view of events, with a simple partition of the epistle between i–ix and x–xiii, removes the problem of xii. 17 f. It avoids unnecessary hypotheses (such as a visit and unfavourable report by Titus, for which we have no evidence). It deals fairly with the various pieces of evidence at our disposal. It is best defended simply by statement, and by the possibility it affords of dealing in detail with some of the special problems that are discussed in the next section of the Introduction. For more elaborate partition theories, see below, III (a).

III. Special Problems

(a) *The History of the Epistle.* The Muratorian Canon, which originated in Rome towards the end of the second century, recognizes the existence of two epistles to the Corinthians:

> Verum Corinthiis et Thessalonicensibus licet pro correptione iteretur, una tamen per omnem orbem terrae ecclesia diffusa esse dinoscitur—[1]

[1] Text quoted from B. F. Westcott, *The Canon of the New Testament* (1896), p. 546.

that is, by the number (seven) of the churches addressed. From this time onward both epistles were accepted without doubt. Half a century earlier Marcion had included 2 Corinthians in his canon of the New Testament; Tertullian in dealing with it (*Adversus Marcionem* V. 11, 12) and using only material whose Pauline origin Marcion himself allowed (*Adv. Marc.* V. 1), quotes, in quite a short discussion, from chapters i, iii, iv, v, vii, xi, xii, xiii. Irenaeus not only quotes 2 Corinthians but refers to it by name. Earlier use of the epistle cannot be proved. It is sometimes claimed that Polycarp shows knowledge of it, but the passages adduced (Polycarp, *ad Phil.* ii. 2; iii. 2; v. 1; vi. 2; xi. 3) are by no means convincing. This does not mean that there is any doubt about the authorship of the epistle.[1] The external evidence, though not as early as that for 1 Corinthians, is good, and the internal evidence is decisive. The circumstances of the 50s of the first century are depicted in a way that no writer of pious fiction could have achieved and, more important, the apostle is painted, 'warts and all', with a frankness for which only he can have been responsible.

The relative lateness (in comparison with 1 Corinthians) with which 2 Corinthians emerges into general use has been held to confirm the belief that it is composite, made up of parts of two or more distinct letters. G. Bornkamm[2] draws attention to this, and to the fact that Clement of Rome, admonishing a still dissident Corinthian church, reminds its members of 'the letter [singular] of the blessed Paul, the apostle' (1 Clement 47. 1). It would have been useful to quote 2 Corinthians; that Clement did not do so is probably due to the fact that it was not yet publicly known, and had probably not yet been put together. Dr Bornkamm concludes, 'I would suggest therefore that our 2 Corinthians was not put together till after the dissemination of 1 Corinthians, and did not immediately become known generally but only in a restricted circle. The character of the compilation however points certainly to the post-apostolic period, that is, to the period at which Acts and the Pastoral Epistles were composed (the end of the first or beginning of the second century)' (op. cit. p. 34).

It is probably true that 2 Corinthians came into general use later than 1 Corinthians. This however does not prove (though it is

[1] On the authorship of vi. 14–vii. 1 see pp. 193–203.
[2] 'Vorgeschichte', pp. 33 f.

consistent with) the belief that 2 Corinthians is a composite work. This must be shown by other arguments. There was good enough reason for withholding 2 Corinthians from publication, whatever the process by which it was composed.

The popular theories regarding the composition of 2 Corinthians, with the observations on which they are based, have already been set out. They cannot be proved incorrect (though it is worth noting that the argument (p. 13) that x–xiii must precede i–ix because there are corresponding passages in the two parts is seriously damaged if, with a number of more recent writers, we add ii. 14–vii. 4 to x–xiii to make up the 'Severe Letter'). Three further points may be brought against these theories.

(1) The exegetical difficulties of the points of transition (ii. 13/14; vi. 13/14; vii. 1/2; vii. 4/5; ix. 15/x. 1) have been exaggerated, and the abrupt transitions themselves (except perhaps the last) can be satisfactorily explained. For this, see the commentary at the points indicated.

(2) ii. 14–vii. 4; x. 1–xiii. 13 does not correspond to what might be expected of the contents of the Severe Letter. 'The event, which, according to 2 Cor. ii. 3-5, 9, was dealt with in the intermediate epistle, is not treated in x–xiii; and, conversely, 2 Cor. ii. 3 ff. and vii. 8 ff. do not speak of how the congregation reacted to the polemic against the "superlative apostles" in x–xiii, which could hardly have been omitted if x–xiii belonged to the intermediate epistle.'[1]

(3) Finally, it is not clear why or how the epistle should have been put together in the complicated way presupposed by the more elaborate literary hypotheses. This objection does not apply very strongly to the view that i–ix and x–xiii were originally separate letters, especially if it is held (as in this book) that i–ix was earlier (and only a little earlier) than x–xiii. They might have been put together for convenience, or because one of the letters lost its epistolary opening and ending. But no reason has been given why an editor should within the framework of i–ix first insert ii. 14–vi. 13; vii. 2-4; and viii, and then, within his first insertion, insert vi. 14–vii. 1, taking care at each point so to interrupt the argument as to leave what are held to be impossible sequences. Such stupidity in a responsible editor is hard to credit. Dr Bornkamm, it is true, attempts to explain the editor's motive and method. He explains

[1] Kümmel, *Introduction*, p. 213.

first the placing of the sharply polemical chapters x–xiii at the end of the epistle, noting the widespread early Christian belief that false prophecy and teaching were a sign of the End, and that 'the announcement that false prophets and heretical teachers would come, and the warning against them, often occur at the end of particular writings and sections' (op. cit. p. 25). This determined the placing of chapters x–xiii by the editor. We cannot say that Paul himself would for the same reason have placed these chapters in this position, for they do not use characteristically apocalyptic language, or represent the false apostles as nightmare figures (*Schreckgestalten*) of the time of the End.

Dr Bornkamm's explanation of the surprising transition in chapter ii is as follows. 'This unexpected transition fits as well (so it seems to me) into the conception of a later compiler and editor, who, looking back, saw even that journey of Paul's from Ephesus, through Troas, to Macedonia in the light of the triumphal procession [ii. 15] which the apostle of the Gentiles accomplished, as it is inconceivable from the standpoint of Paul himself. This point must have seemed to the former particularly suitable for the immediate introduction of the first apology, whose last confident words, already cited above, made easily possible for him the continuation of the interrupted narrative in the transition from vii. 4 to 5' (op. cit. pp. 30 f.).[1]

It cannot be said that these explanations are convincing. Dr Bornkamm, in effect, destroys his own argument with reference to x–xiii: these chapters are not apocalyptic warnings of what is to be expected in the last days, but a straightforward attack upon contemporaries; not a paraenetic warning (comparable with Acts xx. 29 f.), but polemics. And it is difficult indeed to see how anyone could have regarded ii. 12 f. as the description of a triumphal procession. If the editor had at this point added vii. 6 the argument might have had more weight, but this verse is deferred till after the 'interpolation', which is preceded only by the statement that Paul was so upset that he was unable to carry out the programme of evangelization that he had planned, even though there were good facilities for it.

[1] Of the insertion of vi. 14–vii. 1 Bornkamm offers no explanation, and says only, 'The short apocalyptic exhortation, vi. 14–vii. 1, abruptly introduced and breaking the connection, has to be recognized as the single unpauline piece, for whose unpauline terminology and thought the Qumran texts have now produced surprising parallel material' (op. cit. p. 32).

It may be that no limit should be set to the stupidity of editors, and one cannot expect always to understand their motives; but it cannot be said that any good explanation of the process that led to the composition of 2 Corinthians out of disordered fragments has yet been given. This must remain not indeed a decisive but a significant argument against partition theories.

(b) *The Collection.* The chronology of the collection made by Paul for the poor saints in Jerusalem is discussed in the notes on chapters viii and ix. The view taken in the commentary is as follows.

(1) The Corinthians heard of the project and made inquiries about it.

(2) Paul gave them preliminary instructions in 1 Cor. xvi. 1-4.

(3) Instead of completing the matter himself when he visited Corinth (as proposed in 1 Cor. xvi. 5-9), Paul asked Titus, when he conveyed the Severe Letter, to deal with the collection too.

(4) Titus left Corinth with the work unfinished; Paul asked him to return, accompanied by two brothers, to bring it to a conclusion.

(5) The work was further interrupted by the troubles reflected in 2 Cor. x–xiii.

(6) But it was brought to a successful conclusion by Paul himself during the three-month visit to Greece mentioned in Acts xx. 3; see Rom. xv. 26, which (written in or near Corinth) speaks of the Achaean contribution to the fund.

It remains here to inquire into the purpose and meaning of the collection. Evidence outside the Corinthian letters that must be borne in mind is as follows.

Acts xi. 27-30; xii. 25: the help sent from Antioch to Jerusalem.

Acts xxiv. 17: Paul declares that many years after his conversion he had come to Jerusalem to bring alms for his people.

Rom. xv. (16), 25-8, 31: After writing to Rome, and before setting out on his journey to Rome and Spain, Paul will go to Jerusalem with a gift for the poor saints, to which Macedonia and Achaea have contributed.

Gal. ii. 10: It was part of Paul's agreement with the 'Pillars' in Jerusalem that 'we should remember the poor'. This he was eager to do.

The collection has recently been discussed, independently but in considerable agreement, by D. Georgi and K. F. Nickle;[1] it is not possible here to summarize these detailed works, both of which repay careful study. The following note is indebted to both, though it differs from them in important respects.

Paul's procedure was not without Jewish parallels, the evidence for which is set out by Dr Nickle (op. cit. pp. 74–99), who mentions the half-shekel temple tax, general charitable provision for the poor made within local communities, the patriarchal tax (collected by 'apostles', but too late to be of direct relevance), and various features of the common life of the Qumran sect. He concludes (op. cit. p. 99) that Paul 'borrowed most heavily for the organization of his collection from the Jewish Temple tax'. There are however important differences, to which Dr Nickle draws attention, 'in view of the attempt to interpret Paul's collection for Jerusalem as a tax imposed upon him and his Gentile communities by the leaders of the Jerusalem church' (op. cit. p. 90). He makes, rightly, the following points. (1) The Jewish tax was levied primarily for cultic purposes; Paul's collection was for the relief of the poor. (2) It was claimed that the Jewish tax went back to Moses; Paul could quote the Old Testament in relation to his collection (2 Cor. viii. 15, 21; ix. 7, 9, 10) but did not seek any legal prescription for it. (3) The tax was highly organized; Paul made only *ad hoc* local arrangements. (4) The tax was collected annually at dates determined by the liturgical year; Paul's was an isolated project which took some years to put into effect. (5) The temple tax called for the payment of a prescribed sum; Paul left each subscriber free to decide what he would give. (6) Some though not all Jews[2] were under obligation to pay the tax, and proceedings could be taken against defaulters; no one was obliged to contribute to Paul's collection.

This list of differences is important and should make it impossible to regard Gal. ii. 10 as the imposition of a new, Christian 'temple tax'; at least, Paul did not view his collection in this light, though it is not impossible that there were some in Jerusalem who would have been glad to do so.

[1] Georgi, *Kollekte*; Nickle, *Collection*; see also K. Holl, 'Der Kirchenbegriff des Paulus in seinem Verhältnis zu dem der Urgemeinde', *Gesammelte Aufsätze zur Kirchengeschichte* II (1928), pp. 44–67, especially 58–62; Munck, *Paulus*, pp. 277–302 (ET, pp. 282–308).

[2] Women, slaves, and minors were exempt.

There should be little doubt that the primary significance of the collection in Paul's eyes was that it brought financial help from Gentile Christians who, though not wealthy (1 Cor. i. 26; 2 Cor. viii. 2), were relatively better off, to Jewish Christians in Jerusalem who were poor. This is a less striking observation than some hypotheses that have been constructed on the subject but it has the advantage of being in accord with what Paul says, and in harmony with his Christian thinking as a whole. He had little interest in cultic expressions of Christian truth, much in the service of the needy (Rom. xiii. 8 ff.; 1 Cor. xiii; et al.); in this, as in other matters, he appears to have understood Jesus himself as well as most. The collection was an act of service (*διακονία*; see viii. 4; ix. 1, 12, 13), and even of grace (*χάρις*; see viii. 1, 6, 7, 19; (ix. 14)), and thus related to the grace of Jesus Christ himself (viii. 9).

Relations between Paul and the church of Jerusalem, and its representatives, are discussed below (III (d)); they were by no means uniformly cordial, and it is probably true that Paul regarded his offering to Jerusalem as a means of demonstrating his fundamental good will (cf. Rom. ix. 1 ff.; x. 1), and thus of keeping the peace. The Gentile church owed the Jewish church an unpayable debt—the first Christians were Jews, and it was they (notably of course Paul himself) who had brought the Gospel to the Gentiles. For this service no adequate recompense could ever be made, and it was certainly not too much to ask the Gentiles to make a material gift to their spiritual benefactors (Rom. xv. 27)—even though some of the 'benefactors' had had no desire to bestow any benefits upon their beneficiaries. This was a matter of fellowship (*κοινωνία*; see viii. 4; ix. 13), and of equality (*ἰσότης*; see viii. 13 f.; for Georgi's view of this word see pp. 226 f.). From Gal. ii. 9 onwards Paul appears to have accepted a measure of separate development for the Jewish and Gentile wings of the church, though it was a separateness that almost inevitably ran into difficulties (Gal. ii. 11), and could not in practice be fully maintained; it was in any case always bridged by practical love, expressed, for example, in the collection.

The material in Romans suggests that the collection 'was intended to play a vital part among the events of the last days' (*Romans*, p. 278), and this theme has been taken further by both Dr Georgi and Dr Nickle. In Rom. xi. 31 Paul sees the conversion of the Gentiles as contributing to the conversion of Israel; their gift to Jerusalem would not only be a concrete proof of the reality of their conversion, those who conveyed it could be thought of as 'an eschatological pilgrimage of the Gentile Christians to Jerusalem by which the Jews were to be confronted with the undeniable reality of the divine gift of saving grace to the Gentiles and thereby be themselves moved through jealousy to finally accept the Gospel' (Nickle, *Collection*, p. 142). Dr Georgi similarly speaks of the provocative character of the collection (*Kollekte*, pp. 84 ff.), and brings it into relation with the purpose of Romans as a whole—it will contribute to the progress of the Gospel further west. These suggestions are on the right lines, though it may be that they press the point too far; by far the most important point to Paul, and the only one that he himself makes explicitly, is that the collection was an act of love for the benefit of those who were in material need.

(c) *The False Apostles.*[1] A good summary account of the attempts that have been made to identify Paul's opponents in 2 Corinthians is given by G. Friedrich (op. cit. pp. 192–6; see also Georgi, *Gegner*, pp. 7–16), who distinguishes three lines of interpretation.

(i) Some (notably Baur, Windisch, Käsemann, and Kümmel) see in Paul's opponents a group of Palestinian Jewish Christians. If the false apostles were not actually commissioned by the 'super-apostles' (Baur), they at least claimed (Käsemann) to draw authority from them, though in fact it was the Jerusalem church that had commissioned them to bring the Gentile mission churches under its authority. They also claimed the authority conferred on them by their knowledge of the historical Jesus, and disparaged Paul because he lacked this knowledge. The fundamental Judaism of these men was perhaps modified by their alliance with the gnostic group that prided itself on its inspiration (Windisch).

Dr Friedrich criticizes this identification. The Corinthian opponents were quite different from those in Galatia. The former show no interest in circumcision, the keeping of the Sabbath, and cultic purity. 'Neither do they bring against Paul the charge of antinomianism, nor does Paul attack their work-righteousness as the chief mark of their false theology. An alliance of the gnostic libertines with the rigorous legalists is hardly conceivable. The designation "servants of Christ" and the appeal to miracles and

[1] See 'Christianity at Corinth', 'False Apostles', and 'Paul's Opponents'; also Käsemann, 'Legitimität'; Friedrich, 'Gegner'; Georgi, *Gegner*.

visions speaks against Palestinian Jews. The rabbinic Jewish Christianity that originated in Jerusalem is not interested in visions, but in observing the written law' (op. cit. pp. 192 f.).

(ii) A second view is that the Corinthian opponents were 'representatives of a gnostic movement of oriental origin. . . . The self-confidence with which they appear, the emphasis upon the possession of the Spirit, on inspired speech, and on ecstasy, may well give rise to the impression that there exists a continuity between Paul's opponents in 1 and 2 Corinthians' (op. cit. p. 193).

But neither will this identification stand examination. 2 Corinthians deals no longer with the various *charismata* insisted on by the 'spiritual' opponents in 1 Corinthians, and Paul no longer has to combat the libertinism apparent in 1 Corinthians. The gnostic understanding of resurrection and the gnostic Redeemer myth are no longer alluded to, since what we have in 2 Cor. xii is common to many types of religion. 'Gnosis is no longer the cause of pride and arrogance as in 1 Corinthians. On the hypothesis that they are gnostics it remains unclear why Paul's opponents should produce commendatory letters' (op. cit. p. 193).[1]

(iii) This leaves open the third possibility, which Dr Friedrich, following Dr Bornkamm and Dr Georgi,[2] accepts: the opponents were Jews, but Hellenistic Jews, who imitated the style of propaganda used by the inspired figures of the Hellenistic world. 'In their behaviour and the style of their preaching they belong to that type of itinerant wandering prophets, magicians, and saviours represented by Apollonius of Tyana, Alexander of Abonuteichos, and Peregrinus Proteus, who gave themselves out to be God's envoys, and sought to exalt themselves by revelations and miracles' (op. cit. p. 196; cf. Collange, e.g. p. 84). Dr Friedrich develops this identification by finding a relation between the false apostles and the movement started by the Hellenist Stephen (Acts vi, vii).

The articles referred to in note 1 on p. 28, and the notes on relevant passages in this commentary, discuss at some length the various possibilities that have been outlined. The view taken in this book is that the arguments of Dr Friedrich (to mention no others) have made it impossible to maintain the position that in 2 Corinthians as well as in 1 Corinthians Paul is confronted by

[1] Note the attack on the position of W. Schmithals on pp. 194 ff.

[2] A similar view is adopted by M. Rissi, *Studien zum zweiten Korintherbrief* (1969), though without additional argument.

gnostics (though the circumstances presupposed by 1 Corinthians cannot have completely ceased to exist, and we shall see that a gnostic element enters into the make-up of the new opponents). The adversaries were certainly Jews. They were moreover Jews of Palestinian origin, who exercised a Judaizing influence. This view cannot be rebutted by the argument that Paul, in his debate with them, says nothing about circumcision and Sabbath. There were Judaizers, of whom Peter at Antioch (Gal. ii. 11) is the most notable example, who maintained a legalist position without insisting upon these expressions of it. A main theme of 2 Cor. xi is that Paul is as good a Jew as any of his opponents; they must have been Jews, and Jews who insisted on their Jewishness. They found themselves, however, in Corinth in an environment in which Gentiles were exercising a fundamentally Gentile judgement on apostolic claimants, and applying Hellenistic criteria in order to determine who were and who were not apostles. In this environment they adopted Hellenistic characteristics, some of which are correctly noted by Dr Friedrich.

The same controversial environment caused Paul to deal with the question which Dr Käsemann makes the title of his essay on 2 Corinthians—'Die Legitimität des Apostels', Apostolic Legitimacy.[1] The treatment of this question supplies the primary motivation, and most of the contents, of 2 Corinthians, and gives the epistle its priceless worth. The apostle's legitimacy appears not in the power of his personality, not in his spiritual experiences, not in his commissioning by the right ecclesiastical authorities, but only in the extent to which his life and preaching represent the crucified Jesus.

(d) *Paul and Jerusalem.* The question of vital importance here is whether Paul uses the terms 'false apostles' (*ψευδαπόστολοι*, xi. 13) and 'super-apostles' (*ὑπερλίαν ἀπόστολοι*, xi. 5; xii. 11) to refer to the same group, or to two different groups. If the former, those whom he describes as the 'servants of Satan' (xi. 15) can only be those who intruded into his mission field at Corinth; they cannot be the Jerusalem apostles, to whom, on this view, Paul makes no direct reference in 2 Corinthians. If the latter, the 'false apostles' will be the intruders, the 'super-apostles' most probably the Jerusalem group.

The majority, probably, of scholars identify the 'false apostles'

[1] See p. 28, note 1. I have dealt with a kindred theme in *Signs*.

with the 'super-apostles'. The principal argument in favour of the identification is based upon xi. 5, where, immediately after speaking of one who comes and proclaims another Jesus, whom we did not proclaim, Paul adds, I consider that I come behind the super-apostles in no way at all. At a first glance it seems that he is referring to those who in Corinth have preached a different Gospel. This is, however, mistaken exegesis, as is shown in the commentary, and it is difficult to resist the force of Dr Käsemann's argument[1] that to say of men who are described as servants of Satan, 'I am not inferior to them' is intolerable. The existence of two groups is implied. One Paul attacks as he does the false brothers of Gal. ii. 4; the other he treats with the same mild irony with which he describes, in the same Galatian context, those who had the reputation of being pillars (Gal. ii. 6, 9). He does not attack them, but he makes it clear that they are not his superiors, and that he owes neither his apostleship nor the duty of obedience to them. They may be identified with the three Pillars (James, Cephas, and John), or possibly with the wider group of the Twelve (or rather, with the surviving members of that group).

As persons and ecclesiastical dignitaries they were an embarrassment to Paul, both in themselves and as those whom his immediate foes claimed as their backers. It must have been impossible to be certain regarding the legitimacy of this claim: had the Jerusalem leaders really given authority to those who were wrecking the Corinthian church? There might seem to be documentary proof of this. But if they had done so, had they given them authority to do what they were in fact doing, or were the intruders acting *ultra vires*? Evidently Paul hoped, and perhaps believed, that they were. In Gal. ii he recounts the agreement he had reached with the Jerusalem authorities, and this had not been wholly annulled by Peter's defection in Antioch. The fact of the collection shows that Paul intended to keep his side of the bargain, and to maintain if he could some kind of *modus vivendi* with Jerusalem. This intention however compelled him to fight in Corinth with one hand tied behind his back; to have renounced Jerusalem would have set Paul free to resist the intruders in an uninhibited way. Probably Paul was not far from this; the different Gospel of xi. 4 recalls the distinction made in Gal. ii. 7 between the Gospel of the circumcision and the Gospel of the uncircumcision. That instead of taking

[1] See 'Legitimität', p. 42/21.

this step Paul in his fight against the false apostles accepted the disadvantage of keeping the peace with Jerusalem shows his belief that the Jerusalem apostles were sound at heart, and that his theology could not dispense with its links with Jesus of Nazareth.

Sound at heart they may have been, but their conception of apostleship was different from his.[1] As agents[2] of Jesus they seem to have taken it to be their task to consolidate his work in Palestine and, as a legitimate extension of his own willingness to have dealings with the occasional Gentile who presented himself,[3] to consolidate in relation with themselves such Gentile churches as might happen to come into existence (cf. Acts viii. 14; xi. 22). For Paul, Jesus was nothing if not universal, a second Adam rather than a second Moses; hence his mission to the Gentiles, which he was able to integrate into the mission to Israel (see above, pp. 27 f.).

Paul's relation with Jerusalem was one of partial agreement and partial disagreement; of embarrassment and some friction; and of loyalty. The view taken in this commentary reveals a situation essentially the same as that which emerges from Galatians, and throws a good deal of light on an obscure subject. If, however, this view is mistaken and the false apostles are to be identified with the super-apostles, 2 Corinthians, apart from its important evidence regarding the collection, contributes little to the question.

(e) *Paul as a man.* Paul never wrote a more personal letter than 2 Corinthians. To say this is not to hand the epistle over to psychological interpretation,[4] for it would be equally true to say that he never wrote a more theological letter. It is simply a letter in which he wears his heart on his sleeve and speaks without constraint, hiding neither his affection, nor his anger, nor his agony. He is always a theological person, for he sees all his affairs and feelings *sub specie Dei*; but equally he is a human person, and no less human because he is theological.

Nothing appears more powerfully in 2 Corinthians than the strength of Paul's vocation. It would have been natural for Paul simply to give up the ungrateful, unruly, unloving, unintelligent

[1] See *Signs*, especially pp. 35–46, 68 f.

[2] On *shaliaḥ* see *Signs*, pp. 12 f., and especially the book and article by K. H. Rengstorf there referred to.

[3] See J. Jeremias, *Jesus' Promise to the Nations* (1958), pp. 28–37.

[4] Cf. C. H. Dodd's handling in *Studies*, pp. 79–82, of the theme of 'boasting' in terms of a 'second conversion'. In many ways this is illuminating, but it does not do full justice to the evidence; see p. 70.

Corinthians, and leave them to their destiny. There is no indication that this thought ever crossed his mind: you are in our hearts, bound up with us in death and in life (vii. 3). The care of all the churches, with its attendant anxiety (xi. 28), was a burden from which he did not seek release. It would doubtless have been a welcome relief if he could have shared the doubts about his apostleship that others felt. But he was the slave of Christ (Rom. i. 1; Phil. i. 1); this made him the slave of his people too (iv. 5), and from this service there was no remission. He knew that Christ spoke in him (xiii. 3), manifesting the truth of the Gospel on every side (ii. 14); if this did not meet with universal acceptance, if it proved sometimes to be an odour issuing from death and leading to death (ii. 16), this was because the god of this age (iv. 4) had been at work: we know his tricks (ii. 11). All this Paul could not prove to those who were unwilling to accept it (see e.g. xi. 16; and *Signs*, pp. 41 f.); in a sense he could not prove it even to himself, for in himself he found no sufficiency for the task (iii. 5)—so much the stronger, therefore, the conviction that kept him at his work.

The brief allusive list of 2 Cor. xi. 23-33 gives some indication of the physical as well as the moral discouragements and disincentives under which Paul worked, and at the same time of the scantiness of the record of Paul's life provided by Acts. iv. 8 ff. and vi. 4-10 fill out the list, in rather less explicit pictures (cf. 1 Cor. iv. 9-13). Men have died as a result of only a small fraction of the punishments and afflictions Paul suffered; he survived, and was to pursue an active and hazardous life for some years more. Beyond doubt, Paul 'must have been pretty tough' (C. H. Dodd, *Studies*, p. 67). Yet he suffered some kind of physical affliction. It must not be assumed that all the passages, even all those in 2 Corinthians, that have been held to be relevant to this matter, refer to the same infirmity. It has been suggested (see the note on xii. 7) that the thorn in Paul's flesh may possibly have been a defect in his speech, that hampered the eloquence that marks his letters and made him unimpressive and indeed contemptible in personal presence. i. 8 (see the note) may well refer to an illness; but diseases are many, and Paul may on this occasion in Asia have suffered from one to which he was not normally subject. Nothing can be deduced from it with regard to his normal health; certainly it gives no ground for thinking that Paul was not as a rule a fit and active man.

2 Corinthians supplies some of the evidence on the basis of

which Paul has been described as a mystic, or visionary; the evidence however is hardly convincing. It is true that xii. 2 ff. describes an experience in which Paul was caught up to heaven and heard words which he was not allowed to communicate to his fellow men; more important than this one instance is the remark that follows (xii. 7)—it was because his visions were so remarkable that, to keep him humble, the thorn was driven into his flesh. It remains significant that, to find a suitably impressive example of visions and revelations of the Lord (xii. 1), he goes back fourteen years (xii. 2); such raptures did not happen to him every other week. Undoubtedly, Paul was an oriental Greek, or Greek Oriental, and as such subject to a good deal of religious excitement; that he spoke with tongues more than anyone in Corinth (1 Cor. xiv. 18) was a pretty large claim to make. But tongues and visions alike were to be measured, he held, in terms of their value not to the individual but to the church, and Paul insisted on keeping his own feet, and the church's, firmly on the ground (1 Cor. xiii. 1 ff.). To keep one's eyes fixed not on things seen but on things unseen (iv. 18) does not mean to abandon common life in the interests of mysticism, but to see the events of this age in the light of the age to come (cf. v. 16, with the note). To Paul, the spiritual world was unmistakably real, and from time to time he experienced it in an ecstatic way; but so far from cultivating this kind of experience he rather disparaged it, and laid no weight on it in his exposition and defence of the Gospel.

2 Corinthians, more than most of the epistles, reveals Paul as a man capable of profound feeling. His love for the Corinthians is revealed not less but more clearly by the fact that it was misunderstood, and the fact that, being misunderstood and spurned, it sometimes drove him to irony and bitterness. Why do you think I refuse to take payment for my ministry? Because I don't love, don't trust you, will not let you share my responsibility? God knows! (xi. 11). He loved the Corinthians; he wanted not their property but only themselves (xii. 14); he made himself their slave (iv. 5); then had to watch them making themselves subservient to false apostles who proved that they were servants of Satan rather than of Christ by their arrogant readiness to gobble up the members of the church (xi. 20). Paul suffered for the Corinthians the agony a father might feel over a loved daughter whom he had betrothed to the best of husbands, only to see her flirting and

apparently about to destroy her virtue, her happiness, and herself with selfish and unprincipled philanderers (xi. 2 f.). In all this, their self-righteousness, and self-confidence that they had no need of him, twisted the knife in the wound. The appearance of Titus with good news, the message that the Corinthians really were on his side and had not been taken in by the deceivers, correspondingly overjoyed Paul:

> Oh! if one soul from Corinth[1]
> Meet me at God's right hand,
> My heaven will be two heavens
> In Immanuel's land.

We rejoice when we are weak, but you are strong (xiii. 9). Paul did not feel this affection for the intruders at Corinth; he attacks them bitterly, on the two grounds, that they were propagating their errors under the cloak of the Gospel,[2] and were corrupting his Corinthians. They were apostles on the cheap, profiting from the suffering and labour of others, more concerned with what they could get than with service given either to God or to men. He speaks of them as he does of false brothers in Galatia (Gal. ii. 4; v. 12), and of Judaizing opponents in Rome (Rom. iii. 8; xvi. 17 f.) and Philippi (Phil. iii. 2 f., 17 ff.).

Paul was accused of acting with fickleness, of saying Yes and No at the same time (i. 17). There was at least an element of plausibility in the charge, which contributes something to our picture of Paul as a man. He had proposed a visit to Corinth (1 Cor. xvi. 5-9); then a double visit (2 Cor. i. 15 f.); but then, when the first half of the visit went badly, he changed his plans and did not return as he had intended and had said that he would (i. 23). It is certainly true that the reason for this change of plan lay with the Corinthians, and that Paul's motive had been excellent —it was, he believed, in the Corinthians' own interest that he should not return. It is arguable that in this he was mistaken: the Corinthians themselves were fickle enough, and it might have been healthy to have one partner in the dispute keeping to an absolutely steady course; his action was sure to be misinterpreted; and to

[1] I substitute Corinth for Anwoth in Anne Ross Cousin's metrical version of 'Some Last Words of Samuel Rutherford'. There was not a little of Paul in Rutherford; see (in addition to the *Letters*) Alexander Whyte, *Samuel Rutherford and some of his correspondents* (1894).

[2] See 'False Apostles', pp. 383 f.

'spare' them is not necessarily the best way to bring spoilt children to their senses. Be that as it may; rightly or wrongly, Paul acted spontaneously, and it was his nature to do so, as it was his nature to lay bare his deepest thoughts and feelings. This could look like fickleness, and it was easy for ill-disposed persons to represent it as fickleness. It is not only more charitable but more accurate to describe it as adaptability.[1] We have already seen the enormous driving force of Paul's conviction and vocation; this force was applied with sensitivity in the direction Paul judged right, with a flexibility that allowed frequent change of plan. The only guiding principle of absolute authority, which serves also as the final description of Paul as a man, has already been given in 1 Cor. ix. 23: Whatever I do, I do for the sake of the Gospel. To this one can only add, in the words of Windisch (p. 290), 'In this part of the epistle [2 Cor. x–xiii] Paul displays the *εἰκών* [image] of the God of the Bible, who is wrathful and punishes and judges, and yet cannot give up his love for the creation which gives him so much toil and trouble.'

IV. Theology at Corinth

(a) *Corinthian Theology.* The term is not without precedent,[2] but it must not be taken to mean that a single coherent theology developed at Corinth, and was held by the whole church. Nothing was more characteristic of the Corinthian church than its tendency to division, and though it may be possible to isolate a few general tendencies it is clear that the non-Pauline factions disagreed with one another as well as with the apostle. Many winds of doctrine blew into the harbours and along the streets of Corinth, and it must have been very difficult for young Christians to keep on a straight course. The town, though a new, Roman foundation was set in the midst of the Hellenistic world, and popular philosophy and popular piety, to say nothing of popular scepticism, were propagated there; how far philosophy and piety had combined in the right proportions and the right context[3] to produce gnosticism need not now be examined. There was a synagogue (see above, p. 2), presumably of Hellenistic Jews, which provided a spring-

[1] See H. Chadwick, 'All Things to All Men', *N.T.S.* i, pp. 261–75.

[2] See especially A. Schlatter, *Die korinthische Theologie* (1914).

[3] See R. McL. Wilson, *Gnosis and the New Testament* (1968), p. 10.

board for Jewish faith to leap into the Hellenistic world (cf. Acts xviii. 4). Corinth undoubtedly received Christian visitors in addition to Paul; some of them preached the same Gospel, others did not. The opening verses of 1 Corinthians make it plain that the church very soon after its foundation showed tendencies to division; the tenets and make-up of the Paul-party, the Apollos-party, the Cephas-party, and the Christ-party cannot be discussed here; see *1 Corinthians*, pp. 43-6. These were not the only lines on which the church divided (1 Cor. xi. 18), and they may not even represent the most characteristic directions of theological thinking. These, in any case, are better discovered by observing Paul's reactions and replies than by speculating on, for example, Apollos's Alexandrian training.

Study of 1 Corinthians is likely to leave the reader in no doubt that some at least of those whom Paul had in mind indulged in speculative theology based on the themes of knowledge (γνῶσις) and wisdom (σοφία). For the use of these words see *1 Corinthians*, pp. 37, 52 ff.; and the index s.vv. There is nothing to suggest that Paul was opposed to everything in the speculative system. He accepted, for example, its monotheism (1 Cor. viii. 6). Its error (in Paul's view) lay in its disparagement of the material, and in the ethical consequences which some if not all of its practitioners drew from it. In its main presuppositions it probably originated outside the Christian field, and when it came into contact with the apostolic Gospel it interpreted the eschatological language of the latter without reference to its future fulfilment. Undoubtedly there were those in Corinth who claimed that they had already entered upon their kingdom; they were full, they were rich (1 Cor. iv. 8). Otherwise expressed, this meant that the resurrection had already happened; if this was so, there was no resurrection to come, and in 1 Cor. xv Paul defends the Christian apocalyptic view of the future. Even Christ has not yet fully achieved his kingdom (1 Cor. xv. 25); death as an enemy still holds the field (xv. 26); its defeat is certain, but as long as it remains sin remains as its sting (xv. 56). It is not clear whether the Corinthians thought that the risen, reigning life they believed they lived had been given them in baptism; if they did so, this would help to account for Paul's references to baptism in 1 Cor. i. 13-17, though these may reflect no more than an exaggerated veneration for the baptizer. There is no doubt that they tended to believe that baptism together with participation in the Lord's Supper gave them immunity from sin and the punishment of it (1 Cor. x. 1-13). Their conviction that as Christians they had no more concern with the material led them not only to the belief (which Paul shared) that eating sacrificial foods (εἰδωλόθυτα) in itself did no harm to the eater, but also to a readiness to participate in idolatrous rites, and a disregard for brothers with weaker consciences, tendencies which Paul condemned (1 Cor. x. 14; viii. 13). The same principle led to a paradoxically twofold attitude to sex. On the one hand, marriage, they thought, ought to be avoided, or, if it had already been contracted, either broken up or emptied of its physical element; on the other, it could do no harm to have intercourse with a harlot—the most spiritual gnostic could use his stomach for food (since neither stomach nor food had any permanent existence), and the sexual appetite and its fulfilment stood on the same basis (1 Cor. vii. 1; vi. 12 f.).

It is not likely that all these features of faith and practice were shared by all Christians at Corinth; it may well be, for example, that one group took an ascetic, another a licentious, attitude to sexual relations, though the combination of spiritual marriage with the use of fornication as a safety-valve is by no means impossible. Again, it is not clear how the emphasis on the showier gifts of the Spirit, especially speaking with tongues, was combined, if it was combined, with the interests mentioned in the last paragraph. It is not necessary here to decide the disputed question whether glossolalia was or was not a feature of the Jerusalem church, insisted on by its travelling representatives as a mark of genuine Christianity.

Glossolalia provides, however, an excellent example of the difficulty Paul experienced in dealing with Corinthian Christianity. It was indeed a gift of the Spirit, and one that he himself possessed to a preeminent degree (1 Cor. xii. 10, 28, 30; xiv. 18); yet as a witness to the Lordship of Jesus (1 Cor. xii. 3) it was of little value, and it did little to build up the church (1 Cor. xiv. 2-5); for this reason Paul preferred to speak five words with his mind to tens of thousands of words in a tongue (1 Cor. xiv. 19). The Corinthian ideas were not all of them wrong, but they were badly out of proportion: even, for example, a firmly held monotheism, which knew that an idol had no real existence, was, to Paul, less important than a loving regard for one's brother. It is, significantly (as we shall see), in his account of his apostleship (1 Cor. iv. 9-13; ix. 15-23) that the difference between him and the Corinthians comes out most clearly.

In all this Corinthian stress upon *opera operata*, and upon human wisdom as the ground of faith and union with God (1 Cor. ii. 4 f.), there is a close analogy with the Judaism whose stress on works Paul combats elsewhere, and it may well be right to see in Corinth an early form of that confluence of Hellenistic, Oriental, Jewish, and Christian streams that makes up full-blown gnosticism.

To suppose that all the errors that can be read on and between the lines of 1 Corinthians came to an end as soon as that epistle was read in Corinth would certainly be a mistake. The Corinthians were not to be corrected so easily. In any case, as we have seen, many of the Corinthian errors were unbalanced developments of views that Paul himself held: he agreed that 'we do speak wisdom among the mature' (1 Cor. ii. 6); that 'an idol has no existence' (viii. 4); that (within certain fairly narrow limits) 'it is a good thing for a man not to touch a woman' (vii. 1); that tongues, and the word of wisdom and of *gnosis*, were gifts (though they were not the only, or the greatest, gifts) of the Spirit of God (xii. 8 ff., 28 ff.); that the resurrection of the dead did not mean the rising of the natural body but involved also transformation (xv. 42-53); and that the cup of blessing was a joint participation in the blood of Christ, the shared loaf a joint participation in his body (x. 16). These were doctrines always open to the possibility of misunderstanding, and no doubt they continued to be misunderstood. So much is clear; it is harder to define the nature of the misunderstanding, partly through lack of evidence, partly because, though it arose in two superficially different quarters, these shared a measure of theological unity. Both Judaism and incipient gnosticism, in reaction to Pauline theology, expressed themselves in an attempt to keep divine, or spiritual, action under human control. On the one hand, God's representatives were authenticated by their commission from human authorities and called for the observance of laws, such as those regarding food; on the other, they sought accreditation by their inspired speech, and taught that since by sacramental and gnostic means God was already at work men could receive, and had received, an irreversible transformation that guaranteed their eternal salvation. This is indeed a very rough generalization, which if it were pressed would invite serious questioning; moreover, it already draws to some extent on the evidence of 2 Corinthians. This is perhaps excusable, since the intention is to show how the very different phenomena of 2 Corinthians are related to the Corinthian situation.

It has already (p. 29) been pointed out that 2 Corinthians shows far less interest—explicitly, at least—in gnosis and wisdom than 1 Corinthians, and the fundamental historical observation has been made: Corinth had become the mission field (though that is perhaps a term not entirely suitable to the facts—it was a secondary mission, which built on foundations laid by others) of a new, non-Pauline apostolate, emanating from Jerusalem, fundamentally Jewish, or Judaizing, but ready as Paul was not to adapt itself to criteria of apostleship proposed, or exacted, by the mainly Gentile church of Corinth (see p. 30). What is to be observed in 2 Corinthians is best explained as the forcing of a Judaizing movement into a mould at least partly Hellenistic. That this was possible has been shown by the last paragraph; the fact is that on each side Paul was dealing with men who wished to be at the centre of, and to control, their own religion, and had not yet learnt what it meant to walk by faith, not sight (2 Cor. v. 7).

This observation means that the 'different Gospel' of xi. 4 must be described in terms of its results in human behaviour. The term itself recalls Gal. i. 6 ff., and the other terms attached to it (another Jesus, a different Spirit), though significant, must not be allowed to obscure the fact that what Paul has in mind is essentially the Judaizing message that subordinated the Gospel of freedom, grace, and faith, based on the act of God in Jesus, to the law. It is surprising that circumcision is not mentioned, but it must not be supposed that the Judaizing message always took the form it assumed in Galatia. The discussion of Moses, and the fading of the law, in 2 Cor. iii is a key-point in the epistle; it leads to the clearest affirmation of Christian freedom (iii. 17) and can hardly have been without controversial intention, embedded as it is in material that charges rival preachers with falsification of the Gospel (ii. 17; iv. 2; see the notes). These preachers arrived in Corinth with letters of commendation which seem to have emanated from Jerusalem, and can hardly have been unconnected with the 'Pillars' (Gal. ii. 9) who stood at the head of the Jerusalem church. This not only establishes their Jewish and Judaizing background (cf. xi. 22), but indicates a hierarchical tendency in their understanding of Christianity. This comes out again in the claim they appear to have made on behalf of the Jerusalem authorities to some sort of suzerainty over the Pauline churches (x. 12-16). Theirs was an apostolate 'from men and through man' (cf. Gal. i. 1), and because it concerned the structure of the church had implications also for the substance of the church's Gospel. Paul did not commend the Gospel on the grounds of authority (which he certainly claimed to possess); it commended itself by the work of the Spirit who operated through it.

'Spiritual commendation' of this kind might bear a superficial, but no more than a superficial, resemblance to other aspects of the authority Paul's opponents claimed (possibly in response to Corinthian requirements). They behaved in an authoritative way, which impressed their hearers (xi. 20); they had visions and received revelations (xii. 1; see the note); they had at their command an inspired oratory that Paul could not match (x. 10; xi. 6); they performed miracles (xii. 11 f.; see the note). All that need be said here of these features of the rival mission is that they are functions of a Gospel that could not commend itself, but rested upon human supports. This was a complete inversion of Paul's understanding of the relation between church and preacher on the one hand, and on the other the word of truth; see iv. 7-18; vi. 3-10, with the notes.

The strange preachers of a 'different Gospel' proclaimed 'another Jesus', and it is not incorrect to argue (see below, pp. 276 f.) that this implies a fundamental difference in Christology. Two passages may be set beside xi. 4.

> Though we have known Christ according to the flesh, yet now we know him in this way no longer (v. 16).
>
> Are they servants of Christ? I am really going out of my wits when I say it, I am even more a servant of Christ (xi. 23).

The latter passage may, but in itself need not, mean that those of whom Paul speaks claimed a special position because they had been disciples of Jesus during his ministry. The former has often been understood (see the notes) to be on Paul's part a disparagement of the significance of the 'historical Jesus' which presupposes on the part of his adversaries what he would regard as an exaggerated emphasis on the importance of contact with Jesus during his earthly life. For Paul's own views and their place in his

Christology see below (pp. 46 ff.), and the commentary; it is not correct that he discounted the importance of the 'historical Jesus'. It may nevertheless be true that the Corinthian opposition valued Jesus, and their relation with him, in the wrong way—in fact, 'according to the flesh'. Precisely what this evaluation was it is impossible now to say, for Paul does not tell us; but there can be no doubt that he would have condemned, as behaviour determined by the flesh, any attempt to claim preeminence or dignity, or a privileged relation with God, on the mere ground of having known Jesus during his ministry, and any tendency to regard him, whether in the role of a superior rabbi or a new Moses, as the fount of a new law which could form the basis of a new legalism.

Further than this we cannot go. Speculative Christology was in its beginnings, and there was no clear-cut line of demarcation between orthodoxy and heresy. There is no indication in 2 Corinthians of a kind of speculation that Paul felt himself obliged on principle to condemn. What provoked his dissent because it constituted a different Gospel was an attitude that treated Jesus as something less than Lord, or found the Lord in someone other than Jesus crucified. The different Gospel, viewed as preaching, as theology, or as ethics, misrepresented Jesus; that was its condemnation.

(b) *Paul's theology in the Corinthian setting.* No attempt will be made here to give a full account of Paul's theology, or even of the theological material that is so richly but so unsystematically scattered through the Corinthian letters.[1] No denial of a valid doctrine of the inspiration of Scripture is involved in the recognition that Paul's theology evolved in concrete situations under the stimulus of events and especially of controversy; and few situations in Paul's career were so eventful and so full of controversy as his struggle with and for the Corinthian church. Nothing made him express so clearly and powerfully his own understanding of apostleship as the mission to Corinth of the false apostles (xi. 16-30, with the notes; also *Signs*, pp. 35–46); few things (but these include the Galatian controversy, and the occasion of the writing of Romans) compelled him to see, state, and apply his own Gospel with such

[1] It should be unnecessary to point out that a commentary differs in this respect from other books. The Introduction may legitimately contain a brief systematic account of the writer's thought, but the commentator must allow the writer to set it out as he chooses and simply follow him with explanatory notes. A commentary is not a monograph.

force and passionate conviction as the 'different Gospel' which the false apostles preached. There is therefore good reason to conclude this introduction with a brief study of Paul's theology, not as a systematic whole, but as certain features of it were forced into prominence in the Corinthian correspondence.

In Corinth, as elsewhere, Paul preached Christ crucified, ostensibly a matter of weakness and folly, but to those on the way to salvation the power and the wisdom of God (1 Cor. i. 23 f.). Those who accepted his Gospel knew the meaning of the grace of the Lord Jesus: for their sake he had become poor that they through his poverty might become rich (2 Cor. viii. 9). Sinners though they were, they had come to occupy a position of righteousness in relation to God, but only because the sinless Jesus had voluntarily taken up a position which, at face value, accused him of sin (v. 21). They were righteous in the sight of God because they were in Christ (1 Cor. i. 2), collectively the body of Christ (1 Cor. xii. 27), into which they had been baptized, receiving at the same time the Spirit of God (1 Cor. xii. 13), which in turn bore witness to Christ in the acclamation, Jesus is Lord (1 Cor. xii. 3). The lordship of Jesus Christ, the Son of God, accepted already by Christians, had still to be consummated as a universal fact in his victory over all his enemies, including eventually death itself (1 Cor. xv. 25 f.).

This pattern of Christian belief was, as we have seen, challenged in Corinth from several angles. The challenges led Paul to develop and clarify his teaching. Most of the particular examples are to be found in 1 Corinthians, and it will suffice to mention them again here briefly, since they play no large part in 2 Corinthians. They do, however, contribute to the understanding of the major challenge presented to Paul as a theologian, and of his reply to it, as these appear in 2 Corinthians.

It is easy, for example, to see Paul's rejection of false notions about baptism and the Lord's Supper; it is not so easy to see how he responded to them, and what he put in their place. For his understanding of baptism, indeed, we can do little unless we turn to Romans (see *Romans*, pp. 121–30). In the Corinthian letters the most important passage is 1 Cor. xii. 13: In one Spirit we were all baptized into one body, whether Jews or Greeks, whether slaves or free men. Baptism is the sign of the one body of Christ, which is informed by one Spirit. This leads us to inquire what Paul means by the body of Christ, and by the Spirit. The Supper points in the same direction; thus 1 Cor. x. 16 f.: The cup of blessing, which we bless, is it not a joint participation in the blood of Christ? The loaf which we break, is it not a joint participation in the body of Christ? Because there is one loaf, we who are many are one body, for we all share in the one loaf. Baptism and Eucharist are both related to the body of Christ; the latter contributes explicitly the thought (which the fuller discussion in Rom. vi shows to belong equally to baptism) that the body of Christ was killed, since the blood that animated it was spilt. The connection with the death of Jesus is made even clearer in 1 Cor. xi; the origin of the Supper lies in the night in which he was handed over to death (xi. 23); the eating and drinking were accompanied by the proclamation of the Lord's death.[1] Paul continues with the theme of judgement, and claims that some Corinthians sleep in death because in their eating and drinking they fail to perceive the body. Baptism and the Supper are accompanied by, and themselves are, a proclamation of the word of the cross; not a guarantee of freedom from sin and from judgement but an incorporation—a corporate incorporation—into the dying of Jesus which his resurrection has made eternal. The fruit of the Spirit (Gal. v. 22 f.) is every kind of self-forgetfulness; it is into this Spirit that men are baptized.

This observation may lead to Paul's teaching on the gifts of the Spirit, which all Christians (1 Cor. xii. 7), in some form or other, have. It seems (see *1 Corinthians*, pp. 36 f.) that Corinth liked best such showy gifts as speaking with tongues; for Paul the most excellent way was love, of which the most characteristic property is that it does not seek its own (1 Cor. xiii. 5). It may be that 1 Cor. xiii had been written before it was included in 1 Corinthians (see *1 Corinthians*, pp. 297, 299, 314 f.), but it was in 1 Corinthians that it was included, and it is part of the development of thought that took place in the Corinthian setting. From love, which is the one comprehensive term that covers all Christian behaviour, it is natural to turn to the more detailed ethical teaching which Paul did not think it superfluous to set alongside the statement of principle. It was, for example, in the setting of Corinthian disparagement of marriage that Paul developed his own belief that marriage was indeed undesirable because it multiplied and com-

[1] It is curious that so many liturgiologists think that the eucharist is primarily about the resurrection.

plicated the troubles of the last days, but was in its uniting of the two sexes part of the divine order (1 Cor. xi. 11) and provided an opportunity for the saving power of God to be put into effect (1 Cor. vii. 16).

The discussion of marriage leads up to and includes the most pointed statement of Paul's eschatological ethics (1 Cor. vii. 29 ff.). Since the outward show of this world is passing away, those who have wives should be as though they had none, those who weep and those who rejoice as though they did no such thing, those who buy as though they did not possess, those who use the world as though they had no full use of it. 'He who can thus live, in service to God and in detachment from the world, is a free man . . . , though his freedom is not that of the Stoic . . . , but of the slave of Christ (cf. vii. 22)' (*1 Corinthians*, p. 177). It is life lived under the eschatological pressure of the last days, and in obedience to God in Christ, that is truly free; Paul's 'as if not' (ὡς μή) is neither a fiction nor a way of escape from the world, but a simple recognition that the world as we know it is moving towards its end, and that in consequence the things that are seen are temporal, whereas the things that are not seen are eternal (2 Cor. iv. 18). Recognition of this eschatological situation leads not to resignation or mystical abstraction but to life freed from anxiety and therefore open to service.

For if anyone was disposed to forget the things that are seen and to live in a haze of future glory it was not Paul but his opponents, whom he exposes with the sharpest irony. Already you have reached satiety; already you have become rich; apart from us you have come to your kingdom. Yes, and I wish you had come to your kingdom, that we too might be crowned with you (1 Cor. iv. 8). Not so the apostles: We have become as it were the world's scapegoats, the scum of the earth, to this day (iv. 13). 'As if not' is truth, not fancy; yet it is not visible truth; and on this Paul insists in the eschatological chapter, 1 Cor. xv. Christ has been raised from the dead, but as first fruits, not finality; resurrection for the rest of men may be anticipated but it is not yet complete; death the last enemy still holds the field and Christ himself waits for the overthrow and subjugation of his foes (1 Cor. xv. 25 f.).

This proposition, which is the core of the chapter on resurrection, might seem to attach no more than penultimate significance to the figure of Jesus. This is certainly not Paul's intention, and it is

Christology that binds together the two epistles and gives unity to their very miscellaneous contents. The Christology of 1 Corinthians can be summed up in the double proposition that Jesus is the Lord (xii. 3), who is in all things, from beginning to end, obedient to his Father (xv. 28). Paul insists upon taking both propositions seriously; and their combination is the root of all satisfactory Christological thinking. Repeatedly, Jesus is bracketed with God, and evidently belongs to the same order of being, an order that is superior to any other that human experience can conceive: there are many 'gods' and many 'lords', yet for us there is one God, the Father, from whom come all things and to whom our being leads, and one Lord Jesus Christ, through whom all things, including ourselves, come into being (1 Cor. viii. 5 f.). In particular, this Lord Jesus Christ is Lord over the church, which is his body; alternatively, he is the foundation, the only conceivable foundation on which the Christian building may rest (1 Cor. iii. 11). This he is, however, as Christ crucified, the Lord of glory who was crucified by the rulers of this age (1 Cor. ii. 8), the sole theme of Paul's preaching (1 Cor. ii. 2). It is the Crucified who was raised, and becomes in the operation of the Christian preaching the power and wisdom of God.

The application of Wisdom terminology, and the necessity of putting right the doctrine of the resurrection (which led to the notion of Christ as the last Adam), gave rise to some Christological advance in 1 Corinthians (see *1 Corinthians*, pp. 17 ff.), but the many-sided anguish perceptible behind 2 Corinthians expressed itself in some of the most striking of Paul's Christological statements. These maintain the same point: Christ is the Lord who expressed his lordship in sacrificial obedience to the Father—this is the fundamental affirmation of Paul's Christology in every epistle, but he seldom shows so personal and existential an apprehension of what his proposition means as he does in 2 Corinthians.

No part of the New Testament makes more forcibly and comprehensively the assertion that Jesus is the fulfilment of the Old Testament: However many God's promises may be, in him is the Yes to them all (i. 20). It follows that great as was the glory that accompanied the giving of the law, it was nothing in comparison with the glory that accompanied the establishment of the new covenant of freedom in the Spirit (iii. 17)—the glory of God in the face of Jesus Christ, who is the image of God (iv. 4), the means, that is, by which the invisible God (cf. Col. i. 15) becomes visible. In this language Paul has already drawn out the full Christological usefulness of Jewish Wisdom speculation, and adumbrated the Logos Christology of the Fourth Gospel. The primitive eschatological conviction of the first Christians—Behold, now is the accepted time, now is the day of salvation (vi. 2)—has already given rise to a Christology that is at least on the way to metaphysics. The eschatology however is not lost; Paul's Christ is one who moves through time, and his movement in time, his acceptance of change, is the measure of grace, and it is grace not metaphysics that constitutes a Gospel. You know the grace of our Lord Jesus Christ, that though he was rich yet for your sake he became poor, that we through his poverty might become rich (viii. 9). To be the image of God is not to be simply in a static inward-directed relation with the Father: It is the God who said, Light shall shine out of darkness, who shone in our hearts with a view to that illumination which consists in the knowledge of the glory of God seen in the face of Jesus Christ (iv. 6). The Gospel which thus conveys the glorious truth that God is creative grace makes its triumphal way through the world (ii. 14), though indeed there are those who are blinded and cannot apprehend it (iv. 3), and others who turn it into a 'different Gospel' (xi. 4), which attempts to take initiative and responsibility out of God's hands and place them where they cannot be borne (see above, pp. 40 ff.).

It was to take initiative and bear responsibility, and to do so in the place where they needed to be taken and borne, that the Son of God (i. 19) entered time, entered this age, and thereby set the powers of the age to come to work within it; he became poor (viii. 9), and experienced the ultimate poverty of weakness and death: he was crucified as a result of his weakness (xiii. 4). This Paul never forgot, and intended that his readers should never forget; the statement in v. 16 that he no longer knows Christ after the flesh certainly does not mean that he has no interest in a Christ who lived and died in human flesh (see the notes). What Paul means is that he now, because of Christ, understands living and dying in a new way; they are both of them more terrible and more glorious than he had—after the flesh—thought. Dying as he did meant that Christ was on our behalf thrust into the position of sin; the result of this was that in him we were brought into the position of righteousness, related to God as men ought always to have been related to him. Christ is the inclusive man, in whom we come to be; because he took on him our sin and made it his we may take his righteousness upon us and make it ours, entering with all the saints, God's holy ones, the church, into the age to come which lies beyond the messianic affliction (see *Romans*, p. 122) of the last days.

This paradoxical interchange of life and death, sin and righteousness, has to be expressed in the dialectic of life in this world. Crucifixion was not the last word in the story of Jesus. He was crucified in his earthly weakness; but he lives by the power of God (xiii. 4). He is alive now, and will judge the world (v. 10). This is a total eschatological programme, which Christians anticipate by faith; but in the present age, and on this side of physical death, it appears not as a consummated process that has already reached its blessed conclusion, but as the interplay of weakness and strength, death and life. We are weak in him, but we shall live with him by the power of God (xiii. 4). As this verse shows, strength and life belong characteristically to the future, but the following words—'and that in relation to you'—show that the future is not simply one that lies beyond present experience. It is, however, in human weakness that the pattern of the Gospel is most clearly shown: 'My grace is enough for you; for power comes to perfection in weakness. Therefore will I most gladly boast rather in my weaknesses, in order that Christ's power may rest upon me' (xii. 9). And Paul constantly bears in his body the death of Jesus—not as an end in itself but as the only way to a manifestation of his life (iv. 10). Human weakness is thus not a thing that may or must be tolerated; Paul boasts about it, as the surest proof of his being a Christian, and a representative of the Christ crucified who is the Lord, not in spite of his having been crucified, nor as a reward for having been crucified, but because being 'Christ crucified', 'the Son of God who loved me and gave himself for me' (Gal. ii. 20), is what God means by being the Lord.

This is the issue that lies behind Paul's wrestling with false apostles, and his wrestling for the Corinthian church. The Corinthians' failure to understand him was a measure of their failure to understand Jesus; Paul and Jesus alike they estimated 'according to the flesh' (v. 16). Paul's apparently alternating subservience (ourselves your slaves, iv. 5) and stubborn insistence upon his rights and status (e.g. 1 Cor. ix. 1 f.; 2 Cor. x. 11; xiii. 10), his refusal to commend himself which looked so much like self-commendation (iii. 1; v. 12; x. 12; xii. 19), his refusal to take gifts from the Corinthians when it seemed so natural, and such an appropriate mark of mutual affection, that he should do so (xi. 7-11; xii. 13), his playing the fool over visions and revelations when he knew very well that he was playing the fool (xii. 1, 11), his vision of triumph in the midst of an unsuccessful mission (ii. 14), his superiority to Moses, whom he recognized as the mouthpiece of God (iii. 13), above all, his paradoxical description of his ministry —through glory and dishonour, through evil report and good report, as deceivers and yet true, as unknown and yet well known, as dying and behold we live, as chastened and yet not put to death, as sorrowing but always rejoicing, as poor but making many rich, as having nothing and yet possessing all things (vi. 8 ff.): all this makes sense only when viewed in the light of Christ crucified, who is the Lord. Paul's apostolic behaviour is a reflection of his Christology.[1]

The behaviour of the false apostles may have reflected their Christology, the Christology of the 'other Jesus' (xi. 4); they may have held a *theologia gloriae* that made their boasting (v. 12; x. 16 f.) natural and their aggressive behaviour (xi. 20) justifiable. We lack adequate information on the question, and should not jump to conclusions. Their behaviour certainly did not reflect Paul's Christology; hence his strenuous opposition. It would be absurd to suggest that he felt no personal hurt when these men insinuated themselves into 'his' church, but his opposition was primarily theological, and his criticism based on his understanding of Jesus (cf. 1 Cor. xi. 1). He was more concerned that the Corinthian church, for which he had a measure of responsibility, created by his authority 'for building you up' (x. 8; xiii. 10), should act on his principles; and to grovel before the false apostles (xi. 20) was as bad a lapse from Christian behaviour as was the latter's arrogance. When the Corinthian correspondence came to an end, the Corinthian church had still not learnt the hardest lesson of the Christian faith; it had not yet discovered that the Christ the church proclaims as Lord is Christ crucified, still crucified as the risen Lord, risen indeed in his wounds (cf. John xx. 25-9); that Christians live by faith, not by sight (2 Cor. v. 7).

[1] It is also a reflection of the gospel tradition, whether or not Paul knew this in anything like the form in which we have it today. See *Signs*, pp. 78–81; also the note in the commentary on the Christological form of x. 1.

This truth above all the letters proclaim and apply; in small things, such as the relative value of glossolalia and prophecy (1 Cor. xiv. 4 f.); in large things, such as the evaluation of love (1 Cor. xiii); in fundamental things, as in the exposition of the being and achievement of Christ (2 Cor. v. 11-21). The church at large, not only the church at Corinth, never has learnt, and never can learn, this truth in such a way as to be beyond the danger of forgetting it, and the Corinthian letters stand in the New Testament as in some respects its clearest and most urgent reminder of this eminently forgettable truth, of the grim fate of a wealthy, spiritual, and successful church that forgets it, and that the only mark of legitimacy[1] in the Christian church is that it carries in and with itself the death of Jesus and the promise of resurrection.

[1] I allude to the title of Käsemann's article 'Legitimität'; see also *Signs*, pp. 85–114.

ANALYSIS OF THE EPISTLE

A. INTRODUCTION i. 1-11

1. i. 1, 2: Address
2. i. 3-11: Thanksgiving

B. PAUL'S PLANS FOR CORINTH, AND THEIR WORKING OUT IN THE PAST i. 12–ii. 13

3. i. 12-22: Paul's boasting; behind Paul's plans lies the fulfilment of God's plan in Christ
4. i. 23–ii. 13: Paul's plans may change but his purpose remains

C. THE PURPOSE EXPRESSED IN MISSION AND MINISTRY ii. 14–vii. 4

5. ii. 14–iii. 3: The Christian mission and its divine support
6. iii. 4-18: The old covenant and the new, the old ministry and the new
7. iv. 1-6: The ministry—the treasure it dispenses
8. iv. 7-18: The ministry—the earthenware vessel in which the treasure is contained
9. v. 1-10: A digression illustrating further the relative unimportance of the earthenware container
10. v. 11-21: The treasure: the ambassador's message of reconciliation and new creation arising out of the death of Christ
11. vi. 1-13: An appeal for a response to God and his ambassador
12. vi. 14–vii. 4: Response to God is exclusive

D. PAUL'S PLANS FOR CORINTH, AND THEIR WORKING OUT IN THE FUTURE vii. 5–ix. 15

13. vii. 5-16: Narrative resumed (cf. 4); penitence opens the door to the future
14. viii. 1-24: The collection (1)
15. ix. 1-15: The collection (2)

E. THE FUTURE THREATENED x. 1–xiii. 10

16. x. 1-6: An appeal for complete obedience
17. x. 7-18: A declaration of war on the counter-mission
18. xi. 1-15: The church at Corinth endangered by rival apostles
19. xi. 16-33: Answering fools according to their folly: (a) Qualifications
20. xii. 1-10: Answering fools according to their folly: (b) Revelations
21. xii. 11-18: Answering objections
22. xii. 19–xiii. 10: The apostle and the church: the truth

F. CONCLUSION xiii. 11-13

23. xiii. 11-13: Last words, and greeting

TRANSLATION AND COMMENTARY

A. INTRODUCTION

1. i. 1-2. ADDRESS

(1) Paul, an apostle of Christ Jesus through God's will, together with Timothy his brother Christian, to the church of God that is in Corinth, with all the saints who are in the whole of Achaea. (2) I wish you grace and peace from God our Father and the Lord Jesus Christ.

For the customary opening formula of a Greek letter, and for Paul's Christian modification and expansion of the formula, see *Romans*, pp. 15–23; *1 Corinthians*, pp. 30–5. Here, as in the other epistles, Paul's name is followed by a reference to his apostleship, his correspondents are given a Christian definition, and his greeting becomes a Christian prayer. In this epistle, as in 1 Corinthians but not in Romans, both writer and readers are joined by others.

Paul describes himself as **an apostle of Christ Jesus through** 1
God's will. On Paul's apostleship see, in addition to the notes on Rom. i. 1; 1 Cor. i. 1 (and other passages in these epistles—see Indexes s.vv.), *Signs*, pp. 35–46; also Introduction, pp. 32 f., 49 f. It would be idle to comment further on the word *apostle* at this stage, since this epistle contains, though by no means the most systematic, the fullest and most passionate account of what Paul meant by apostleship, defined in its own light, in relation to the ministry of Moses under the old covenant, and in relation to others who claimed, some with no more right than Paul, others with no right at all, the same title and office. The relevant passages will be discussed in due course. When these are borne in mind, the words *of Christ Jesus* (genitive of the author, as Bachmann points out), and *through God's will* stand out in clearer light. No man in his right senses would have chosen the kind of life Paul lived, exposed not only to physical danger and hardship but to insult, abuse,

loneliness, anxiety, conflict, and fear, of his own will. Paul had no choice about being an apostle and a preacher (cf. 1 Cor. ix. 16 ff.); apostleship might be hard, but silence under God's goad would be infinitely worse. It is his election *through God's will* that gives him the curious authority ('for building you up, not for casting you down', x. 8; xiii. 10) that he has over against the Corinthians. It is perhaps not surprising that they failed to understand it, and were more impressed (xi. 20) by those whose authority appears to have lain in their own will, their self-election, self-appointment, as apostles. Paul's apostolic authority is not of human origin, and therefore is not expressed in terms of gnostic mysteries, though he was not unskilled in knowledge (xi. 6), of the impressive behaviour of the 'divine man' (*θεῖος ἀνήρ*), though his ministry was accompanied by miracles (xii. 12), or of the paper credentials of those who could claim to be envoys of the Jerusalem church (cf. e.g. iii. 1). His authority resided only in the truth, self-evidencing, or, better, evidenced by the Spirit (cf. 1 Cor. ii. 4), of the word he was commissioned to proclaim, and in the pattern of death and resurrection stamped upon his own life and work (e.g. 2 Cor. iv. 10).

As in 1 Cor. i. 1, Paul is not alone. Like Sosthenes there, **Timothy** here is not, apparently, an apostle—he had not seen the risen Jesus (cf. 1 Cor. ix. 1; xv. 8); but he is a **brother Christian**; literally, *the brother*. For a discussion of this word see *1 Corinthians*, p. 31; it was not a new term for a religious associate, but the Gospel had given it new life. For Timothy and his relations with the Corinthian church see 1 Cor. iv. 17; xvi. 10 f., with the notes; he is mentioned again at 2 Cor. i. 19, which shows that he was known to the Corinthians. This is in agreement with Acts xviii. 5, where Silas (almost certainly to be identified with the Silvanus of i. 19) is also mentioned. Whether Timothy had been in Corinth since this first visit of Paul's is not so easy to determine. He had been sent to Corinth (1 Cor. iv. 17), and the Corinthians had been told how to treat him *if* (on the significance of this word see *1 Corinthians*, p. 390) he arrived. There is no positive evidence to inform us about this visit. In Acts xix. 22 Timothy and Erastus are sent from Ephesus to Macedonia; it is not impossible that this journey was continued to Greece. In Acts xx. 4 Timothy (with others) accompanies Paul on his journey from Greece to Syria; this however is later than the writing of 2 Corinthians. It seems clear that after writing 1 Corinthians Paul received bad news about the deterioration of affairs in Corinth, and heard of disorder there. It is possible that the news was brought by Timothy, possible also, though by no means certain, and perhaps unlikely, that Timothy had received insulting treatment on the occasion of his visit. If this was so, that he should join Paul in prayer for the well-being of the church gains greater significance. Windisch concludes that there was at this time no conflict between Timothy and the Corinthians; this may reflect Timothy's magnanimity rather than lack of provocation.

Paul and Timothy write **to the church of God that is in Corinth.** The same words occur in 1 Cor. i. 2; see *1 Corinthians*, p. 32, and (for further notes on *church*) *1 Corinthians*, pp. 260 f., 287–96. In 2 Corinthians the word *church* (ἐκκλησία) does not occur so frequently: nine times in all. In the other eight passages (viii. 1, 18, 19, 23, 24; xi. 8, 28; xii. 13) it is used in the plural—a clear indication that, at least at this stage in his career, the primary meaning of the word for Paul was that of a local Christian community, though it is also evident that the local groups belong together (e.g., 'all the churches', xi. 28). The occurrences of the word are an inadequate indication of the fact that this epistle, which raises acutely the question of apostleship, raises also the question of the church, and that so radically as to lay bare the core of its being—the Gospel that creates it, the authority under which it stands, the life of its members, and the peril to which it is exposed. See the notes on the passages cited. The genitive *of God* is possessive.

Whereas in 1 Corinthians Paul refers to the whole company of Christians ('all who, in every meeting place, call on the name of our Lord Jesus Christ', 1 Cor. i. 2; this could refer not to all Christians but to every house group in Corinth) he makes here a more practical addition to the address, **all the saints who are in the whole of Achaea.** Probably all these persons would have an opportunity of learning the contents of the letter; according to Héring we must think of a circular letter, but it is better to recall that Corinth was the capital, and that a letter sent to the church there would be likely in due course to find its way to outlying places where there were Christians. *The saints* are the church, chosen and called by God, and by him set apart for his service. They are not all apostles (1 Cor. xii. 29), but all have their place in God's purpose, and their appropriate gift and function (1 Cor.

xii. 7). *Achaea* (cf. 1 Cor. xvi. 15; also Acts xviii. 12, 27; xix. 21; Rom. xv. 26; 1 Thess. i. 7, 8) in pre-Roman times denoted territory lying on the northern coast of the Peloponnese, bounded on the west by Elis, on the east by Sicyon, and on the south by Arcadia. It did not at that time include Corinth. In 27 B.C. the whole of Greece—including the Peloponnese, the islands, Thessaly, Aetolia, parts of the Epirus, Attica, and Boeotia—became a Roman province, bearing the name Achaea. It should not be assumed that it was precisely in this wide political sense that Paul used the term. In the early imperial period there was a good deal of variation in the administrative arrangements for Achaea, and *the saints* were probably not scattered over a very wide area; there is a hint of this in 1 Cor. xvi. 15, where the household of Stephanas, in Corinth, are said to be the first Christians in Achaea. According to Acts xvii. 34 converts, though few, had been made in Athens, which would thus not (in Paul's usage) be included in Achaea.

2 **I wish you grace and peace from God our Father and the Lord Jesus Christ.** Identical words are found in 1 Cor. i. 3; see *1 Corinthians*, pp. 34 f.: 'Grace is the antecedent being and act of God which are the ground of all Christian existence (cf. 1 Cor. xv. 10); peace is the outcome of God's redemptive act, the total state of well-being to which men are admitted (cf. Rom. v. 1). When one Christian wishes grace and peace to another he prays that he may apprehend more fully the grace of God in which he already stands, and the peace he already enjoys. Each comes from God the Father and the Lord Jesus Christ; the Father is the source, Christ the means or agent.' It is worth noting that Paul places the two Persons side by side, without any suggestion that one belongs to a different order of being from the other. *Grace and peace* is a Pauline formula, often used, and not thought out to fit the Corinthian situation; it is, however, particularly appropriate to that situation, in which peace, the fruit of reconciliation (cf. v. 19 f.) was sadly needed.

2. i. 3-11. THANKSGIVING

(3) Blessed is God, the Father of our Lord Jesus Christ, the Father of mercies and the God of all comfort, (4) who comforts us in all our affliction, to the end that we may be able

to comfort those who are in any kind of affliction, through the comforting with which we ourselves are comforted by God; (5) for as the sufferings of Christ overflow to us, so, through Christ, our comforting also overflows to you. (6) If we are afflicted, it is in the interests of your comforting and salvation;[1] if we are comforted, it is in the interests of your comforting, which takes effect in your endurance of the same sufferings that we also suffer; (7) and our hope for you is secure, because we know that as you share in the sufferings so you share in the comfort too.

(8) For, brothers, we do not wish you not to know about our affliction, which happened in Asia; we were weighed down beyond measure, beyond our strength, with the result that we despaired even of life; (9) yes, we ourselves have received within ourselves the sentence of death, that we should trust no more in ourselves, but in God who raises the dead. (10) It is God who rescued us from so threatening a death, and will rescue us, God in whom we have set our hope; and[2] he will yet deliver us, (11) if you too cooperate on our behalf by your prayer, in order that from many people[3] thanks may be rendered to God on our behalf for the gift of grace bestowed on us through the agency of many.

The pattern that has been observed in Romans and 1 Corinthians is followed here also; as in many Greek letters, an address in the conventional form is followed by a thanksgiving; see *Romans*, pp. 23 f.; *1 Corinthians*, p. 35. Nowhere however in the Pauline letters is the conventional form animated by such profound feeling; Paul gives thanks not simply for the progress of the Gospel in general but for a special deliverance from death which he himself has recently experienced. He sees this experience in relation to the

[1] In verses 6*b*, 7*a*, there is in the MSS a good deal of variation in the order of words, but this makes no substantial difference to the general sense of the passage.

[2] I omit ὅτι with 𝔓[46] B D* 1739 Or. If it is read this sentence depends on the preceding verse, and we must render *we have set our hope that he will* .... This is more awkward and repetitive than the text of the old authorities followed here.

[3] So most MSS; a few (including 𝔓[46]) have ἐν πολλῷ προσώπῳ, the meaning of which is far from clear. There is little to be said for a badly attested reading, and a conjecture, both of which mean 'in the general assembly' of the church, though they are supported by Héring.

progress of the Gospel, but for him personally it has meant a sentence of death and a last minute reprieve—a sequence that helps to manifest the apostolic Gospel. He expresses his thanksgiving in a form that probably owes something to Jewish liturgical usage.

3 **Blessed is God.** Paul's word (εὐλογητός) is frequently used in the Old Testament, not least in the Psalms, to render the Hebrew *baruk*. This observation leads to later Jewish liturgical material, notably the Eighteen Benedictions of the synagogue service, all cast in a form that may be illustrated by the first:

> Blessed art thou (*baruk 'attah*), O Lord our God and God of our fathers, God of Abraham, God of Isaac, and God of Jacob, the great, mighty and revered God, the most high God, who bestowest loving-kindnesses, and possessest all things; who rememberest the pious deeds of the patriarchs, and in love wilt bring a redeemer to their children's children for thy name's sake (Singer, p. 44).

The Hellenistic synagogue no doubt used corresponding formulations in Greek. The parallel, as well as indicating Paul's own background in pious Judaism, is probably decisive (so Kümmel) on the question whether Paul's sentence (which in Greek has no verb) should be understood as indicative or optative: Blessed is, or blessed be, God. The former is preferable, though the language equally permits the latter (which is preferred by Bachmann and Windisch). For the indicative, cf. Rom. i. 25; (ix. 5); and see Robertson, p. 396. The distinction may be to some extent unreal; the invocation of blessing is blessing.

Blessed is God could be a purely Jewish utterance; Paul defines his meaning in a Christian sense by the words that follow. God is **the Father of our Lord Jesus Christ.** Literally the clause runs, *Blessed is the God and Father of our Lord Jesus Christ*, and this could be taken, and has been taken, in the sense, Blessed is he who is the God of our Lord Jesus Christ (the God whom Jesus acknowledged and served), who is also the Father whom our Lord Jesus Christ recognized. This is unlikely; Paul shows no interest in the personal religion of Jesus. He retains his personal address to God as Abba (see Rom. viii. 15, with the note; Gal. iv. 6), but probably because it had already become a part of Christian usage. It is more probable that we have here a Christian version of a Jewish blessing: Blessed is God; but the God of the Old Testament, the God of our fathers, is now known to us as also the Father of the Son whom he sent into the world (Gal. iv. 4), Jesus Christ. In view of the fact that two other New Testament authors (or one, if Ephesians was written by Paul) use precisely the same words (Eph. i. 3; 1 Pet. i. 3) it seems that the formula had achieved widespread liturgical and devotional use. This is not surprising since it expresses the fundamental conviction that Jesus signifies not the contradiction but the fulfilment of the faith of the Old Testament and of Judaism; the reference to Jesus Christ determines both the way in which God is God and the way in which he is Father (Bachmann). Equally fundamental is the description of Jesus Christ himself as *our Lord* (cf. Rom. x. 9; 1 Cor. xii. 3, with the notes). Though *Lord* (*κύριος*) no doubt became conventionalized with use it denoted the absolute authority of Jesus and his right to require unquestioning obedience from those who, though his younger brothers (Rom. viii. 29), were also his slaves (Rom. i. 1).

Paul now strikes out on his own, applying the Blessing to the circumstances that led him to his act of thanksgiving. God is **the Father of mercies.** Cf. Wisd. ix. 1 (*κύριος τοῦ ἐλέους*); but the language is still that of Jewish liturgy. The prayer (*'ahabah rabbah*, 'With abounding love') that introduces the Sh^e^ma' in the synagogue service includes the words, 'O our Father, merciful Father (*ha'ab ha-raḥ^a^man*), ever compassionate, have mercy upon us'. Cf. 1QH x. 14, the God of mercies (*'el ha-raḥ^a^mim*), and for other parallels see J. Jeremias, *Abba* (1966), p. 30, note 62. According to Jeremias (op. cit. pp. 30 f.), we have to do here not with an address to God as Father, a Father described by the adjectival genitive as merciful, but with 'Father' as a word giving individual effect to the quality mentioned: 'Du Inbegriff der Barmherzigkeit', 'Thou who art the epitome of mercy'. Windisch similarly says that God is the 'creator and primal origin of mercy'. In the New Testament 'mercies' (*οἰκτιρμοί*) is a mainly Pauline word, used nearly always (Rom. xii. 1; 2 Cor. i. 3; Phil. ii. 1; Heb. x. 28; the exception is Col. iii. 12) in the plural, probably because it is so used in the LXX as the translation of a Hebrew plural (*raḥ^a^mim*). Paul evokes this Old Testament background in the description of his own circumstances and the deliverance (see verses 8 ff.) that God has wrought for him; cf. e.g. Ps. xxxix (xl). 12 (with, in verse 14, the verb ῥύεσθαι, used in 2 Cor. i. 10); lxviii (lxix). 17 (with θλίβεσθαι, used in 2 Cor. i. 6); lxxviii (lxxix). 8 (again with ῥύεσθαι in the next verse). God delivers the afflicted, not because he is under obligation to do so, but of mercy, pity, alone. The thought is taken a little further, from God's inward property of mercy to his outward actions, when he is described as **the God of all comfort.** The noun (παράκλησις), with the cognate verb (παρακαλεῖν), occurs fairly frequently in 2 Corinthians; no single translation will suffice. At viii. 4, 17 (the noun); ii. 8; v. 20; vi. 1; viii. 6; ix. 5; x. 1; xii. 8. 18 (the verb) the meaning is quite different from that of noun and verb in the present paragraph (with which cf. ii. 7; vii. 4, 6, 7, 13; and perhaps xiii. 11). The alternation is somewhat harsh (especially between ii. 7 and ii. 8) but by no means impossible; the Greek word can bear the various meanings required by the contexts. The present context, of affliction, peril, and deliverance, determines the sense here as comfort. This occurs in a number of important Old Testament passages, notably Isa. xl. 1; li. 3, 12, 19; the existence of these passages, and the quasi-technical messianic use of the corresponding Hebrew (*niḥam*) and its cognates, makes it probable that Paul saw his own comforting and deliverance not as a single act of God wrought out of special favour for himself but as part of the total messianic comfort and deliverance. This is confirmed by the use he proceeds to make of it in verses 4, 6, 7. It is clear that comfort means not that Paul is consoled *in* his afflictions but that he is delivered *out of* them.

God is the ultimate source of every act of comforting, but
Paul moves quickly from the general (it may be that the established
4 formula continues up to the end of verse 3) to the particular: **who**
(the relative is perhaps causal—'because he comforts'; so Calvin) **comforts us in all our affliction.** Some detail about the affliction Paul refers to is given in verses 8 f.; cf. also vii. 6, and the longer and more explicit list of afflictions in xi. 23-7. Not only the immediately following verses but the whole epistle brings out the fact that Christian existence, manifested most plainly in the life of an apostle, consists in this paradoxical combination of affliction and comfort—both of which are not of self-contained interest but of wider application. The plural *us* reflects this application; Paul is speaking in the first instance of himself, but his affairs are not a purely private concern. This point must be remembered at several places in this epistle, in which the use of singular and plural often

raises considerable problems. The purpose of the comfort Paul receives is **that we may be able to comfort those who are in any kind of affliction.** In this verse a Greek word (πάσῃ) changes its meaning from *all* to *any*. The latter use is probably due simply to repetition, not Semitic influence (Beyer, p. 190); indeed, it hardly needs explanation (M. iii. 200; B.D. §275. 3). The apostle stands in a position which is unique because it is determined by its relation to the unique saving action of God. It is probably true that many elements contributed to the notion of apostleship as this developed in primitive Christianity—the Jewish *shaliaḥ*, the philosophical and gnostic missionary, and the 'divine man'—but none of these played so fundamental a part in Paul's understanding of his mission as his special relation with the eschatological event of Christ crucified and risen, which is manifest alike in his carrying about the killing of Jesus (iv. 10) and in his deliverance from death (verse 10), which gives visible, historical form to his trust in God who raises the dead. These things, not his personal merit, make him an example, and universalize the chastening and the comfort he receives. The thought here is thus more profound than the non-Christian parallels which Allo illustrates by quoting Virgil, *Aeneid* i. 630; 'non ignara mali miseris succurrere disco' (Schlatter similarly refers to Ketuboth 8b; there are more examples in Windisch). Paul comforts others not through his own strong personality but **through the comforting** (παράκλησις, a *nomen actionis*) **with which we ourselves are comforted by God**. Cf. vii. 6, though this refers to a different occasion.

The sufferings of Paul, and, less obviously, of other Christians too, have the significance Paul ascribes to them because they are
not their own sufferings. **As the sufferings of Christ overflow** 5
to us (that is, abound in our direction, abound so as to reach us; the metaphor in the English *overflow* is not too strong to express this), **so, through Christ, our comforting also overflows to you** (the last two words are not in the Greek but are needed in order to complete what appears to be the sense; see below). *The sufferings of Christ* may be taken in two ways; probably both are right and should be combined. (a) The sufferings are those *experienced by* Christ; these are extended so as to reach and be shared by others. (b) The phrase is closely analogous to the Hebrew 'sufferings of the Messiah' (*ḥeble ha-mashiaḥ*), which means not sufferings personally borne by the Messiah (so that we

should not, with Goudge, translate 'the sufferings of the Christ') but sufferings associated with him, 'messianic sufferings' ushering in the messianic age in a period of woe preceding eternal bliss. Perhaps the most primitive form taken by Christian belief about the death of Jesus was that he had taken this suffering upon himself and endured it on behalf of the elect; Paul himself developed his doctrine of the atonement from this source (*Romans*, p. 122). The continuation of life in this world after the death and resurrection of Jesus, often, for Christians, in uncomfortable circumstances, could most easily be explained on the supposition that some of *the sufferings of Christ* had been allowed to reach, and to be endured by, his followers. There is little doubt that Paul, even if Col. i. 24 is judged not to have been written by him, held this view, and believed that his own sufferings, as indeed his work in general, had eschatological significance. For him, the suffering was a matter not of apocalyptic speculation but of historical fact (iv. 8 ff.; vi. 4 ff.; xi. 23 ff.). This was true, too, in some degree, of the church as a whole; its being was characterized by such suffering. The 'holy cross' (Luther) is a mark of the church.

So is *comforting*; and Paul's comfort *overflows* to the Corinthians; cf. iv. 12, Death is at work in us, but life in you. The suffering of Jesus is redemptive; so in a subordinate degree is the suffering of the apostle, and brings comfort to his converts. No experience of
6 his is without value to the church (cf. v. 13). **If we are afflicted, it is in the interests of** (ὑπέρ; B.D. §231.2; Moule, *Idiom*, p. 65, 'with a view to') **your comforting and salvation**—because our being afflicted leads to our being comforted, and this we share with you; and our common comforting is not human cheerfulness but an aspect of the whole movement from death to life which marks the last days. More explicitly, **if we are comforted, it is in the interests of your comforting.** Clearly it would be pointless to speak of the comforting of the Corinthian Christians with the same kind of comforting that Paul enjoys if they did not experience, and endure, sufferings analogous to his; we can only guess, however, what these may have been. The comforting **takes effect** (for the verb ἐνεργεῖσθαι cf. e.g. iv. 12; Gal. v. 6) **in your endurance of the same sufferings that we also suffer**. Profoundly conscious as he is of his special apostolic vocation, Paul does not draw an absolute distinction between himself and the ordinary Christian who is not an apostle; the special thing about an apostle is that a

common Christian pattern comes in him to a particularly sharp focus. This pattern, of suffering and comfort, of death and resurrection, is not a matter of bad and good fortune, but of God's
intention; hence **our hope for you is secure** (for the adjective, 7
βέβαιος, a common commercial term, cf. Rom. iv. 16, 'that the promise might be secure'; and cf. i. 21 for the cognate verb); it is founded on God's mercy, and confirmed by present fact. **Because we know** (the nominative participle, εἰδότες, is not properly constructed in the sentence, since it does not refer to the subject of the main clause; it agrees with the subject of a variant form of the sentence, and is causal, 'We hope . . . because we know . . .'; there are many parallels in Paul, classical literature, inscriptions, and the papyri—see Bachmann for examples) **that as you share in the sufferings, so you share in the comfort too.** In the last clause (which has no expressed verb) it would be possible to understand a future instead of a present tense: 'as you share in the sufferings, so you will share in the comfort too'. If this alternative is accepted it becomes necessary to drop *because*, and to suppose that *we know* (oddly expressed by a participle instead of a finite verb) repeats *our hope*: 'Our hope is secure; we know that you will share . . .'. But on all counts this way of taking the clause is less probable. Affliction and comfort are experienced at the same time—though this does not exclude the thought of a future deliverance.

From what has been said in verses 3–7, and especially from the proposition in verse 6a, it follows that Paul's sufferings should be a source of strength to his converts. He has no motive for
concealing them, as if they were tokens of failure and defeat. **For,** 8
brothers (for this address cf. viii. 1; xiii. 11, and the note on i. 1), **we** (in these verses the first person plural hardly differs from the singular) **do not wish you not to know** (cf. viii. 1, and, as closer parallels, Rom. i. 13; xi. 25; 1 Cor. x. 1; xii. 1; 1 Thess. iv. 13) **about** (another use—cf. verses 6, 7—of the hardworking preposition ὑπέρ; see Moule, *Idiom*, p. 65, and cf. viii. 23; xii. 8) **our affliction, which happened** (many MSS add, to us, which undoubtedly gives the sense) **in Asia** (that is, the Roman province, whose capital was Ephesus). The reference must be to a particular event, or sequence of events, but it is impossible to identify it with certainty. It cannot have been the incident referred to in 1 Cor. xv. 32, for it seems that Paul is now informing the Corin-

thians of it for the first time (though Schlatter thinks that the lack of detail here means that the Corinthians must have known already what Paul had in mind). If it refers to the riot of Acts xix. 23-40 this must have been far more dangerous to Paul's life than Acts allows us to see; this is quite possible. We may recall also the various perils of xi. 23 ff. As good a suggestion as any is that Paul has been seriously ill; Clavier (*Studia Paulina*, p. 77) draws attention to hints in the narrative that suggest a peril arising within rather than without. Allo reaches a similar conclusion; it is not clear why Strachan should think of physical violence, perhaps lynching. The nature of Paul's supposed illness has elicited many conjectures; see xii. 7, with the note. None of these is more than a conjecture, but it is certain that Paul's life was in serious danger, as the following words make clear. **We were weighed down** (like an overloaded ship) **beyond measure** (*καθ' ὑπερβολήν*: the noun and its cognates are particularly characteristic of 2 Corinthians—i. 8; iii. 10; iv. 7, 17; ix. 14; xi. 23; xii. 7; in the rest of the New Testament five times in all), **beyond our strength, with the result that we despaired** (*ἐξαπορηθῆναι*; cf. iv. 8, and, for the construction, Dionysius of Halicarnassus, *Ant. Rom.* vii. 18. 2, *ἐξαπορεῖσθαι ἀργυρίου*, to be at a loss for money) **even of life.** The purpose of this experience has already been indicated (verse 6).
9 **Yes** (*ἀλλά*, adversative to what is implied in the preceding: 'We could no longer hope for life, but on the contrary . . .'), **we ourselves** (this strengthens the reflexive which is about to be used; cf. x. 12, and see B.D. §283.4) **have received** (or 'accepted'—fighting against it no more; so Héring) **within ourselves the sentence of death.** The verb (*ἐσχήκαμεν*) is in the perfect tense, not the aorist as might be expected, possibly because (M. i. 145; cf. 248) the aorist (*ἔσχον*) is nearly always ingressive, though B.D. §343.2 (cf. Allo) consider that here (though not in all places in the epistle where it is used) there is good reason for the perfect. The meaning will be that though the sentence was not immediately carried out it remained in force, so that Paul knows that henceforth his only hope lies in resurrection. This is most natural if the threat was illness. *Sentence* is here the probable meaning of a word (*ἀπόκριμα*) that seems to have been often used of favourable imperial decisions. M.M. (s.v.) develop this thought: 'Dittenberger defines these [*ἐπιστολαί, ἀποκρίματα, διατάγματα*] successively in the context [cf. *O.G.I.S.* 494. 19 f. (II 131)] as dispatches

addressed by the proconsul to the Emperor, the Senate, etc., replies given to deputations of provincials to him, and *edicta*, or documents addressed to the people at large, and not to individuals . . . Paul . . . may be taken as meaning that he made his distressed appeal to God, and kept in his own heart's archives the answer—"ἀποθάνῃ· τὸ δὲ ἀποθανεῖν κέρδος [You are to die; but to die is gain]", as we might reconstruct it.' The thought is pleasing, but fanciful. *Sentence* is the right translation in this context (see Lietzmann's quotation from Theodoret); Paul could hardly have used the more explicitly condemnatory word (κατάκριμα) in view of Rom. viii. 1. According to Héring, what Paul feared was not death itself, but a premature end to his Gentile mission; but this is not what Paul goes on to say.

The next clause is introduced by a word (ἵνα) that normally denotes purpose, and there is no need to suppose (as some do) that it here expresses result, though purpose achieved in events in the past is result, intended result. The affliction and the deliverance took place in order **that we should trust no more** (the perfect subjunctive, πεποιθότες ὦμεν, with the negative, suggests the discontinuance of an existing condition) **in ourselves, but in God who raises the dead.** Death marks the frontier of human existence. Within the area thus defined man has, or at least appears to have, a certain scope for self-confidence; but to approach the frontier, as Paul had done, is to recognize not merely the limits but the ultimate self-deception of such self-confidence. It is because this epistle as a whole moves on this boundary line between life and death that it contains so much persistent questioning of all human security, and is so uncomfortable a document. If, however, it dismisses all human comfort, security, and confidence, it is in the interests of the only true comfort, security, and confidence. It is *God who raises the dead* (cf. Deut. xxxii. 39; 1 Sam. ii. 6). This was Jewish commonplace: R. Johanan said, Three keys are in God's hand, which are not put into the hand of any representative of his: the key to the rain (Deut. xxviii. 12), the key to the womb (Gen. xxx. 22), and the key to the quickening of the dead (Ezk. xxxvii. 13) (Taanith 2a; for many parallel passages see S.B. i. 523, and cf. the second of the Eighteen Benedictions: Thou, O Lord, art mighty for ever, thou quickenest the dead, thou art mighty to save (Singer, p. 44)). Cf. Rom. iv. 17. Paul however is not simply citing a familiar formula.

> To be dead means not to be. Those who are not, cannot will and do, nor can they possibly be objects of the willing and doing of others. *ἀνάστασις ἐκ νεκρῶν* [the resurrection of the dead] is not one possibility of this kind with others. Where it takes place, God and God alone is at work. To raise (*ἐγείρειν*) the dead, to give life (*ζωοποιεῖν*) to the dead, is, like the creative summoning into being of non-being, a matter wholly and exclusively for God alone, quite outside the sphere of any possible cooperating factors (Heb. xi. 19; 2 Cor. i. 9; Rom. iv. 17) (Barth, *C.D.* IV i. 301).

Physical illness, the shadow of death, the failure of his work in Corinth, were among the causes that led to the breaking down of a man who, if any had ground for confidence in the flesh, had more (Phil. iii. 4; cf. 2 Cor. xi. 22 f.). The church at Corinth, like many another since, thought it could by-pass affliction on the way to comfort; the theme of the epistle is that this is impossible (cf. Acts xiv. 22). Christian discipline means, for an apostle and for the church as a whole, a progressive weakening of man's instinctive self-confidence, and of the self-despair to which this leads, and the growth of radical confidence in God.

Confidence in God grows through experience of his power to
10 deliver. **It is God who rescued** (cf. Rom. vii. 24; xv. 31; Col. i. 13; 1 Thess. i. 10; 2 Thess. iii. 2) **us from so threatening** (literally, 'so great', but the colourless adjective is not appropriate here in English; perhaps 'so terrible') **a death** (Bachmann and Kümmel accept the plural, read by 𝔓[46] and some other MSS), **and will rescue us** (the present tense, *καὶ ῥύεται*, found in a large number of MSS, and the omission of the words by a few, is probably due to the occurrence of the future later in the verse; it was felt—as Allo still feels—that a sequence of past, present, and future was suitable). God had rescued Paul (it seems) from physical death; Paul is not confident that God will do this whenever circumstances threaten him—he is content to be absent from the body and present with the Lord (v. 8). The present act of deliverance had the effect of providing Paul with a comfort he could communicate to the Corinthians, and educating him out of confidence in himself and into confidence in God. What future rescues might mean only the future would show; but **God** can be defined as the one **in whom we have set our hope**. The sentence

ends here; see note 2 on p. 57. *Hope* is confidence (in God) understood with special reference to the future; cf. the use in Rom. iv. 18, in a context similarly determined by confidence in God's power to bring life out of death.

The closing words of this verse must be attached to verse 11, the text (see notes 2, 3 on p. 57) and construction (see Moule, *Idiom*, p. 108) of which are doubtful and obscure. Paul first reaffirms his confidence in God as Saviour: **and he will yet deliver us**; then remembers that God acts through the prayers of his people, and that if he (Paul) can minister comfort to his people, his people may also minister to him in that their prayers secure God's gifts for him, and that they may join in the chorus of thanksgiving for what God gives and does. The opening clause
(a genitive absolute) is clear enough: **if you too cooperate** 11
(probably, with me; possibly, with one another; according to Schlatter, with God) **on our behalf by your prayer.** It seems most natural to take this *prayer* in the sense of intercession; and Kümmel's argument that it refers (as does the latter part of the verse) to thanksgiving is hardly supported by the passage he quotes from Sifre Deut. 27 (on iii. 24) (71 a) (If the prayer of one individual for many is heard in such a way, much more will the prayer of many for one individual). Intercession helps (in a way Paul does not stop to explain) to set in motion the divine act, and this in turn leads to thanksgiving. This is the sense of the final clause (introduced by ἵνα) that follows: **in order that from many people thanks may be rendered to God** (the last two words are not in the Greek; there is no question that they are intended, and in English it seems better to make them explicit) **on our behalf for the gift of grace** (χάρισμα; the word has many meanings—see *Romans*, pp. 113, 134, 237, and *1 Corinthians*, p. 38; here it refers primarily to the act of rescue) **bestowed on us through the agency of many** (translating as if Paul had written τὸ διὰ πολλῶν—as Denney points out, a usage not uncharacteristic of him; if we take the text as it stands, without the article, διὰ πολλῶν reduplicates ἐκ πολλῶν προσώπων; Moule, *Idiom*, p. 108, sets out the grammatical problem very clearly). *From many people*: Paul could well have been content here with a pronoun (ἐκ πολλῶν); it is true that the noun he adds (προσώπων) had become common in Hellenistic Greek for 'person', but this does not explain the addition. It may be that he thinks of it in its primary sense of

'face'—many faces upturned to God in prayer; or he may think of it in the sense it has in drama—there are many different characters in the play, but all cooperate to the same end and join in the same thanksgiving when it is achieved. The verb 'to give thanks' (εὐχαριστεῖν) is seldom used (as here) in the passive; according to Kümmel the only true parallels to this passage are Justin, *I Apology* lxv. 5; lxvi. 2; cf. also Hermas, *Similitude* vii. 5, where the active has a direct object. Judith viii. 25 hardly supports the meaning 'to pray' (Héring).

According to Bachman, Paul begins his dispute with Corinth by referring to the affliction which was the first event in the period during which the relations discussed in the epistle developed. From here up to chapter vii Paul unfolds them chronologically. This may to some extent oversimplify the structure of chapters i–vii, but is not far wrong.

B. PAUL'S PLANS FOR CORINTH, AND THEIR WORKING OUT IN THE PAST i.12–ii.13

3. i. 12-22. PAUL'S BOASTING; BEHIND PAUL'S PLANS LIES THE FULFILMENT OF GOD'S PLAN IN CHRIST

(12) For our boasting is this: it consists in the testimony of our conscience, that it was in the simplicity[1] and sincerity that come from God, not in fleshly wisdom but in God's grace, that we behaved in the world, and especially in relation to you. (13) Sincerity—yes, for we are not writing to you anything different from what you read and indeed recognize;[2] and I hope you will go on recognizing to the

[1] *Simplicity* translates ἁπλότητι, the text of D G lat sy; other MSS, including 𝔓[46] B ℵ, have ἁγιότητι (*holiness*). The words, especially when written in uncials, look much alike (ΑΠΛΟΤΗΤΙ: ΑΓΙΟΤΗΤΙ); confusion would be easy. Reasons for preferring *simplicity* are given in the exposition; see also Lietzmann.

[2] *And indeed recognize* is omitted by 𝔓[46] B, probably through homoeoteleuton.

end, (14) as indeed you have recognized in part, that we are your boasting just as you are ours in the day of our Lord Jesus.

(15) It was in this confidence that I decided to come to you at first, that you might get a second kindness,[1] (16) and to go on by way of you to Macedonia, and again from Macedonia to come to you, and by you to be sent on my way to Judaea. (17) Do you think, then, that, when I made this decision,[2] I was acting with fickleness? Or the plans I make, do I make them according to the flesh, so as to say at the same time, Yes, yes, and No, no?[3] (18) God is to be trusted, and he will bear witness that our word to you is not Yes and No. (19) For God's Son, Christ Jesus, who was proclaimed among you by us, by me and Silvanus and Timothy, did not prove to be Yes and No; on the contrary, in him a final Yes has been pronounced. (20) For however many God's promises may be, in him is the Yes to them; for this reason it is through him too that the Amen to God, to his glory, is pronounced by us. (21) And he who guarantees us, along with you, for Christ, and made us share his anointing, is God, (22) who also sealed us, and in the Spirit put in our hearts the first instalment of our full blessedness.

The thanksgiving Paul offered (i. 3-11) was sincere; he was the kind of writer who means what he says because he is constitutionally incapable of saying what he does not mean. But he was certainly capable of putting a situation in the best rather than the worst possible light, and imputing the highest motives even when he had reason to suspect something a good deal lower. He had spoken of the comfort the Corinthians had received through his experiences, of their intercession for him, and of the thanksgiving they will offer in recognition of the gift of grace their prayers have won for him. He must however have been aware that there was, or had been, a different atmosphere in Corinth, that he had been accused

[1] So almost all MSS; B has *joy* (χαράν instead of χάριν). This is probably a slip; the difference in meaning is not great. It has however been argued that joy is original and that the more familiar theological word was substituted for it.

[2] D it sy have *when I made this plan* (βουλευόμενος, instead of βουλόμενος), probably through assimilation to the latter part of the verse.

[3] 𝔓[46] and the Vulgate have simply Yes and No. This is preferred by Kümmel, but see Dinkler, p. 100, note 3. The short text is probably due to assimilation to verses 18 and 19.

there of levity and fickleness, of writing one thing, saying another, and doing a third. There is something to put right, and he proceeds to put it right.

So far from being exposed to rebuke, he has something to boast
12 about: **Our boasting is this**. Words of the 'boasting' root (καυχᾶσθαι, καύχημα, καύχησις) are particularly common in 2 Corinthians. Altogether they occur in 2 Corinthians 29 times; in Romans 8 times; in 1 Corinthians 9 (10) times; in Galatians 3 times; in Philippians 3 times; in 1 Thessalonians once; nowhere else in the genuine Pauline letters. There must be some reason for this relative frequency. C. H. Dodd (*New Testament Studies* (1953), pp. 73–82) explains Paul's inward development in terms of the psychological necessity he felt of having a ground of boasting (καύχημα); it was only a 'second conversion', falling between the writing of 2 Cor. x–xiii and i–ix (on the critical view of the epistle involved see Introduction, pp. 12 f., 19–25) and caused by the affliction of i. 8, that finally freed him from this mental and spiritual constraint. Apart from the literary and historical problems raised by this reconstruction of events, it harmonizes ill with the distribution of the words in question; the verb (καυχᾶσθαι) is more frequent in chapters x–xiii than in i–ix, but both nouns (καύχημα, καύχησις) are more frequent in chapters i–ix. It should be remembered that the words are used in the Old Testament in a good sense (e.g. Ps. xxxi (xxxii). 11, Boast (καυχᾶσθε), all you who are upright in heart), and that where the Old Testament discourages the wrong kind of boasting it does so by encouraging the right (Jer. ix. 22 f., quoted at 1 Cor. i. 31; 2 Cor. x. 17). The latter of these passages shows that in the Corinthian situation Paul had to deal with opponents who (in his view) boasted in the wrong way; partly by subconscious reaction, partly in order to put the matter right, Paul found himself talking frequently in terms of boasting (or glorying, or exulting—it is hard to maintain uniformity of rendering in English). This seems the most probable explanation. Paul's grounds for boasting are the sincerity and integrity of his behaviour.

His boasting **consists in the testimony of our conscience**; that is, he can boast that his *conscience* testifies to what follows. For *conscience* (συνείδησις) cf. iv. 2; v. 11. As at Rom. ii. 15 the word 'implies man's ability to detach himself from himself and view his character and actions independently. He is thus able to act as a witness for or against himself. His conscience is not so much the bar at which his conduct is tried, as a major witness, who can be called on either side as the case may be' (*Romans*, p. 53). See also Sevenster, *Seneca*, pp. 92 f., 99 ff., especially for the difference between the Stoic and the Pauline understanding of conscience; and Stoic passages cited by Windisch. Paul's conscience bears witness **that it was in** (this word (ἐν) is causal—Schlatter) **the simplicity and sincerity** (cf. Phil. i. 10 for the cognate adjective) **that come from God** (literally, 'in simplicity and sincerity of God'; the genitive, τοῦ θεοῦ, must denote the author), **not in fleshly wisdom but in God's grace, that we** (Paul refers primarily to himself, but verse 19 shows that his colleagues are in mind too) **behaved in the world, and especially in relation to you.**

The textual problem is this clause (see note 1 on p. 68) is very difficult to resolve. 'Holiness' (ἁγιότης) may be right, though it is not a word Paul uses elsewhere (he uses ἁγιωσύνη at Rom. i. 4; 2 Cor. vii. 1; 1 Thess. iii. 13), and in the present context a more specifically ethical notion seems to be in place; Paul is defending himself against a charge of duplicity, and an appeal to singleness of mind is particularly appropriate. If, however, Paul did use 'holiness' here he used it with strong ethical overtones, so that the variation makes little difference to the exegesis. Paul never had any intention of deceiving the Corinthians in any way; the point of this denial will appear in due course. Indeed, he had never deceived anyone; sincerity was the mark of his action throughout the world. Why the special reference to Corinth? Simply because it was to Corinth that he was writing? But Paul seems in at least one other respect to have treated Corinth as a special case: it was especially in Corinth, or more generally in Achaea, that he refused to accept any payment from the church he had founded (cf. e.g. xi. 8: I robbed other churches by taking pay from them in order that I might be able to serve you). There may have been good reasons for special care on Paul's part in his relations with Corinth. There is no difficulty in supposing that he was sensitive enough to perceive in his converts there the seeds of future trouble; the trouble duly arose, notwithstanding his circumspection.

His first point is ethical: he acted in *simplicity* and *sincerity*. The next clause describes his work from a more theological angle: *not in fleshly wisdom but in God's grace*; cf. 1 Cor. ii. 5 (That your faith might not depend on men's wisdom, but on God's power).

Wisdom (σοφία) occurs here only in the second epistle, frequently in the first (see *1 Corinthians*, pp. 17 f.), where *fleshly wisdom* finds parallels in e.g. 'the world's wisdom' (i. 20; ii. 6; iii. 19), 'men's wisdom' (ii. 5). This kind of wisdom was a local, Corinthian peril; the Corinthians themselves were the sort of people who fancied that they could achieve salvation by a wisdom of their own making and under their own control; this peril Paul had guarded against from the start, and it had been to some extent at least overcome, if we may judge from the fact that it is not again referred to in 2 Corinthians, which deals rather with a peril threatening Corinth from without (though it is evident that it found no difficulty in evoking echoes within, perhaps not unrelated to the old interest in wisdom). The counterpart to *fleshly wisdom*, which in turn helps to define it, is *God's grace*. *Grace* (χάρις) is well illustrated in chapters viii, ix, which deal with Paul's collection: it denotes free, active love (cf. *Romans*, p. 76, and passim). It is also used for the special gift that fitted and equipped Paul for his apostolic ministry (e.g. Rom. xii. 3), and for the special divine act and gift that, when received, make a man a Christian (2 Cor. vi. 1), and the continuing divine favour that enables the Christian life to persist. It goes too far, however, to regard it, as Windisch does, as almost synonymous with the power of God. Paul's behaviour was not lacking in wisdom, for there is a divine wisdom, paradoxically consistent with the foolishness of the message of the cross (1 Cor. i. 18), a way of thinking (and consequently of behaving) that is formed, both in dependence and in imitation, by God's grace. The wisdom Paul rejects is *fleshly* (σαρκικός) *wisdom*. For the meaning of 'flesh' (σάρξ) see *Romans*, pp. 157 f. As grace means an outgoing concentration of attention and care upon another, regardless of any legal claim that other may have upon the gracious person, flesh denotes an inward concentration of the *fleshly* person upon (neither God nor his neighbour but) himself. It does not mean a part of man, or his physical existence over against his soul or spirit, but the whole man wrongly directed, with his mind set (Rom. viii. 5 ff.) on that which is not God.

Paul, then, has a good conscience with regard to his relations with the Corinthians, and though he knows that this is no ground of justification (1 Cor. iv. 4) he can be proud of the fact. Out of the theology of the grace of God emerge, as gifts from God himself, the ethical virtues of *simplicity* and *sincerity*. This is the foundation of Paul's argument in this paragraph; and it ought to be recognized by the Corinthians themselves.

Sincerity (this word is not represented in the Greek but helps to 13
bring out the connection with the preceding verse)**—yes, for we are not writing to you** (cf. x. 9 ff. for a distinction between Paul's letters and his presence) **anything different from what you read and indeed recognize** (for the omission by some old MSS of the last three words see note 2 on p. 68). For *what you read* it might be possible to translate *what you perfectly well know* (taking the ἀνα- in ἀναγινώσκετε to have intensive force; Moule, *Idiom*, p. 89). The sense would then be, 'I am saying nothing new, but only reminding you of what you already know'. In the context however it appears that the Corinthians are accusing Paul of having deceived them, and it is perhaps best to take as his meaning, 'There are no hidden meanings in my letters, nothing to read between the lines; what I mean anyone can read straight out of the text'.

From his letters the Corinthians can—and do—recognize the sincerity of his intentions and the straightforwardness of his plans; but there should be more in their recognition than that. **I hope**
you will go on recognizing to the end, as indeed you have 14
recognized in part (Windisch shows that *in part*, ἀνὰ μέρος, must limit the degree of recognition)**, that we are your boasting** (cf. Jer. xvii. 14; Deut. x. 21; Judith xv. 9—Schlatter) **just as you are ours** (cf. v. 12; Paul puts them on the same level as himself) **in the day of our Lord Jesus.** These facts the Corinthians cannot fail to have recognized to some extent; it would make an apt counterpart to this if *to the end* (ἕως τέλους) were taken to mean *completely*: 'You have recognized in part; I hope you will recognize completely'. This is a possible meaning of the phrase, and it is so taken by Allo; its sense, however, is determined by the reference to *the day of our Lord Jesus*. It points to the future; Paul hopes that recognition will not be withdrawn, though he has some reason to fear that it may be.

He puts first the confidence that *we are your* ground of *boasting*: this was less likely to occur to the Corinthians (cf. 1 Cor. iv. 8-13) than that they were Paul's. Cf. 1 Cor. ix. 2; 2 Cor. xiii. 5; the Christian status of each confirmed that of the other. The epistle contains much evidence (e.g. ii. 1; iii. 1; vi. 4-10; x. 1-16; xi. 1; xii. 11, 16 ff.; xiii. 3) that the Corinthians were apt to disparage Paul, but they owed their faith to him, and therefore could not afford to despise his apostolic office, or its results. For his part, he could boast of them as the fruit of his work. *The day of our Lord Jesus* is the day of judgement, when all will appear before Christ's tribunal (v. 10). The phrase is common in the Pauline letters (1 Cor. i. 8; v. 5; Phil. i. 6, 10; ii. 16; 1 Thess. v. 2; 2 Thess. ii. 2), and rests upon the Old Testament 'day of the Lord', which has more than one connotation, but points to the time when God's action will be no longer hidden but manifest; in the New Testament period it was understood in an apocalyptic sense.

The last three verses have dealt in generalities; but the Corinthians have made a specific attack on Paul's sincerity, and it calls for a specific answer. He has failed, they say, to carry out the plans he announced for visiting them. Paul begins to deal with the charge but is carried away by a theological line of thought. He comes back to the charge at i. 23, in fact admitting it, but claiming that his motive was good, and conceived in the interests of the Corinthians. For the argument of i. 15-24 see, in addition to the commentaries, the essay by W. C. van Unnik in *Studia Paulina*, pp. 215–34.

15 **It was in this confidence** about you, and our mutual relations, **that I decided to come to you at first, that you might get** from me **a second kindness.** It is far from easy to disentangle from Paul's words in this paragraph exactly what he planned to do, failed to do, and in the end did. He writes allusively, for readers who, at least in outline, knew the facts, even though they misinterpreted them, and may possibly have misrepresented them. This verse states the aim, the next verse the details, of Paul's plan. Paul *decided* (giving βούλεσθαι its strong sense; it implies an act of will, a decision) to visit Corinth twice on a journey he was making (probably from the other side of the Aegean, from Ephesus or some other place in the province of Asia) to Macedonia, on the outward journey and again on his return. This plan suggests that *at first* (here better than 'formerly', or 'on the earlier of two occasions') should be taken with *come* rather than with *decided*, though the latter is suggested by the order of words. The second intended visit is described as a second kindness (χάρις; see verse 12); the word is used in a variety of ways, especially in this epistle, of God's generosity (e.g. viii. 9) and of man's (e.g. viii. 6). 'Favour' would suggest a condescension Paul would be unlikely to intend; 'gift' would be a good rendering if not taken in too concrete a sense; a 'second mark of his esteem' (Allo).

Paul's intention, then, was to visit Corinth first, **and to go on** 16
by way of you to Macedonia, and again from Macedonia to come to you, and by you to be sent on my way to Judaea. This plan is probably a development of that given in 1 Cor. xvi. 5 ff.; this is more probable than that 1 Cor. xvi is itself the complained of variation. There indeed Paul's meaning seems to be that he will not call in Corinth on his way to Macedonia, because he does not wish to see the Corinthians in passing but to spend some time with them; but he might well have changed his mind and decided to visit Corinth twice, on the outward journey as well as on the way back to Judaea. The journey which, according to Acts xx. 1 ff., took Paul from Ephesus first to Macedonia, then to Greece, and finally back to the East, falls at a later point, but this may only mean that the journey to Judaea (on which, presumably, Paul would be conveying the fruits of his collection for the poor saints) was deferred because of troubles in both Ephesus and Corinth.

Do you think then (this is an attempt to give the sense of *οὖν* 17
... *μήτι ἄρα*) **that, when I made this decision** (possibly the decision to add the extra visit to Corinth, more probably the decision to make the journey to Corinth and Macedonia as a whole), **I was acting with fickleness** (perhaps, since *fickleness* has the article, *the fickleness with which you charge me*—Windisch)**?** This was not quite the point. The Corinthians had not, it seems, objected to his making a plan to visit them, or to his changing this plan so as to visit them twice rather than once, but to his cancelling the visit or visits of which he had given notice. Reading between the lines, it appears that Paul is saying: I was going to Macedonia; I did not need to pass through Corinth either way, but in fact I planned to go out of my way to visit you, and then changed my plans to visit you twice; does that suggest that I am neglecting you? But he is in some difficulty because, however excellent his motive, he had changed his plans. Naturally this does not mean that he had not had good reasons for doing so. **The plans I make** (Paul now uses the related but different verb *βουλεύεσθαι*; it may be a synonym, but I take it that he intends a small difference in meaning)**, do I make them according to the flesh** (for the word *flesh*, *σάρξ*, see i. 12, with the note)**, so as to say** (*ἵνα* for the consecutive infinitive, though M. i. 210 regards it as final; see B.D. §391.5, and cf. Luke ix. 45) **at the same time** (these four words are essential to the argument, but have to be introduced into the

text) **Yes, yes, and No, no?** A man who lives a self-centred existence is necessarily undependable; he will at any moment change his mind and his plans if it appears to suit his own interest to do so. Paul knows well that it was not self-interest that led him to change his plans, but does not explain the matter till i. 23; his 'Yes, yes' and 'No, no' (which recall James v. 12; Matt. v. 37, though Paul's point is different) lead him off on a theological digression—which is not a digression in the sense that it makes the fundamental point that his behaviour is rooted in his message, in which there is no ambiguity.

18 Paul is not the only witness to his own integrity. **God is to be trusted** (van Unnik compares the Hebrew *n^e'eman*, which provides a link with verses 20 ff.), **and he will bear witness** (the last five words are not in the Greek but are needed to make sense of the sentence; for *God is to be trusted*, cf. 1 Cor. i. 9; x. 13; 1 Thess. v. 24; 2 Thess. iii. 3; for God as witness, cf. i. 23; xi. 31; Rom. i. 9; Phil. i. 8; 1 Thess. ii. 5, 10; the two together make up a kind of oath) **that our word to you is not Yes and No.** *Our word* is both 'what we say about our plans' and 'our preaching'. Once the latter theme is suggested Paul cannot refrain from developing it. The present verse provides no basis (notwithstanding Stauffer, pp. 137 f.; E.T., p. 158) for a discussion of the question whether the Christian message may or may not be described as dialectical. What Paul means is simply that there is no ambiguity about it. God's promises are plainly intelligible, and what he promises he performs. There is no fickleness about him. Hence—'Contradictoria non sunt in Theologia' (Bengel). Since Jesus Christ is the theme of the Gospel this is preeminently true about him.

19 **For God's Son, Christ Jesus, who was proclaimed among you by us** (according to Moule, *Idiom*, p. 119, there is throughout verses 15–24 a careful distinction between the singular and the plural of the first person; certainly the plural is here differentiated into its constituents—that is, it is a genuine plural), **by me and Silvanus and Timothy** (Why is Apollos not mentioned? Calvin asks, and answers that Paul, Silvanus, and Timothy had been more vilified; we may add the guess that Apollos's preaching appealed more strongly to the Corinthians), **did not prove to be** (ἐγένετο; perhaps simply 'was not') **Yes and No.** It is as God's Son that Jesus affirms the being and purpose of his Father. According to Acts xviii. 1-4 Paul arrived in Corinth alone, and

began to preach. In xviii. 5 he is joined by Silas and Timothy, who share his work. It is hardly open to doubt that Silas and Silvanus are the same person. xviii. 5 is the last of 13 (12) references to Silas in Acts; Silvanus joins Paul and Timothy in 1 Thess. i. 1; 2 Thess. i. 1. Timothy is mentioned as co-author with Paul of the present epistle; see i. 1 and the note. All these preached the same Gospel, and this Gospel was Christ. The message reached the Corinthians in the demonstration of the Spirit and of power (1 Cor. ii. 4). There is no equivocation in Christ; **on the contrary, in him a final** (the adjective is inserted in order to bring out the force of the perfect γέγονεν) **Yes has been pronounced.** The meaning of this Yes is brought out in the following verses (see also Cerfaux, *Christ*, p. 334; E.T., p. 446); it is not an affirmation of man's desires, or even of man's supposed needs, but of God's design. And to say Yes to God may mean saying No to man.

Paul's meaning is that it is in Jesus Christ that the purposes of
God, previously announced in the Old Testament, are fulfilled.
However many God's promises may be, in him is the Yes 20
to them; that is, whatever God has promised finds its fulfilment
in Christ. This will be understood in the first instance personally:
Jesus himself is the promised scion of the house of David (Rom.
i. 3; ix. 5), the deliverer who will come out of Zion (Rom. xi. 26).
Paul's thought however is more profound and subtle than this;
he seldom uses the simple 'testimony' method of adducing the
authority of the Old Testament. Jesus is the counterpart of Adam
(Rom. v. 14; 1 Cor. xv. 22, 45–9), the fulfilment of that to which
the figure of Adam could only point; he is the seed of Abraham
to whom the promise was made (Gal. iii. 16); he is Wisdom and
Torah. He constitutes the goal to which the whole history of Israel
pointed—the end of the law with a view to righteousness (Rom.
x. 4), himself the divine gift of righteousness, the necessity of
which the law could show, though it lacked the life-giving power
actually to achieve it (Gal. iii. 21). God has not yet finished his
work (in the present epistle see e.g. i. 14; iv. 14, 18; v. 1-10;
xi. 15; xiii. 4), but what he still has to do will be done through
Jesus. **For this reason, it is through him too** (or, For this reason
too, it is through him; but this gives a less satisfactory connection)
that the Amen (equivalent, as van Unnik points out, to Yes) **to**
God, to his glory, is pronounced by us. Compare 1 Cor. xiv. 16;
Amen suggests a liturgical context (cf. Moule, *The Phenomenon*

of the New Testament (1967), pp. 54, 68); upon the words 'through Jesus Christ God's Son' (see verse 18), the congregation say *Amen* (the 'customary Amen'—Plummer, noting the article). Certainly *Amen* (except in its unparalleled use as an introduction to sayings of Jesus) is a liturgical word, employed in Judaism and going back to the Old Testament (e.g. Deut. xxvii. 15-26; Jer. xi. 5; Ps. xli. 14), and its use in Christian worship may well have brought it to Paul's mind. No further explanation is needed, or probable; the '*–m–n* acrostic which some find in 1QS x. 1-4 is itself doubtful, and so is its messianic interpretation (Braun). The fulfilment of God's purposes, of which the person and work of Jesus constitute the primary affirmation, is reaffirmed by Christians, but reaffirmed by them through Jesus, in whom they are related to God and his purposes (1 Cor. i. 30; see Barth, *C.D.* IV iii, 12). Their *Amen* is thus, like his *Yes*, acted as well as spoken; God is glorified in the obedience of his people. The liturgical hint in *Amen* suggests that **by us** refers to the Christian community at large; in verse 19, however, *by us* means by Paul, Silvanus, and Timothy, the apostolic group, and in verse 21 *us* is distinguished from *you*. That Paul's apostolic labour is an outstanding Amen to God, and to his glory, is true, not because Paul is an outstandingly devoted Christian but because his apostolate is created by the Gospel of God's faithfulness to and fulfilment of his promises (cf. Rom. i. 2 ff.). But it is probable that here (as in verse 22) Paul is associating his fellow Christians with himself.

The word *Amen*, based on the Hebrew root '*-m-n*, suggests solidity, firmness; the significance of this is emphasized by van Unnik, whose essay has already been referred to. After resting his own impugned trustworthiness on the faithfulness of God in Christ, Paul, for the moment setting aside the question of his changed plans (it will be resumed in verse 23), develops the theme theologically. There is no question of God's faithfulness; but how is it communicated to men? It is God himself who effects the
21 steadfastness of both apostle and people. **He who guarantees us, along with you, for Christ, and made us share his anointing** (cf. 1 John ii. 20, 27), **is God** (or, less probably, God, who guarantees . . . , is also he who seals . . .). Cf. i. 7 and the note; the verb 'to guarantee' (βεβαιοῦν), with its cognates, is very common in commercial and legal papyri. It occurs very infrequently in the LXX; it is a sense, not a linguistic connection, that

links it with verse 20, for the few passages in Symmachus noted by van Unnik (p. 227) can hardly be said to bridge the gap. The word, however, is a Pauline word, for which 1 Cor. i. 6 ff. is particularly important: God verifies, confirms, the Gospel, by fulfilling its promises for preacher and hearers alike. They are guaranteed as Christ's property by God himself, whose being and faithfulness are pledged for theirs. God also *made us share* the *anointing* of Christ, himself the Anointed One. There is a play on words in the Greek (Χριστός . . . χρίσας) which the English only clumsily represents; it cannot have been accidental. See Cerfaux, *Christ*, p. 374, E.T. p. 498. Pagan parallels (Firmicus Maternus, *de Err. prof. Rel.*, 22—'habet diabolus christos suos') are relatively unimportant. The anointing of the Messiah, or Christ, means his election by God to office and function, and his equipment for carrying out the work to which he is called—the assurance of vocation and the guarantee of ultimately successful mission. Christians, being in Christ (that Paul here writes 'into Christ', εἰς Χριστόν, not 'in Christ', ἐν Χριστῷ, may be due to the commercial metaphor; we are, as it were, 'entered to Christ's account'), share his vocation and mission and as themselves anointed are assured of this not by the steadfastness of their own faith, or by the warmth of its emotional accompaniments, but by God himself. On the manner in which this guarantee is given, see below, pp. 80 f. Denney thinks that the anointing is to the apostolic office. The Corinthians are specifically included in 'guarantees', and this has the effect of excluding them from 'anointed'. It seems more probable that the second *us* includes both the *us* and the *you* of the previous clause.

Once embarked upon his commercial analogy, Paul proceeds to
use it to the full. God **also sealed us.** Abundant evidence is cited 22
by M.M. (s. v.; see also G. A. Deissmann, *Bible Studies* (1901), pp. 238 f.) for the use of sealing in the Hellenistic world. The seal, given and preserved intact, was a proof that a document had not been falsified, or goods tampered with in transit. It was also a mark of ownership; and the Christian, sealed (as the next verse suggests) with the Spirit, was both visibly marked out as God's property, and secured ready to meet examination at the day of judgement. Cf. also Ezek. ix. 4; 4 Ezra vi. 5; viii. 57 ff.

It is natural to think of both anointing (cf. Isa. lxi. 1) and sealing in terms of the Spirit; but in speaking directly of the Spirit Paul uses a further commercial metaphor—also connected with security (βεβαιότης) by Philo (*De Fuga et Inventione* 150 f., though the sense here is different—see Windisch). **In the Spirit** God **put in our hearts the first instalment of our full blessedness;** literally, he gave the earnest (ἀρραβών) of the Spirit in our hearts. *Earnest*, which seems to be no longer in current use in this sense, means money paid on account, the first instalment of a total sum due, itself part of the sum and the pledge that the whole amount will in due course be paid. For the use of Paul's Greek word in this sense, see M.M. (s.v.). The genitive *of the Spirit* is here taken to be appositional (see Robertson, p. 498; M. iii. 214): the earnest consisting of the Spirit. It would be possible (see N. Q. Hamilton, *The Holy Spirit and Eschatology in Paul* (1957), p. 32, on Rom. viii. 23) to take it as a partitive genitive: the first instalment of the whole Spirit. This however seems improbable in itself (Paul does not think of the Spirit as given in parts), and also misses the connection both here and in v. 5 (where the same word is used; see the notes) with the future. The Spirit is the divine agent that realizes resurrection (i. 9), 'eschatological existence', the life of the age to come, in the present. In other words, life in the Spirit (cf. Rom. viii. 1-13, with the notes) is life centred not upon self, or upon man, but upon God. This is the ultimate destiny of the human race in the future, and it is already anticipated before the arrival of the age to come.

In verses 21 f. Paul uses four images: the guarantee, anointing, sealing, the first instalment. They follow upon the summary of his preaching as the announcement that Christ is the final affirmation of all God's promises, and the *Amen* with which this proclamation is welcomed by the believer. *Amen*, as we have seen, has itself a liturgical ring, and it is often maintained (see especially Dinkler, pp. 99–117) that Paul's account of God's confirmation of the believer's faith is also expressed in liturgical language, with special reference to baptism. 'Among the four verbs that Paul uses, βεβαιοῦν [to guarantee] in the present denotes the total action of the baptismal event, whose particular aspects and motifs are described in the three verbs that follow in the aorist tense. What Paul means to express is that baptism is a transaction of a legal kind which unites the newly baptized person with all the rest of the baptized, whereby God himself establishes them all in Christ, and sets in motion a process which the Christian—borne by the χαρίσματα [spiritual gifts]—must ever anew lay hold of' (Dinkler,

p. 115; see also G. W. H. Lampe, *The Seal of the Spirit* (1951), pp. 3–7). There is a measure of important truth in this view, but it appears to have been exaggerated. The fact that the first participle (*who guarantees*) is in the present tense takes some weight off any possible baptismal allusion (unless the intention is to say: 'God confirms us . . . because we can recall the fact that he did in our baptism anoint . . . seal . . . give'). It is possible to find (as Dinkler convincingly does) baptismal elements in the usage of all four words, but there are other elements too. Thus 'to guarantee' may have a remote connection with baptism at 1 Cor. i. 6, 8; Col. ii. 7, but is quite differently used at Rom. xv. 8; the cognate adjective (βέβαιος) is not connected with baptism at either Rom. iv. 16 or 2 Cor. i. 7; the cognate noun (βεβαίωσις) is used once only, at Phil. i. 7, which has nothing whatever to do with baptism. 'To anoint' is used nowhere else by Paul. 'To seal' (σφραγίζειν) has no connection with baptism at Rom. xv. 28; it has at Eph. i. 13; iv. 30, but these should be regarded as post-Pauline. The cognate noun (σφραγίς) is used with reference to circumcision at Rom. iv. 11, and at 1 Cor. ix. 2 in a quite different way. 'To give an earnest' (ἀρραβῶνα διδόναι) may be connected with baptism in the post-Pauline Eph. i. 14; it could be so connected at 2 Cor. v. 5, but the interest of the passage in which this verse occurs lies not in baptism but in the future life. I have dealt here only with Pauline references, which for our purpose are the most important; the inclusion of others would make no noticeable difference. It is probable that, though Paul had not directly concerned himself in the matter, most of his Corinthian converts had been baptized (see *1 Corinthians*, pp. 47 ff.); their baptism had given outward expression to the faith they had come to hold, and doubtless had been an occasion when the work of the Spirit had confirmed their relation to Christ. But the present passage, which does not contain the word baptism, though it would have been easy to include it if Paul had wished to remind his readers of this particular event, refers more probably to the whole complex of their entry into the Christian life—conversion, faith, baptism, the reception of the Spirit. A similar view is taken by Héring, who aptly quotes Chrysostom, 'What does "He annointed, and he sealed" mean? That he gave the Spirit'.

Plummer and Hughes point out the Trinitarian implications of verses 21 f.

4. i. 23–ii. 13. PAUL'S PLANS MAY CHANGE BUT HIS PURPOSE REMAINS

(23) I invoke God as witness against my soul for the truth of this: it was with the intention of sparing you that I did not come again to Corinth. (24) This does not mean that we are lords over your faith, but we work together with you for your joy; for it is by faith that you stand. (1) But[1] I made up my mind to this, that I would not come to you again in sorrow. (2) For if I cause you sorrow, then who is it that makes me happy but he who is caused sorrow by me? (3) Moreover, I wrote to just this effect, that I might not come and be caused sorrow by those from whom I ought to have had joy, for I was confident in respect of all of you that my joy was the joy of all of you. (4) For I wrote to you out of much affliction and distress of heart, with many tears, not in order to inflict sorrow upon you, but that you might know the love that I have specially for you. (5) But if anyone has caused sorrow, he caused sorrow not to me, but to some extent—that I may not exaggerate—to all of you. (6) This reproof delivered by the main body is sufficient for the person in question, (7) so that on the other hand you ought rather to forgive and comfort him, lest he be swallowed up in excessive sorrow. (8) So I ask you to confirm your love for him; (9) for I wrote to you to find out how you would stand the test, whether[2] you were obedient in all things. (10) But to whom you forgive anything, I do too; for indeed what I have forgiven—if I have forgiven anything—I have forgiven on your account in the presence of Christ, (11) lest Satan should take advantage of us; for we are not ignorant

[1] Instead of *but* (δέ), $\mathfrak{P}^{46}$ B 69 have *for* (γάρ). This reverses the course of the argument if it is taken to connect with i. 24; it may, however, have been intended to connect with i. 23, i. 24 being a parenthesis: I acted so as to spare you . . . for I had made up my mind . . . . This could be the original sense and reading (cf. Kümmel).

[2] In place of *whether* (εἰ), B A have the Greek letter η, which could be taken either as a variant spelling of εἰ, or as the dative feminine singular of the relative pronoun (ᾗ), *in which* you were obedient . . . . See Robertson, p. 194; M. ii. 72.

of his designs. (12) But when I came to Troas to proclaim the Gospel of Christ, although a door stood open to me in the Lord, (13) I got no relief for my spirit because I did not find Titus my brother; instead of making full use of the opportunity I said Goodbye to them and went off to Macedonia.

At i. 15 Paul began to explain what his plans with respect to
Corinth had been, and why he had changed them. His vindication
of his own integrity led him to speak of the Gospel, which dictated
his plans, and of Christ who is the Gospel. He may, in view of these
profound connections of thought, be acquitted of digression, but
it remained nonetheless important to return to the simple point
and explain why he had not done what he had told the Corinthians
he would do. That Paul saw how important this was appears in the
opening words of the new paragraph (for the whole of which see
Schweizer, *C.O.N.T.*, 721). **I** (the pronoun is emphatic—Plummer 23
concludes that Silas and Timothy are not in mind here) **invoke
God as witness** (Schlatter points out the close verbal parallel in
Josephus, *Antiquities* i. 213) **against my soul** (myself—Bultmann,
E. & F., p. 153; my life—Moule, *Idiom*, p. 185) **for the truth of
this.** Similar asseverations occur at xi. 31; xii. 19; cf. Rom. ix. 1;
Gal. i. 20. Paul calls upon God as witness in Rom. i. 9; Phil. i. 8;
1 Thess. ii. 5, 10. They reflect Paul's energetic habit of speech
and his passionate nature, also a common rhetorical figure (see
Betz, *Lukian*, p. 117); but they correspond with his belief that his
life is exposed to God's scrutiny—cf. v. 11, We stand open to God.
God who looks upon the heart knows the truth of Paul's motives
better than the Corinthians do, and Paul sets his testimony above
theirs; and he is prepared for divine punishment if he should lie.
It was not because he made his plans *according to the flesh*, or
acted *with fickleness* (i. 17) that Paul had postponed his proposed
visit to Corinth. **It was with the intention of sparing you that
I did not come again to Corinth.** 'Intention' would be more
naturally expressed by the future participle (φεισόμενος), whereas
Paul uses the present (φειδόμενος), and it would be possible to
translate, I was sparing you when I did not come again; this,
however, would imply an intention to spare. What Paul means by
'sparing' is made clear by verse 2; had he come he would have
found it necessary to make the Corinthians unhappy, and this he
was unwilling to do. For an interesting parallel see Augustine,

Epistle CCXI. 2, quoted by Hughes. *Not . . . again* (οὐκέτι; the variant οὐκ probably arose in translation) with a verb in a frequentative tense would more naturally mean 'came no more', that is, 'gave up coming'; with an aorist (ἦλθον) it must mean, 'did not, on a specific occasion, come again'. An attempt to identify the specific occasion must be deferred to the note on verse 1. For the moment Paul turns aside to consider the possible implication of apostolic visits, planned, made, and not made. They might suggest that he is a dictatorial spiritual director who believed it to be desirable that he should be constantly available to order the life of
24 the church. Not so: **This does not mean that we are lords over your faith.** We might have expected (Lietzmann), 'We are not lords over you', and personal domination is indeed rejected, or rather reversed, at iv. 5 (see the note). Compare *Signs*, pp. 41–4; also Denney: 'Those who have received the Gospel have all the responsibilities of mature men; they have come to their majority as spiritual beings; they are not . . . subject to arbitrary and irresponsible interference on the part of others'. In this Denney is following (no doubt, consciously) the lead of Calvin ('This is always a settled principle—that pastors have no special lordship over men's consciences because they are ministers and helpers and not lords'); but both follow 1 Pet. v. 3. Allo translates 'your masters on the subject of the faith'; but this hardly does justice to the genitive (τῆς πίστεως). The reference to *faith* is appropriate, **for it is by faith that you stand**; that is, you have your existence as Christians by faith, and your Christian existence in faith is determined by no man, but by God only. The apostolic proclamation evokes faith, but there is no apostolic domination that can command it. Faith 'per dilectionem operatur, non per dominium cogitur' (Anselm, quoted by Goudge). All the apostle can do is to **work together with you for your joy**; literally, 'we are fellow-workers of your joy', *with you* not being expressed in Greek. It is possible that Paul may mean, 'we work together with one another', that is, Paul, Silvanus, and Timothy; or he may think of himself as working together with God (cf. 1 Cor. iii. 9—so Schlatter); but the present statement is an alternative to *lords over your faith*, and some kind of relation (not that of master and slave) with the Corinthians is probably intended. *Joy* is suggested by *spare*: If we had not acted so as to spare, the result would have been anything but joyful. Paul is no tyrant to make men tremble; he works

with them that in faith they may stand on their own feet (Calvin), and thereby have joy. For the connection between faith and joy see Phil. i. 25; also Rom. xiv. 17; xv. 13; Gal. v. 22; Col. i. 11; 1 Thess. i. 6. Paul does not say here, 'You are doctrinally sound', but, If you stand as Christians at all, it is by faith: *it is by faith that you stand.*

Paul returns to the examination of his plans. I am no lord over
your faith, ordering you what to do and believe, **but**, on the con- 1
trary, **I made up my mind** (ἔκρινα—reached a decision) **to this, that I would not come to you again** (πάλιν) **in sorrow**. *Again* occupies an ambiguous position, and the translation is intended to reproduce the ambiguity of the Greek. Paul may mean: 'I resolved not to come to you again in such circumstances that my coming would, on this occasion, be in sorrow'; or, 'I visited you once in sorrowful circumstances, and resolved that I would not repeat such a visit'. The latter is the more probable interpretation (ἐν λύπῃ immediately follows πάλιν); the former cannot be absolutely excluded, but unfortunately leads to no possibility of reconstructing the events behind 2 Corinthians. Paul's words could (on this interpretation) refer to any point after his first visit to Corinth: he simply resolved not to come to Corinth on a painful visit. If the latter interpretation is adopted we learn that Paul had already paid a painful visit to Corinth. This can hardly have been the first, founding, visit. This doubtless was not without its difficulties (however sceptically Acts xviii. 1–18 is regarded it is probably in this respect not far wide of the mark), but it could hardly be characterized as on the whole sorrowful (ἐν λύπῃ); 1 Corinthians gives no hint to this effect. Thus after the writing of 1 Corinthians Paul had visited Corinth again, and in painful circumstances. The fact of the second visit is confirmed by passages in 2 Corinthians which suggest that Paul's next visit will be his third (see xii. 14; xiii. 1, with the notes), also by passages which speak of an injury done to Paul, apparently when he was in Corinth (see verses 5-11; vii. 9, 12; x. 10). Thus the second visit must fall between 1 Corinthians and 2 Corinthians. We know that when Paul wrote 1 Cor. xvi. 5 ff. (cf. iv. 18-21) he was planning a visit to Corinth; in the present paragraph he is explaining why he had not paid an expected visit to Corinth. This (though it has grown—in intention—into a double visit) is so clearly similar to 1 Cor. xvi. 5 ff. that we must suppose that the two passages refer

to the same (intended) event. We may now choose between the following two possibilities. (1) After writing 1 Corinthians Paul paid an extra (unannounced) visit to Corinth. This had unfortunate consequences, and with a view to sparing the Corinthians Paul abandoned the projected (double) visit. (2) It was on the first member of the projected double visit that Paul ran into trouble in Corinth; he therefore abandoned the second member. Both alternatives are possible, but (2) is preferable, not only as the more economical, but also because it suits the 'not again' (that is, 'no more', οὐκέτι) of verse 23, and fits well into Paul's justification of himself. He had promised the Corinthians a visit, to be made on his return from Macedonia to Ephesus (1 Cor. xvi. 5 ff.); out of pure *kindness* (χάρις, i. 15 and note) he had changed his route and visited them on his way to Macedonia, intending to visit them on his way back also; it was only because of what happened in Corinth that he had not called on the return journey. They had thus been promised a visit, and had received one, earlier than they had been led to expect; what right had they to complain if the treatment Paul had experienced prevented them from receiving an additional visit—especially since in the circumstances this must have been a visit painful alike for him and for them? For further discussion of what may have happened on the 'sorrowful visit' see Introduction, pp. 7f., 18f. The immediately following verses suggest that the fault cannot have lain entirely with the Corinthians.

2 **For if I cause you sorrow,** as I should have done by paying you a visit at the time in question, **then who is it that makes me happy**, as you do, **but he who is caused sorrow by me?** This verse, unless Paul is writing in an impossibly flattering vein, must mean that relations between himself and the Corinthians were fundamentally good, and that not only at the time of writing (which might perhaps be explained by reversing the order of chapters i–ix and x–xiii—see Introduction, pp. 12 ff., and pp. 242–5) but also at the time referred to. If Paul had paid the visit, the cancelling of which had given rise to misunderstanding and complaint, the representative Corinthian (note the singular participles, ὁ εὐφραίνων and ὁ λυπούμενος—not a special defender of Paul in Corinth, or, as Denney thinks, the penitent offender), who by his Christian faith gave happiness to Paul, would have been hurt; that is, there was trouble in Corinth for which this representative Corinthian was not responsible. This may be confirmed by the

construction at the end of the verse, which is here translated *he who is caused sorrow by me. By* translates not the usual preposition (ὑπό), but one that ordinarily means *out of* (ἐξ); and, though it would be unwise to build on this suggestion, the choice of preposition might suggest not 'sorrow caused directly by my agency', but 'sorrow that arises from me, on my account, sorrow that is occasioned rather than caused by my presence'. This would be consistent with the view (see below, pp. 212 ff., and 'The Injury'. p. 155) that it was not a native Corinthian but a visitor who had injured Paul.

The circumstances were such that to visit Corinth would do harm, and to stay away would do harm (as it manifestly had done). Paul had sought to deal with this difficult situation by writing a letter, though it was a letter that cost him much pain, part at least of which may have been due not to anger but to virtual certainty
that whatever he said would be misunderstood. **Moreover, I** 3
wrote to just this effect .... It is uncertain how the words that follow the verb (τοῦτο αὐτό) are to be taken. There are three possibilities. (1) They may be adverbial (adverbial accusative, or accusative of respect; cf. Plato, *Protagoras* 310 E), and translated: 'I wrote for precisely this reason'. They would then be taken up in the final clause that follows: 'namely, in order that I might not come ...'. This makes the words logically redundant (for all that Paul is saying is, 'I wrote in order that ...'), but they add force and vigour to the sentence. So B.D. §290.4; cf. Robertson, p. 699. (2) They may be the direct object of *I wrote*, and refer to a quotation from the painful letter. If this view is accepted the quotation might be, 'It was to spare you that I did not revisit Corinth' (verse 23); or, 'I am determined not to come to you again in sorrow' (verse 1); or, looking ahead, 'I am writing in order that I may not come and be caused sorrow ...'. (3) They may summarize the content of the letter: 'I wrote to just this effect ...'. The surrounding verses would on this view be taken not as quoting the words of the letter but as repeating its main drift. This seems to be the best way to take the words in question (so, e.g., Bachmann). The possible quotations (mentioned above under (2)) relate rather to the situation of 2 Corinthians (when the complaint was made that Paul had not visited Corinth) than to the situation of the letter that replaced the visit. There was no need to expound *just this effect*; the Corinthians had read the letter and knew what it contained.

Paul wrote as he did **that I might not come and be caused sorrow** (in verse 2 he was afraid of causing sorrow; doubtless the effect would have been mutual) **by those from whom I ought to have had joy.** After verse 24 this cannot mean that Paul was afraid that he would find the Corinthians less subservient than he hoped, and that his dignity would thereby be offended. His sorrow would be caused by the discovery that they (misled by false apostles; see xi. 13) had adopted a false Gospel and were failing to live as Christians. The situation was a delicate one, for fear that a visit would lead to sorrow was accompanied by confidence. Paul believed that his letter would be successful, **for I was confident** (causal use of the participle πεποιθώς) **in respect of all of you** (not a loyal minority) **that my joy was the joy of all of you;** that is, that you would be happy that I was happy, that, in fact, we should share a common happiness in the Gospel. This confidence at the time of writing must be remembered in the discussion of the unhappy incident at Corinth and of Paul's relations with the Corinthian church. There are trouble-makers there, but the church as a whole (*all of you* may well be a kindly exaggeration; see verses 5 f.) was sound.

Paul was confident in the Corinthians themselves, yet the
4 situation was a serious one, **for I wrote to you out of much affliction** (the word of i. 8) **and distress of heart, with many tears, not in order to inflict sorrow upon you** (literally, in order that you might be grieved), **but that you might know the love** (this word is in a very emphatic position) **that I have specially for you.** That *I wrote* (ἔγραψα) is not an epistolary aorist, referring to the present ('I now write'—in the present letter) is shown by vii. 8, which also shows that, though this was not Paul's purpose, the Corinthians were grieved by what he wrote. There are circumstances, and these seem to have been among them, in which to see, in a person one has treated far from well, persistent love and confidence can be salutarily (as Paul says in vii. 9) painful. It seems (see above, pp. 86 f.) that the injurious action was committed by a visitor to Corinth, and though the content of Paul's sorrowful letter can only be conjectured it may well have contained an assurance that Paul could not believe that the Corinthians had really supported, and would continue to support Paul's opponent, and that he still loved them. This assurance would prick their consciences (see vii. 9 ff.). That Paul

should specially love the difficult Corinthians is in no way unlikely; problem children often evoke love. Compare Paul's refusal to accept payment in Corinth (see especially xi. 11).

Paul may have been the occasion of pain; its real cause was the man who (it seems) had stirred up trouble in Corinth. Paul refuses to regard this as a personal matter—a clear sign (as Lietzmann points out) that that is what, by ordinary standards, it must have seemed. Paul, however, thinks of the injury done to the church, and is concerned to 'gain his brother' (Matt. xviii. 15; cf. Dodd,
Studies, p. 59). **But if anyone has caused sorrow, he caused** 5
sorrow not—as you might suppose—**to me, but to some extent** (ἀπὸ μέρους, limiting not the number of persons affected but the extent of the effect—so Kümmel against Lietzmann)—**that I may not exaggerate** (better than 'bear hardly on' him, or you)—**to all of you.** Who is the person referred to in this verse, and what did he do? Neither of these questions can be answered with certainty because, even when vii. 12, which apparently refers to the same incident, is included, the evidence is insufficient. We must collect such evidence as there is; see the summaries on pp. 93, 212 ff. From the present verse we learn that the offence, though ostensibly directed against Paul, was truly, in Paul's eyes, an offence against the church. This seems to exclude a reference back to the case of incest mentioned in 1 Cor. v. 1 (though such a reference was already seen by Tertullian, *De Pudicitia* 13); and it is not probable that Paul would write in this way if his position and authority had been attacked indirectly in the person of one of his assistants, such as Timothy. We should probably think of an occasion during the second visit—a sorrowful one (cf. verse 1)—when Paul was insulted and his authority flouted. This would have been an attack on the whole church, which was founded on the Pauline Gospel. By whom was the attack made? We are not yet in a position to answer this question, but *all of you*, if taken strictly, would suggest that the attack was made by someone who was not a member of the Corinthian church. This conclusion cannot at this stage be pressed; if the offender stood alone and his action had been repudiated by all his fellow Christians, *all of you* could hardly be called a gross exaggeration for 'all of you minus one': the rest had all been grieved by the fact that one of themselves should have acted in this way. This however is only a possible conclusion, not the most probable.

The weight of probability so far is in favour of the view that the offender was a stranger; this conclusion however is often thought to be incompatible with the next verse, since only a member of the church would be liable to punishment by the church (see e.g. Kümmel, *Introduction*, p. 208). The verse however is full of difficulties, and these must be considered before conclusions are
6 drawn from it. A **reproof** has been delivered (no verb is expressed in the Greek; it would be possible to say that the reproof had been 'decided on') against the offender. The word *reproof* (ἐπιτιμία) is often (e.g. Authorized Version, Revised Version, Revised Standard Version, Jerusalem Bible; New English Bible has 'penalty'; cf. Hatch, *Essays*, p. 4) rendered 'punishment', but it may be questioned whether this impressive consensus is correct. In the Greek Bible the word occurs only here and at Wisdom iii. 10; the Vulgate renders it here as *objurgatio*, at Wisdom iii. 10 as *correptio*, neither of which suggests punishment. The only other source cited by L.S. for the meaning 'punishment' is *O.G.I.S.* 669. 43 (II, p. 402). It is true that the cognate verb (ἐπιτιμᾶν) means, among other things, 'to lay a penalty upon a person', and that cognate nouns (ἐπιτιμή, ἐπιτίμημα, ἐπιτίμησις) occasionally suggest this thought. But this is not the primary meaning of the group of compounds, and when these acquired a new sense in addition to the 'enjoyment of civil rights and liberties' this was as often 'rebuke' as 'punishment'. This is confirmed by the general New Testament usage of the verb (ἐπιτιμᾶν), which occurs 30 (29) times, but only once (Jude 9) where it could possibly mean 'to impose a punishment', and especially by Luke xvii. 3 (cf. Matt. xviii. 15, with the verb ἐλέγχειν), which provides an important parallel to Paul's treatment of the present situation. An offending brother must be rebuked, or reproved; and as soon as possible forgiven. We may therefore translate not 'punishment' or 'penalty' but reproof.

Paul says **this** *reproof*. The bearing of the demonstrative adjective is not perfectly clear, but it tends to confirm the view we have just taken. 'This punishment', with nothing for *this* to refer to, would be impossible writing, even if we observe (with Lietzmann) that Titus must have told Paul (vii. 13) what had happened, and that Paul could assume that the Corinthians would know what he meant. But, though *this reproof* also hangs somewhat unhappily in the air, it could not unreasonably be claimed that simply by dissociating themselves from his action the Corinthians had reproved the offender, and thus that *this reproof* was implied in the the context.

Paul adds that *this reproof* was **delivered by the main body** of the church. An alternative rendering (of the Greek ὑπὸ τῶν πλειόνων) would be 'by the majority' (or even 'by a considerable number'; so Windisch, who deduces a gathering at which the church voted; see B.D. §244.3, and cf. ix. 2); this would imply a minority which either sided with the offender, or wished for sterner measures—or possibly two minorities, one on each side of the main body. The Corinthian church (which had known other divisions) may have been divided in this way, but the words used do not require this conclusion. Paul's phrase (for the Greek usage see L.S. s.v. πλείων I, 2) is sometimes used for the main body of persons concerned in any matter without the necessary implication of a minority, though the main body are sometimes distinguished from their leaders. The phrase may also reflect the use of 'the many' (*ha-rabbim*) for the community in Qumran literature (the usage is very common—see Kuhn s.v., and e.g. CD xiii. 7, and cf. Josephus's account of the Essenes in *War* ii. 146). Paul did not however borrow the usage from the Qumran sect (cf. Black, *Scrolls*, p. 177; Delcor, in *P. & Q.*, pp. 79 f.); its roots are already to be found in the Old Testament (see especially Dan. xii. 3), whence no doubt both Paul and the Sect derived it—see Braun. We conclude that the main body of Corinthian Christians had, if not at once yet in due course, taken Paul's side against would-be leaders who had imposed themselves upon the church; such at least was Titus's possibly too favourable and optimistic report (see vii. 7-11, with the notes). This conclusion is not formally incompatible with the view that the reproof was approved by a majority rather than the whole; but the emphasis is different.

The *reproof* **is sufficient** (the adjective, which is neuter, does not agree with the substantive, which is feminine, a fact noted but not explained at M. iii. 311; Hughes thinks it a Latinism, *satis*; it might not be wrong to translate, 'is sufficient treatment for') **for the person in question** (literally, 'for such a man'; cf. verse 7). Paul is quickly satisfied, and does not wish to record the offender's name (unless, much less probably, we are to suppose that the name originally stood here and was removed by Corinthian
editors). The time for reproof is now past, **so that on the other** 7

hand you ought (supplying δεῖν; see Moule, *Idiom*, p. 144) **rather to forgive** (χαρίζεσθαι is normally 'to give'; *forgive* is 'peculiar' to Paul (Windisch)) **and comfort him.** Cf. Luke xvii. 3: If your brother sins, reprove him, and if he repents forgive him. Paul shows no awareness that he is putting into practice words of Jesus; cf. Rom. xiii. 8 ff. (and the note). Instead of citing authority he gives a reason for the course of action he recommends: **lest he** (again, literally, 'such a man', ὁ τοιοῦτος) **be swallowed up in excessive sorrow.** He has already felt the effect of the reproof (Lietzmann) and might be so overwhelmed by grief and remorse as to abandon his faith and relation with his fellow Christians
8 altogether. Compare verse 11. **So**, Paul resumes, **I ask** (the same verb, παρακαλεῖν, as that just translated *comfort*, a hard but legitimate change of sense) **you to confirm** (κυρῶσαι; for this legal word cf. Gal. iii. 15) **your love for him.** It would be possible to take *for him* (εἰς αὐτόν) with *confirm*, and translate 'to him'. There is a similar pair of possibilities at Rom. v. 8; see *Romans*, pp. 106 f. Paul's usage points decisively to the translation given. Bachmann notes the contrast between the legal *confirm* and the non-legal *love*. Perhaps there is a deliberate contrast with what the Corinthians might have expected Paul to say—'Confirm the sentence'. Denney thinks of 'some formal action'.

This injunction might seem inconsistent with the tone of Paul's
9 earlier letter (see vii. 8), but it is not so, **for I wrote to you** not so much in order to secure the punishment of the offender as **to find out** (ingressive aorist, γνῶ—'to get to know') **how you would stand the test** (literally, 'the proof of you', δοκιμή; see *Romans*, p. 104). This purpose is consistent with the suggestion that the offender was not a Corinthian; Paul was less concerned about him (troublesome though he might be) than about the Corinthians, concerning whom he wished to know **whether you were obedient in all things.** Paul does not say to whom the Corinthians should be obedient, but after i. 24 it is scarcely possible that he should be speaking of obedience to himself, except as to the one in whom the authority of Christ was represented to the church.

10 **But** at present the main thing is forgiveness; and Paul does not intend to be behindhand with this. **To whom you forgive anything, I do too.** Paul (no apostolic 'lord'—i. 24) will accept the Corinthians' judgement in this (as he evidently hopes—verse 7—that they will accept his). Indeed he has not waited for them.

For indeed what I have forgiven—if I have forgiven anything (cf. verse 5—Paul implies that the offence was not against him but against the church)—**I have forgiven** (this verb is a necessary supplement, not in the Greek) **on your account** (that is, for your good) **in the presence of Christ;** that is, Paul's forgiveness has been granted (a) not in order to meet his own convenience by disposing of an awkward situation and placating an enemy, but with a view to the building up of the Corinthian community (cf. x. 8; xiii. 10), and (b) not irresponsibly, but as an act performed in the presence of (cf. Prov. viii. 30 for ἐν προσώπῳ; the meaning at iv. 6 is different) Christ, and under his judgement (calling on Christ as witness—Windisch). Paul returns (cf. verse 7)
to and develops his reason for insisting on forgiveness: **lest Satan** 11
(see Rom. xvi. 20; 1 Cor. v. 5; vii. 5, and the notes; also 2 Cor. xi. 14; xii. 7; Paul uses the name also at 1 Thess. ii. 18; 2 Thess. ii. 9) **should take advantage** (πλεονεκτεῖν; for cognate nouns see Rom. i. 29; 1 Cor. v. 10 f.; vi. 10, and the notes) **of us** (perhaps, that is, of Paul—so Hughes; more probably of Paul and the church jointly). It is Satan's object to seize Christian believers and make them his own; this he would succeed in doing if the offender were *swallowed up in excessive sorrow*, and despaired; equally, if Paul and the Corinthians were unforgiving. But Satan will be forestalled; **for we are not ignorant of his designs.** It is part of Paul's apostolic business to know what Satan is after, how he plans to achieve his goal, and thus to prevent his success (cf. Allo). The *we* however is not a purely 'apostolic' *we*; all Christians in some measure have this knowledge.

Several of the important historical themes of this passage will be raised again in the exposition of chapter vii; see pp. 212 ff., also Introduction, pp. 7 f. For the present it will be worthwhile to note (a) that Paul's opponent was probably (like himself) a visitor to Corinth; (b) that Paul understood the Corinthian church to be essentially on his side; (c) that so far from using his apostolic authority to dictate what should be done he left it to the Corinthians to take action, and accepted what they had done, contenting himself with the giving of advice. 'Ecclesia gerit claves' (Bengel, on verse 6).

The next two verses are included in this paragraph because they are part of Paul's account of his changing travel plans. This is confirmed by the fact that in Greek *Troas* has the article, probably because Troas was in mind, though not mentioned at i. 23 (so

B.D. §261.1; this is more probable than that Paul means 'the
12 Troad'). **But when I came to Troas to proclaim** (literally, 'for', εἰς) **the Gospel of Christ** (note that Paul's purpose was to preach, not to get news of Corinth), **although a door stood open** (perfect tense; for the metaphor cf. 1 Cor. xvi. 9—there was an opportunity for evangelism) **to me in the Lord** (Paul's success in
13 evangelizing was due to the Lord—Schlatter), **I got** (the same tense as 'we received' in i. 9; see a long note in Robertson, pp. 900 f.—Paul's intention may be to stress the continuous anxiety up to the arrival of Titus; but see Moule, *Idiom*, p. 14—*received* is parallel to the aorist *went off*) **no relief for my spirit,** that is, for myself. This use of *spirit* is infrequent in Paul; see however Bultmann, *E. & F.*, p. 154. Cf. vii. 5, where the word 'flesh' is used, with no evident difference in meaning; and vii. 1, where 'spirit' and 'flesh' are used side by side. Paul proceeds to give the cause of his anxiety (suprisingly using the accusative and infinitive construction, though he is himself the subject of the infinitive): **because I did not find Titus my brother** (for the Christian use of this word see i. 1, and the note; for Titus, see 'Titus').

It seems that when Paul did not visit Corinth (i. 23; ii. 1) Titus did so, possibly conveying the letter Paul wrote with many tears (verse 4). Paul had presumably returned to Ephesus (without paying the expected second visit to Corinth), but had left once more. Whether he was on his way to Corinth he does not say; certainly the letter (written after he had in the end made contact with Titus, vii. 6) was written before he reached there. It would have been wholly unnatural if he had not been anxious to hear news of Corinth from Titus, but the time was one of general strain (cf. vii. 5: not only fears within, which might have related to Corinth, but also fightings without, which on this occasion could not have been against Corinthian adversaries), and Paul says explicitly that this was due to the non-arrival of Titus, who had been engaged on the collection and would have been a likely prey for bandits (cf. 'Titus', pp. 9 f., 13). Wendland's 'Anxiety about the church drove him on' is not justified. Paul's Corinthian troubles at this stage have often been overdrawn. He had (it seems) been attacked at Corinth by another travelling preacher—with xi. 13 in mind, we may say, by a false apostle (cf. 'The Injury', p. 155). He cancelled his second visit to Corinth (itself an afterthought) in order not to provoke more trouble, and wrote a letter to test the attitude of the church, believing, at least hoping, that it remained loyal. When Titus (perhaps carrying the letter) set out for Corinth on the business of the collection Paul went out of his way to tell him what good people the Corinthians were (vii. 14); and the Corinthians did not let him down. So at least it seemed; and when it became evident that the Corinthians had fallen for the false apostles (e.g. xi. 4, 20) the shock to Paul was all the greater.

For the present Titus did not appear, and in his anxiety, **instead of making full use of the opportunity** (a supplement, to bring out the force of the Greek ἀλλά) **I said Goodbye to them** (that is, the Christians in Troas—now, and at Acts xvi. 8, he had made some use of his opportunities) **and went off to Macedonia.** This may have been an unwise step. From Troas Paul could reach Macedonia either by sailing straight across the Aegean to Neapolis, Amphipolis, or Thessalonica, or by taking the longer land route round the northern end of the sea. How could he be sure that he would not miss Titus on the way? There may have been an arrangement with Titus, but neither this, nor which route Paul actually took, is known. See 'Titus'. Knox, *P.G.*, p. 144, writes: 'Paul must have left Troas . . . when he realised that Titus had missed the last boat and would have to come through Macedonia.' This would date the event in the autumn.

C. THE PURPOSE EXPRESSED IN MISSION AND MINISTRY ii.14–vii.4

5. ii. 14–iii. 3. THE CHRISTIAN MISSION AND ITS DIVINE SUPPORT

(14) But thanks be to God, who goes always at our head in a triumphal progress in Christ, and through us manifests, like an odour, the knowledge of himself in every place. (15) For we are the sweet savour of sacrifice that rises from Christ to God, and that among those who are on the way to salvation and among those who are on the way to destruc-

tion; (16) to the latter it is an odour issuing from[1] death and leading to death, to the former an odour issuing from[1] life and leading to life. And who is sufficient for these things? (17) For we are not, like the majority,[2] watering down the word of God; no, we speak as out of sincerity, as from God himself, before God, and in Christ.

(1) Are we beginning again to commend ourselves? Or do we need (as some do) commendatory letters, to you or from you? (2) You are our letter, written in your[3] hearts, known and read by all men, (3) because it is manifest that you are a letter of Christ, supplied by us, a letter written not with ink but with the Spirit of the living God, not on stone tablets but on tablets that are hearts of flesh.[4]

That the epistle as we read it in the MSS here takes a sharp turn is beyond doubt. The story of Paul's anxious wait for Titus is abruptly dropped, and we hear no more of it until it is taken up, in language similar to that of ii. 12 f., at vii. 5. The hard transitions have led to the view (see Introduction, p. 11) that ii. 14–vii. 4 (or more strictly ii. 14–vi. 13; vii. 2-4, since most of those who hold that ii. 14–vii. 4 is an interpolation believe that vi. 14–vii. 1 is an interpolation within the interpolation) is a fragment of a different letter from that contained in i. 1–ii. 13; vii. 4–ix. 13, perhaps, with chapters x–xiii, a part of the 'severe' letter, written with many tears. There is no *a priori* reason why pieces of different letters should not have been combined in a single document, though it is not easy to see why or how this happened; the truth or false-

[1] *Issuing from* renders the preposition ἐκ, which is omitted by D G and the majority of MSS. The text without the preposition is simpler: a smell of death (life) that leads to death (life); the longer text, though it raises difficulties of interpretation (see the notes) is Pauline (cf. iii. 18), and to be preferred.

[2] For *the majority* (οἱ πολλοί; see the note), many MSS (including 𝔓[46] D G) and Marcion have *the rest* (οἱ λοιποί). There is little difference in meaning; the extraordinary charge implied in *the majority* is scarcely weakened if the other reading is accepted.

[3] *Your* is weakly attested (by ℵ 33). *Our* (the alternative read by the great majority of authorities) may be due to assimilation to vii. 3. *Your* both gives the required sense, that the Corinthians themselves are—even though unwillingly—Paul's commendation, and leads to the next stage in the argument (for which see the notes). See Bultmann, *Theol.*, p. 218, E.T. i. 222.

[4] There is textual confusion here; some (e.g. M. iii. 214) prefer καρδίας to καρδίαις, others a conjecture (e.g. Bultmann, *Theol.*, p. 218, E.T. i. 222). The awkward Greek of the text is probably due to the Old Testament allusion; see the notes.

hood of the hypothesis must be determined by the possibility or impossibility of understanding the transitions, and by the suitability of the contents of the passage in question to one context or another. The issue therefore is fundamentally one of exegesis, and though the arguments are summed up in the Introduction the question will be dealt with in more detail in the Commentary.

Perhaps the most acute question of all is why Paul should abandon his description of the situation at Troas (ii. 12 f.) and go on to speak of the triumph of Christ, in which he shares. It is quite reasonable to suppose that an editor has here joined two documents together; but it is not necessary to do so. The reference to Titus emphasizes the feeling of doubt, uncertainty, and insecurity in which Paul wrote his letter, and which continued after he had sent it (cf. vii. 8); but already the preceding paragraph reflects the relief Paul had now come to feel (prematurely perhaps), and he begins to speak of forgiveness and love, and of his confidence in the Corinthian church as a whole. It would have been (at least for some writers) natural to conclude the story with an account of Titus's return as the ground for Paul's happier mood; but it is not unlike Paul to jump to the conclusion, avoiding the intermediate stages (which the Corinthians knew, because they knew what message Titus was taking back to Paul), and to burst out in a theological expression ('nobilissima digressio'—Bengel) of the foundation on which the new relations between himself and his converts rested. It may be noted that the outburst of praise (according to Windisch, a hymn) is not at all suited to the 'severe' letter, to which some ascribe ii. 14–vii. 4. Allo thinks that the mention of Macedonia (with its faithful Christians) prompted the outburst of praise. Héring suggests that ii. 13, 14 were originally placed immediately before vii. 5, and were displaced into their present position. He notes that ii. 11 and ii. 14 join well.

But (one may reasonably underline the adversative sense of the 14
particle δέ; cf. Hughes, and T. W. Manson in *Studia Paulina*, p. 161), notwithstanding all fears, anxieties, problems, and rebuffs, **thanks be to God, who goes always at our head in a triumphal progress in Christ.** The meaning is not perfectly clear. Paul's verb (θριαμβεύειν, which Georgi, *Gegner*, p. 225, thinks Paul may have taken over from his opponents) is derived from the Latin *triumphus*, and means 'to celebrate a triumph'.

When used with a direct object it means 'to triumph over someone' (and is used in this sense at Col. ii. 15), also 'to lead (as a prisoner of war) in one's triumphal procession', and hence 'to expose to shame, disgrace'. It can scarcely mean (though some translators take it so) 'to cause to triumph'. None of these meanings is entirely appropriate here. Paul did think of himself as a slave of Christ (e.g. Rom. i. 1), and indeed as a prisoner of war (Rom. xvi. 7; Col. iv. 10; Phm. 23), but in this verse he is describing himself and his colleagues as collaborating with God, and not as exposed by him to disgrace. Notwithstanding the lack of supporting lexical evidence it is right to follow L.S., Allo, and Kümmel in taking Paul to represent himself as one of the victorious general's soldiers sharing in the glory of his triumph. But there is a paradox here; Paul did not forget (1 Cor. xv. 9; Gal. i. 13, 23) that he had fought on the wrong side, and that his position in the triumphal progress was due to a reversal by grace of his deserts. 'By the grace of God I am what I am, and his grace towards me did not prove vain, but I laboured more abundantly than all of them; yet not I but the grace of God with me' (1 Cor. xv. 10).

The thought, or rather the imagery, takes an abrupt turn. God, who leads us in his triumphal procession, **through us manifests** (the word suggests something that will be apprehended by the organs of sight, not those of smelling), **like an odour** (for the image cf. Betz, *Lukian*, p. 41), **the knowledge of himself** (literally, the odour of the knowledge of himself, that is, the odour that consists of the knowledge of himself; but English idiom will hardly stand this) **in every place.** The best explanation of the new figure (see Windisch and Lietzmann; also Knox, *P.G.*, p. 129, with important references) is that the use of incense was customary in triumphal and quasi-triumphal processions, both royal and religious. Goudge rightly raises the question whether this practice was one that would have occurred to a Jew, such as Paul, but it is hard to think of a better explanation. The apostolic procession is a spectacle to the world (1 Cor. iv. 9); it also makes itself known through smell. See further below, pp. 99–102. What in fact is diffused by Paul and his colleagues is the *knowledge* of God. In every passage in which *knowledge* (γνῶσις) occurs in the second epistle (ii. 14; iv. 6; vi. 6; viii. 7; x. 5; xi. 6) it is used in a good sense, and has lost the bad associations that cling to it in the first (see *1 Corinthians*, pp. 37, 144 f., 189 f.)—an indication that the situation and problems in Corinth have changed. Paul now speaks of the revelation of God in the person of Christ; it is in Christ crucified (cf. 1 Cor. i. 18, 23 f.; ii. 2) that God is known, and that the crucified is also the risen and exalted one is a mark of the paradoxical character of the being of God. The revelation is displayed *in every place*. The same words (ἐν παντὶ τόπῳ) occur in 1 Cor. i. 2 (see the note); it is impossible however to give them the same meaning here. They correspond to *always* earlier in the verse: God is at work in the apostolic mission at all times and in all places. This proposition requires further elucidation.

The manifestation of the knowledge of God is *in Christ* (cf.
iv. 6), but it is *through us*; **for we are the sweet savour of** 15
sacrifice that rises from Christ to God. The thought of incense suggested in verse 14 is now developed as Paul uses a fresh word for odour, which is here rendered as *sweet savour of sacrifice*. It is regularly used in descriptions of sacrifice in the Old Testament (e.g. Gen. viii. 21; Exod. xxix. 18; Lev. i. 9; Num. xv. 3; Ezek. vi. 13; Dan. iv. 34; Wendland notes the 'odour of wisdom' at Sirach xxiv. 15; xxxix. 14; cf. 2 Baruch lxvii. 6), and is used metaphorically in the New Testament (Eph. v. 2; Phil. iv. 18). Its meaning can hardly be other than sacrificial here, and for this reason the word *sacrifice* has been introduced into the translation. Paul's Greek also includes a simple genitive (Χριστοῦ) and a dative (τῷ θεῷ), and it seems inevitable that one should fill out the picture by taking Paul's sense to be that the apostles are the smoke that arises from the sacrifice of Christ to God, diffusing as it ascends the knowledge of God that is communicated in the cross. The image (which has somewhat remote rabbinic analogies—see S.B. iii. 497) would seem much less violent in Paul's day than it does in ours,[1] and one may (with Schlatter) compare such passages as Rom. xii. 1; xv. 16; Phil. ii. 17, where Paul speaks of himself or others as a sacrifice. Its meaning is in substance clear enough. (a) The preaching of the Gospel is part of the Gospel itself (cf. *Romans*, p. 28). The process that begins with the crucifixion and resurrection of Jesus is continued in the apostolic testimony to

[1] One may be allowed to recall one of E. C. Hoskyns's sayings (designed no doubt to arouse and stimulate): '. . . it was almost to be regretted that we could not sacrifice a bull once a year, preferably on a hot day in summer, in order to enable theological students to understand the meaning of the word "sacrifice" in the Old Testament' (*Cambridge Sermons* (1938), p. xxiii).

him. (b) There is in principle an identity between what is seen in Jesus, crucified and risen, and what is seen in Paul, since Paul always carries about in his body the death of Jesus, that the life of Jesus too may be manifested in him (iv. 10). Paul is conformed to the death of Jesus (Phil. iii. 10; and see also *Signs*, pp. 80 f.). The life of suffering and of devotion to God that Paul lives is (in secondary continuation of the life of Jesus) a manifestation of the nature and purpose of God. Where Paul's mission advances, the smoke of Christ's sacrifice ascends; it reaches, and is well-pleasing to, God, and at the same time it communicates the truth to men. Here, as regularly (see Käsemann, *Freiheit*, p. 201; E.T. p. 112), Paul applies the language of cultus to life and preaching; priests, sacrifices, incense, in the conventional cultic sense, are of little or no interest to him; see Introduction, p. 27.

The manifestation of the knowledge of God does not mean that all in the immediate environment accept it, know God, and thus attain life and salvation. It takes place both **among those who are on the way to salvation and among those who are on the way to destruction.** The wording repeats that of 1 Cor. i. 18. 'Both groups are described by present participles, and although the latter is from a compound verb with a "perfectivizing" preposition (*ἀπολλυμένοις*; see M. i. 114 f.) neither process can be thought of as complete. It is nevertheless true, as Kümmel points out (comparing Phil. i. 28 and Rom. viii. 24), that both terms, and the distinction between the two groups, are eschatological.[1] Destruction and salvation (cf. Rom. i. 16, 18) are consummated at the last day (cf. Rom. ix. 22; xiii. 11)' (*1 Corinthians*, p. 51). The present verse simply observes the existence of the two groups, and the distinction between them, and the observation was based on Paul's missionary experience: the same preaching of the same Gospel led some to acceptance, and some to mocking rejection (cf. Acts xvii. 32 ff.). The choice of language, in the writing of a theologian like Paul, shows, however, that the observation is not merely empirical. It is God who saves and God who destroys, and neither process can take place independently of his will; but it is only in the next verse that Paul brings out this fact, and even there he does little to explain it, contenting himself with an extension of his metaphor.

16 **To the latter it is an odour** (Paul now reverts to the word,

[1] Compare also Wilckens, *Weisheit*, pp. 22 f.

ὀσμή, of verse 14) **issuing from death** (on the text see p. 96, note 1) **and leading to death, to the former an odour issuing from life** (on the text see p. 96, note 1) **and leading to life.** The same *odour*, that is, the same preached message, is both. The stench of death itself breeds disease, and kills; the breath of life creates and quickens. *Issuing from* translates the preposition *from* (ἐκ), which, as Schlatter says, here has causal force. The Gospel, as Paul understood it, emanates from a scene of death which is itself paradoxically a scene and source of life. It would oversimplify the matter to say that the distinction between those who are *on the way to salvation* and those who are *on the way to destruction* is that the former do and the latter do not accept the resurrection of Jesus, but it would nevertheless provide a valid pointer to a more complicated distinction. If Jesus is taken to be a dead Jew and nothing more the message about him will be rejected, and those who reject it will become as dead as they suppose Jesus to be. If however he is recognized as 'Christ Jesus—who died, or rather was raised, who is at the right hand of God, who actually is interceding on our behalf' (Rom. viii. 34), he becomes the source of life. The issue whether to any given hearer the same person is a dead Jesus or a living one is the profound mystery of predestination, for it cannot be supposed independent of the knowledge and intention of God (see *Romans*, pp. 170 f., 220 f., 227); Paul will return to this theme (e.g., iii. 16 f.).

As a Jew, Paul was not unfamiliar with the notion of a message that could be both healing and poisonous in its effects. Several passages describe Torah in this way; for details, see T. W. Manson, in *Studia Paulina*, pp. 155–62. For example, Deuteronomy Rabbah i. 6 (so Manson, but the passage appears to be in i. 5) plays on the first words of Deuteronomy ('These are the words', *'elleh ha-d^ebarim*): 'As the bee (*d^eborah*) reserves her honey for her owner and her sting for others, so the words of the Torah are an elixir of life (*sam ḥayyim*) for Israel and a deadly poison (*sam ha-maweth*) to the nations of the world' (Manson's translation). The Hebrew word *sam* has the ambiguity of the English *drug*. Elsewhere (Manson quotes Shabbath 88b; Yoma 72b; Taanith 7a; other passages will be found in S.B. iii. 498 f.; there is a similar argument in Schlatter, who however quotes only Taanith) the distinction between those for whom Torah is life-giving and those for whom it brings death is made not (as in

Deuteronomy Rabbah, above) on the basis of race, but on personal grounds: one must accept Torah in obedience, and study it for its own sake. The double effect of Torah is on any showing an important parallel to what Paul says about the Gospel. Manson (cf. Stumpff, *T.W.N.T.* ii. 809 f.) goes further, observing that *sam* may also mean 'perfume' or 'spice', and thus obtaining a connection not only in substance but in imagery with the present passage in 2 Corinthians. This is rejected by Kümmel, on the ground that *sam* means medicine, not odour; this is true of Yoma 72b, to which Kümmel explicitly refers, and, it seems, of post-Biblical Hebrew in general, but in the Old Testament the word is used of the constituents of anointing oil (e.g. Exod. xxv. 6) and incense (e.g. Exod. xxx. 7), and this might have helped Paul to form the connection. Greek parallels also can be cited: Windisch quotes Aristotle, *De Mirab. Auscult.* 147 (845b), and Aelian, *Hist. Animal.* III 7.

The precise affiliation of Paul's metaphor is interesting but not important in comparison with the horrifying truth he has stated. By preaching the Gospel he leads some to life, and at the same time sentences others to death. It is not surprising (though Windisch finds the connection difficult) that he proceeds by asking, **And who is sufficient** (ἱκανός) **for these things** (that is, for bearing and discharging such responsibilities as those described)**?** The question arises naturally out of the context, but the notion of sufficiency—adequacy for the apostolic vocation—is characteristic of 2 Corinthians (the adjective occurs here and at iii. 5; the noun, ἱκανότης, at iii. 5; the verb, ἱκανοῦν, at iii. 6; the only comparable passage elsewhere in Paul is 1 Cor. xv. 9). Georgi (*Gegner*, pp. 220–5), who, like Windisch, thinks the transition abrupt, and notes the fact that Paul, having asked this question, goes on immediately, in verse 17, to compare himself with others, draws the conclusion that Paul's adversaries 'must have said', We are sufficient. 'Over against this confident assertion Paul sets his critical question . . . The opponents had probably spoken very confidently of their sufficiency, and brought this into quite immediate relation with God' (p. 224). This observation forms part of Georgi's argument that the opponents were regarded as 'divine men' (θεῖοι ἄνδρες; see Introduction, p. 29, and 'Paul's Opponents', p. 234). These suggestions are to some extent justified, but require qualification. Verse 16a makes the question of 16b readily intelligible, as we have seen. That Paul's opponents prided themselves on their self-sufficiency (which is no doubt true) does not prove that they defined themselves, or were defined by others, as 'divine men'. Georgi's analysis of Paul's reaction to them is nevertheless sound, and he is right in recognizing that the question, Who is sufficient for these things? implies the answer, No one is—certainly I am not.

This makes the opening of the next verse intelligible. I make no
claim to self-sufficiency, **for we are not, like the majority,** 17
watering down the word of God. It is only those who do this who can claim to be self-sufficient; those who handle the word of God in its purity know how inadequate they are for the task. *Watering down* attempts to convey the two aspects of Paul's verb (καπηλεύειν; Calvin and Schlatter recognize only the first of the two meanings given below), which suggests (a) the practice of making profit out of preaching the word of God, and (b) the adulteration of the word of God. The word was specially though not exclusively used of the wine trade, and 'watering down' involves both adulteration and excessive profit. Behind Paul's use of the word lies a long tradition of philosophical usage, in which the sophist is rebuked for selling his intellectual wares for cash (cf. e.g. Plato, *Protagoras* 313 CD; Philostratus, *Life of Apollonius* i. 13); and the two ideas that seem to be included here are brought together by Lucian, in *Hermotimus* 59: Philosophers sell their teachings, like the wine sellers (κάπηλοι), the majority (οἱ πολλοί) mixing (their product with water), and adulterating it (δολώσαντες; cf. iv. 2), and giving bad measure (cf. 'False Apostles', pp. 384 f.). See also Betz, *Lukian*, p. 114. T. R. Glover (*Paul of Tarsus* (1925), p. 103) compares Aristotle, *Politics* i. 9. 2 (1257B); the whole of i. 9 (1257AB 1258A) should be read. Strachan compares Lucian's *Peregrinus* 13, but adds that the men in question may not have been out for money. 'They may have loved power over other men's lives; . . . They may have sought admiration for their own intellectual powers'. W. D. Davies, p. 133, thinks Paul may be hinting at the activities of Jewish missionary traders.

This kind of behaviour Paul ascribes to *the majority* (οἱ πολλοί—which it is hardly satisfactory to explain as 'many as compared with the small number of authentic apostles' (Hughes); on the text, see note 2 on p. 96) of preachers. This extraordinary charge occurs not in a passage of passionate invective, but in one where the reference to other preachers arises incidentally. Doubtless

Paul is not writing with numerical precision, and is thinking especially of the situation in Corinth; yet preachers who visited Corinth (cf. xi. 4) will have visited other places too. There is little in the present passage to identify the preachers in question, though iii. 4-18 (which compares Paul and Moses) suggests that they were Jewish Christians, and this is confirmed by the fact that they took pay for their preaching—1 Cor. ix. 5-14 indicates that this was the practice of Jewish apostles such as Cephas. On the identity and activities of the preachers who visited Corinth and worked in opposition to Paul, see pp. 28 ff.; also 'Paul's Opponents'.

Whatever the majority may do, Paul will have nothing to do with such practices. **No** (ἀλλά)**, we speak as out of sincerity** (cf. i. 12)**, as from God himself, before God, and in Christ** (cf. xii. 19). This clause describes Paul's preaching in contrast with that of his rivals; reference back to the theme of 'sufficiency' is minimal, rather than determinative (as Georgi, *Gegner*, p. 222, suggests); it is nevertheless right to compare iii. 5. It is because Paul speaks *from God* that he neither needs nor wishes to reckon any sufficiency as proceeding from himself. *Sincerity*, as i. 12 indicates, is a divine gift, but not a distinctively divine characteristic. Paul is anything but a 'divine man'. God, a being other than himself, inspires his speech; but so far is he from identifying himself with a god that he confesses that he acts *before God*, in the presence of God, that is, so as to be seen and judged by God. Above all, it is *in Christ* that he speaks, that is, as a Christian, as one whose act is determined not by himself but by Christ. For this common and characteristic phrase see *Romans*, pp. 127, 236. Windisch's comment, that to speak 'in Christ' is equivalent to speaking 'in the Spirit' (cf. 1 Cor. xii. 3) is perhaps nearly, but not quite exact.

Georgi thinks that Paul, in representing his preaching as itself a divine act of revelation (*Offenbarungsgeschehen*), makes use in ii. 14-17 of gnostic and apocalyptic motifs (*Gegner*, p. 225). As gnostic motifs Georgi mentions: '(1) The universal character of the revelation (perhaps also θριαμβεύειν [to lead in triumph] as a concept of revelation). (2) Perfume as a symbol (*Kennzeichen*) of revelation, and also as a symbol of the λογικὴ λατρεία [spiritual worship]. (3) Identification of the event of revelation and the event of proclamation. (4) Revelation as destiny. (5) Dualistic motifs. (6) The notion of direction (ἐκ–εἰς [from–to]).' This is a by no means convincing list. The meaning of (1) and (6) is not clear. (2) calls for demonstration. Evidence that perfume was a metaphor peculiar to, or even specially characteristic of, gnosticism is not adduced, and Rom. xii. 1 f. shows that Paul was capable of developing the notion of non-cultic worship (including the transferred use of cultic terminology and imagery) in a context not determined by gnosis. In (3), (4), and (5) parallels with gnosis can be seen, but the material in itself is too Pauline to be easily ascribed to gnostic motifs operating upon him. That Paul lived and thought in a partly gnostic environment is true, and is reflected in this paragraph; but it is reflected to the same extent in many other paragraphs, so that the observation loses much of its value. Georgi mentions only two apocalyptic motifs: '(1) The Χριστός [Christ] title. (2) The pair of opposites σωζόμενοι–ἀπολλύμενοι [those on the way to salvation—those on the way to destruction], which are to be understood futuristically.' The former point has no weight: Christ is a common title in Paul. The latter is important, and has been noted above (p. 100); it provides an important corrective to elements of gnostic dualism that the paragraph might suggest: the distinction between believers and unbelievers is expressed in their decision and not in their being, yet rests ultimately upon God's decision (not theirs), and is therefore not absolute in the present but awaits the day of judgement. The conclusion to be drawn (by no means in complete disagreement with Georgi) is that Paul is dealing with a particular situation in Corinth, is dealing with it (as he would say) *in Christ*, that is, with fundamentally Christian insight and motivation (affected only slightly by gnostic motifs), and that his opponents were Jewish rather than gnostic. The two terms 'Jewish' and 'gnostic' are not to be regarded as mutually exclusive; features proper to each were probably combined, but the weight lies on the former. On the chapter as a whole, and its relation with Jer. xxxi, see Dodd, *A.S.*, p. 45.

Paul continues to deal with his adversaries in Corinth. They may
have preached a false Gospel, but they were armed with excellent
credentials. These Paul lacked; and was open to the charge of
manufacturing his own. **Are we beginning again to commend** 1
ourselves? Or possibly, with little difference in meaning, Are we
beginning to commend ourselves again? Paul has just described
himself as acting in sincerity, in the power of God, responsibly

before God, and in Christ; this could indeed look like self-praise; but that was not Paul's intention. Presumably he had on an earlier occasion been accused of self-commendation; we cannot say when this was—quite possibly on the sorrowful visit, or when the severe letter was received (so Schlatter). But see 1 Cor. iv. 4: take *before God* (ii. 17) seriously, and self-praise is impossible. Equally, the praise and commendation of other men become irrelevant. On the one hand, it cannot vie with divine approval; on the other, no more than a clear conscience can it justify before God. But Paul had little choice or freedom of movement. 'Self-defence is almost impossible without self-commendation. S. Paul's opponents at Corinth made the former necessary, and then blamed him for the latter' (Goudge). **Or do we need (as some do) commendatory letters, to you or from you?** The use of commendatory letters was as widespread in antiquity as it is today. Ample evidence for the use of Paul's words (the adjective *συστατικός*, and the verb *συνιστάνειν*) is provided by M.M., s.vv., and for the practice in Windisch. The substance of such letters is well illustrated by a Latin papyrus quoted by Deissmann (*Light from the Ancient East* (1927), pp. 197–200; P. Oxy. I 32): Already some time ago (iam . . . et pristine) I commended (commendaveram) to you Theon my friend, and now also I beg, sir, that you may have him before your eyes as myself; for he is such a man as may be loved by you. For he left his own people, his affairs and business, and followed me, and through all things he has kept me safe. And therefore I pray you that he may have access to you . . . . Jews also used such letters; see S.B. ii. 689, and Schoeps, *Paulus*, p. 70 (E.T. p. 75). Paul needed no such letters, but had no objection to the practice, which in itself could be a useful one; he was willing to supply commendatory letters. See Rom. xvi. 1 f., with the note. 1 Cor. xvi. 3 (see the note), 10 f.; 2 Cor. viii. 22 f.; Col. iv. 7 ff. are similar commendations, though the technical words are not used.

Some implies that missionaries, not in connection with Paul, had reached Corinth, and had established themselves there by means of commendations from recognized authorities; also that they had sought commendations from the Corinthian church to take them on the next stage of their journey. We cannot on the basis of this verse conjecture who these persons were, nor may we, with Lietzmann, conclude that the Corinthians complained that Paul had no commendatory letters to show; see further the notes on iv. 2, and the summary in the Introduction, pp. 32ff. It is probable though not certain that the holders of commendatory letters should be classed with *the majority* of verse 17; that is, Paul not merely ranks them differently from himself (who has no need of the supports they use) but considers that they trade upon an adulterated message. His language is not yet, however, as severe as it will become in chapters x–xiii; if he is there speaking of the same persons the situation must have developed.

But if Paul has no need of a commendation to indicate his position in Corinth, or of the services of Corinth to commend him elsewhere, what sign of authority does he bear? He can indeed
produce a 'letter'. **You are our letter, written in your** (on the 2
text see note 3 on. p. 96) **hearts** (if 'our' is accepted instead of *your* the plural *hearts* becomes difficult, though not impossibly so—see Kümmel; it could include Timothy), **known and read** (or 'clearly known'; see the note on i. 13, where the same word is used) **by all men.** Compare 1 Cor. ix. 2, You are the seal of my apostleship in the Lord. 'The Corinthian church does not make Paul an apostle, and his apostleship does not depend on it (any more than on the Jerusalem church—cf. Gal. i. 1), but its existence is a visible sign of his apostleship' (*1 Corinthians*, p. 201). Compare 2 Cor. xiii. 5, with the note. The only distinguishing feature of the present passage is that Paul, having spoken of the letters used by others, naturally describes the Corinthians' testimony to his apostleship in terms of a letter, written in the hearts of his converts. As such it is accessible to *all men*—Paul's rivals in the work at Corinth may have regarded their commendations as confidential. In any case, a letter written with pen and ink will be read only by a limited number.

In this verse we see Paul's thought moving in the direction it will take in the next paragraph. His *letter* was not written in ink on papyrus; it was natural to say that it was written *in your hearts*; cf. Rom. ii. 15; Philo, *Spec. Leg.* iv. 149 (Knox, *P.G.*, p. 130). But this suggests the prophecy of the New Covenant (Jer. xxxi. 33, I will put my law in their inward parts, and in their heart will I write it; cf. also Ezek. xi. 19; xxxvi. 26), which in turn evokes the contrast with the law given to Moses and written on tablets of stone (Exod. xxxi. 18; xxxii. 15 f.), and thus the contrast between the old covenant and the new. In the new paragraph (iii. 4-18) there are other Old Testament and extra-biblical allusions and parallels, and various cross-currents of thought; these will be noted in due course, but it is well to observe here how naturally Paul's mind moves from the *ad hominem* argument of iii. 1 f. to the theological exposition that follows.

3 Paul can say to his readers *You are our letter*, **because it is manifest that you are a letter of Christ;** literally, 'since you are manifested (*φανερούμενοι*; Héring takes this to be middle, and translates, 'Manifestement vous êtes une lettre . . .') that you are . . .'. This is intolerable as English and must therefore be paraphrased, but the participle shows that the thought continues from verse 2a, and thus provides some slight confirmation of the reading *your* (see above). The existence of the Corinthian Christians in Christ is a communication from Christ to the world, a manifestation of his purpose for humanity; this communication incidentally has the effect of commending Paul as a trustworthy bearer of the word of Christ. It is at this point that Paul's metaphor begins to be rather too much for him, for in a sense what he has just said means that he has written his own letter of commendation. This may account for the curious word that he now uses: the letter was Christ's (subjective genitive) but it was **supplied** (*διακονηθεῖσα*; for the rendering see L.S., s.v. II) **by us.** Paul uses this verb elsewhere only of his collection (viii. 19, 20; Rom. xv. 25), but the cognate noun (*διακονία*), which is particularly frequent in 2 Corinthians (twelve times; seven times in the remaining Pauline epistles, once in Ephesians, three times in the Pastorals), represents his apostolic ministry in general (e.g. iv. 1), and indeed Christian service at large (e.g. Rom. xii. 7; 1 Cor. xii. 5). Both 'to write' and 'to deliver' (Lietzmann, not Kümmel) would be too narrow. Paul means to suggest (and perhaps compresses the thought too severely for clarity) that it was through his work that the *letter of Christ* came into being. This is in fact part of the total argument: Paul's ministry was validated by the word he spoke, and by the fruit of that word in those who heard it.

The distinction between the *letter* that commended Paul and those of other missionaries now leads him, by its natural and scriptural associations, towards the argument of the next paragraph. It was **a letter written not with ink but with the Spirit of the living God,** for it was the Spirit who was the agent of the Corinthians' conversion (a theme developed later in the chapter; see the notes on iii. 6, 8, 17, 18); it was written **not on stone**

tablets but on tablets that are hearts of flesh (for the text see note 4 on p. 96). The contrast in the last clause recalls that of Ezek. xi. 19; xxxvi. 26, though it is not identical with it. 'Imperceptibly the picture changes again, for what is written is now no longer a commendatory letter but the Gospel which stands over against the law, and is written in men's hearts through the Spirit' (Lietzmann). For 'Torah in the heart' see W. D. Davies, p. 225.

6. iii. 4-18. THE OLD COVENANT AND THE NEW, THE OLD MINISTRY AND THE NEW

(4) We have the confidence to make such a claim through Christ before God. (5) It is not that we are of ourselves sufficient to consider any part of this process as proceeding from ourselves; rather, our sufficiency comes from God, (6) who gave us our sufficiency to be ministers of a new covenant, based not on letter but on Spirit; for the letter kills but the Spirit gives life. (7) But if the ministry of death, engraved in letters on stones, came into being in glory, so that the children of Israel could not gaze on the face of Moses because of the glory of his face, glory which was in process of abolition, (8) does this not mean that, even more, the ministry of the Spirit will be in glory? (9) For if the ministry[1] of condemnation was a matter of glory, much more shall the ministry of righteousness abound in glory. (10) For that which has been glorified in the past has not been glorified at all in comparison with the surpassing glory. (11) For if that which is in process of abolition was accompanied by glory, much more shall that which abides continue in glory. (12) Since then we have such hope, we exercise great freedom, (13) and do not act as Moses did, who put a veil on his face, that the children of Israel might not gaze upon the end of that which was being abolished. (14) But their minds

[1] *The ministry*, nominative, ἡ διακονία, is read by B it and the majority of MSS. Many excellent witnesses (including 𝔓[46] א D G) have the dative, τῇ διακονίᾳ, giving the rendering, If glory pertained to the ministry of condemnation, much more .... The sense is unchanged, the construction greatly eased by this variant which, notwithstanding its strong support, must be regarded as a secondary 'improvement' of the text.

were hardened; for up to this very day the same veil remains unremoved at the reading of the old covenant, for in Christ it is being abolished. (15) But to this day, when Moses is read, a veil lies upon their heart; (16) but whenever it turns to the Lord, he takes away the veil. (17) Now 'the Lord' is the Spirit; and where the Spirit of the Lord is, is freedom. (18) But we all, with unveiled face, behold as in a glass the glory of the Lord, and are transformed into the same image, from glory to glory, as from the Lord, the Spirit.

We have seen that in the last few verses Paul moved from the
thought that the Corinthian Christians were themselves his letter
of commendation, a letter written not with ink on paper but by
the Spirit of God in their hearts, to the recognition that this matter
was no merely personal commendation but the fulfilment of the
prophecy that under the new covenant the word of God would be
written not on tablets of stone but in men's hearts—that in fact
the Gospel and its effects were his authorization. This close connection is not inconsistent with the view of W. D. Davies, *C.O.J.*,
p. 175, that Paul here casts a critical glance at Qumran, and the
suggestion of Moule, *Birth*, p. 54, that he incorporates a synagogue
sermon, but it tends to diminish their force. That Paul is still
thinking in the terms suggested by ii. 16–iii. 3 is shown by verses
5 and 6; we may therefore take verse 4 as follows: What we have
just said amounts to the claim that your existence as Christians is
both the seal (1 Cor. ix. 2) of our apostleship, and replaces the
4 tables of the law as the new testimony to the new covenant; **we
have the confidence to make such a claim** (literally, 'We have
such confidence') **through Christ before God.** The last two
words (translating πρὸς τὸν θεόν) might be 'in God'; certainly
Paul means that his confidence is not self-confidence. It is not
based upon his own character or qualifications; it is given him
through Christ, that is, through his relation with Christ and the
work Christ does through him (cf. iii. 3, 'supplied by us'), and if
he has this confidence *before God* it is at the same time confidence
in God (cf. i. 9, where Paul uses a verb, πεποιθότες ὦμεν, cognate
with the noun, πεποίθησις, used here).

Verse 5a brings out the negative, verses 5b and 6 the positive
5 aspect of this. **It is not that we are of ourselves sufficient**
(cf. ii. 16) **to consider any part of this process** (literally, 'any-

thing', τι, but Paul is writing within the limits of the topics under discussion) **as proceeding from**, and therefore dependent on, **ourselves.** The sentence doubles back on itself. Paul means, We do not consider that any part of our sufficiency arises within ourselves. Nothing stands to our own credit. The counterpart of this follows: **rather, our sufficiency comes from God.** That is, ability to bear the burden of responsibility imposed by the apostolic mission (see the notes on ii. 16), and to execute the mission itself, comes from God. This is an intelligible, self-contained thought. It may be however that it was given shape by the use in the LXX of the 'Sufficient One' (ὁ ἱκανός) as a name or title for God, representing (by false but current etymology) the Hebrew name El Shaddai. See Knox, *P.G.*, p. 131, who also points out that 'the thought is common in Philo, cf. *Leg. Alleg.* i. 44; *De Cher.* 46; *De Mut. Nom.* 27, 46'. Dodd, *B.G.*, p. 15, goes further, seeing in the usage of *sufficiency* a link with the theme of *covenant* which is pursued in the following verses; this is more doubtful, and in any case the verbal links with the Old Testament are less important than the thematic link; in the Old Testament and the New God takes ultimate responsibility for his own word. It is true that Paul is here in effect answering the question of ii. 16, 'We are'. But to describe this as 'Selbstgenügsamkeit' (Schmithals, p. 151) seems about as remote from Paul's meaning as it is possible to be.

Whatever the link, Paul re-expresses the thought of *sufficiency*
in terms of the new covenant. *Sufficiency* comes from God, **who** 6
gave (or 'also gave', but unless Lietzmann and Allo, who translates *réellement*, are right in thinking that καί simply emphasizes the following verb the sentence becomes grossly repetitive) **us our sufficiency** (Paul, having used the adjective in ii. 16; iii. 5a, and the noun in iii. 5b, now uses the verb, ἱκανοῦν, but 'made us sufficient' is even clumsier than the translation given; for the thought cf. 1 Tim. i. 12) **to be ministers** (the noun, διακόνους, cognate with the verb translated 'supplied' in iii. 3) **of a new covenant.** The thought runs back to ii. 14 ff. No human being can bear the burden of proclaiming a Gospel that is at the same time 'an odour issuing from death and leading to death, and an odour issuing from life and leading to life'. Only God himself can make men sufficient for such a task. It is this task that is now redefined as that of *ministers* (servants, agents) *of a new covenant.* In reverse,

it appears that the primary duty of ministers is the proclamation of the word.

It may be that the notion of *sufficiency* suggested the terminology of *covenant* (see above); it is perhaps more likely that this arose out of the picture of a letter written in the heart, which suggested Jeremiah's new covenant prophecy of the law written in the heart (Jer. xxxi. 31-4), a prophecy fulfilled in Christ. The meaning of covenant (διαθήκη) cannot be deduced from the word itself but only from its biblical usage. Ordinarily it means 'testament', but it can refer to a one-sided arrangement or disposition (see G. Quell and J. Behm in *T.W.N.T.* ii. 106-37, and Kümmel), and in this sense is used as an equivalent of the Hebrew *b^erith*, normally rendered 'covenant'. This is the relation, initiated and determined by God, between himself and his people; hence naturally connected with service (Wendland). There had been various covenants in the Old Testament (see Rom. ix. 4, with the note; that Paul in 2 Corinthians but not in Romans refers to a *new* covenant is due to the fact that he is dealing with Judaizers—so Bachmann and Denney), and the New Testament in general (especially Heb. viii) claims that the prediction of a new and better covenant was fulfilled in Jesus, and witnessed to by the wine of the Supper (Matt. xxvi. 28; Mark xiv. 24; Luke xxii. 20; 1 Cor. xi. 25). Paul also uses the word at Rom. ix. 4; xi. 27; Gal. iii. 15, 17; cf. Eph. ii. 12, but its meaning in the present passage must be sought in the passage itself. The covenant is **based not on letter but on Spirit.** The distinction in Paul's mind has been much disputed; see *Romans*, pp. 60, 138. It is best to proceed in terms of the context. In iii. 3 Paul says that the Corinthians are themselves a letter of Christ, written not with ink but by the Spirit of the living God; in this statement he is contrasting the letters, written by men with pen and ink, which his rivals carried as their authorization, with the work of the Spirit of God in the hearts of the Corinthian converts, which was the only authorization upon which he could depend. The contrast is thus between human opinion and performance, and the work of God by his Spirit. The contrast between *letter* and *Spirit* will be essentially similar. It was certainly not Paul's intention to suggest that the Old Testament law was merely a human instrument; it was, on the contrary, spiritual, inspired by the Spirit of God (Rom. vii. 14). But it was easy to misuse it —easy for the Jew to assume that, simply because he possessed it, he was himself superior to the rest of mankind (Rom. ii. 17 ff.), easy to treat it, not as a divine gift (Rom. ix. 4), but as an indication of human achievement. Indeed, the law itself, by its preceptual character, pointed in this direction, and the point is noted in Jeremiah's new covenant prophecy (so that Windisch can describe the present clause as a gloss on Jer. xxxi). *Letter* thus points to the way in which (in Paul's view) many of his Jewish contemporaries understood the law on which their religion was based, and through this to man-made religion in general, whether legalistic or antinomian and mystical (cf. Bultmann, *E. & F.*, p. 159; Käsemann, I, p. 222; Stuhlmacher, *Gerechtigkeit*, p. 93); *Spirit* points to the new action of God in Christ, where man by faith leaves God to act creatively, no longer expecting to fend for himself. Calvin rightly insists that the contrast between letter and Spirit has nothing to do with allegory. 'By the letter he means an external preaching which does not reach the heart, and by the Spirit life-giving teaching which is, through the grace of the Spirit, given effective operation in men's souls.'

When *letter* and *Spirit* are understood in this way as human and divine action respectively, the next clause follows at once: **the letter kills but the Spirit gives life.** Compare Rom. viii. 2 (The religion which is made possible in Christ Jesus, namely that of the life-giving Spirit), with the note; also Rom. viii. 6 (To have one's mind set on the flesh results in death, but to have one's mind set on the Spirit results in life and peace). See also Rom. vii. 11 (so Benoit, II, p. 20; and compare A. Feuillet in *Mélanges Bibliques en hommage au R. P. Béda Rigaux* (1970), pp. 340–5). Existence that is man-centred can only die, because it is cut off from the source of true life; existence that is centred upon God is given life by him. It is also true, as Hughes points out, that the law kills because it is not obeyed; but whatever *the letter* may mean it seems in this context to be somewhat disparaged, and for Paul the law is in itself good (Rom. vii. 12, 14). The covenant theme is characteristic of the Qumran literature, but the parallel with Paul is slight. W. D. Davies (loc. cit.) points out that the sect appear to have interpreted the covenant in terms of letter *and* Spirit; Braun is properly critical of the suggestion that Paul was combating Qumran influence in Corinth.

The contrast he has now stated in the simplest terms Paul proceeds to elaborate in a midrash on Exod. xxxiv. 28-35; the suggestion that he is using a sermon he had preached in a synagogue (Moule, *Birth*, p. 54) has been noted above; less convincing perhaps is the view that he is correcting an already existing midrash (S. Schulz, *Z.N.T.W.* xlix. pp. 1–30; against this, see Collange, pp. 67 f.). According to Exod. xxxiv. 28, Moses spent forty days with God on the holy mountain, fasting, and 'he wrote upon the tablets the words of the covenant' (LXX, these words upon the tablets of the covenant, τῆς διαθήκης). Both Hebrew and LXX suggest in this verse that Moses himself wrote the words, but this is inconsistent with xxxi. 18 (written with the finger of God) and xxxii. 16 (the tablets were the work of God, and the writing was the writing of God, graven—κεκολαμμένη—upon the tablets), unless we are to think, by analogy with 2 Cor. iii. 3, that the writing was God's, *supplied* (διακονηθεῖσα) by Moses. Moses (Exod. xxxiv. 29) came down from the mountain with the tablets in his hand, not knowing that the skin of his face was shining (LXX, that the appearance of the skin of his face had been glorified—δεδόξασται; Sifre Numbers 140 (on xxvii. 20) (52b): Moses's face was as the face of the sun) because of his converse with God. Aaron and all the children (LXX, elders) of Israel were afraid to approach Moses (xxxiv. 30); Moses however summoned them, and passed on to them the commandments God had given him. When he had finished speaking with them (and presumably not before, xxxiv. 33), he put a veil (κάλυμμα) on his face. But when (xxxiv. 34) Moses went in to speak to the Lord, he took off (περιῃρεῖτο) the veil until he came out (when presumably he put it on again, though the Old Testament does not say this); he then handed on commandments to the Israelites. xxxiv. 35 now surprisingly continues, And the children of Israel saw that the face of Moses shone (LXX, δεδόξασται) —which implies that when speaking to them Moses had not worn a veil. The Greek could be taken in a pluperfect sense (they had seen—at the first encounter), but the Hebrew (*w^{e}ra'u*) could not be translated in this way, but rather implies habitual seeing. Finally this verse, the last in the story, notes that Moses put (περιέθηκεν) the veil (back) on his face when he went in to speak with God. The best we can make of this (though it hardly fits the Hebrew verb quoted above) is that when Moses returned from God to the people there was a brief, terrifying interval in which the people saw his glorious face, but that he quickly veiled himself until he went back to solitary conversation with God. Nothing is said or implied about the disappearance of the radiance from his face, and a Jewish tradition maintained that it remained until his death (S.B. iii. 515; Targum Onkelos, Deut. xxxiv. 7: Moses was 120 years old when he died; his eye had not grown dim, and the splendour of the glory (*ziw yᵉqara*) of his face had not changed). S.B. go on to say (iii. 516), 'We have met no passage in the old rabbinic literature in which there is a reference to "Moses's veil";' and it seems that Paul's exegesis is not based on traditional Jewish themes (apart from the Old Testament account of Moses's shining face), but is a new Christian interpretation; there is no reason to think of it as anything but his own work, produced with polemical intent against a Judaizing threat (see Introduction, pp. 29f.).

The interpretation begins with a resounding contradiction of the
Jewish understanding of Sinai, which saw it not as a **ministry of** 7
death (a *Henkersamt*—Windisch) but as a gift of life; so for example Exodus Rabbah xli. 4 (97c), God engraved the tablets for them in order to give them life (other passages are quoted in S.B. iii. 502; for Torah as the source of life see also John v. 39; Rom. vii. 10, with the notes; cf. Gal. iii. 21). For *ministry*, see iii. 3, 6. Paul has begun with his own work as a ministry, or service (διακονία), and on this basis describes that of Moses in the same terms. Moses's ministry was a *ministry of death* because it was **engraved in letters on stones**, and, in the sense described above (verse 6), *the letter kills*. This was not the intention of God in giving the law, but 'the very commandment which was intended to produce life resulted for me in death' (Rom. vii. 10). This was the fault of sin (Rom. vii. 13), but the ultimate result was good, since 'I through the law died to law that I might live to God' (Gal. ii. 19). Moses's ministry was to prove lethal in its effects, yet it **came into being in glory, so that the children of Israel could not gaze on the face of Moses because of the glory** (according to J. Jervell, *Imago Dei* (1960), pp. 176 f., glory is bound up with authority; see pp. 176–80 for the paragraph as a whole; J. A. Fitzmyer, *Mélanges Rigaux*, pp. 422 ff., connects glory with Spirit and power) **of his face.** Here Paul is simply summarizing the Old Testament story; behind his use of the narrative lies his conviction that the law (whatever else may have to be said about it) is 'holy, righteous, and good' (Rom. vii. 12)—precisely because it is the law of God (see Wendland). He cannot

however leave this statement unqualified; the glory **was in process of abolition** (literally, 'was being done away', *καταργουμένην*). The word is one Paul uses frequently, other authors hardly at all; he uses it here not because the story he is working on contained a reference to the fading of the glory (this could be better described by other words) but because the main theme of his argument is that the law (at least, the law understood in terms of letter) and the covenant based on law are being done away and replaced by a new covenant based on Spirit; see verses 11, 13, 14. It is in these verses therefore that the word calls for exposition.

There is, as we have seen, a negative element in Paul's argument, but its main drift is positive. If the covenant of law was accom-
8 panied by a manifestation of divine glory, **does this not mean that, even more, the ministry of the Spirit** (cf. 'ministry of righteousness' in verse 9) **will be in glory?** For the exegetical basis of the *a fortiori* argument see verse 11 (Bonsirven, *Ex.*, p. 317). *Will be* is a logical, not a chronological future, and does not point to the *parusia*. The *ministry of the Spirit* is already operative; see i. 21 f. and the note. This is not a subjective genitive; the meaning is analogous with *ministry of death* in verse 7. The service of Moses in the law is marked by death; the service of Paul and his colleagues in the Gospel is marked by the Spirit; compare verse 3. The Spirit is given to those who accept the message, and in them constitutes a God-centred life.

9 The contrast is now repeated in different terms. **For if the ministry of condemnation was a matter of glory, much more shall the ministry of righteousness** (for this word see *Romans*, pp. 29 f., 73, etc.) **abound in glory.** The *ministry of death* and the *ministry of the Spirit* now become respectively the *ministry of condemnation* and the *ministry of righteousness*. The law condemns by setting side by side God's requirement and man's failure to meet it; cf. Rom. iii. 19 f. In this verse, righteousness is defined by contrast with condemnation; it means acquittal, justification, the act by which God puts man in the right relation with himself. As usually in Paul (cf. also v. 21), it is not an ethical but a relational word. It is also however to be defined by the parallel with *Spirit* in verse 8; that is, *righteousness* is not a merely mechanical rearrangement of relationships, but divine power. After citing this passage, with vi. 7 and Rom. v. 21; vi. 19 f.; x. 3, Käsemann (II, p. 186; E.T., p. 174) writes: 'The gift imparted here is not and never can

be separable from its giver. It partakes of the nature of power, so far as in it God himself comes on the scene, and with it remains on the scene. So claim, obligation, and service also are inseparably bound up with it.' I question whether this (though right as far as it goes as a general observation) does justice to the meaning of *ministry*, which again is not fully explained by the passages quoted by Stuhlmacher (*Gerechtigkeit*, p. 158) from the Dead Sea Scrolls (1QS iv. 9; 1QH vi. 19: ‘^{a}*bodath ṣedeq*). Paul does not mean that righteousness is being served, any more than he means that death, condemnation, or the Spirit is being served. He is speaking rather of kinds of service (that of Moses, and that of the apostolic preachers of the Gospel) in which these are characteristic features. Stuhlmacher cuts too many corners when he says (p. 76), ‘The new world of the church is for Paul, like every world, a power structure. The power that determines this world Paul calls δικαιοσύνη θεοῦ [the righteousness of God],' and goes on to quote 2 Cor. iii. 8 f. as making the essential connection between *righteousness* and *Spirit*. Yet he is right when he says immediately before, ‘The forensic situation is the way by which this new world and creation, characterized by freedom, is reached'. *Righteousness* is God's action, but here at least Paul is concerned with the result of this action, which is justification and the status of righteousness thereby conferred on man. This is the objective aspect of the Gospel; *Spirit* points to the subjective apprehension of it in the re-creation of man. Moses could not justify his people (Exod. xxxii. 32 f.), and could only pray that the Lord would put his Spirit upon them all (Num. xi. 29); the new ministry is in every respect more glorious.

Paul develops the theme of the superiority of the new covenant.
For (the *καί*, untranslated, adds emphasis) **that which has been** 10
glorified (not simply Moses's face, but the setting of the old covenant as a whole) **in the past** (a supplement, to clarify the English and bring out the tense of the Greek participle) **has not been glorified at all in comparison with the surpassing glory** (literally, ‘in this respect, namely, as far as concerns . . .'), that is, the glory that attends the Gospel. The Greek is somewhat clumsier than this English representation of it, but the meaning is sufficiently clear: looked at in itself, Mount Sinai is a scene of glory, but it is nothing in comparison with the clearer revelation of God's mind in the Gospel. This disparagement, even though it

be a relative disparagement, of Torah is an extraordinary observation to come from the pen of a Jew, and must be borne in mind in any final assessment of Paul's attitude to the law. Schlatter makes 'in this respect' (or 'in this part', ἐν τούτῳ τῷ μέρει) more precise—possibly too precise: 'What Moses received by way of glory was and remained limited "in this matter", namely in that Moses did not yet have the ministry of the Spirit and of righteousness, but was entrusted only with the ministry of condemnation and of death.'

11 The next verse adds a further contrast. **For if that which is in process of abolition** (cf. verse 7) **was accompanied by glory** (διὰ δόξης; but it is doubtful whether Paul means anything different from ἐν δόξῃ, in this verse, and verses 7, 8; cf. vi. 8, and Moule, *Idiom*, p. 58), **much more shall that which abides continue** (no verb is expressed but one describing a continuous state is called for) **in glory.** The law was a transient phenomenon belonging to a past age; compare Rom. x. 4; Gal. iii. 19-25; and the remarks in *Adam*, p. 65. The Gospel, the new covenant, is permanent; it is God's last word and deed, and cannot be superseded; compare Mark xiii. 31.

Since the facts are as described, a difference in behaviour
between Moses and Paul follows. For the remainder of the paragraph, verses 12-18, see the article by W. C. van Unnik, 'With
12 Unveiled Face' (*Nov. T.* vi. pp. 153–69). **Since then** (the new
development, or practical application—Windisch, is grounded in
what has just been said) **we have such hope** (hope that is based
upon the abiding glory of the new covenant), **we exercise** ('let
us exercise' would be grammatically possible, but does not suit
the context) **great freedom** (παρρησία: for this word see
W. C. van Unnik, *The Christian's Freedom of Speech in the New
Testament* (1962), and *De Semitische Achtergrond van* ΠΑΡΡΗΣΙΑ
in het Nieuwe Testament (1962); also the article by H. Schlier in
T.W.N.T. v. 869–84, and a long note by Windisch)—that is, we
can preach and speak to you Corinthians with complete frankness;
13 **and** in this we **do not act as Moses did, who put a veil on his
face.** Literally the last clause runs, 'and not as Moses put a veil
on his face'. This clearly demands a supplement if the connection
of thought is to be intelligible. As van Unnik says (*Nov. T.* vi,
p. 159), Paul makes a jump; but it is perhaps not quite as daring
a jump as he thinks, nor is the exegesis implied by the supplement

a mere guess. B.D. §482 point out that omissions are common in comparisons, and in such a sentence as that which Paul writes here, with its ***not as*** (οὐ καθάπερ), it is more than an implication that what Moses did we do not do. There is, however, a leap, and van Unnik has made it intelligible by drawing attention to the Aramaic idiom 'to uncover the face, or head' (*galleh 'appin*, *rosh*). '"To cover the face" is a sign of shame and mourning; "to uncover the head" means confidence and freedom; in the Targumim e.g. "with uncovered head" has the same meaning as "in freedom" . . .'. The '"unveiling of the head or the face" comprises openess [*sic*], confidence and boldness' (p. 161). Compare verse 18, and the notes there. Moses did not act towards the children of Israel with the same complete frankness that Paul employed towards the Corinthians (for Paul's insistence on this cf. e.g. i. 18 f.; vi. 11 ff.). In order to make this point Paul reads into the Exodus narrative more than is explicitly stated there. Indeed, Exodus suggests that Moses veiled his face out of consideration for the people's fear (Exod. xxxiv. 30); Paul says that he did so **that the children of Israel might not gaze upon the end of that which was being abolished**—that is, on the simplest understanding of the words, that they might not see the glory come to an end and thus be led to disparage Moses as being of no more than temporary importance. This, as Lietzmann says, 'undoubtedly contradicts the intention, though not absolutely the letter, of the Old Testament narrator'. Certainly this proceeding, as described by Paul, was less than perfect frankness—unless, possibly we should think of the purpose in question as not that of Moses, but God's; but Paul is not concerned with (and almost certainly did not intend) a moral indictment of Moses. *That which was being abolished* (τοῦ καταργουμένου, neuter—conceivably masculine, but it would be hard to make sense of this) is not the glory (δόξα, feminine) of Moses's face; we must go back to the neuter participles of verses 10, 11, and see here a reference to the old covenant, or dispensation, as a whole, the religious framework of law under which Israel was constituted as a people. It was out of this that Moses's behaviour sprang, just as Paul's different behaviour was rooted in the different religious framework of the new covenant, which is based on the Gospel, not law (cf. i. 19). Viewed in this way, Paul's thought appears to be consistent, but it becomes obscure because he uses the same imagery in order to express both the theological, and the moral, or behavioural, aspects of it. Héring thinks that *end* (τέλος) should be interpreted, as at Rom. x. 4, in the sense of 'goal'; but this does not seem to make good sense here. Ragnar Bring (*St. Th.* xxv. 35) takes *end* to mean the 'climax of the splendour'; compare *St. Th.* xx. 13, but his view is not convincing. The complication of the argument increases as Paul proceeds to use the image of the veil in a new way.

14 **But their minds** (the word is the same—*νοήματα*—as that of ii. 11, but must here be translated differently) **were hardened**—made obtuse, uncomprehending. Compare Isa. vi. 9 f. (Lindars, pp. 159–67). *But* is a truly adversative *but*. Moses acted as he did not with a view to concealing the truth but in order to persuade the children of Israel to accept it; they would be more likely to do so if they did not see the end of the glory. *But*—his well-meant attempt failed, because a different kind of veiling was added. The power of the beholders to perceive was diminished. The Old Testament, though less clear than the New, was a genuine revelation of God; the hearers themselves (but see iv. 3 f.) contribute to its failure to achieve its goal. This is stated first in direct terms, and Paul then returns to the image of the veil—prompted, it may be, by practices of the synagogue, such as the veiling of the Torah scrolls, or the covering of the head, during prayer, with the *ṭallith* (Bachmann). **For** (this explains how and why *their minds were hardened*) **up to this very day the same veil** (presumably that which Moses placed on his face, in the sense of 'that which prevents clear vision and understanding') **remains unremoved at the reading of the old covenant** (what Israel fail to see is that the old covenant is old—Wendland), **for in Christ it is being abolished.** The sentence is full of obscurity and ambiguity, and the translation given cannot be regarded as certainly correct. Thus it would be possible to take *at the reading* (ἐπὶ τῇ ἀναγνώσει) to mean 'upon the reading'; the veil lies upon the law (as originally it had lain upon the face of the law-giver); see Knox, *P.G.*, p. 131, and compare Bornkamm, *Paulus* (1969), p. 131. But in verse 15 Paul writes that *a veil lies upon their heart*, and this should probably be taken to determine the sense here. In the translation, *unremoved* represents a participle with the negative (μὴ ἀνακαλυπτόμενον). This is neuter, and is taken here to be in agreement with *veil* (κάλυμμα): the veil remains, not being taken away. This leads to the rendering of the next clause, *for* (ὅτι) *in Christ it is being*

abolished (so, e.g., Windisch). Here, however, lies the difficulty that leads some commentators (e.g. Plummer) to abandon this construction, for how can it be said that the veil remains because it is being abolished? And is it not the law, or the glory of the law, that is being abolished? The veil is *taken away* (verse 16). The answer to the objection is to stress the phrase *in Christ*. As Israel hears the law in the synagogue the veil of unbelief remains, for it is in Christ and in Christ only that the veil is removed. If this answer is not thought satisfactory, the alternative is to regard the participle as absolute (so Allo): 'the veil remains, it being not revealed (that is, since it is not revealed) that (an equally possible meaning for ὅτι) it (the law; the glory, or the dominance, of the law) is being abolished in Christ'. This is possible though not attractive grammatically; in substance it would be true only if the participle were limited by 'to them', or in some such way. At *this day* it has been revealed but only to believing Christians, not to unbelieving Jews, that the law was fulfilled and done away in Christ.

The old covenant implies what we call the Old Testament, and could be so translated (for the bearing of the whole paragraph on the doctrine of the inspiration of Scripture see Barth, *C.D.* I ii. 514 f.); Paul is however writing with special reference to the covenant that was made at Sinai in terms of the commandments given to Moses on the tablets of stone. He does not here use the term 'new covenant' (see 1 Cor. xi. 25), but it is implied. The old covenant of the law is preached in the synagogue. Paul preaches the new covenant of God's justifying righteousness and of the Spirit. This carries with it the abolition of the law (in the old, legalist, sense).

Paul depicts the present situation more explicitly. **But** (the 15
antithesis is most naturally taken to be with the last words of the preceding verse: the law is done away in Christ, nevertheless . . .) **to this day, when Moses is read** (publicly read in the synagogue, or studied, that is, by Jews; though Reicke, *Diakonie*, pp. 288 f., thinks Paul is attacking a Christian Judaizing interpretation of the Old Testament), **a veil lies upon their heart.** Some take the *but* to be intensive: yes, to this very day . . .; Lietzmann takes the intensification to lie in the change (see above, p. 120) from a veil on the law to a veil on the Israelites' hearts. Reading from the Torah was a part of every synagogue service; see especially P. Billerbeck, 'Ein Synagogengottesdienst in Jesu Tagen', *Z.N.T.W.*

lv. pp. 143–61. The Torah contained the truth, but it could not penetrate through the veil to the hearers' hearts.

The veil may however be removed (as Paul knew, since God had
16 revealed his Son to him, Gal. i. 16). **But whenever it** (referring to the *heart* of verse 15; or possibly to Israel, or to Moses, or to any man) **turns to the Lord** (for the reinterpreting of this word to refer to Christ, see Bousset, *Kyrios Christos* (1913), pp. 122, 145), **he takes away the veil.** It is in the Lord (that is, Christ) that the meaning of all Scripture becomes clear (Calvin). The closeness of this verse to the language of Exod. xxxiv. 34 lends it obscurity, but at the same time provides a necessary clue to its interpretation. The Old Testament verse runs: But whenever Moses went in before the Lord to speak with him, he would take off (περιῃρεῖτο) the veil. 'He' must be Moses, and the verb (rendering the Hebrew *yasir*) must be in the middle voice: 'He took the veil off himself'. Paul however is no longer thinking of Moses, but of the conversion of Israelites (ultimately of the conversion of Israel as a whole, but here, as *whenever* shows, he is thinking not so much in terms of Rom. xi. 26 as of Rom. xi. 14; cf. 1 Cor. ix. 20); hence he changes 'went in before the Lord' to *turns to the Lord.* Since Moses is gone from the protasis he cannot be retained in the apodosis. Recognizing this, most commentators take the verb to be passive, and translate, 'the veil is taken away'. But in form it can equally well be middle, and the LXX suggests that this is in fact so. This yields the translation *he takes away the veil,* in which the subject can hardly be other than *the Lord* of the preceding clause. Of course, an agent, and indeed this agent, is implied by the passive verb, but to take the verb as is done here facilitates the transition to the next verse and the solution of the notorious problem it contains. It is God himself who opens men's minds to the Gospel; conversion rests ultimately upon the mercy of God (cf. e.g. Rom. ix. 16). 'An existence freed from empirical Judaism under an Old Testament interpreted on the basis of the Crucified who is known as the living Lord . . . is the abiding foundation of Christian existence' (Goppelt, p. 111).

17 **Now 'the Lord' is the Spirit.** The use of inverted commas is intended to make clear that the article with *Lord* (ὁ κύριος) is anaphoric (see Turner, *Insights*, pp. 126 ff.; also Kümmel, *Theologie*, p. 149), and directs the reader's attention to *the Lord* in verse 16. This was virtually a quotation from the Old Testa-

ment; Paul interprets it (somewhat in the manner of the Qumran *p^esharim*, e.g. 1QpHab xii. 7: The city is Jerusalem, *ha-qiryah hi' y^erushalaim*; cf. Gal. iv. 25; 1 Cor. x. 4) with reference to Christ. 'The Lord', as we have seen, is not only the divine figure to whom penitent Israel turns but the agent who by removing the veil from their heart makes this turning possible. The latter function is pre-eminently, in Paul's understanding, the work of the Spirit, who accompanies the apostolic preaching and gives it its power so that it is no longer a merely human word but the word of God (1 Thess. ii. 13; cf. 1 Cor. ii. 4), and thus inscribes the truth of the Gospel of the new covenant in the hearts of believers (iii. 3). If this view is correct, there is no occasion to draw the conclusion that Paul identified the exalted Christ with the Spirit, and so taught a binitarian, and excluded a trinitarian, doctrine of God. It is certainly true that for Paul Christ the Lord, and the Spirit, were two very closely related terms, each of which was unthinkable apart from the other, since the objective status of being in Christ carried with it the subjective accompaniment of receiving the Spirit, who was manifested in particular gifts (e.g. 1 Cor. xii. 7); he was however capable of distinguishing them, as for example in the phrase 'Spirit of Christ' (Rom. viii. 9). It is in the realm of action (cf. 1 Cor. xv. 45) rather than of person (or of substance, as Lietzmann says) that the terms *Lord* and *Spirit* are identified. Earlier in the chapter the Spirit was contrasted with *ink* (iii. 3) and with *letter* (iii. 6, 7, 8); the work of the Spirit is to replace the authority (as κύριος) of the written law, thus fulfilling Jeremiah's 'new covenant' prophecy of the law written in men's hearts. For a full account of the many interpretations of this sentence see Allo, pp. 94 ff., 107-11. Allo himself stresses the letter-spirit contrast of verse 6, as does Bachmann, who also gives a full note on various interpretations. See further W. D. Davies, p. 196; also J. G. D. Dunn, in *J.T.S.* xxi, pp. 309-20, reaching a conclusion similar to that given here.

The Spirit is thus *Lord*, with the right to direct; yet **where the Spirit of the Lord is, is freedom.** The end of the dominance of the written law means liberty. *Freedom* is an important theme in 1 Corinthians (ix. 1, 19; x. 29; see the notes) but is mentioned here only in 2 Corinthians. See also Rom. vi. 18, 22; viii. 2, 21 (with the notes); Gal. ii. 4; iv. 22-31; v. 1, 13. It is freedom from law, from sin, and from death; Käsemann I, p. 21 (E.T., p. 119) contrasts the

Lord who gives freedom with Ananke (necessity, destiny). The context, with its elaborate discussion of Moses on Mount Sinai, shows that here it is freedom from the law that is in mind, though there may also be a glance back at verse 12 (*freedom*, παρρησία), and a reference to the bold confidence that characterizes Paul's apostolic work. Compare Lucian, *Piscator* 17 (cited by Bachmann), where truth, freedom, and boldness (ἀλήθεια, ἐλευθερία, παρρησία) are brought together. The Christian, in whose heart God's law is written by the Spirit, is not bound by legalistically conceived religion; the apostle, whose work is done in the power of the Spirit, does not need to hedge his preaching and his relation with the churches by little-minded considerations of expediency and appeasement. Since this freedom is evidently anything but licence to do what one pleases regardless of the will of God, there is a measure of attractiveness in the suggestion of Turner (*Insights*, pp. 126 ff.) that the opening word of the sentence (here translated *where*, οὗ) should be written differently (οὐ) and translated 'not', so that the sentence would mean 'The Spirit is not independence of (freedom from) the Lord'. Linguistically, however, the suggestion is not convincing. Paul expresses 'freedom from' not by means of a genitive but by a preposition (ἀπό, Rom. vi. 18, 22; vii. 3; viii. 2, 21; ἐκ, 1 Cor. ix. 19), or by the dative (Rom. vi. 20), and 'independence' does not seem to be an exact rendering. The usual translation of the verse should be retained. So should the text; it is unnecessary to emend to 'Where the Spirit is sovereign' (reading κύριον for κυρίου), or to follow Héring, who emends and punctuates, 'Where the Lord is (οὗ δὲ ὁ κύριος), the Spirit is; where the Spirit is, is the Lord's freedom (οὗ δὲ τὸ πνεῦμα, κυρίου ἐλευθερία)'.

In winding up the paragraph Paul moves away from the main theme of the apostolic ministry, which contrasts with that of Moses (see J. Jeremias, in *T.W.N.T.* iv. 872 f.), to that which is
18 common to all Christians. **But we all** (not a single person, such
as Moses, not apostles only), Jews and Gentiles, have turned to the Lord and received the freedom created by the Spirit, and thus **with unveiled face** (since the Lord, the Spirit, takes away the veil—see the article by van Unnik, referred to on p. 118), **behold as in a glass the glory of the Lord.** An alternative translation is, 'reflect as a mirror the glory of the Lord'; this however is less probable. The verb (κατοπτρίζεσθαι) is not a common one,

so that usage is not decisive—Chrysostom appears to combine both interpretations (Denney). But the ancient VSS support *behold* rather than 'reflect', and 'the translation "we reflect" ... removes the contrast of the Christians with the Jews, who because of their veil cannot see' (Kümmel; similarly Windisch; cf. Wilckens, *Weisheit*, p. 74).

To behold the glory of God, and to receive knowledge of him (cf. iv. 6), is to be transformed. For the relation of this proposition with gnosis, see the note on iv. 6. If the result of the transformation is not apotheosis (Bousset, *Kyrios Christos* (1913), p. 203) it is not far away from it. Kümmel (*Theologie*, p. 199), however, rightly insists that the thought is not properly mystical; the believer remains distinct from God. We **are transformed** (Betz, *Lukian*, p. 132) **into the same image, from glory to glory.** The word *image* is suddenly introduced; see Rom. viii. 29; 1 Cor. xi. 7; xv. 49, with the notes in each case; also Col. i. 15 (*Adam*, p. 86). Compare 2 Cor. iv. 4. According to J. Jervell, *Imago Dei* (1960), pp. 173–6, iii. 18–iv. 6 is an exposition of Gen. i. 26 f.; more probably the word image was suggested by the reference to the looking-glass, in the context of wisdom speculation; see especially Wisdom vii. 26. What Christians behold is not God, viewed directly: such direct vision is not for this world. They see his glory as in a glass; in fact, what they perceive is the knowledge of the glory of God in the face of Jesus Christ (iv. 6); in other words, they see not God but Christ the image of God (that is, the means by which the invisible God becomes visible, not the wisdom hypostasis of speculation but the historic person of Jesus); and seeing Jesus the image of God they are, not deified but, *transformed into the same image*, the glory they share with him ever increasing (*from glory*, that is, one stage of glory, *to glory*, that is, to a higher stage). Compare 2 Baruch li. 3, 7, 10 (... they shall be changed ... from beauty into loveliness, and from light into the splendour of glory). Alternatively, one may think of present glory giving place to future; and Schlatter, noting the next *from* (in *from the Lord*), thinks that both are causal: glory comes from glory. Compare Collange, p. 123.

Transformation takes place **as from the Lord, the Spirit.** In the last few clauses Paul has taken up a good deal of the language of gnosis (for Jervell's view that he is providing a midrash on Gen. i see above, and below, pp. 132–5). He here ties up the end of the paragraph with the beginning (iii. 3, 8): the agent of transformation, of glory, is the Spirit. That the Spirit is involved in the renewal of human nature is clear, but the precise meaning of Paul's words is not. After the preposition *from* two genitives stand side by side (ἀπὸ κυρίου πνεύματος). The equation of the two nouns at the beginning of verse 17 probably justifies the view that they are here in apposition: *from the Lord*, that is, *the Spirit*. Alternative possibilities are (1) the Spirit of the Lord, (2) the Lord of the Spirit, and (3) a Spirit who is sovereign (since both words are anarthrous κυρίου may be treated as adjectival; see Knox, *P.G.*, pp. 131 f.). It is perhaps best to suppose that Paul wishes to affirm that the work is of God, who, whether one thinks in terms of the Father, the Son, or the Spirit, is Lord; and to add that the divine work of transformation is in fact to be ascribed to the third of these agencies.

'With verse 18 Paul has really proved too much' (Lietzmann). Lietzmann means that Paul began by affirming the dignity and self-sufficiency of his apostolic office; he needs no commendatory letters. He finishes by speaking of the status not of apostles but of all Christians. This is true, but the transition is one that is inherent in Paul's thought. As an apostle he has authority (x. 8; xiii. 10), but he is not a superior kind of Christian; in some respects the reverse of this is true (1 Cor. iv. 8 ff.), and it is only superficially that what he says here about the vision of glory and the transformation of the believer seems incompatible with the humble picture of apostolic life painted in chapters iv and vi (cf. 1 Cor. iv. 11 ff.). The vision of God remains qualified (v. 7), and it is the Spirit as first instalment who anticipates (i. 22; v. 5), but without fully realizing, the glory that belongs to the future. Paul is not without a *theologia gloriae* (*Signs*, p. 105), and indeed has his own paradoxical kind of 'triumphalism' (ii. 14).

7. iv. 1-6. THE MINISTRY—THE TREASURE IT DISPENSES

(1) For this reason, and since in the mercy of God we have this ministry, we do not neglect our duty,[1] **(2) but, as far as**

[1] Many, but inferior, MSS have instead of *neglect our duty* (ἐγκακοῦμεν), 'grow weary' (ἐκκακοῦμεν).

we are concerned, we have renounced the behaviour that shame hides; we do not practise knavery or adulterate the word of God, but in the sight of God we commend ourselves to the conscience of all men by showing forth the truth. (3) If moreover our Gospel is veiled, it is veiled for those who are on the way to destruction, (4) in whom the god of this age has blinded the minds of those who do not believe, in order that they may not see[1] the illumination of the Gospel of the glory of Christ, who is the image of God. (5) For it is not ourselves that we proclaim, but Christ Jesus as Lord, and ourselves as your slaves for Jesus' sake. (6) For it is the God who said, Light shall shine[2] out of darkness, who[3] shone in our hearts with a view to that illumination that consists in the knowledge of the glory of God seen in the face of Christ.

The preceding paragraph has contrasted the ministries of
Moses and of Paul (as a representative apostle), the fading glory
of the law, which as a means by which man may hope to be related
to God is being done away, and the transforming power of the
Spirit, which actually creates in man the glorious image of God
which the law could only demand in vain. Moses was a minister
of the Law, Paul is a minister of the Gospel—'the Gospel in which
Christ's glory shines' (Calvin on verse 4). **For this reason,** 1
because the Gospel is good news of the glory of God (or possibly,
if διὰ τοῦτο looks forward, because of what is said in the next
clause), **and since in the mercy of God we have this ministry**
—the ministry of life, glory, the Spirit—**we do not neglect our**
duty. This is a paraphrase, which puts together the clauses 'having
this ministry' and 'as we received, or were treated with, mercy';
it would be possible to connect the latter (καθὼς ἠλεήθημεν) more
closely with what follows: as God dealt with us in pity, so we for
our part . . . . But probably Paul is merely saying rather emphati-
cally what is said in the paraphrase. It was of God's mercy that he,

[1] See the note on this verse. The verb (αὐγάσαι, or καταυγάσαι, or διαυγάσαι) is determined in the sense 'shine upon' by the addition of the pronoun αὐτοῖς in many MSS and VSS. The older MSS however do not have the pronoun, and its addition probably reflects a mistaken interpretation of the verb.

[2] So (λάμψει) 𝔓⁴⁶ B ℵ * A D*; 'May light shine' (λάμψαι) is probably due to assimilation to the creation narrative (Gen. i. 3).

[3] The relative (ὅς) is omitted by D* G it Marcion, probably in order to produce a smoother sentence.

the persecutor, was called into the ministry; compare 1 Cor. xv. 9 f.; Gal. i. 13; 1 Tim. i. 15 f. See also 1 Cor. vii. 25.

We do not neglect our duty: see note 1 on p. 126. Compare iv. 16; Luke xviii. 1; and especially Gal. vi. 9; in each passage the same textual variation occurs. Not only are the Greek words alike; the thoughts are related, since weariness could well be the cause of neglect of duty. W. L. Knox (*P.G.*, p. 133) has 'behave treacherously', but this does not seem to be the normal meaning of the word. *Our duty* is evidently to proclaim the Gospel in all its purity and power; this thought leads naturally to the next verse.

2 **As far as we are concerned** (these words are an attempt to bring out the force of the (unusual) middle, ἀπειπάμεθα)**, we have renounced** (this can hardly in the context carry the implication that Paul had previously practised them) **the behaviour that shame hides,** literally, the hidden things of shame; Paul refers to things one may do, but will do only under cover, and with shame if found out—he has in mind the practices condemned in the next clause. The force of the middle may be to refuse something offered to one; in this case Paul would be thinking of the courses he describes as genuinely open to him and rejected by him. **We do not practise knavery.** Paul's word (πανουργία; cf. xii. 16, where the adjective is used) means literally 'readiness to do anything', usually any bad thing; as we say, 'to stop at nothing'; in view of what follows it may be significant that it and its cognates are used by Galen and others in the sense of adulterating medicines. Paul may therefore be specifying rather than adding when he continues, We do not . . . **adulterate the word of God.** Compare ii. 17; here, as there, there are probably two implications: (a) Paul had been accused of adulterating the Gospel (probably by not requiring all, Gentiles converts included, to observe the law of Moses), (b) in Paul's view there were Christian preachers who did falsify the word of God. This means that the (probably mutual) accusation of xi. 13 (see the note, also 'False Apostles'), where Paul describes some of his rivals as *false apostles*, was already in circulation. The next few verses (see the notes) clearly presuppose a polemical background, but are hardly explicit enough to enable us to describe the adversaries Paul has in mind. Verse 2b however implies that they were the same persons who carried commendatory letters (see iii. 1 f., and the notes), and verse 3 suggests that Paul was charged with preaching a 'veiled' Gospel.

He may have been charged by Judaizers not only with adulterating the Gospel (Schoeps, *T.G.J.*, p. 68) by not demanding obedience to the law but also with preaching a gnostic version of the Christian message, accessible only to the gnostic few. Such a charge would find its rebuttal in the next clause.

Others may pervert the Gospel; others may bring this charge against us; the truth is that **in the sight of God**, whose judgement alone matters (cf. 1 Cor. iv. 4), **we commend ourselves** not as some, such as Judaizers, may do, to the prejudices but **to the conscience of all men** (literally, to every conscience of men; all —πᾶσαν—brought forward for emphasis) **by showing forth the truth,** that is, the Gospel, or word of God (cf. Bultmann, *Exeg.*, p. 143). Almost every word in this sentence is significant both positively and negatively. Paul has not yet finished with the theme of commendation, which evidently played an important part in affairs at Corinth. There is only a superficial contradiction between this passage and others in which Paul says that he does not and will not commend himself. The distinction between Paul's self-commendation and that of his rivals is that he acts *in the sight of God.* And he appeals to the *conscience*; on this word (συνείδησις) see *Romans*, p. 53; *1 Corinthians*, pp. 102, 241-4; also, in addition to C. Maurer in *T.W.N.T.* vii. 897–918, Bornkamm, ii. 111-18. Paul refers here to the capacity for moral judgement, which apparently he attributes to non-Christians as well as Christians (Windisch); the man who does not accept Paul's sincerity as an apostle will in the end condemn himself for not recognizing the truth. Paul's appeal is universal; there is no question of his seeking approval from a small group of partisans. Any man who has a conscience should be able to recognize Paul's good faith, because he appeals to the conscience by *showing forth the truth*; cf. v. 11. As always (cf. Gal. i. 8 f.; and see *Signs*, pp. 85 f.), Paul sees his ministry as validated by the Gospel he proclaims, not *vice versa.* The choice, however, of the word *truth*, which has a much wider range of meaning than Gospel, is significant; Paul commends himself not by spinning a tale about his own importance but simply by telling the truth; compare xii. 6. A parallel to this phrase, literally 'by the manifestation of the truth', has been found in CD ii. 12 f., translated by Millar Burrows (*The Dead Sea Scrolls* (1956), p. 350), 'He caused them to know by his anointed his Holy Spirit and a revelation of truth'. The reading however is uncertain; see the discussion by Murphy-O'Connor in *P. & Q.*, pp. 198 f.; it is probably best to accept Lohse's reading, *w^ehoze 'emet*, 'seers of truth', that is, 'True seers'. There is no need to seek in Qumran the origin of Paul's use of the word *truth*; 'the truth' is a very natural term for the 'true message', which one believes.

What Paul has just said ought to mean that all men believe his message, and thus accept Paul himself as a true and faithful messenger. This is not so. Even the Jews, who should have understood it most clearly and accepted it most readily, did not do so; there was a veil on their hearts (iii. 15). That Paul's Gospel
3 has been rejected does not however prove that it is false. **If moreover** (or, Even if) **our Gospel is**—as some say—**veiled** (ἔστιν κεκαλλυμένον could be a periphrastic perfect, 'has been veiled', but is probably descriptive; cf. Moule, *Idiom*, p. 18)**, it is veiled for** (Paul's ἐν might be rendered 'among', but probably stands for the simple dative; see B.D. §220.1; M. iii. 264) **those who are on the way to destruction.** Compare ii. 15 f., and see the note; also 1 Cor. i. 18; Mark iv. 11 f. Here, as in the earlier chapter, Paul sees men's response to the Gospel as lying ultimately within the decision of God himself. According to Lietzmann Paul is referring to his adversaries, the false apostles of xi. 13, who refuse to accept his understanding of the Gospel. This is unlikely; here and in the next verse ('those who do not believe') Paul uses language that he normally applies not to false brothers but to those who are outside the Christian fellowship. He has not yet developed his thought about the divine use of a negative response to the Gospel as he does in Rom. ix–xi; unbelief is due to the devil's
4 action. These persons *on the way to destruction* are those **in whom** ('in the case of whom' is possible, and might fit better the rest of the sentence, which is certainly awkward) **the god of this age** ('grandis sed horribilis descriptio Satanae'—Bengel) **has blinded the minds** (νοήματα, as at iii. 14, not ii. 11) **of those who do not believe.** *The god of this age* is a bold expression for the devil (cf. 1 Cor. ii. 8), based on the commonplace apocalyptic presupposition that in the present age the devil has usurped God's authority, and is accepted as god by his fellow rebels; only when in the age to come God establishes his kingdom will the devil be driven out. The life, death, and resurrection of Jesus have dealt a decisive blow at Satan and his subordinates, but they are not yet com-

pletely defeated or fully reconciled; they attack Christians (*Romans*, pp. 174, 244 f.; *1 Corinthians*, pp. 236 ff., 357 f.), and also prevent men from becoming Christians; compare 2 Thess. ii. 9, 10 (also the next verse, which states the other side of the matter—God sends a force to deceive them; cf. *Adam*, pp. 13 f.). Compare also the so-called Freer logion at Mark xvi. 14. *Those who are on the way to destruction* are the victims of Satan; yet they are also *those who do not believe* (the word ἄπιστος occurs twelve times in 1 Corinthians, three times in 2 Corinthians, nowhere else in Paul—relations with the outside world were evidently particularly important in Corinth); that is, the fault that leads to their destruction is also their own; see on this an interesting note in Conzelmann, *Theol.*, pp. 216 f. The only solution of this paradox is in God, but, as was noted above, Paul does not here work this out. It is true that some have taken *the god of this age* to mean the one true God—the only God there is, and therefore the God of this as of every age; but this does not seem to be what Paul means. His language is superficially dualistic, but only superficially so. Against his own will the prince of evil is made to serve God, so that true dualism is excluded (Lietzmann). Irenaeus, *Against Heresies* III 7. 1 applies *of this age* to the *minds of those who do not believe*, avoiding the difficulty and missing the point (Bousset, *Kyrios Christos* (1913), pp. 234, 444; see also N. Brox, in *Z.N.T.W.* lix. 259 ff.).

Satan has blinded the minds of these men **in order that** (taking εἰς τὸ μή to be final; it could equally be consecutive—'with the result that'; see Moule, *Idiom*, p. 143; a description of Satan's purpose, behind which stands God's suits the context better) **they may not see** (this meaning of αὐγάζειν is clear in Sophocles, *Philoctetes* 218; Philo, *De Vita Mos.* ii. 139; see also note 1 on p. 127 and cf. iii. 13 and iii. 18, κατοπτρίζεσθαι) **the illumination of the Gospel** (genitive of origin; see B.D. §168.2; M. iii. 218) **of the glory of Christ** (this heaping up of genitives is Jewish Greek—Schoeps, *Paulus*, p. 26; E.T., p. 36). Most of the terms used in this sentence recur somewhat more explicitly in verse 6; see the notes on that verse. Paul is adopting the language of gnosticism (γνῶσις, verse 6), but makes it clear that those who do not accept the Gospel are not to be dismissed as by nature incapable of doing so; they have been blinded by an alien power. Light streams from the Gospel that Paul preaches because the theme of the Gospel is Christ (see the next verse), and Christ, the vehicle of God's glory, is himself a glorious figure. Divine *glory* is conventionally represented in the Bible and elsewhere in terms of light (e.g. Isa. lx. 1; Acts xxii. 11); biblical and gnostic imagery can thus be united, but they are united in such a way that the essential light-darkness dualism of gnosticism becomes a dualism of decision (H. Conzelmann, in *T.W.N.T.* ix. 337).

The divine *glory* appears in Christ (and thus derivatively in the Gospel) because Christ **is the image of God.** See the note on iii. 18, and compare Heb. x. 1. According to Jervell (*Imago Dei* (1960), p. 209; cf. pp. 194–7, 214–18) there is here not a quotation of but a reference to such Christological hymns as are quoted in Phil. ii. 6-11 and Col. i. 15-20; that Christ was the image of God (in the form of God) was a regular constituent of such hymns (cf. also John i. 1, 18; Heb. i. 3; and see Bultmann, *Theol.*, p. 131, E.T., i. 132). There is a formal relation with the gnostic conception of the image, which is actually God, Deus manifestus, and is incarnate in the heavenly Anthropos (Jervell, p. 215). Notwithstanding the verbal similarity, however, Paul's conception of God is different from the gnostic, and so too is his use of the term *image*. Jervell is right when he continues (p. 216), 'The divine *doxa* is . . . the way God exists and acts, that is, God himself. If the *doxa* of Christ is mentioned, that means that God himself is present in Christ.' It is unfortunate that he goes on to interpret this in terms of the Johannine Prologue and Hebrews, instead of confining himself, in the search for illustrative material, to Paul. Thus he reaches the conclusion (p. 218), 'As we see from 2 Cor. iv. 1-6, Christ's being in the image of God leads to the result that men should come thereby to recognize the divinity (*Göttlichkeit*) of Christ.' It would be nearer to Paul's thought to say that through Christ as the image of God men come to apprehend the *Göttlichkeit* of God—that is, to understand what it means really to be God. Compare Barth, *C.D.* III i. 201 f. Kümmel, *Theologie*, p. 145, referring to Wisdom vii. 26, rightly says, 'This leads to the result that the origin of the concept makes in the highest degree unlikely an equation of the Son of God with God, and Paul plainly uses this concept precisely because by means of it he can say clearly that in God's Son God himself is encountered, yet at the same time remains the Invisible One.' It is impossible to draw together into a unity the various occurrences in the Pauline writings of the word *image*. Paul was aware of its use in the Old Testament creation narrative, and in the Wisdom literature (Jervell is right—pp. 215 f., note 165—in rejecting Procksch's suggestion that the use of the word is based on Ezk. i); and though he can hardly have been ignorant of the gnostic material that may already have affected primitive Christian hymnology, it is primarily the biblical material that influences him. In for example 1 Cor. xi it is the creation narrative that is in mind; here in 2 Cor. iv (and in Col. i. 15) he uses the concept of Wisdom as the means by which the unknown God is revealed. As verse 6 shows, he has in mind both the analogy of creation (Light shall shine out of darkness) and the story of his own conversion (shone in our hearts); Wisdom was God's agent in creation (Prov. viii. 22, 30; Wisd. vii. 21), and also 'entered into holy souls, making them friends of God and prophets' (Wisd. vii. 27)—that is, Wisdom was also the agent of conversions. Before Paul makes these allusions, however, there is a further charge to answer.

He must speak of Christ in this way, **for it is not ourselves that** 5
we proclaim. (Lietzmann thinks that *ourselves* is not governed by *proclaim*, but that another verb—λογιζόμεθα—must be understood: We consider ourselves not lords but slaves). Compare iii. 1; v. 12; it might appear (Paul himself allows) that he was commending himself. 'His opponents are not altogether wrong in accusing Paul of proclaiming himself' (Bousset, *Kyrios Christos* (1913), p. 155). Paul's position was a difficult one, which it must have been impossible to explain to anyone who did not begin from the same presuppositions. These were not gnostic, though to some extent they led him to speak in gnostic terms (Schmithals, p. 150). Grace had been given (e.g. Rom. xii. 3) to Paul to act as an apostle; apostleship had been given him (Rom. i. 5); but, on Paul's understanding of apostleship, this meant that the Gospel had been entrusted to him (Gal. ii. 7) in order that he might preach it (Gal. i. 16); and the Gospel consisted precisely in this, that though neither Paul nor any man could merit the favour of God this had been given freely without respect of persons in Christ crucified and risen. Paul could not deny his commission without surrendering the Gospel; nor could he practise his vocation as an apostle without denying to himself any personal status or privilege. His apostolic authority could be manifested only by the renunciation of all the commonly recognized marks of authority. Hence the next two clauses: *It is not ourselves that we proclaim*, **but Christ Jesus as**

Lord (κύριον without the article will be predicative), **and ourselves as your slaves for Jesus' sake.** It would be hard to describe the Christian ministry more comprehensively in so few words. Paul's primary vocation was as a preacher; this by no means excluded pastoral responsibility (cf. xi. 28), in which the aim is to see that Christ is truly Lord of the church, though it did mean that Paul had little interest in such matters as baptism (1 Cor. i. 14-17). For 'Jesus is Lord' as a summary of Christian belief see Rom. x. 9; 1 Cor. xii. 3, with the notes. It expresses trust and obedience rather than doctrine, though it has doctrinal implications. As the substance of Christian proclamation it means that the crucified Messiah has been exalted by God (through the resurrection—cf. Rom. x. 9) to a position of lordship in heaven; the agent of atonement (Rom. iii. 25; 2 Cor. v. 19 ff.) and proof of God's love (Rom. v. 8) is now the merciful ruler of the world, and victor over all evil powers. To accept him as what he is thus means release from sin, law, and death; it also means to become his slave, and Paul introduces himself as the slave of Christ (Rom. i. 1; Phil. i. 1). But to be the slave of Christ means concretely to be the slave of those who are Christ's, a readiness to 'spend and be spent up' (xii. 15) on their behalf. Paul has already renounced the thought of being himself a lord over the Corinthians' faith (i. 24, using the verb κυριεύειν cognate with the noun κύριος, lord); here he expresses his relation to them positively. It was a relation which the Corinthians were probably ready to accept with some complacency (though they also admired an apostle who was prepared to handle them roughly—xi. 20), and Paul was doubtless wise to add that he served them not because they were such pleasing masters, or had in themselves any claim upon him, but *for Jesus' sake*. Jesus had become a 'servant of the "circumcision"' (Rom. xv. 8; see the note); his apostle had a similar vocation.

The basis of Paul's apostolic ministry is stated in the next verse.

6 **For it is the God who said, Light shall shine out of darkness** (cf. Gen. i. 3, though the wording there—Let there be light—is different; see Ps. cxi. 4, LXX), **who shone in our hearts with a view to** (πρός) **that illumination that consists in the knowledge** (taking τῆς γνώσεως as an appositional genitive) **of the glory of God seen** (this word is not in the Greek) **in the face of Christ.** Paul still has in mind the theme of Christ as the Wisdom-image of God (cf. verse 4); this facilitates the comparison between

the first creation and the new creation (see v. 17). The main theme here, however, as Bultmann (*Exeg.*, pp. 374 f.) has rightly seen, is not that salvation runs parallel to creation, but that Paul's apostolic activity resembles the creation of light. 'It is thus creation and the apostolic office that are parallel.'

The one God is responsible for all light; it was the Creator who *shone* (λάμπειν; a compound form, περιλάμπειν, is used in the account of Paul's conversion in Acts xxvi. 13, not however in Acts ix or xxii) in Paul's heart, revealing Christ to him (Gal. i. 16—this answers the problem felt by Bachmann and Héring—that the Father cannot be immanent), and disclosing the Gospel that he was to preach. The creation of light in Gen. i was for the illumination of the world; the revelation of light in Paul's conversion was for the dissemination, through Paul's apostolic work, of knowledge (γνῶσις); compare ii. 14, with the note. Gnosis 'is here . . . nothing other than the Gospel' (Jervell, p. 218, note 172). Paul's use of the word is probably a polemical appropriation of current (probably Corinthian) usage. *Illumination* also suggests a gnostic (less probably a mystery-religion—Bousset, *Kyrios Christos* (1913), p. 203) background (it is unlikely that the word had already become a term for baptism, though from the time of Justin it did so—see Michel on Heb. vi. 4). Philo compared the kindling of fire from fire with the handing on of knowledge (ἐπιστήμη; *De Gig.* 25); Paul sees his ministry as the means of bringing light to the world; that which illuminates the world, in the spiritual sense, is *knowledge*; *knowledge* is knowledge of the glory (not simply the majesty but the saving acts) of God; and this is to be seen *in the face*, that is, in the person (contrast the use of ἐν προσώπῳ at ii. 10—Moule, *Idiom*, p. 184, but cf. Moses in iii. 7) *of Christ*. As the image of God he is the place where God himself, the invisible, is known.

Thus the paragraph, which begins—and may be said to continue up to verse 5—as a justifying comment on Paul's apostolic ministry, ends with an account of the content of the Gospel. As at the creation light broke out from the darkness and illuminated the world, so through Paul's apostolic ministry the knowledge of God is diffused in glory. 'The light created by God is implicitly what the apostolic office is explicitly—the sign and witness of God Himself at the heart of the cosmos' (Barth, *C.D.* III i. 120; cf. II i. 42). In Christ the glory of God is revealed. Paul has not forgotten (as verse 5 shows) that it is through persons like himself, weak, and often evil spoken of, that this glory is revealed. He will have more to say about the earthenware containers in which the glory is conveyed in the next paragraph.

8. iv. 7-18. THE MINISTRY—THE EARTHENWARE VESSEL IN WHICH THE TREASURE IS CONTAINED

(7) But we have this treasure in earthenware vessels, in order that the preeminence of power may be God's, and not derived from us. (8) At all times and in every way we are afflicted but not crushed; we are at a loss but not completely baffled; (9) we are persecuted but not deserted; we are struck down but not destroyed. (10) We are always carrying about in the body the killing of Jesus, in order that the life of Jesus too may be manifested in our body. (11) For we living men are continually[1] being handed over to death for Jesus' sake, in order that the life of Jesus too may be manifested in our mortal flesh; (12) and so death is at work in us, but life in you. (13) But since we have the same Spirit of faith as that referred to in the Scripture passage, I believed, therefore I spoke, we too believe, and therefore also speak, (14) for we know that he who raised up Jesus[2] will also raise up us with Jesus, and will make us stand before himself with you. (15) For all these things are done on your account, in order that the grace, when it has expanded through the majority, may cause gratitude to abound to the glory of God. (16) Therefore we do not neglect our duty;[3] but though our outward man is decaying, yet our inward man is being renewed day by day. (17) For the light and momentary burden of affliction

[1] *Continually* is ἀεί, and is the first word in the sentence. Instead of it, 𝔓[46] G pesh Irenaeus Tertullian Ambrosiaster have εἰ, if. This may well be right, *continually* being perhaps due to assimilation to the *always* of verse 10. If εἰ is read, the translation will run: For if we living men are handed over to death for Jesus' sake, it is in order that the life of Jesus . . . .

[2] This is the reading of 𝔓[46] B 33 vg Origen Tertullian. Most MSS have 'the Lord Jesus'—a pious expansion.

[3] The same variation occurs as at iv. 1; see note 1 on p. 126.

produces for us out of all proportion an eternal load of glory, (18) as we keep our eyes fixed not on things seen but on things unseen; for the things seen are temporary, but the things unseen are eternal.

Paul's ministry has encountered much detraction, but so far from proclaiming himself he preaches not even the great though passing splendour of the law but the glory of God in the face of Christ, thus enlightening men with true knowledge. The glory however belongs entirely to the Gospel that is preached, and not at all to the apostle who preaches it. God has indeed shone in our hearts;
but we have this treasure in earthenware vessels. The 7
metaphor is not uncommon, but it is used in various senses. It does not seem relevant that earthenware vessels were in use in the Temple (Lev. vi. 28; xi. 33; xiv. 50). In 2 Tim. ii. 20 f. the point seems to be that whether a vessel is made of gold, silver, or earthenware, it may be clean and thus ready for honourable service to its owner. At Isa. lxiv. 8 it is emphasized that the vessel does not make itself—God resembles the potter, his people the potter's vessel; Lam. iv. 2 (cf. Jer. xix. 11) brings out the fragility of earthenware. The Qumran parallels alleged (1QS xi. 22; 1QH iii. 20 f.; iv. 29; x. 5; xi. 3) are somewhat remote. In Hellenistic usage the metaphor usually describes the body as a vessel that serves as a container for the soul; thus Cicero, *Tusc. Disp.* I 22, 52: 'corpus quidem quasi vas est aut aliquod animi receptaculum'; compare Marcus Aurelius viii. 27. A similar usage recurs in Philo (*De Migr. Abr.* 193; *Quod Det. Pot.* 170; *De Somn.* i. 26), though, as Windisch (on this passage) observes, Philo is somewhat nearer to Paul in that the soul contained in the body is not an independent human existence but something that exists in virtue of a relation to God ('Our mind has not created the body, but is the workmanship of Another; and it is therefore contained in the body as in a vessel': *De Migr. Abr.*, loc. cit.). None of these lines of interpretation quite fits Paul's use of the metaphor. It is true that in chapter v he goes on to speak of the body as the integument of a being that survives death, and that his language there may owe something to Hellenistic usage (see the notes); and even nearer, at iv. 16, he contrasts the outward and the inward man. In the present verse, however, his main concern is to emphasize not the fragility of the earthenware vessels (Allo) but the contrast between the infinitely

precious treasure of the Gospel (see iv. 6), and the human bearers of it. This is rightly seen by Bachmann; and there is a fairly close parallel in Sifre Deut. 48 (on xi. 22) (84a): As it is not possible for wine to be kept in golden or silver vessels, but only in one which is the least among vessels, namely, an earthenware vessel, so also the words of Torah can be kept only with one who humbles himself. The plural *vessels* suggests that Paul is thinking not only of himself but also of his colleagues. T. W. Manson (*Studia Paulina*, p. 156) recalls iv. 6 and mentions the small earthenware lamps of antiquity, perhaps rightly; but there is no point in going back to ii. 14 and citing Plutarch, *Aemilius* 32, where we learn that at Aemilius's triumph large sums of money were carried in jars (ἐν ἀγγείοις). Collange (p. 146) notes the Old Testament use of *k^e^li* for human beings.

The contrast between the wealth of the Gospel and the bearers of it was intended by God, **in order that the preeminence of power may be God's, and not derived from** (ἐξ) **us.** No one looking at Paul's insignificant person would suppose him to be the source of power working towards salvation (Rom. i. 16); this would therefore be attributed to its proper source. *Illumination*, *knowledge*, *glory* have now given place to *power*; all are closely related to Paul's understanding of the Gospel.

The next verses bring out the double fact that Paul himself looks like anything but the actual source of divine power, for he is a feeble sufferer, and yet is also the scene of such a display of divine power as delivers him from the natural consequences of his
8 suffering. **At all times and in every way** (an elaborate but
necessary rendering of ἐν παντί, which applies to all four contrasts
—see Windisch; the same expression occurs at vii. 5) **we are**
afflicted but not crushed; we are at a loss but not completely
baffled (Paul repeats the word—ἀπορούμενοι—for *at a loss*,
adding the prefix ἐξ; for the perfective force of this see M. i. 237;
9 ii. 310; Robertson, p. 596); **we are persecuted but not deserted;**
we are struck down but not destroyed. It is possible to construct this sequence of participles with the verb (ἔχομεν) in verse 7, but more probable that they are absolute. For similar accounts of Paul's apostolic work see 1 Cor. iv. 9-13 and 2 Cor. vi. 3-10. The pattern of Christian existence, which becomes particularly clear in the life of an apostle, is determined by crucifixion and resurrection. Sometimes (notably in chapter vi) the two elements in the

pattern are paradoxically described as different features of the same experience; here they are more prosaically combined: affliction is serious, but not fatal; perplexity is real, but Paul can still find his way; persecution is fierce, but the Lord stands by his servant; even the most devastating thrust does not prove mortal. Windisch and Kümmel rightly bring out both the parallel between Paul's language and that of the Stoics, and the difference in substance. Windisch quotes Seneca, *Ep.* lxxi. 25 ff., with the significant last sentence, 'stat rectus sub quolibet pondere . . . vires suas novit'. It is not his own strength that Paul knows, but the power of God, which delivers him out of distress that would otherwise prove too severe for him (cf. i. 10). Thus his life, in addition to his preaching, is a clear witness to the Gospel.

It is theologically important that Paul can thus describe his experience of crucifixion and resurrection in simple historical as well as in dialectical terms. The latter prevent the former from developing into the wrong kind of *theologia gloriae* (see *Signs*, pp. 104 f.), but the former prevent the latter from becoming a merely intellectual abstraction; God does actually deliver his servant from the power of evil. This is not mythology but fact, even though it remains true that in this age the believer remains in a world characterized by sin and death. It may be that Paul makes this point against Corinthian gnostics who undervalued the body, and proclaimed themselves—as spirit; see Schmithals, pp. 74–8.

As a historical statement these words may be placed with xi. 23-7; persecution was fiercer, and Paul suffered more severely, than Acts (for whatever reason) permits us to see.

Paul takes up the pattern of life and death in more explicit terms.
We are always carrying about in the body the killing of 10
Jesus. Compare i. 5; xiii. 4; Rom. viii. 17; 1 Cor. xv. 31; Phil. iii. 10. When Paul means to speak of death he uses (forty-five times, including verses 11, 12) the common Greek word (θάνατος); here (and elsewhere only at Rom. iv. 19) he uses a different word (νέκρωσις), and it is reasonable to suppose that he does not simply mean death. The word suggests a process, the making dead (νεκρός), and it is probable that Paul's meaning is that one who observed his life as a Christian apostle (Cerfaux, *Christ*, pp. 245 f., E.T. p. 327, emphasizes that Paul speaks here of apostolic rather than ordinary Christian experience) would see, constantly repeated,

a process analogous to the killing of Jesus. This, in a context that deals with persecution, is to be taken literally ('The sufferings which come upon him daily in his work for Jesus are gradually killing him' (Denney); cf. Schweizer, *Beiträge*, pp. 175, 228; and see Gal. vi. 17), though behind the physical suffering lay a 'dying with Christ' which gave it meaning. Bultmann, *E. & F.*, p. 328, contrasts Paul's understanding of this with Ignatius's *imitatio* (Ignatius, *Romans* vi. 3). It goes beyond the bounds of probability to suggest (Turner, *Insights*, p. 94; cf. xii. 7) that Paul had actually been crucified at Perga; stoning, scourging, and the like added up to a sufficient total. Killing, or something very near to it, was a regular part of Paul's Christian experience; it was not however an end in itself. We share Christ's death **in order that the life of Jesus too may be manifested in our body.** As verse 14 shows (against Schmithals), the primary reference here is to future resurrection (cf. Barth, *C.D.* III ii. 494); the life of Jesus will be manifested when our natural bodies are transformed into spiritual bodies (1 Cor. xv. 35-49). It is however part of Paul's understanding of this process that it was already anticipated through the work of the Spirit (see especially i. 22; v. 5); to this extent and in this way *the life of Jesus* was already being *manifested*, in the deliverance Paul has already described (verses 8 f.), and in the inward renewal of verse 16. The destruction of the earthenware vessel (verse 7) reveals more clearly the treasure it contains.

The next verse repeats the thought of verse 10, with slight
11 variations. **For we living men** (Paul uses the article, οἱ ζῶντες—
we who have not died before the *parusia* but expect to witness it; cf. 1 Cor. xv. 51 f.) **are continually being handed over** (παραδιδόμεθα; cf. Rom. viii. 32, and many other passages where it is used for the handing over of Jesus to death; it is also used for his betrayal by Judas, but the thought of treachery does not seem to be in mind here) **to death for Jesus' sake**—that is, our being Christians exposes us to constant risk of being no longer *the living*. Paul does not wish to die before the *parusia* (cf. v. 4, with the note) but inevitably exposes himself to the danger of doing so; this is (as in verse 10) to be understood of literal sufferings undergone *for Jesus' sake*, that is, in the execution of apostolic tasks, but it also points to a community of experience with Christ crucified—not to mysticism (though the term is often used) but to faith which conforms itself to the pattern of existence provided in Jesus. 'As Jesus'

herald, he told the story of his passion; he not only told it, but experienced it too; compare Phil. iii. 10' (Schlatter). As in verse 10, purpose is expressed: **in order that the life of Jesus too may be manifested in our mortal flesh.** This corresponds closely to verse 10 except that for *our body* is substituted *our mortal flesh*. On this Kümmel writes that here 'σάρξ [flesh] stands in the sense of σῶμα [body], an exception to Paul's normal usage; in the parallel statements of verse 10 and 11 σάρξ [flesh] and σῶμα [body] denote the individual being, which awaits the σῶμα πνευματικόν [spiritual body] at the resurrection.' For Paul's customary use of *flesh* see above, p. 72. Unless the change from *body* to *flesh* is due to mere desire—possibly subconscious stylistic desire—for variation, it should probably be understood to underline the point made above (pp. 137 f.); the manifestation of the life of Jesus, though perfect only in the resurrection at the end, is already begun and shines through the sin and suffering of the present life—it appears even in the context of *flesh*. Even our present self-centred, man-centred, existence shows signs of the transforming power of the Spirit who brings freedom (iii. 17). So far as Paul is united with Christ he is set free from the old self (cf. verse 16) and lives to God (e.g. Rom. vi. 11; Gal. ii. 19).

A new contrast now appears. At first it seems that Paul intends
simply to restate and sum up the contents of verses 10, 11: **And so** 12
(writing ὥς τε; see Moule, *Idiom*, p. 144) **death is at work in us**
—not simply imposed from without by persecution, but working itself out from within, from our union with the crucified Jesus; **but**, Paul continues, **life** is at work **in you.** Up to this point Paul has been speaking mainly of his experience as an apostle. T. W. Manson is perhaps not wrong in saying (*P. & J.*, p. 74), 'It is conceived not as something confined to a spiritual *élite* within the community, but as the normal thing for all Christians'; but the whole context is about Paul's apostolic ministry, and it is in the apostle that what is in fact the essence of Christianity for all Christians becomes most clearly visible. As the manifest ringleader of the Christian movement, the apostle draws upon himself the heaviest experience of suffering; as the one in whom the Gospel is manifested he can say that the life of Jesus not only will be revealed in the resurrection at the last day but already begins to become visible in his *mortal flesh*. Here however he appears to reserve death for himself, life for his readers. This may mean (Dodd,

Studies, p. 110) that Paul himself expected to die before the Advent but that his readers would survive to experience it as living men. This would mean (as Dodd points out) a significant change of view from that of 1 Cor. xv. 51 f. In view of v. 8 the change is not impossible. The alternative is the interpretation which Lietzmann, though he adopts it, thinks can be given trivial expression in the words 'Physically, things go steadily worse with me, in consequence of my work in the mission . . . . , but spiritually, for the same reason, they are always going better for you'. This becomes less trivial if it is compared with Col. i. 24: Paul endures (vicariously—Windisch) what is left over of the messianic afflictions (see above pp. 61 f.) that the church may not have to bear it, absorbing suffering into his own person, as Jesus has done (Mark x. 45). The passage in Colossians (which some hold not to have been written by Paul) only makes explicit what is hinted at elsewhere, not least in verse 15 of this paragraph—all these things are done on your account. Bachmann interprets somewhat similarly, with the suggestion that verses 10b, 11b (body, flesh) give not the place where but the means by which life is manifested, not in Paul, but through Paul—that is, *in you.* It does not seem necessary to conclude, with Calvin, that Paul is writing ironically.

In such circumstances, is it worth while to continue as an apostle? The work entails much suffering, and, as the whole Corinthian context shows, it brings little thanks. The answer to the question is that faith both lays the missionary obligation upon Paul (cf. 1 Cor. ix. 16), and assures him that present suffering is not the end.
13 Hence he continues to preach the Gospel. **But** (notwithstanding the fact that all we appear to get out of it is death, though you get life) **since we have** (in Greek a participle, ἔχοντες, which, awkward as the connection is, must presumably be coordinated with πιστεύομεν; see Robertson, p. 1134) **the same** (that is, the same as the Psalmist, though Strachan, and Calvin, who thinks Paul is here correcting the irony of verse 12, take Paul to mean, the same as you—Corinthians; but Paul thinks of faith that leads to speech) **Spirit of faith** (that is, the same divine Spirit, who engenders faith; Bultmann, *Theol.*, p. 326; E.T. i. 330, thinks of the Spirit proper to faith) **as that referred to in the Scripture passage . . . .** This (κατὰ τὸ γεγραμμένον) is a citation formula not used elsewhere by Paul (who usually has καθὼς, or καθάπερ, γέγραπται). The variation may be insignificant—it corresponds

closely to the very frequent rabbinic 'according to that which is written' (*sheha-kathub*, k^{e}*kathub*, and the like). G. A. Deissmann, *Bible Studies* (1901), p. 250, sees legal parallels in the papyri. The Scripture runs, **I believed, therefore I spoke.** Paul quotes the LXX (Ps. cxv. 1) exactly; the Hebrew (Ps. cxvi. 10) differs somewhat. S.B. iii. 517 can find no reference to it in the old rabbinic literature. Paul pays no heed to the context, but picks out the two significant words. **We too believe, and therefore also speak.** 'Faith must bear witness, it cannot keep silence' (Wendland). Paul does not say what he believes, or what he speaks. It is sufficiently obvious. What he believes is the Gospel, and what he speaks is the Gospel, which, as it must, to be effective, meet with faith on the part of the hearers (Rom. x. 14 ff.), must also proceed from faith.

Faith and speech are both related to knowledge. Paul acts as he
does because **we know that he who raised up Jesus** (cf. Rom. 14
x. 9; 1 Cor. xv. 11—this is a central element in Christian life and
proclamation) **will also raise up us with Jesus** (cf. Rom. vi. 5;
viii. 11; 1 Cor. vi. 14), **and will** (in the future 'us with you';
contrast verses 10, 12) **make us stand** (cf. the intransitive use of
the same verb—παρίστημι—at Rom. xiv. 10; and cf. further 2
Cor. v. 10) **before himself with you.** *With Jesus* clearly cannot
mean 'at the same time'; the resurrection of Jesus lies in the past;
the death, not to say the resurrection, of Paul and his readers still
lies in the future. The phrase points (as such expressions—with
Jesus, with the Lord, and so on—commonly do in Paul) to the
eschatological future; Christians will be raised up as Christ was
raised up, so as to be for ever with him; compare 1 Thess. iv. 17.
This means that Paul and his readers will be together (*with you*),
and all will be in the presence of God (this is already implied by
the παρά in παρίστημι). It does not seem necessary to choose (as
Lietzmann thinks we must) between appearing before God's
judgement seat and sharing in his triumph; both are elements in
the last events; but the stress does not here lie on judgement (as it
does at v. 10). Paul speaks boldly, knowing that beyond earthly
tribulation lies God's victory (cf. verse 17), and that God who
justifies us will make us stand blameless in his presence (1 Thess.
v. 23).

Paul does not forget that he is writing about his apostolic ministry. His believing, speaking, suffering are not for his own

15 sake. **All these things** (not 'all things' in general, but those described in the preceding verses) **are done on your account.** Paul returns to the theme of i. 6 (cf. v. 13); see the notes. All his experiences, of affliction and of comfort, may be turned to the advantage of his people, and he knows that it is the business of a good minister to use them so. This is part of 'proclaiming ourselves as your slaves' (iv. 5). There is however a motive beyond even that of building up the community: in all his work Paul seeks the glory of God. So much is clear, but there are obscurities in Paul's language, which partly recalls i. 11. His aim is **that the grace, when it has expanded through the majority** of the church, **may cause gratitude to abound to the glory of God.** In Greek (as in the English, which seeks to imitate it) there is a play between the words *grace* (*charis*) and *gratitude* (*eucharistia*). Paul has not in this context defined what he means by *grace*; in this epistle we may point to the comprehensive account of the word jointly supplied by viii. 9 and ix. 8: *grace* is in the first place the act of loving condescension which took place in the willing humiliation of Jesus Christ, and in the second place the divine supply which meets all the needs of those who belong to the people of Christ. Here the latter thought is in mind, though Paul knew well that *grace* as the supply of man's need rested entirely upon *grace* as the favour of God. Paul speaks of *grace* as expanding, using the verb (πλεονάζειν) of which sin is the subject at Rom. v. 20; as that verse shows, Paul does not make a sharp distinction between the two verbs here rendered *expand* and *abound* (περισσεύειν; in Rom. v. 20 ὑπερπερισσεύειν is used). *Grace* increases in quantity, and spreads; *expands* covers both senses. It *expands* so as to cover a wider area; it is therefore an attractive suggestion that we should translate (Moule, *Idiom*, p. 108; cf. Bent Noack, *St. Th.* xvii. pp. 129–32), 'through the increasing numbers', that is, of converts. The more converts, the greater the supply of grace, and correspondingly the greater the measure of thanksgiving. The suggestion would be convincing were it not for the use of the word *majority* (οἱ πλείονες) at ii. 6 (and at ix. 2; 1 Cor. x. 5; xv. 6; Phil. i. 14; in a different sense only at 1 Cor. ix. 19). These passages seem to determine Paul's usage. Normally at least he refers either to the *main body*, or to the *majority*, of the church (as was noted at ii. 6, the difference is one of emphasis). Does this however make sense? It is intelligible enough to speak of a rebuke determined on by the

majority of the church; but does not grace extend, by definition, to all members of the church? The point is that (as at Rom. v. 20) grace may multiply in depth as well as area; and Paul would probably have been thankful indeed if a majority of the church at Corinth had grasped their dependence on the grace of God; they would have had a less exaggerated opinion of themselves. *Abound* (περισσεύειν) is here transitive (that is, *cause to abound*) with grace as its subject and thanksgiving as its object. To receive and understand God's grace is necessarily to thank him, and thus to glorify him; not objectively to increase his glory, which would be impossible, but to recognize it and make it known.

Paul turns back to the point made at the beginning of the chapter (see iv. 1), but at greater depth. It is one thing to fulfil one's apostolic vocation in the light of the treasure of the Gospel, another to do so with reference to the fragility of the earthenware vessel in which the treasure is contained, and the suffering one incurs in the work of evangelism. In iv. 1-6 Paul said, in effect, After God has revealed himself in the glory of conversion, we cannot neglect our duty. Here he says, Not even the decay of the body and the discouragement of outward things will lead us into
dereliction of duty. **Therefore** (in view of our faith that God will 16
raise us up with Jesus) **we do not neglect our duty** (the same word, with the same textual variant, as at iv. 1); **but though our outward man** (the metaphor is no more perspicuous in Greek than in English, and it seems better to retain it in translation and attempt to explain it in the notes than to paraphrase) **is decaying, yet our inward man is being renewed day by day** (ἡμέρᾳ καὶ ἡμέρᾳ is described by B.D. §200.1 and M. iii. 243 as a Hebraism, but the usual Hebrew expression is *yom yom*, not *yom wayom*, and when the latter phrase occurs, at Est. iii. 4, it is not translated by the LXX ἡμέρᾳ καὶ ἡμέρᾳ, whereas ἡμέρᾳ τῇ ἡμέρᾳ is used in Modern Greek for 'day by day'). If Paul's *day by day* is less of a Hebraism than may at first sight appear, his *outward man* and *inward man* may be less Greek. See Rom. vii. 22; vi. 6, with the notes. *Inward man* recalls such passages as Plato, *Republic* IX 589A: The supporter of Justice makes answer that he ought rather to aim in all he says and does at strengthening the man within him (ὁ ἐντὸς ἄνθρωπος) (Jowett). Compare Epictetus II vii. 3: Have I not the seer within (τὸν μάντιν ἔσω) who tells me the nature of good and evil? viii. 14: If an image of God were present you would not

dare to do any of the things you do. But when God himself is present within (ἔσωθεν) and beholds and hears all things, are you not ashamed to be thinking and doing these things . . .? *Corpus Hermeticum* xiii. 5: The mortal form changes daily. Similar language was used by Hellenistic Judaism; see for example Philo, *Quod Det. Pot.* 22 f. (. . . This man, dwelling in the soul of each of us . . . convicts us from within . . . (Colson and Whittaker)); for many more quotations see Windisch. That Paul is using language that would be familiar in his non-Christian, and non-Jewish, environment is certain; but he supplies it with his own, Christian, meaning, which can only be ascertained if the whole range of expressions (not only *outward* and *inward man* but also *old* and *new man*—note *renewed* in this verse) is taken into account; Rom. vii. 22 and 2 Cor. iv. 16 must be interpreted in terms of Rom. vi. 6 (and Col. iii. 9—cf. also Eph. iii. 16; iv. 22, 24). *Inward* and *outward man* are not the elements of a psychological dualism (of which hardly any trace is to be found in Paul's writing as a whole) but refer to the man of this age and the man of the age to come (cf. the natural body and the spiritual body of 1 Cor. xv. 44). They thus provide a clear example of the way in which Paul combines the two strands in his doctrine of salvation (see *Adam*, passim, especially pp. 92–119), that which, rooted in Jewish and primitive Christian eschatology, is expressed in cosmic and mythological terms, and that which treats existentially of the being of man. It is clearly impossible to treat the inward (or new) man as a purely eschatological being, belonging to the future; he already exists, since he *is being renewed day by day*. That is, the peculiar Christian eschatology, which insists that the age to come has already (though not completely) come into the present, makes it both possible and necessary to adopt, from the Hellenistic world, a quasi-mystical turn of speech. This however does not imply, in the ordinary sense, mysticism, or that Paul is thinking of the body as a material (and therefore evil) integument or envelope enclosing the soul (immaterial, and therefore divine). From one aspect, Paul as a whole is the *old man* (B.D. §184 rightly say that ἡμῶν is possessive, not dependent on ἔξω), subject to a thousand troubles and under sentence of death; from another aspect, Paul as a whole is the *new man*, whose very being is Christ (cf. Gal. ii. 20; Phil. i. 21), the heavenly man (1 Cor. xv. 47). The outward man can only decay (for Paul's word, διαφθείρεται, cf. 1 Cor. xv. 42, 50, 53: φθορά, φθαρτός), not simply because of such attacks as are described in verses 8 f. but because it belongs to a world that is passing away (1 Cor. vii. 31). The inward man experiences constant renewal. 'According to the rabbinic notion, the ethical renewal of man belongs only to the future, which alone can bring the promised new Spirit, or the new heart' (S.B. iii. 600 f.); that is, the renewal Paul speaks of is an anticipation of eschatology. For the verb to renew (ἀνακαινοῦσθαι) compare Rom. xii. 2 (ἀνακαίνωσις), though here the thought is different. In Romans, the mind, the intellectual aspect of human nature, must be renewed in order to form correct moral judgements; here Paul thinks of the daily renewal of Christian existence, which is not guaranteed by an act of faith, or by baptism, in the past, but continues only in virtue of continual contact with the Lord.

I have given here the interpretation of *outward man*, *inward man*, that seems to me probable. Others have taken Paul's language differently. On the interpretation of iv. 16–v. 10 as a whole see J. A. T. Robinson, *The Body* (1952), pp. 75–8. According to Bachmann, the two terms are psychological, used instead of 'body' and 'soul' to make clear that the same 'I' is the subject of both bodily and spiritual experiences. Many distinguish between the terms *outward man* and *old man*; see for example Calvin ad loc.; Conzelmann, *Theol.*, p. 202; Bultmann, *E. & F.*, p. 155, and *Theol.*, pp. 198–200, E.T., i. 200-3 (the inward man is the true self). Rissi, pp. 66 f., compares the present passage with Rom. vii, and thinks that we have to do not with two parts of the person, but two aspects of the same reality (*Wirklichkeit*). The *inward man* is man as thinking and willing subject; *outward man* is the same subject realized on earth in historical existence.

From what is said in verse 16 the remainder of the paragraph follows. It enables, first, a suitable balance to be drawn up between
present suffering and future glory (cf. Rom. viii. 18). **The light** 17
and momentary (there is a full note on this word, παραυτίκα, in Bachmann) **burden of affliction** (literally, the momentary lightness—neuter adjective, ἐλαφρόν for abstract noun—of affliction) **produces for us out of all proportion** (a double expression, which cannot be literally translated; Paul uses the former part of it, καθ' ὑπερβολήν, at Rom. vii. 13; 1 Cor. xii. 31; 2 Cor. i. 8; Gal. i. 13) **an eternal load of glory.** It is in comparison with *glory* that the *affliction* appears light; in itself it was heavy enough—see

i. 8, We were weighed down beyond measure (καθ' ὑπερβολήν). The word *load* (βάρος) was probably chosen to form a suitable contrast with the description of the affliction. It could be used in the sense of 'abundance' (see L.S., s.v. VI), and may have suggested to Paul (Moule, *Idiom*, p. 186) a play on the Hebrew word for *glory* (*kabod*), whose root meaning is 'heaviness'. *Produces* (κατεργάζεται) is not simply a futuristic present; the glory is already in part present, in the daily renewal of our *inward man*. This bears upon the interpretation of the next verse.

The future glory is prepared, and it is in a measure experienced,
18 **as we keep** (the participial clause could be rendered Since we
keep, or Provided that we keep; it seems best to leave it open) **our eyes fixed** (the construction is very awkward, a genitive absolute following upon the dative, ἡμῖν, at the end of verse 17; the nominative, σκοποῦντες, read by D* F G, and thought possibly right by B.D. §423.5, does not mend matters) **not on things seen but on things unseen,** treating them as a 'mark to aim at' (Denney; cf. Schlatter). Like *outward* and *inward man* this sentence at first sight suggests a dualistic distinction between the material and the spiritual, but Paul is still thinking of the afflictions that formed the visible part of his daily experience and the glory that was to come, and was already visible, though only to the eye of faith. Compare Rom. viii. 24 f. It is in this sense that he continues, **for the things seen are temporary, but the things unseen are eternal.** This is not metaphysics, but eschatology (and *temporary* is a better translation than 'temporal' (Hughes)); the life to which Paul's observation leads is not one of abstraction, but of faith (cf. v. 7). 'Here too the contrast is not the Hellenistic one between the visible world without and the invisible world within, but that between the transient present age and the abiding age to come, which in hope is already present; it is in this "Not yet" and in the certain hope of the eschatological fulfilment that faith lives' (Kümmel). Compare Rom. viii. 18; Wisd. iii. 5; also 2 Baruch xliv. 9, 12; lxxxi. 3; and other passages given in Bousset-Gressmann. And see the *Acts of Peter and Paul* 84: All things here are temporary (πρόσκαιρα); the things that are there are eternal.

9. v. 1-10. A DIGRESSION, ILLUSTRATING FURTHER THE RELATIVE UNIMPORTANCE OF THE EARTHENWARE CONTAINER

(1) For we know that if our earthly house, a tent, is taken down, we have a building that comes from God, a house not made with hands, eternal, in the heavens. (2) For in this tent we groan, longing to put on over our body our habitation which comes from heaven, (3) in the hope that,[1] when we have put it on,[2] we shall not be discovered to be naked. (4) For we who are in the tent, burdened as we are, groan, because we do not wish to strip, but rather to put on over our body the habitation that comes from heaven, that what is mortal may be swallowed up by life. (5) He who prepared[3] us for this very purpose is God, who, in the Spirit, gave us the first instalment of his whole gift.

(6) We are always confident, therefore, since we know that while we are at home in the body we are absent from the Lord (7) (for we conduct our lives on the basis of faith, not the appearance of things); (8) we are confident, I say, and content to be absent from the body and present with the Lord. (9) For this reason also we make it our ambition, whether we are present or absent, to be pleasing to him; (10) for we must all appear before the judgement seat of Christ in order that each one may receive recompense for the things he has done by means of his body[4]—recompense,

[1] Instead of εἴ γε, 𝔓[46] B D G have εἴπερ, implying more strongly that the 'supposition agrees with the fact' (L.S., s.v. εἴπερ): 'since, when we have put it on, we shall not . . . '. This reading is certainly old, and may well be correct.

[2] For 'when we have put it on' (ἐνδυσάμενοι) the Western Text (D* G it Marcion; and Chrysostom) has 'when we have taken it off' (ἐκδυσάμενοι). This reading of course implies that 'it' is 'this tent', not the 'habitation that comes from heaven'. Bultmann, *Probleme*, p. 11, thinks that only the Western variant yields a clear sense; but in fact the difference is primarily one of emphasis.

[3] The Western Text (D G lat) has 'he who is preparing' (the present participle, κατεργαζόμενος).

[4] For the difficulties of this sentence see the note. 𝔓[46] and the Latin versions have τὰ ἴδια τοῦ σώματος, which differs from the text translated only by the addition of an ι: 'the things proper to his body'.

that is, in relation to things he has done, whether good or evil.[1]

This paragraph (which is notoriously difficult; see a full note on the history of its interpretation in Allo, pp. 137–55; also
1 Knox, *P.G.*, pp. 136–43) takes up, with the word **For** (γάρ), the conclusion of the preceding one, which dealt with the visible and the invisible, the present and the future which is already to some degree present in the renewal of the inward man. This was a sketch of the pattern of Christian existence in general, and was so intended by Paul, who throughout chapter iv was speaking of the treasure of the Gospel and of the earthenware vessel, humble and frail, in which it was contained, even when entrusted to an apostle. It has however a special application to the question of life after death. Neither here nor in 1 Cor. xv does Paul deal with this question in a systematic way. It has been maintained (notably by Schmithals, e.g. pp. 227 f.; see the observation by E. Brandenberger, *Adam und Christus* (1962), p. 73) that Paul completely failed to understand the dualism of his adversaries; in fact, in both epistles his real concern is focused upon the way Christians are to live here and now (see verses 6 f., 9 f.). He uses the Christian hope for the future to bring out the meaning of the present, affirming that Christians 'von dem leben, was sie noch nicht sind, was aber ihrer wartet' (they 'live by something they are not yet, something that still awaits them'; Bornkamm, *Paulus*, p. 230).

Why do we focus our attention upon that which is invisible and eternal, rather than upon that which is temporary and visible? Because **we know** (it seems that Paul can assume that the problems that gave rise to 1 Cor. xv are no longer causing trouble) **that if our earthly house, a tent** (taking τοῦ σκήνους as a genitive of apposition; there is no reason to think that the image was suggested by the proximity of the Feast of Tabernacles; see in addition to the passages discussed below Isa. xxxviii. 12; Ascension of Isaiah ix. 1, 2, 9-13; 2 Enoch xxii. 8 ff.), **is taken down, we have a building** (οἰκοδομή; in view of the immediately following *house*, οἰκία, it is impossible to stress, as Turner, *Insights*, pp. 130 f., does, the contrast between this word as denoting process

[1] ℵ A have the word φαῦλον, used by Paul elsewhere only at Rom. ix. 11; the majority of MSS (including 𝔓[46] B D G) have the commoner and more positive κακόν (cf. xiii. 7), which is probably secondary. See the note.

and *οἰκητήριον*, the thing built, in the next verse) **that comes from God, a house not made with hands** (and thus one of the invisible things of iv. 18; cf. Mark xiv. 58; from this description follows the next adjective), **eternal, in the heavens** (for the plural, cf. xii. 2). *We know* does not necessarily imply that the teaching to be given was traditional and already familiar to the Corinthians; Paul's habitual reminder is a question, for example, 'Do you not know . . . ?' (Rom. vi. 3; vii. 1). We cannot therefore, with J. N. Sevenster, *N.T.S.* i. 295, conclude that Paul is not suddenly introducing the Greek doctrine of immortality—though the conclusion itself is correct. When in 1 Cor. xv. 11 Paul recalled the universal Christian preaching of the resurrection he did not express himself as he does here; there has been new thinking, catalysed, in all probability, by controversy with thought of a gnostic kind (so e.g. Bultmann, *Probleme*). Collange (p. 187) thinks that when he says *we know* Paul is referring to the saying of Jesus (cf. Mark xiv. 58) about the Temple.

A *tent*, with its suggestion of impermanence and insecurity, is a common picture of the earthly life and its setting in the body: Wisd. ix. 15 (the only place in the LXX where Paul's word, *σκῆνος*, not *σκηνή*, is used); 2 Peter i. 13 f.; also Plato, Philo, and other philosophical writers (see references in Windisch). The usual meaning is that the tent is the body, a temporary dwelling-place for the immortal soul. It is well to be rid of it: You do well to make haste to take down the tent (*λῦσαι τὸ σκῆνος*; *Corpus Hermeticum* xiii. 15). It is not, however, as will appear, Paul's desire to release the soul (or whatever the non-material part of man should be called) from all corporeal containment. If the tent *is taken down*: this may be in death, or at the transformation of the living at the time of the *parusia* (1 Cor. xv. 51). Bultmann (*Probleme*) seems to think that only one of these possibilities can be in mind; on the contrary, the context suggests that both are considered, though Paul regards the latter as preferable. In either case, further accommodation is provided by God himself—the word order suggests (Bachmann) that Paul means a 'building-from-God' rather than 'we-have-from-God'; *not made with hands* virtually repeats *that comes from God*. This building *we have* (*ἔχομεν*, present tense); that is, we have it in hope, the present tense expressing confident certainty (Lietzmann, Allo). Schlatter, however, argues that the verb expresses neither the future nor contemporaneity; it means, We have—at the moment of death. E. E. Ellis (*N.T.S.* vi. 211–24; the whole article, on 2 Cor. v. 1-10, should be read) believes that the new building is a corporate body, the Temple of 1 Cor. iii. 16; vi. 16 ff.; this view leads to some difficulty in explaining the earthly tent.

The relevance if not the truth of the proposition that we have a building that comes from God is shown by our desire for such a
2 building; hence the **for** with which the new sentence begins. **In this tent** (no noun is expressed, but the demonstrative is either masculine or neuter, and the only possible antecedent is σκῆνος, tent—unless we take the antecedent to be the preceding sentence (cf. e.g. John xvi. 30), and the phrase to mean 'at this time', or 'in this longing', or 'for this reason'; but verse 4 strongly suggests *in this tent*) **we groan**—because it is the scene of affliction (i. 8; iv. 8-12; xi. 23-7), and because we long for the time of fulfilment when God will terminate the course of this age and establish his reign—compare Rom. viii. 23, the only other occurrence of the verb (στενάζειν) in Paul. The only possible reaction of the Christian to the present age is that he should die to it; this he does in union with Christ. *Groaning* however has a mainly positive content; it means that we are longing for something to happen—**longing to put on over our body** (the last two words are not in the Greek, but *to put on over* alone is not tolerable in English, as ἐπενδύσασθαι is in Greek) **our habitation** (the word, as used by Paul, is synonymous with *building* in verse 1; see the note) **which comes from heaven** (according to verse 1, it is now in heaven, whence it will come to us at the right moment; Turner, *Insights*, p. 130, distinguishes *heaven* (plural) in verse 1 from *sky* (singular) in verse 2—it seems doubtful whether this distinction was in Paul's mind). The metaphor is hopelessly mixed; *putting on* is concerned with clothes (Héring notes the use of the metaphor of celestial clothing in the Mandaean texts), but we do not wear *buildings*. This does not mean that the metaphor is unclear, though it becomes clearer as Paul proceeds.

Bultmann (*Probleme*, p. 11) thinks that the word translated *to put on over* means in fact only 'to put on', basing his view on verse 4; that verse however rather supports the view taken in the present translation—see the notes. We may think of a man wearing clothes; he wishes to put on another garment over those he is already wearing. We may think of a man living in a house or tent; he wishes to put up another, larger house or tent round the one he already inhabits. Paul longs therefore to receive the new dwelling, which awaits his use in heaven without having to give up the old; that is, he hopes not to have the old tent taken down in death, but, by surviving till the *parusia*, to receive the new dwelling in addition—to put it on like an overcoat. In the language of 1 Cor. xv. 51, he hopes to be one of those who do not fall asleep in death and lie in the earth till they are raised incorruptible in a spiritual body, but survive till, with the return of Christ, they are changed, that is, exchange their natural body for a spiritual without any interval. (See the article by C. F. D. Moule, referred to below in the note on verse 5).

Paul, reverting to the image of clothing, now states his hope
explicitly. We long thus to put on the new building **in the hope** 3
that (εἴ γε καί; this expresses assurance rather than doubt—see Thrall, pp. 85-91; on the text see note 1 on p. 149), **when we have put it on** (ἐνδυσάμενοι, repeating the sense of the compound verb of the preceding verse—M. i. 115; on the text see note 2 on p. 149), **we shall not be discovered to be naked.** *When we have put it on* can hardly be interpreted except in terms of the preceding verse and 1 Cor. xv. 53 f., though Dr Thrall (pp. 82-95) takes it to refer to baptism, in which the believer puts on Christ, the new man: we are confident that, whatever happens, we shall not be found to be naked, since provision has already been made to safeguard against this. This however leaves the *put on over* (ἐπενδύσασθαι) of verse 2 unexplained. On the verse as a whole see J. N. Sevenster, *Studia Paulina*, pp. 202–14.

Paul's desire not to be found *naked* reveals not only a characteristically Jewish horror of nakedness, but also that, though he uses in this context a quantity of Hellenistic language, he does not use it in its normal Hellenistic sense. Outside the Jewish and Christian field, the nakedness of the soul was not dreaded but longed for—at least, among philosophical thinkers. With the man in the street it was perhaps different: It seems to me that in many ways men are mistaken about the power of this god [Hades], and that it is not right to fear him. For they are afraid because, when once any of us dies, he is always there [with Hades], and because the soul, stripped (γυμνή) of the body goes to be with him, of this too they are afraid (Plato, *Cratylus* 403 B; cf. *Gorgias* 523, 524; *Phaedo* 67 DE, cf. 81 C; *Republic* IX 577 B—all these passages should be carefully studied). See also Betz, *Lukian*, pp. 84, 93: man enters the ship of the dead naked. In Hadrian's famous (and untranslatable) poem the soul is naked at death:

Animula vagula blandula
hospes comesque corporis,
quae nunc abibis in loca
pallidula rigida nudula?
nec ut soles dabis iocos

(*Historia Augusta*, *Hadrian*, xxv).

Stripping was necessary if the soul was to enter the highest heaven. 'Then, stripped (γυμνωθείς) of those qualities which the spheres have wrought in him, man reaches the ogdoatic nature [outside the seven spheres, in the immediate presence of God]' (*Corpus Hermeticum* i. 26; cf. x. 18: When the mind is separated from its earthly body, immediately it puts on its proper clothing, which is made of fire). The thought may be of Persian origin; see F. Cumont, *Oriental Religions in Roman Paganism* (1911–1956), pp. 159 f., note 54. Philo shared the Greek view of the nakedness of the soul as a desirable thing: He [Moses, at the end of his life] began to pass over from mortal existence to life immortal and gradually became conscious of the disuniting of the elements of which he was composed. The body, the shell-like growth which encased him, was being stripped away and the soul laid bare (ἀπογυμνουμένης) and yearning (ποθούσης; Paul's word in verse 2 is ἐπιποθεῖν) for its natural removal hence (*de Virtutibus* 76 (F. H. Colson); cf. *Leg. Alleg.* ii. 57, 59). See also Lucian, *Hermotimus* 7.

This was not Paul's view; *nakedness* was to be abhorred and if possible avoided. But what did he mean by nakedness? According to E. E. Ellis (*N.T.S.* vi. 221; cf. W. Grundmann, *N.T.S.* viii. 24 ff.) Paul was thinking of the shame of exposure at the *parusia* and judgement, but this does not seem consistent with Paul's argument (cf. Schweizer, *C.O.N.T.*, n. 288). It seems clear (see especially the discussion in Kümmel, *Theologie*, p. 214), in the light of 1 Cor. xv, that Paul is thinking of a possible period between death and the coming of the Lord at the End. According to Kümmel, however, he is thinking not of bodiless existence, but of a 'preliminary waiting for the appearance of Christ'. But surely it is precisely bodilessness that makes this period of waiting undesirable in Paul's eyes. Already in this life we are waiting; we do not wish to do this in a bodiless state. 1 Cor. xv. 35 ff. shows that bodilessness was for Paul undesirable, and a condition that could not last for ever, but it does not show that it was unthinkable. In the event of death 'a natural body is sown, a spiritual body is raised up' (1 Cor. xv. 44). But raising up does not follow immediately upon sowing; what of the interval? This is the period of waiting (cf. 1 Cor. xv. 37, 'a bare (γυμνόν) grain'), and what makes it undesirable is that the natural body has perished in death and the spiritual body has not yet been conferred (though it is anticipated in the *inward man* of iv. 16; see the note). It is true (as Kümmel points out) that not even death can separate us from the love of God (Rom. viii. 38 f.), but rather means being 'with Christ' (Phil. i. 23); but we must probably conclude that Paul had not yet fully integrated his eschatological programme with his conviction that God was Lord over life and death alike and that those who were in Christ could not be separated from him. Whether they are fully integrable is a fair question. Schmithals's argument (pp. 227 f.), that Paul shows in this verse misunderstanding of a Corinthian gnostic position, depends on the view that he is endeavouring to show (by adducing man's longing for a future life, which, in Paul's view, could not conceivably be a longing for nakedness) that his adversaries are involved in a logical absurdity. But Paul is not arguing in this way; he writes out of the Christian longing to finish with this age of sin and death and enter upon the age to come.

This interpretation of Paul's thought seems to be borne out by
the next verse. **For we who are in the tent** (that is, the *tent* of 4
verse 1, the earthly body), **burdened as we are, groan** (as Paul says in Rom. viii. 23, We ourselves also, who have the first-fruits of the Spirit, we ourselves also groan inwardly, while we still look forward to our adoption as God's children, the redemption of our body), **because we do not wish to strip, but rather to put on** (for the imagery cf. Knox, *P.G.*, p. 138) **over our body the habitation that comes from heaven** (the last eight words, not in the Greek, are needed in English to make sense of *put on over*, ἐπενδύσασθαι; cf. verse 2). Interpretation of this verse must turn on the meaning of the words translated *because* (ἐφ' ᾧ). Here they are followed by a present tense (cf. Rom. v. 12, where they are followed by an aorist). In classical usage, the same words followed

by a future mean 'on condition that', and Dr Thrall (pp. 94 f.) would retain this meaning here, and see a caution against gnosticism. It seems however that when the idea of a condition relating to the future is moved into the present, 'on condition that' becomes 'in view of the fact that' (so M. i. 107; cf. Robertson, pp. 604, 963; M. iii. 272; Turner, *Insights*, p. 131). If we accept the meaning *because* it will follow that *burdened* does not mean 'fastened to a physical body we should like to get rid of'; *we do not wish to strip* off our body. It must be observed too that Paul does not say, 'Not because we wish' (*οὐκ ἐφ' ᾧ θέλομεν*), but *because we do not wish* (*ἐφ' ᾧ οὐ θέλομεν*), and though his word order is occasionally eccentric we must (until the contrary is proved) assume that he means what he says. He thus differs radically from the Hellenistic view described above—and from 4 Ezra xiv. 13 f. We can hardly interpret *burdened* (*βαρούμενοι*) in terms of the *load* (*βάρος*) *of glory* in iv. 17; it is better to look back to i. 8: We were weighed down (*ἐβαρήθημεν*) beyond measure, beyond our strength, with the result that we despaired even of life. The *groaning* and the *burden* are the fear of death—though fear, in the case of a man of such heroic courage, is manifestly an inadequate term. Paul is not in the ordinary sense afraid of death; he dreads it precisely for the reason he proceeds to give—because it would be a much happier thing to survive till the *parusia*, that is, not to die, be buried, pass some time *naked*, and then be raised up, but to be transformed immediately (1 Cor. xv. 51) by the substitution of a spiritual for the natural body (1 Cor. xv. 44), to put on the new dwelling over the old. On the notion of heavenly clothing and a heavenly body, and Paul's horror of nakedness, see the note in Windisch, pp. 164 f.

The content of Paul's wish is **that what is mortal may be swallowed up** (*καταποθῇ*; cf. 1 Cor. xv. 54, Death has been swallowed up in victory) **by life.** The parallel with 1 Corinthians confirms that Paul is thinking of what will befall those who are still living when the *parusia* takes place. Even for those who die (and Paul goes on to face this possibility), death is not the end (and they will not be anticipated by the survivors, 1 Thess. iv. 15); but it is better to survive, and to witness and share in the victory of life, that is, of God himself. When Christ has overcome the last enemy, death, God will be all in all (1 Cor. xv. 28). Compare Isa. xxv. 8.

Paul's hope for the future is rooted in the past and the present.
He who prepared (see note 3 on p. 149) **us for this very purpose** 5
is God (construction as at i. 21), **who, in the Spirit** (as at i. 22 I take Spirit, *πνεύματος*, to be an appositional genitive), **gave us the first instalment of his whole gift.** For this description of the Spirit see i. 22, and the note; it is particularly appropriate here in a context in which Paul is dealing with God's promises for the future. The aorist participles, *prepared* (*κατεργασάμενος*) and *gave* (*δούς*), point to decisive actions on God's part; it is natural to think of conversion and baptism, but unwise to confine Paul's thought within narrow limits; compare pp. 80 f.

This verse is the key-point in C. F. D. Moule's discussion of Paul's teaching on the resurrection (*N.T.S.* xii. 106-23). That for which God prepared us is a process which begins with the corruption of the physical body, which is complete at death, when a new spiritual body is provided. Man would prefer 'addition' (*ἐπενδύσασθαι*), but God has planned 'exchange', which involves nakedness, a state man dreads with the instinctive fear that perhaps his hope may in the end be mocked by God's failure to provide the new, spiritual body. In this respect, Moule thinks, 2 Cor. v marks a change in comparison with 1 Cor. xv. There is great value in his discussion of dualism in Paul, and his view may be right; but is it satisfactory to regard verse 2 as a 'spasm of unbelief'?

Paul now proceeds to draw practical inferences from what he has said. The earthenware vessel in which the Gospel is contained is indeed fragile; it may or may not survive till the *parusia*, but will certainly not last beyond it. But so great is the glory of its contents, and so sure the divine promise of which a foretaste is given in the
Spirit, that there is no room for despondency. On the contrary: **We** 6
are always confident (the finite verb renders a Greek participle, *θαρροῦντες*, which is in anacolouthon; Paul presumably intended to say, Being always confident we do so-and-so, forgot how the sentence was going, and began again in verse 8), **therefore** (Paul's *οὖν* refers back to verses 1-5), **since we know** (another participle, *εἰδότες*, used causally) **that while we are at home in the body we are absent from the Lord.** Paul uses the verb *to be confident* (*θαρρεῖν*) only in 2 Corinthians, at v. 6, 8; vii. 16; x. 1, 2; it includes the notion of boldness. He now drops the metaphor of the tent and speaks simply of the body, meaning the natural body which we use in this world. We face the dissolution of this body

with boldness partly because we are confident that God will supply a superior replacement for it, partly also because we know that life in the body, familiar as it is, has disadvantages. Goudge indeed says that 'to be at home in the body' is a 'deplorable translation. The present body is quite unworthy of the name of home'. It is however the home we must at present be content with. For the life of exile in this world see Knox, *P.G.*, pp. 140 f., with many references.

At this point Paul's sentence breaks down and he has to start again. To be present in the body is to be absent from the Lord: Paul cannot mean that in this life the Christian is separated from Christ; he has used too often such expressions as 'in Christ'. He thinks however of Christ as reigning in heaven, and so long as the Christian lives on earth in this age he cannot be in the full sense *with Christ* as he will be when he departs (cf. Phil. i. 23; this is Paul's characteristic use of *with Christ*). This is part of Paul's
7 understanding of the nature of Christian life: **for we conduct our lives** (literally, walk; for the idiom cf. iv. 2) **on the basis of faith, not the appearance of things.** Paul is explaining what he means by *absent from the Lord.* It is in the absence, or it might be better to say, in the invisibility of Christ, that faith is conceivable; compare Rom. viii. 24, A hope you can see is no hope at all. Faith does not proceed on the basis of an objectively authenticated Christ (for example, on a firm demonstration of the fact of the resurrection; see *1 Corinthians*, pp. 341, 349); it trusts the absent and undemonstrable Christ, whose history has already vanished into the past and whose coming lies in the unknown future (cf. 1 Cor. xi. 26). It believes in life when nothing is visible but death (Rom. iv. 17-22), and is content therefore to be baptized into Christ's death (Rom. vi. 3), and to carry about with it the killing of Jesus, confident that his life also will be manifested when and as God wills (iv. 10; cf. Col. iii. 4). This does not mean that faith is unreal; it is as real as the absent Christ is real. It does mean that it really is faith. The corresponding negative statement is that we do not trust to *the appearance of things.* The translation of Paul's word (εἶδος) is uncertain. It is often given an active meaning, *sight*, and this makes good sense: *sight* is a good counterpart to *faith.* This however is not the usual meaning of the word (see L.S., s.v.). Kümmel has answered Kittel's suggestion (*T.W.N.T.* ii. 372; see also Windisch, who quotes Num. xii. 8, Face to face I

will speak to him, ἐν εἴδει καὶ οὐ δι' αἰνιγμάτων) that the word is passive in the sense that Christians 'do not yet walk in the sphere in which their eschatological glory has become visible' (Kümmel's wording). But the word can be taken in its usual passive sense in a way that is not open to the same objection: We live by believing in the absent and invisible Christ, not by looking at visible forms. This seems to be Paul's meaning. Compare 1 Cor. xiii. 12; and the discussion in *1 Corinthians*, pp. 306-11.

Paul now takes up again the sentence that began with the
participles in verse 6, and broke down. **We are confident, I say** 8
—that is, in the face of the possibility of death; see verse 6; not only so (or perhaps, because we are confident), we are **content to be absent from the body and present with** (the use of the preposition πρός is not an Aramaism) **the Lord**, or possibly, stressing the aorist tenses, to leave the body and come home to the Lord, that is, by dying. Since the position is that which Paul has described, to die is gain (Phil. i. 21), and we are well pleased to look forward to it. It is important to see the resemblance between what is said in this chapter, and 1 Cor. xv. on the one hand, and Philippians on the other. There is little sign of development in Paul's thought on this subject beyond the fact that as time advanced he found that he must take with increasing seriousness the possibility of his own death, and in doing so took also with increasing seriousness the sense in which even the dead are with the Lord.

The thought that for all, living and dead alike, the coming of Christ will give final meaning to their existence is full of comfort and confidence, but it is also a challenge to Christian living. The coming of Christ means judgement, and for this it is the Christian's
business to be ready. **For this reason also we make it our** 9
ambition, whether we are present or absent (it makes little difference whether we supply 'the body' or 'the Lord'; *him* suggests the latter, but against this Kümmel notes the order of the participles), **to be pleasing to him.** 'Also for his people in heaven, Jesus is Lord' (Schlatter), requiring their obedience—an obedience it will always be a joy to give. One's physical condition, whether in life or death, becomes ultimately irrelevant (Conzelmann, *Theologie*, p. 186); compare 1 Thess. v. 9 f.; Phil. i. 21. Paul gives no indication at this point of the kind of behaviour likely to be pleasing to Christ; it is only the principle he is con-

cerned with. The thought that his future is in the hand of God does not lull the Christian into false security but makes him the more determined to be obedient. Paul states once more his familiar theme, Become what you are, and then makes the thought of judgement as explicit as possible. We must endeavour to be
10 pleasing to Christ, **for we must all** (M. iii. 201 notes the order of words, *τοὺς πάντας ἡμᾶς*, the sum total of us—without exception) **appear** (the word, *φανερωθῆναι*, is used of appearances in court; C. F. D. Moule, *The Phenomenon of the New Testament* (1967), p. 92; cf. Calvin, 'It is almost as if he were citing them to that heavenly assize') **before the judgement seat of Christ.** Compare Rom. xiv. 10, We shall all stand before God's judgement seat; also Rom. ii. 16, The day in which, according to my Gospel, God judges the secret things of men through Jesus Christ. The lack of formal consistency (not only between the epistles but within Romans) is not insignificant Christologically. God carries out judgement, but he carries it out through Jesus Christ; Jesus Christ judges, and his judgement is the judgement of God. Judgement is universal, and includes Christians (according to Héring, this passage refers only to Christians). Its purpose is **that each one** (the individualism of *each one*, *ἕκαστος*, corresponds to the universalism of *we must all appear*; see Bornkamm ii. 74) **may receive recompense for the things he has done by means of his body—recompense, that is, in relation to** (or, 'in proportion to'; see Moule, *Idiom*, p. 53) **things he has done, whether good or evil.** The construction is not clear. I have taken the view that here (as at Lev. xx. 17; Eph. vi. 8; Col. iii. 25) 'to receive something' (*κομίζεσθαί τι*) means 'to receive the reward for something'. The alternative (which gives substantially the same sense) is to suppose that the words of the sentence should be rearranged (as if Paul had written *τὰ πρὸς ἃ διὰ τοῦ σώματος ἔπραξεν*) and rendered, literally, 'the things (that is, the rewards) corresponding to the things he has done through the body'. There is further ambiguity in the words (*διὰ τοῦ σώματος*) which I have rendered *by means of his body*; they might mean, 'in the course of his bodily life'. On the text see note 4 on p. 149.

These difficulties are, from the linguistic point of view, serious; they do not at all affect the fact that Paul teaches that all men must prepare for judgement (see Windisch for an interesting note on Greek and Jewish notions of judgement, individual and collective), which will be executed by Christ, and that they will be recompensed, evil for evil, good for good. Is this consistent with his doctrine of justification by faith? The problem is clearly brought out by Knox, *P.G.*, p. 141; Stuhlmacher, *Gerechtigkeit*, pp. 57, 67; but see also E. Jüngel, *Paulus und Jesus* (1964), pp. 66 ff. Paul saw no inconsistency, for his references to judgement are much too frequent, and are too closely connected with Christ, to be dismissed as an unthinking recollection of his now abandoned Jewish past. He never ceased to think that obedience to the command of God was required of all men, not least of Christians; such obedience is not abrogated but made possible by justification. This is the foundation; on it men may build, and what they build is exposed to judgement (1 Cor. iii. 10-15). Worthless building is destroyed, but the builder is not destroyed with it. It may be significant (see note 1 on p. 150) that Paul uses, along with *good*, a word that means evil in the sense of poor, paltry, worthless (contrast Eccles. xii. 14). This observation, however, does not provide an adequate explanation (as if Paul were saying, When Christians are judged, God does not have to decide between absolute good and absolute evil, but between good and not so good), for 1 Cor. ix. 27 shows that Paul considered the possibility that he himself, and therefore any Christian, might, on the basis of his life, be rejected. 'The decision of faith has constantly to be made anew, up to the moment of the judgement' (Rissi, p. 98).

Bachmann (following Calvin) takes the new paragraph to begin not at v. 11, but at verse 9; in fact, verses 9, 10 may properly be regarded as a transition.

10. v. 11-21. THE TREASURE: THE AMBASSADOR'S MESSAGE OF RECONCILIATION AND NEW CREATION ARISING OUT OF THE DEATH OF CHRIST

(11) Since then we know the fear of the Lord, we persuade men, but we stand open to God; and I hope that we stand open in your consciences too. (12) We are not commending ourselves to you again, but giving you an occasion of boast-

ing on our behalf,[1] in order that you may have something to set against those who boast in appearance, and not in heart. (13) For if we are beside ourselves, it is for God; and if we are of sound mind, it is for you. (14) For the love of Christ controls our action, since we have made up our minds on this, that one died on behalf of all. That means that all died; (15) and he died on behalf of all in order that the living might live no longer for themselves, but for him who on their behalf died and was raised. (16) The consequence of this is that henceforth we know no one according to the flesh; though[2] we have known Christ according to the flesh, yet now we know him in this way no longer. (17) A further consequence is that if anyone is in Christ, there is a new act of creation: all old things have gone, behold, new things have come into being.[3] (18) All these consequences come from God, who reconciled us to himself through Christ, and gave us the ministry of reconciliation, (19) which bears the message that it was God who in Christ was reconciling the world to himself, not counting their transgressions against them, and put in us the message[4] of reconciliation. (20) We therefore act as ambassadors on Christ's behalf, as if God were exhorting you through us; on Christ's behalf we beg you, Be reconciled to God. (21) Him who knew not sin he made sin on our behalf, that we might become God's righteousness in him.

[1] Instead of *on our behalf* (ὑπὲρ ἡμῶν), 𝔓[46] B ℵ have 'on your own behalf' (ὑπὲρ ὑμῶν). This reading, which has such excellent attestation, is often written off as meaningless; it could mean, 'All that I am and do is on your account; what may look like self-commendation is truly for your benefit, and it thus provides you with something to boast about on your own account.' It is true that one would have expected ὑπὲρ ὑμῶν αὐτῶν, or ὑπὲρ ἑαυτῶν; yet how is it that the error, if error it is, is found in hardly any but the oldest and best MSS?

[2] *Though* translates εἰ καί, read by 𝔓[46] B ℵ* D*; εἰ δὲ καί in the majority of MSS would make little difference, but καὶ εἰ, 'even if', in G and the Latin, and εἰ δέ, 'but if', in K, do change the emphasis if not the sense. Collange (p. 262) takes καί in a comparative sense, and translates '. . . in the same way that, if we knew Christ according to the flesh, we now no longer know him so.'

[3] The great majority of MSS add τὰ πάντα, requiring the translation, 'All things have become new'. This reading was used by Marcion, and may well have originated in his desire to have done with everything old—including the God of the Old Testament. But Paul is concerned with new creation, rather than with renovation.

[4] For *the message of reconciliation* 𝔓[46] has 'the Gospel of reconciliation', and D G conflate the two readings—'the Gospel of the message of reconciliation'. 𝔓[46] rightly gives the sense of *message.*

Throughout the central part of the epistle (and indeed, though less clearly, throughout the epistle as a whole) Paul's thought moves paradoxically between the treasure of the Gospel and the mean earthenware vessel in which it is contained, the message and the messenger; but the same paradox extends to cover the dignity and authority of Christ's ambassador, matched with his meek acceptance of the status of slave to the self-satisfied Corinthians, and the fact that the Gospel itself, which is the power of God unto salvation, manifested in his Son, is focused on the unintelligible historical event in which God's Son is treated like a sinner and killed. These three paradoxes are all set out in the present paragraph, which is one of the most pregnant, difficult, and important in the whole of the Pauline literature. It is clearly connected both with what precedes and with what follows, yet has a certain independence; parts of it (see below) may have been already formulated, and quoted, more or less exactly, at this point. This however is a quite uncertain and perhaps unnecessary hypothesis; it may be enough to say that Paul is moved by the subject with which he is dealing to write in an exalted style that suggests the language of hymn or liturgy.

He has just said that *we must all appear before the judgement seat*
of Christ (v. 10), and not unnaturally continues, **Since then we** 11
know the fear of the Lord, as our judge. *The fear of the Lord* has a familiar, weakened sense, in which it means little more than piety (e.g. Job xxviii. 28; Prov. ix. 10); the context forbids this weakened sense here. So far as we are to be judged by our deeds we may well be afraid of what is to come. It is in this fear that **we persuade** (conative, perhaps: we try to persuade) **men.** Compare Gal. i. 10, Are we now persuading men or God? This verse suggests that Paul may have been accused of *persuading men* in a bad sense, that is, of winning them over to his side in an unscrupulous way that would bear examination neither before God nor at the bar of the human conscience. Bultmann (*Probleme*, p. 13; cf. Wendland) suggests that the word must be Paul's opponents'; he would have used 'exhort' (παρακαλεῖν, vi. 1). To this Paul replies, It is precisely in the fear of God, and in full awareness that we must stand before his judgement seat, that we persuade men to accept a message that is not ours but his. This may well be the meaning of the verse; there is no doubt that many accusations against Paul circulated at Corinth. It is not however a necessary

meaning. The paragraph goes on to describe Paul as Christ's ambassador, begging men to be reconciled with God, and it may be that he is advancing his argument by a simple statement of fact: It is the thought of the great judgement day that makes us press on with the work of evangelism (Schlatter). Or it may be (so Hughes) that Paul is thinking here not of evangelism, but of persuading men of his integrity and apostolic status. In either case, he claims, we keep in mind our responsibility before God and men. Whatever men may think or say of us, **we stand open** (the same word, φανεροῦσθαι, as in v. 10) **to God;** it is in his court we must stand, to be acquitted or condemned (cf. 1 Cor. iv. 4). We may try to persuade men to think as we wish them to do, but we appear to God as we are (Bachmann). He can judge the purity of our motives, and it is his judgement that counts; for practical purposes, however, it is not unimportant that the Corinthians (in their own interests) should come to a correct judgement regarding Paul. Accordingly, **I hope that we stand open** (here, as in the preceding clause, the perfect tense is used, suggesting that Paul has taken and still takes his stand in complete openness, untouched by reasonable suspicion) **in your consciences too.** Compare iv. 2, with the note. If the Corinthians will reject prejudice, they will be obliged, Paul *hopes* (followed by the perfect infinitive this almost amounts to *thinks*—see B.D. §350), to recognize the purity of his motives.

A different line of interpretation is followed by Schmithals, pp. 153–8, who thinks that Paul is defending, against gnostic criticism, his rational (non-ecstatic) method of communicating the Gospel. In the present verse *we persuade men* and *we stand open to God* are parallel respectively to *we are of sound mind* and *we are beside ourselves* in verse 13. This interpretation will be taken up again in the notes on verse 13, but it may be observed here that it is much better to take *we stand open* (πεφανερώμεθα) in the sense given by *appear* (φανερωθῆναι), in verse 10, than in a sense somewhat doubtfully ascribed to the cognate noun (φανέρωσις) in 1 Cor. xii. 7. On the rest of the chapter, and especially on the use of the first person singular and plural, see Cerfaux, *Christ*, p. 137; E.T. p. 176.

Paul's appeal to the consciences of his readers is not to be mis-
12 understood. **We are not commending ourselves to you again.**
Paul has already made this disclaimer (iii. 1; see the notes). He is

in a difficult position, for though he has no intention of using any commendation beyond that of the Gospel itself, which authorizes those who preach it, it is necessary, or at least desirable, in the interests of the apostolic mission, that his good faith should be recognized by those who form the churches founded by him. The present verse is of great importance because it shows that this necessity arises out of the presence of others who work on different lines. Compare iii. 2, and the development of the argument in chapters x–xiii—the situation which in these four chapters flares up and is discussed with vehemence and some bitterness is already present in germ in the earlier part of the epistle. Allo writes of these verses: 'The eagle is beginning to look down from above on the martins and foxes; but he is not yet ready to pounce down on them in vertical descent'. 1 Corinthians shows that the Corinthians could be troublesome enough on their own (though already outside influences were at work); the different situation (see the sketch in the Introduction, pp. 5-11) reflected by 2 Corinthians arises primarily out of the activities of a rival apostolate. But if Paul's action is not self-commendation (but only, as Bultmann, *Probleme*, p. 14, points out, apparently self-commendation), what is it? We are **giving** (Paul uses a participle where a finite verb is called for, as at vii. 5, 7; viii. 19, 20, 24; ix. 11; Rom. v. 11; cf. Moule, *Idiom*, p. 179) **you an occasion of boasting on our behalf** (that is, about us; cf. i. 14), **in order that you may have something to set against** (or, something to say to) **those who boast in appearance, and not in heart** (for the contrast between *appearance* and *heart*, πρόσωπον and καρδία, cf. Gal. ii. 6; 1 Thess. ii. 17). Paul is doubtless well aware that what he is doing must look very much like self-commendation; indeed it is self-commendation in the sense that he is representing himself as a faithful and trustworthy preacher of the true Gospel. More accurately, it is commendation of the Gospel as he himself represents it, for its motivation is to be found not in himself but in the Corinthian situation, in which others are boasting not sincerely and truthfully (*in heart*) but in matters that are external, and only apparently related to the truth. Who these persons were is a question that cannot be answered on the basis of this verse alone; evidence must be collected throughout the epistle. For a summary see 'Paul's Opponents', and Introduction, pp. 28 ff. It is not unreasonable, in the light of verse 16, to suggest that part of their boasting rested upon contact with the historical Jesus (cf. Gal. ii. 6), but we may add their commendation from official sources, their forceful characters, their visions,—and achievements that were not their own (see x–xiii, passim). Boasting as such is not expedient (xii. 1), and Paul himself means to boast only in the Lord (x. 17), but it was an important feature of the Corinthian situation that the Corinthian Christians, who at best were not too loyal to the apostle, should not be swept off their feet (as in the end they were—xi. 20) by his showy and plausible rivals. They needed an answer. The answer Paul provided—that in the fear of God he faithfully preached the Gospel entrusted to him, proclaiming Christ as Lord and himself as a slave (iv. 5)—does not seem to have been thought adequate. Compare xi. 6, 22 f.

At this stage (later in the epistle he will go further) all that Paul is willing to claim for himself is that he forgets himself: all that he does is in the service of God and for the benefit of the Corinthians.
13 **If we are beside ourselves** (in speaking with tongues, 1 Cor. xiv. 18, or in visions, 2 Cor. xii. 1-7)**, it is for God** (1 Cor. xiv. 2); **and if we are of sound mind, it is for you.** The man who speaks in tongues holds private conversation with God, which benefits him but is of no use to the community; rational discourse may instruct and build up the church (1 Cor. xiv. 3 f., 19). In neither case is the speaker seeking to glorify himself; the Corinthians, however, could boast of having such an apostle, who seeks only the glory of God (Schlatter). 'Here evidently the realm of the private religious life, which culminates in ecstasy, is marked off from the realm of apostolic service to the community, which is described as *σωφρονεῖν* [being of sound mind]' (Käsemann, 'Legitimität', p. 67/61).

This simple interpretation of the verse may in fact be as much as can confidently and usefully be said about it, but it raises further questions. *We are beside ourselves* translates a word (*ἐξέστημεν*) which may (as at Mark iii. 21) refer to a settled or habitual state (We have gone out of our minds, and stay out of our minds), or to a specific past occasion on which 'We went out of our minds'. Commentators are sharply divided. Denney for example thinks that Paul refers to 'the spiritual tension in which he habitually lived and wrought'. Allo on the other hand insists that the aorist (*ἐξέστημεν*) must refer to a specific occasion. It has even been suggested that the reference is to an occasion on the 'sorrowful visit' when Paul became mad with rage; less improbably, when he commended himself (Bachmann). *We are of sound mind* is unquestionably a continuous tense, but we cannot be sure whether this carries the other verb with it, or is intended as a contrast. Schmithals (see the note on verse 11) believes that Paul is rebutting an argument that since only ecstatic speech demonstrates its divine origin his sober instruction of the community has no apostolic authority; No, Paul replies, ecstasy is for God, what you need is plain reason. If such an argument was current Paul no doubt rebutted it, but this is not the main drift of his thought. It may be that 'to be of sound mind' has been too closely connected with speech and instruction. Plato, *Phaedrus* 244A (ὁ μὲν μαίνεται, ὁ δὲ σωφρονεῖ; cited by Windisch) illustrates the normal use of the word, and Paul's main point may be paraphrased as follows: My Christian and apostolic experience may be divided into the ecstatic and the rational; these are directed respectively towards God and towards you, so that neither is undertaken for my own benefit or glory. Compare verse 15—Paul at least will live no longer for himself. Understood in this way the verse falls into a coherent place in the paragraph as a whole.

At this point Paul ceases either to commend himself or to labour the proof that he is not doing so, but turns to the motive that lies behind all his behaviour as a Christian and apostle. This is not a private but a universal motive (though it is indeed individually felt), and it leads to a fundamental statement of Christian doctrine.

Why do we act as we do—for God, for you, and not for ourselves? As Schlatter puts it, Why is there nothing but love in Paul's heart? This is more probable than Bultmann's view (*Probleme*, pp. 14 f.) that Paul now gives the reason why *boasting in*
appearance (verse 12) is excluded. **The love of Christ controls** 14
our action. *The love of Christ* may be subjective genitive (so Robertson, p. 499)—Christ's love for us, or objective genitive—our love for Christ. Lietzmann (cf. Allo) thinks that it has a mystical double meaning. See the article by C. Spicq (*St. Th.* viii. pp. 123-32). The fundamental thought here must be that of Christ's love for us, since this alone can provide a suitable introduction to what follows. God's (Christ's) love for men is proved by the death of Christ (Rom. v. 8; Gal. ii. 20), and it is to this that Paul immediately turns in the second part of the verse. Spicq however is right when he observes (p. 124) that Christ's love for

Paul evokes Paul's love for Christ. The verb in this clause (συνέχειν) is used by Paul elsewhere only at Phil. i. 23, where his action is constrained by two conflicting motives. The thought here is certainly of control (though V. P. Furnish, *Theology and Ethics in Paul* (1968), p. 167, takes it to mean 'sustain'); the word hardly justifies the translation, 'keeps us from' (excess of ecstasy, or self-praise).

Love for Christ may play its part, but it is Christ's love that sets in motion such behaviour as Paul's. Behind the behaviour lies a perception of the meaning of the death of Jesus. **We have made up our minds on this, that one**—Christ—**died on behalf of all.** This is the historical fact of the crucifixion, interpreted as in the primitive, certainly pre-Pauline, belief expressed in 1 Cor. xv. 3: Christ died for our sins according to the Scriptures. There is no reference here to the Scriptures, and instead of 'for our sins' we have *on behalf of all*; compare Gal. ii. 20; 1 Tim. ii. 6; Mark x. 45. That Christ's death was for the benefit of mankind as a whole (whether this was expressed by 'all' or 'many') was common ground; the meaning of *on behalf of* (ὑπέρ), the way in which the death of one could benefit others, and the way in which the benefit could be appropriated—these were questions awaiting elucidation. The next few verses make a notable contribution to their interpretation.

Starting from the bare proposition that Christ *died on behalf of all* Paul continues: **That means that** (an expanded translation of ἄρα, therefore) **all died.** *On behalf of* thus means as a representative, or perhaps as a substitute (Robertson, pp. 630 ff.); but it should be noted that Paul does not say, All were as good as dead, or All were regarded as if they were dead, or All did not need to die because one died in their place. Neither representation nor substitution, therefore, says exactly what Paul means to say. Perhaps it is best to be content with the statement that, on account of the death of Christ, all men became potentially dead in the sense about to be described in the next verse. 'He died for us that we might die to ourselves' (Calvin). Compare Rom. vi. 3 ff., where the death of Christ means through baptism a death to sin. It is worth noting that in the present passage there is no reference to baptism; Kümmel observes (*Theologie*, p. 192), 'These texts in the Pauline epistles [in addition to 2 Cor. v he mentions Rom. vii. 4, 6; Gal. ii. 19 f.; iii. 13; iv. 4; v. 24 f.; vi. 14 f.], which base the

Christians' death and new life with Christ on God's historical act of redemption and do not mention baptism, show clearly that for Paul it is not the rite of baptism that effects this dying with Christ and the new creation, but that baptism can only be the visible expression of a more comprehensive event.' Compare F. Büchsel, *Theologie des Neuen Testaments* (1937), p. 107; M. Dibelius and W. G. Kümmel, *Paulus* (1951), p. 113.

Christ died for all; therefore all died. In what sense did all die? To have died is 'to have become free for a new life with new aims and new purposes' (Windisch). Paul continues by repeating the initial proposition, and then stating its purpose in a final clause.
He died on behalf of all in order that the living might live no 15
longer for themselves. *The living*, a descriptive subject, where 'men' or 'all men' might have sufficed, brings out the fact that the death all died in the death of Christ was not like his a physical death; rather it was the kind of death he had died (since he was sinless, verse 21) long before his physical death. Common human life since the time of Adam (see *Romans*, pp. 36 f., 111-19) has been lived by men for themselves, for their own benefit. This precisely was the sin of Adam, who instead of living for his Creator sought to control life by and for himself. This is the way men have lived, and it issues in death (Gen. ii. 7; Rom. vi. 23), so that the only hope for mankind is that, in relation to this old life, and in relation to themselves, men should die. Whereas Christ died, he died to sin once for all (Rom. vi. 10a). His once-for-all death to sin is the death of all men, so far as they are willing to die with him; there is no question of such a change taking place apart from the realm of actual obedience and unselfish living.

The final clause continues: men are no longer to live for themselves, **but for him who on their behalf died and was raised.** To the historical fact of the crucifixion is added the historical fact of the resurrection. Whereas Christ lives, he lives to God (Rom. vi. 10b), and corresponding to this is the new life lived in indebtedness and obedience to Christ by those who have died in his death and risen in his resurrection. Because Christ, being the person he was, died and was raised, there exists the universal possibility (*he died on behalf of all; all died*) of a new kind of human existence, no longer centred upon self but centred upon Christ. This is what may be called the subjective core of this paragraph; there is also an objective core, which we have not yet reached. Before we come to it, Paul works out the subjective consequences in two consecutive clauses (both introduced by ὥστε), in verses 16, 17. It is wrong to describe verse 16 as a parenthesis (as does Lietzmann; Kümmel disagrees, as does Bultmann, *Probleme*, pp. 16 f.); the two consequences (in verses 16, 17) are coordinated, and both depend on what is said in verses 14, 15.

16 **The consequence of this is that henceforth** (not from the time of writing but 'from the time at which he saw that One had died for all'—Denney) **we know no one according to the flesh.** One result of dying to self and living for Christ crucified and risen is that one has a new kind of knowledge. It may be (see below) that Paul makes this general statement in order to prepare for the (probably polemical) second half of the verse; this does not make the general statement meaningless. For the meaning of *flesh* (σάρξ) see i. 12, 17; iv. 11, with the notes. 'To have one's life "determined by the flesh" is not simply to live a corporeal existence (Christ himself did this) but to have one's gaze focused upon all that flesh means, and limited thereby to this world; "to have one's mind set" . . . upon existence apart from God' (*Romans*, p. 157). Flesh signifies 'human nature perverted—not perverted because it is material but because as a totality it has fallen away from God and is living anthropocentrically' (*1 Corinthians*, p. 149). If this is the meaning of *flesh* it is easy to see what *knowledge according to the flesh* is. It means that one's estimates are based upon purely human, and especially self-regarding, considerations. The man who knows his fellows thus will behave towards them in a corresponding way. It is possible that Paul is making here a thrust against Corinthian gnosis (see Introduction, pp. 38 f.), but there is little to suggest gnosticism in the technical sense. Such gnosis is in truth (however spiritual it may appear) knowledge according to the flesh, for gnosticism is essentially self-regarding. But a legalist, Judaizing, view would also involve *knowledge according to the flesh*, and what Paul has said is worth saying as a piece of pastoral advice in any context. Moreover the next clause suggests a different kind of polemic.

Though (on the text and translation see note 2 on p. 162) **we have** in the past **known** (ἐγνώκαμεν; the change of verb is not significant; Paul now needs a perfect, and εἰδέναι provides none) **Christ according to the flesh, yet now we know him in this way no longer.** The meaning of these words has been discussed at very great length. The vital step is to see that, even though Paul may have had them in mind from the beginning, they are given almost parenthetically, and are a special case of what is said in verse 16a. Once we estimated men in general (not Christians only, as Wendland suggests) in a way that can be described as *according to the flesh*; we now do so no longer. Similarly we once estimated Christ in this way; we now do so no longer. When the disputed words are approached thus it is clear at once that *according to the flesh* must be treated as adverbial (qualifying the verb *to know*) and not as adjectival (governing the noun *Christ*). Men in general have not ceased to have a historical existence, and 'he is not saying that we can no longer know Christ's flesh, but rather that we are not to judge Him after the flesh' (Calvin). It is fleshly knowledge that Paul repudiates; this means that the view, based on a false interpretation of this verse, that Paul had no interest in the Jesus of history, must be dismissed. It is however necessary to take seriously Bultmann's view (*Theol.*, p. 234; E.T. i. 239) that 'a Christ known κατὰ σάρκα [according to the flesh] is precisely a Χριστὸς κατὰ σάρκα [Christ according to the flesh]', and Schoeps' (*Paulus*, p. 107; E.T., p. 108; cf. *T.G.J.*, p. 427), 'Jesus according to the flesh belongs to the past'. Windisch too agrees that in 'fleshly' knowing subject and object cannot ultimately be distinguished (his note, on p. 185, is important); similarly Cerfaux, *Christ*, p. 211; E.T., p. 278. The trouble with Bultmann's remark is that it is by no means clear what 'Christ according to the flesh' means. Bultmann, and the same is true of Schoeps, seems to understand it to mean 'the Jesus of history'. In fact, if Paul had understood the expression at all (he does not use it at Rom. ix. 5), he might well have understood it to mean the military kind of Messiah whom some Jewish groups imagined in order to satisfy their own nationalist longings—that is, a Messiah anthropocentrically conceived. It is fair to add that a heavenly Son-of-man figure could be conceived in just as 'fleshly' a way. This is not the Jesus of history; it is not even (though this may come nearer) a Messiah historically conceived. What Paul rejects is man's habit (which affects Christians as well as Jews) of making a Messiah in his own image. To reject this is almost the same as rejecting a Messiah so made, but neither way of taking Paul's sentence tells us much about his concern, or lack of it, for the Jesus of history. The time referred to must be before his conversion (see the note above, on *henceforth*); whether he is thinking of his false estimate of Jesus, or of his hope for a coming Messiah, cannot be certainly determined. The former is more probable: he saw Jesus (1 Cor. ix. 1; xv. 8).

In practical terms, Büchsel (op. cit. pp. 98 f.) is right when he says that what Paul rejects is 'a knowledge of Jesus that does not lead to control (*Beherrschtsein*) by the love of Christ (verse 14), to a life for him who for us died and was raised (verse 15)'; and there is little exaggeration in Barth's comment (*C.D.* III ii. 57, cf. 450) that Paul's words could have been said in the name of the evangelists. J. L. Martyn (in *Christian History and Interpretation* (edited by W. R. Farmer, C. F. D. Moule, and R. R. Niebuhr, 1967), pp. 269-87) emphasizes the eschatological aspect of the new knowledge, and J. W. Fraser, in an article that brings the discussion up to date (*N.T.S.* xvii. 293-313), concludes, 'The basic meaning is that Paul, with others, had a new, fuller understanding of the "whole Christ" by the Spirit and by faith; and he sees others in a new way according to their standing with Him, in the new eschatological situation, in the "new creation"' (p. 312).

This however is not the end of the matter. Lietzmann compares this passage with Gal. i, ii, and concludes that we have here an allusion to the same persons who appear in that epistle. Reicke, *Diakonie*, pp. 267, 275-8, thinks of the Christ party in 1 Cor. i. 12. Lietzmann writes, 'The Judaizers, supported by disciples of Jesus, attack Paul, "because he had not known the Lord personally". Paul answers, Through Christ's death all have died, so that for me there is no longer anyone whose earthly circumstances are of any concern to me; even the circumstances of the earthly life of Christ do not concern me.' This, however, if taken strictly, Paul cannot possibly have intended to say immediately after saying that Christ died (a historical act) on behalf of all men. Not only the fact that Christ is now the Lord in heaven, but also the fact that he had lived and died on earth, was a matter of concern to Paul, though, so far as we know, he showed no interest in the details of his earthly life. What he resists, both in Galatians and here, is the notion that the mere accumulation of information about the earthly life of Jesus in itself constitutes faith. This, however, is not because there is anything beneath his theological dignity in the earthly life, but because the accumulation of historical knowledge is a human achievement and is thus a hindrance rather than a help to faith.

So much for knowledge. There is a more fundamental way of
expressing the new thing that has come into the world through the
death and resurrection of Jesus. **A further consequence** (ὥστε; 17
but it is better to link this with verses 14 f. than to try to derive verse 17 as a consequence from verse 16; Allo rightly sees that verses 16 and 17 are parallel, and regards them as positive and negative statements of the same truth) **is that if anyone is in Christ, there is a new** (cf. iii. 6) **act of creation.** For the phrase *in Christ*, which is of great importance in Paul's understanding of Christianity, see *Romans*, p. 127; the eschatological interpretation of the phrase advocated there is the only one that makes adequate sense of the present passage. Paul is thinking neither of mysticism ('ἐν Χριστῷ is not a mystical but an eschatological formula' —Bultmann, *Probleme*, p. 17) nor of ecclesiastical institutions but of a transference by faith in Christ, who experienced the messianic affliction and was raised from the dead as the firstfruits of the resurrection, from the present age into the age to come. Such a transference is properly described as a new act of creation, since the only conceivable analogy to God's act in inaugurating the new age is his creation of the world at the beginning of its story; compare Gal. vi. 15. This was an image familiar in Judaism, in that parallels were drawn between the original creation and God's final act of redemption. These parallels go back at least as far as Deutero-Isaiah: Isa. li. 9 ff.; liv. 9 f. The same book contrasts old and new, as Paul does here: Isa. xlii. 9; xliii. 18 f. For the rabbinic use of the term new creation (*b*^{e}*ri'ah ḥ*^{a}*dashah*) see W. D. Davies, pp. 119 f., and add the reference given by S.B. iii. 519 to Midrash Psalms 18 §6 (69a): R. Simon (c. A.D. 280) said: Not every one who wishes to make a Psalm may do so; rather is it certain with regard to everyone to whom a marvel happened and who made a Psalm, that his sins have been forgiven and that he has become as it were a new creature. See also Schoeps, *Paulus*, p. 224; Stauffer, *Theol.*, pp. 121 ff.; E.T. pp. 141 f.; W. Grundmann, in *P. & Q.*, p. 110. Paul's usage is not as close to the rabbinic as is sometimes suggested, since the rabbis seem to have used *b*^{e}*ri'ah ḥ*^{a}*dashah* in the sense of 'new creature', whereas for Paul the sense is rather *nova creatio*, not a new creature but (as in the translation) a *new act of creation.* Such considerations make it unlikely that Paul was simply borrowing a rabbinic expression (in any case we cannot prove its use by rabbis contemporary with Paul); it is still less likely (not-

withstanding Knox, *P.G.*, p. 144, cf. p. 94) that Paul was alluding to the recent celebration (whether Knox dates the epistle rightly is another question) of the Day of Atonement, though he would certainly have agreed that 'it was not the Day of Atonement . . . which brought the forgiveness that amounted to a new creation or the beginning of the new age' (p. 144). The attempt to relate Paul's teaching here with that of the Qumran sect is also unconvincing; see Braun ad loc. Stuhlmacher, *Gerechtigkeit*, p. 75 (cf. Schweizer, *Beiträge*, p. 190) thinks that Paul is here drawing upon a baptismal tradition; this view is possible, but there seems to be no concrete evidence for it.

Just as *all died* (verse 14) is a universal statement that becomes actually true by individual participation (see p. 169 above), so also is *new creation*; it is when a person comes to be *in Christ*, that is, on his conversion, that in respect of him the new creation, which in another sense has taken place in the death and resurrection of Jesus Christ, takes effect. This is brought out by the alternative punctuation, adopted by Bachmann and Héring, If anyone is a new creature in Christ, old things have passed . . . . One may look back to the description of the Spirit in v. 5, and see this expressed in the next words: **all** (this is not in the Greek but expresses the fact that Paul uses the article—not some old things, but old things as a body, the entire set of them) **old things have gone, behold, new things have come into being** (cf. Rev. xxi. 4 f.). It is not true that the material creation has been swept away, or that history has been annihilated (hence we can hardly draw conclusions from Paul's words here about the significance for him of the historical Jesus); what is gone is the world of relationships that is characterized by *knowledge according to the flesh* (verse 16). To know one's environment in a new way, and to be newly related to God through justification, is to live in a new world; a new set of relationships has come into being. To say this is not to deny the objectivity of what God has done in the death and resurrection of Jesus; of this Paul will speak later. At this point he is relating this objectivity to its subjective appropriation by the man who comes to be *in Christ*. Such a man is no longer concerned with such things as circumcision and uncircumcision (Gal. vi. 15); his relation to God (here we may see the connection between the thought of new creation and righteousness—see below, p. 181) now stands on a different basis. Because however he still lives in a world which to all appearance is unchanged, and himself still bears many traces of his former sinful existence, he must conduct his life on the basis of faith, not the appearance of things (v. 7). Christian existence means that by faith one lives in the midst of the old creation in terms of the new creation that God has brought about through Jesus. Compare 1 Cor. vii. 29, and the exposition of Paul's 'as if not' in *1 Corinthians*, pp. 176 f.

In the rest of the Chapter Paul returns to deal more directly with the theme of the apostolic ministry entrusted to him, the treasure deposited in the earthenware vessel, and to a new attempt to express, in fresh terminology, the objective act of God in Christ.

All these consequences: in Greek simply 'all things' (τὰ 18
πάντα), but Bengel is right with 'haec autem omnia, quae a versu 14 dicta sunt'; similarly Windisch; the reference is mainly to verses 16, 17. Héring and Barth (*C.D.* III i. 33) take 'all things' to refer to the universe, creation as a whole, and the proposition that it is the Creator who reconciles is theologically correct; it does not however seem to be what Paul is saying at this point. The new knowledge, the new creation, **come from** (ἐκ; cf. Rom. xi. 36; 1 Cor. viii. 6) **God.** Bachmann notes how, after so many statements about Christ, God now becomes the ultimate and supreme cause. Compare i. 21; ii. 14; iv. 6; v. 5. Up to this point Paul has been describing the work of God *in nobis*, that is, the new creation that takes effect in and for a man who by faith comes to be in Christ. This is however a consequence that flows from God's work *extra nos* and *pro nobis*; objectively, God **reconciled us to himself through Christ.** For reconciliation, see Rom. v. 10, and the note. It is closely related to justification, and thus leads directly to the mention of God's righteousness in verse 21. To reconcile is to end a relation of enmity, and to substitute for it one of peace and goodwill. It is not necessarily implied that the enmity existed on one side only, but it is plainly stated that in this case the initiative to reconciliation was God's, who found in the death of his Son (Rom. iii. 25 f.) a way in which his love for the sinner and his wrath against sin could be accommodated, so that he might both be righteous himself, and justify the man—the sinful man—who relies on faith in Jesus. Further explanation is given in the next verse. For examples of the rabbinic terminology (*pis*, *raṣah*) see S.B. iii. 519 f.

God *who reconciled us* (that is, potentially at least, all men—verse

14) **gave us** (that is, presumably, Paul and his colleagues, though the change from *us* Christians is abrupt and difficult) **the ministry of reconciliation.** We have already heard a good deal of ministry, or service (διακονία); see iii. 7, 8, 9 (see Benoit II 23); iv. 1; also vi. 3; other passages relate mainly to the collection. The several ministries, of Moses and the apostles, have to do with the relating of men to God, whether by the law or the Gospel; there may in this sense be some parallel with 1 QS viii. 5-10, where the Qumran community (or perhaps the group of twelve men and three priests) make atonement for the land (*lᵉkapper bᵉʿad ha-ʾareṣ*). Paul understood it to be his task to preach the word of the cross (1 Cor. i. 18); this is the message of God's love for sinners (cf. Rom. v. 8), and thus inevitably includes the offer of reconciliation (Rom. v. 9 f.). Reconciliation, if located within God's court and expressed in forensic terms, becomes justification—another pointer to the reference to God's righteousness in verse 21. 'Ministerium dispensat sermonem' (Bengel, referring also to verse 19); the proclamation of reconciliation is the service the church owes to the world (Büchsel, *Theologie*, p. 149).

19 The sense of the next verse is on the whole clear, but it contains a number of grammatical difficulties. The opening words (ὡς ὅτι), which connect it with verse 18, are disputed. Paul uses the same combination at xi. 21 and 2 Thess. ii. 2; in these two clauses the difficulty is not so great, for in them the words introduce a proposition which is not, or is not wholly, true: We have been weak; The day of the Lord is already here. Paul cannot completely affirm either of these statements, and indicates the fact by saying not simply *that* (ὅτι), but *as if it were that* (ὡς ὅτι). This construction is akin to that used in verse 20 (ὡς with following participle), and according to B.D. §396, verse 19 (ὡς ὅτι) should be taken in the same way. The difficulty is that the statement made in verse 19a is not one on which Paul would wish to cast doubt. It is better either to follow the Vulgate (quoniam quidem) and give the words a causal sense; to note (with e.g. M. i. 212; iii. 137) that in late Koine the combination is used where in ancient times one word alone (ὅτι) sufficed; or to adopt the view of Bachmann that the first word (ὡς) retains some comparative force (. . . gave us the ministry of reconciliation, *as* could and did happen, *because* . . .). In the translation I have (though without complete confidence) adopted the first of these courses, partly on the ground that it fits

with the suggestion that Paul is here making use of an existing form of words. It also accords with the view of Kasting, pp. 140 f., that verse 19 is a central verse—the ground of verse 18, whereas verse 20 is the consequence of verse 19. Similarly Barth; detailed exegesis of verses 19 ff. will be found in *C.D.* IV i. 73-8. For the view that verses 19(18)-21 is a quotation from a hymn see E. Käsemann in *Zeit und Geschichte* (ed. E. Dinkler, 1964), pp. 47-59, and the criticism of this in Stuhlmacher, *Gerechtigkeit*, pp. 77 f.

Grammatical difficulties are not at an end, for the words thus introduced may be rendered, as in the present translation, **it was God who in Christ was reconciling the world to himself**; or, God was in Christ, reconciling the world to himself; or, God in Christ was reconciling (taking ἦν καταλλάσσων as a periphrastic imperfect) the world to himself. None of these renderings is impossible; M. iii. 88 chooses the third. The first may be preferred as continuing the thought of verse 18: The new creation comes from God himself, since, according to the message of reconciliation, it was God who . . . . The only new thought (as we move from verse 18 to 19) is that *us* is expanded into *the world*; this says no more than verse 14, *he died on behalf of all.* The absence of the article (κόσμον καταλλάσσων) has the effect of emphasizing the nature rather than the particularity of the object of the verb—it was a whole world he reconciled—including perhaps the rebellious heavenly powers of Col. i. 19 f. (A. Richardson, *An Introduction to the Theology of the New Testament* (1958), p. 213).

Reconciliation is now explained in the same way that justification, or the imputation of righteousness, is explained in Rom. iv. In reconciling the world to himself God was **not counting** (λογιζόμενος; for the verb cf. Rom. iv. 3-8, with the notes) **their transgressions** (παραπτώματα; sin that has become visible in concrete acts—see *Romans*, p. 113) **against them** (the plural pronoun takes up *the world*). The non-reckoning of sin (that is, forgiveness) is equivalent to the reckoning, or imputing, of righteousness; see verse 21. Since transgressions no longer counted against men (cf. Exod. xxix. 10) the way was open for reconciliation; nothing remained but for men to take it. This however they could not do unless they were informed of the possibility now open to them. This brings Paul back (in verses 19b, 20) to the theme of his ministry.

Having made reconciliation possible, God **put in us,** committed to us (cf. Gal. ii. 7), put in our mouths, **the message** (word, λόγος; cf. 1 Cor. i. 18, the word, or message, of the cross) **of reconciliation.** This restates verse 18c, and is expanded in verse 20. *Put*, treated as a finite verb in English, represents a participle in Greek (θέμενος); it may be coordinated with *was* (ἦν) at the beginning of this verse, though it is not easy to see how this can have, as it should, the sense of a pluperfect (M. iii. 89). Some, for example Windisch, who compares 1 Cor. xii. 28, and Conzelmann, *Theologie*, p. 232, take this verse to refer to the establishing in the church of the office of preaching; so in a sense it does, but Paul is thinking not in general terms but specifically of his own ministry.

Since we have been entrusted with this message of reconciliation,
20 **We therefore act as ambassadors** (cf. Phm. 9; Eph. vi. 20; the word seems very suitable as a description of Paul's work; he may have usually avoided it because it suggested a position of privilege and immunity which he did not enjoy; for his disuse of 'herald' see 1 Tim. ii. 7; 2 Tim. i. 11, with my notes) **on Christ's behalf** (ὑπέρ, in his interest, almost in his stead; this is important for the understanding of the word in verses 14, 15), **as if** (ὡς followed by the participle; see the note on ὡς ὅτι in verse 19; another possible translation is 'seeing that it is God who exhorts . . .') **God were exhorting** (on this verb see p. 60) **you** (there is no pronoun in the Greek; Windisch thinks of an address to the still unconverted world, but see the *you* later in the verse, and vi. 1; 'receiving' must be constantly renewed—Bultmann, as quoted below, and *Probleme*, pp. 18 f.) **through us**, as his agents (Kasting, p. 74, refers to the Jewish *shaliah* institution)**; on Christ's behalf we beg you, Be reconciled to God,** that is, accept the reconciliation (which cannot be complete unless accepted on both sides) he offers.

This verse adds little to the theology of the paragraph, but it sums up the picture of Paul's apostleship. On the one hand, Paul has no importance, and indeed no message, of his own. He does not act on his own behalf, but Christ's. His place is that of Christ's slave, and for this reason he is the slave of his hearers (iv. 5); he is no lord over their faith, but works to increase their joy (i. 24). On the other hand, where Paul is at work, Christ, whom he represents, is at work; where Paul speaks, God speaks. The same act that effected reconciliation, committed to Paul the word and ministry of reconciliation. 'With the cross, God instituted the office of reconciliation, the word of reconciliation (2 Cor. v. 18 f.); in other words, the preaching itself also belongs to the event of salvation. It is neither a narrative account of a past event, that once happened, nor is it instruction on philosophical (*weltanschauliche*) questions; but in it Christ is encountered, God's own word to man is encountered: "So we act for Christ, while God at the same time preaches through our mouth, Be reconciled to God!" (2 Cor. v. 20)' (Bultmann, *Exegetica*, p. 228). The whole of this profound and eloquent passage should be read.

Paul has not yet explained to his own satisfaction how Christ
crucified constitutes a message of reconciliation. His final contribution to the explanation is set out in a carefully balanced pair of
parallel lines, which also exhibit chiasmus (J. Jeremias, *Abba*
(1966), p. 278). This observation does not prove that the passage
is to be regarded as verse, or that Paul is quoting existing material
(though this is possible; see above, p. 163). Certainly there are
no grounds for taking the last two words to be a sacramental
formula, as Jüngel, *Jesus und Paulus* (1964), p. 45, does; *in Christ*
is much too common a Pauline formula for that. Compare
Schweizer, *C.O.N.T.* n. 361, 'the "in Christ" ... defines the
validity for the Church today of what took place on the cross'.
The verse may first be set out as prose. **Him who knew not** 21
(that is, had no personal participation in; cf. Rom. vii. 7; also
Yoma 22b, As a one-year-old child, that has not tasted sin) **sin**
(for the sinlessness of the Messiah cf. Ps. Sol. xvii. 40 f.; Test.
Judah xxiv. 1; Test. Levi xviii. 9) **he made sin on our behalf,**
that we might become God's righteousness in him. This may
now be set out as follows, if the order of the Greek is reproduced
in a way intolerable in English idiom:

a	b	c	d
Him who knew not sin	on our behalf	sin	he made

that

a	d	c	b
We	might become	God's righteousness	in him.

It will be seen that though the parallelism is close, the chiasmus is imperfect.

'Quis auderet sic loqui, nisi Paulus praeiret?' (Bengel). For the sinlessness of Christ compare Rom. viii. 3 (which in other respects also recalls the present verse); John viii. 46. That it early became an article of belief is shown by the embarrassment evinced by the evangelists with regard to the baptism of Jesus. It is only as sinless that Christ can, in Paul's view, bear the sins of others. That the merits of the (at least relatively) righteous could be used for the benefit of the sinful was a belief current in Judaism; see Bousset-Gressmann, pp. 198 f., 387. Paul develops the thought in terms of an exchange: Christ was made *sin*, that we might become *God's righteousness*. It is important to observe that the words Paul uses are words describing relationships (cf. Calvin: 'Here righteousness means not a quality or habit but something imputed to us, since we are said to have received the righteousness of Christ. What then is meant by sin? It is the guilt on account of which we are accused before the judgement of God'; see also the discussions of these words in *Romans* and *1 Corinthians* passim). Paul does not say, for by definition it would not have been true, that Christ became a sinner, transgressing God's law; neither does he say, for it would have contradicted all experience (not least in Corinth) that every believer becomes immediately and automatically morally righteous, good as God is good. He says rather that Christ became *sin*; that is, he came to stand in that relation with God which normally is the result of sin, estranged from God and the object of his wrath. Bachmann has shown conclusively that *sin* (ἁμαρτία) does not here mean 'sin-offering', and there is no clear reference to Isa. liii. 6 (*pace* O. Cullmann, *Christologie des Neuen Testaments* (1957), p. 75; E.T., p. 76); Windisch's reference to Rom. viii. 3 is more useful. We correspondingly, and through God's loving act in Christ, have come to stand in that relation with God which is described by the term *righteousness*, that is, we are acquitted in his court, justified, reconciled. We are no longer his judicial enemies, but his friends. Compare the similar pronouncement in Gal. iii. 13 f.: Christ redeemed us from the curse of the law when he became a curse [Paul, notwithstanding his quotation, does not say, accursed] on our behalf, for it is written, Cursed is every one who hangs on a tree; in order that the blessing of Abraham might come to the Gentiles in Jesus Christ.

This interpretation turns upon the forensic meaning of the word *righteousness* (δικαιοσύνη; see Bultmann, *Theol.*, p. 273; E.T., i. 276 f., and the treatment in *Romans* referred to above). As Bauer (*Wörterbuch*, s.v.) says, in this verse *righteousness* (δικαιοσύνη) is equivalent to *justified* (δικαιωθέντες). A new interpretation of *righteousness* however has been proposed by

Käsemann (II pp. 181-93; see also Stuhlmacher, *Gerechtigkeit*, pp. 74-8, 208, 222). For Käsemann, God's righteousness is essentially a manifestation of his power. 'The believers are the world that has been brought back under God's dominion, the flock under the eschatological justice (*Recht*) of God, the flock in which therefore, in accordance with 2 Cor. v. 21, God's righteousness is manifested on earth' (p. 193). For criticism of this view see Bultmann, *Exegetica*, pp. 470-5, especially 472 f. According to Stuhlmacher, 'By the righteousness of God Paul understands the faithfulness of the Creator to his creature. 2 Cor. v. 21 showed that Christ was the embodiment of this faithfulness of the Creator. Ontologically this faithfulness was always to be seen as spiritual power (*pneumatische Dynamis*)' (p. 208). Here it must suffice to say that these views of God's righteousness, at least when viewed in relation to the present verse, seem neither so positively related to the Old Testament background on which Paul works, nor so true to Paul's argument, as that set forth here. The *new creation* of verse 17 and the *righteousness* of verse 21 are not synonymous; the latter is the ground of the former. The new relation to God (righteousness) is the basis of the new creation and its manifestation in renewed moral life; it is not itself the renewed moral life. Allo is right in saying that whereas Christ was incapable of actual sin, 'man really is capable, when God puts it into effect, of true righteousness', but the emphasis must lie on 'when God puts it into effect' (Dieu l'opérant), and in the present passage Paul's thought has not yet reached this stage. He is still thinking of the primary process by which sinful man is related to God.

On this verse see especially the article by Dr M. D. Hooker (*J.T.S.* xxii. 349–61), which emphasizes the representative (rather than vicarious) nature of the work of Christ in both his incarnation and his death, and the overflow of blessing from the man (not only the apostle) in Christ to others.

11. vi. 1-13. AN APPEAL FOR A RESPONSE TO GOD AND HIS AMBASSADOR

(1) Working thus with God we also exhort you not to receive the grace of God in vain. (2) For he says: In an acceptable time I listened to you, and on a day of salvation I brought you help. Behold, now is the welcome time, now is the day of salvation! (3) In thus exhorting you we endeavour to give no offence of any kind, that the ministry[1] may not be censured; (4) on the contrary, in every way we commend ourselves as God's servants should, in much endurance, in afflictions, in anguish, in distresses, (5) beaten, imprisoned, mobbed, labouring, sleepless, hungry, (6) in purity, in knowledge, in patience, in kindness, in a holy spirit, in undissembled love, (7) in the word of truth, in the power of God; with the armour of righteousness to right and left; (8) through glory and disgrace, through good report and ill; as deceivers yet true men, (9) as unrecognized yet recognized, as dying, yet see—we are alive, as undergoing punishment[2] yet not put to death, (10) as sorrowing but always rejoicing, as poor yet making many rich, as having nothing yet possessing all things.

(11) Corinthians, I have let my tongue run away with me, my heart is wide open to you. (12) If there is any lack of space it is not on my side, but in your own feelings; (13) as a recompense of like kind—I am speaking as to my children—do you be wide open to me.

The opening verses of this paragraph are closely connected with the preceding one. We have seen that, in Paul's view, his preaching was itself part of the eschatological event he proclaimed (cf. Bultmann, *E. & F.*, p. 164; *Exeg.*, p. 467). This adds urgency to

[1] The Western Text (D G lat sy sa) has *our* ministry—a not unnatural emphasis. But Christian service (ministry, διακονία) is a wider thing than Paul's, and he is concerned lest faults of his should bring censure upon this wider activity.

[2] The Western Text (D* G it Ambrosiaster) has for *undergoing punishment* (παιδευόμενοι) the more commonplace 'undergoing trial' (πειραζόμενοι).

his appeal; it also makes clear the way in which the first word in
the new paragraph must be taken. **Working thus with God** 1
(God is not mentioned in the Greek, but *working with*, συνεργοῦντες, requires a complement in English, and after v. 19 ff. this, though some take it to be 'you', or hearers in general, can only be God; so e.g. Calvin; cf. 1 Cor. iii. 9) **we also exhort you** (that is, we are in this addressing Christians as well as others) **not to receive the grace of God in vain** (cf. 1 Cor. xv. 10). Nothing the Corinthians can now do, or fail to do, can alter the fact that Christ died for all, and that potentially all men died in his death (v. 14); it is no forgone conclusion that all will cease to live to themselves and live henceforth for Christ (v. 15). If they fail to do this, as far as they are concerned God's free favour will have been bestowed upon them in vain. Since Paul is writing to Christians we must suppose that they have made some sort of response to God's grace; the more pity if in pursuit of their own concerns they now fail to conform to it, or adhere to another Gospel (xi. 4; Denney). See the note on v. 20.

The appeal is backed up with a quotation from the Old Testament (Isa. xlix. 8, cited in verbal agreement with the LXX, which differs a little from the Hebrew), the point of which is that the appeal of Paul's preaching may properly now be made, since the time of fulfilment, which means the time of salvation, has now
come. I make my appeal, **for he** (that is, God; no subject is 2
expressed, and it would be possible to translate, 'Scripture says', hardly to follow Goudge, who thinks the subject is the Servant, identified by Paul with Jesus; but Isaiah says 'thus saith the Lord', and represents God himself as addressing his people) **says: In an acceptable time** (a time looked forward to and greeted with pleasure; or rather, giving a better parallel, a time when God in his mercy accepts men) **I listened to** (the verb, ἐπακούειν, is a technical term for hearing prayer: Betz, *Lukian*, p. 61) **you, and on a day of salvation I brought you help.** Paul claims that the prophecy is fulfilled: **Behold, now is the welcome** (a strengthened form, εὐπρόσδεκτος, of *acceptable*, δεκτός) **time, now is the day of salvation!** Compare Rom. x. 6 ff.; there is no need to force God's hand, to bring his Son from remote and inaccessible places; since the coming of Christ God is waiting to accept men, to reconcile them to himself (v. 20), and all that is needed is for men to accept his offer, that is, to accept his grace (verse 1).

Conzelmann (*Die Mitte der Zeit* (1954), p. 27; E.T., p. 36) contrasts this quotation with the use of Isa. lxi. 2 (to proclaim the acceptable—δεκτός—year of the Lord) in Luke iv. 19; for Luke, but not for Paul, the acceptable time is that of the ministry of Jesus. This is probably a misunderstanding of Luke's thought (see I. H. Marshall, *Luke: Historian and Theologian* (1970), pp. 120 f.). Compare also Cullmann (*Heil als Geschichte* (1965), p. 226; E.T., pp. 254 f.), who argues that the 'present moment of decision' which Paul emphasizes here is not inconsistent with a *heilsgeschichtlich* view of the New Testament message. 'We can say precisely this, that Paul's *heilgeschichtlich* faith provides at every moment the foundation for the existential decision, for which undoubtedly room remains'. This is certainly true in the sense that it is the word of reconciliation through the cross that calls for decision, and that the decision relates to the new eschatological age that originates with the resurrection and opens the way to eschatological existence.

Windisch suggests that vi. 3 should be preceded by vi. 14–vii. 1 (a passage which in any case constitutes a problem; see below, pp. 193 ff.). But the thought of vi. 3 connects with chapter v (Kümmel), verse 2 is (grammatically at least) a parenthesis, and the participle of verse 3, the first of an extraordinary series extending to verse 10, is coordinated with the finite verb (*we exhort*) of verse 1. On these participles see M. iii. 343. I supply four words at the beginning of verse 3 in order to make the necessary con-
3 nection, which the Greek implies. **In thus exhorting you we endeavour to give** (assuming a conative sense for the present tense; cf. 1 Cor. x. 32 f., with the note) **no** cause of **offence of any kind** (taking ἐν παντί, as we must, to be neuter; the Vulgate, with *nemini*, makes it masculine—giving no offence to anyone), **that the ministry may not be censured.** Paul does not say, That we may not be censured. His ministry (cf. v. 18), not his person, is what matters. He was not successful in the attempt to avoid giving offence. His message was itself offensive (1 Cor. i. 23), but this is not what he has in mind. Corinth (and not Corinth alone) was too ready to think in terms of personalities rather than in terms of the Gospel, and Paul, paradoxically, offended the Corinthians by not being offensive enough (xi. 20 f.).

After all that he has said (iii. 1; v. 12; cf. x. 12) about self-commendation it is superficially surprising that Paul continues,

In every way we commend ourselves as God's servants 4
(διάκονοι, nominative; not therefore 'we show ourselves to be God's servants', but 'we, as God's servants, commend...'; Robertson, p. 454) **should.** How does a servant of God commend himself? The answer is in the epistle as a whole. Not by self-praise, violence, ambition, ruthlessness; not by letters of authority from any human source; but by the purity of his motives and behaviour, the sufferings he endures for the sake of others, and the wealth he is able to bring them through the Gospel. Thus the self-commendation Paul indulges in here is not inconsistent with what he has already written. For Paul as God's servant (διάκονος) see iii. 6; xi. 23; 1 Cor. iii. 5; Col. i. 23, 25; and compare Epictetus III xxiv. 65: Diogenes loved men—how? As it was proper that the servant (διάκονος) of Zeus should, at the same time caring for men and acting in subjection (ὑποτεταγμένος) to God. For parallels between the Christian notion of apostleship and that of the Stoic sage and missionary see W. Schmithals, *Das kirchliche Apostelamt* (1961), pp. 100-3.

There follows an account of what Paul's apostolic life had meant to him; compare iv. 8 ff.; xi. 23-9; 1 Cor. iv. 9-13. '2 Cor. vi. 4-10 is an impassioned and almost lyrical passage, where precision in the interpretation of the prepositions is probably impossible because the "catalogue" has lured the writer into repeating a preposition in some instances where in sober prose it might have been unnatural' (Moule, *Idiom*, p. 196). This description (undoubtedly correct as far as the prepositions go) must be partially qualified by the observation that here too Paul appears to be following Stoic models; see especially Dio Chrysostom viii. 15 ff. Paul's life as an apostle has been passed **in much endurance** (cf. Rom. ii. 7; v. 3, with the notes; also 1 Clement v; in the present epistle cf. i. 6), **in afflictions** (the word is characteristic of this epistle: i. 4, 8; ii. 4; iv. 17; vii. 4; viii. 2, 13, but is not uncommon in the other letters), **in anguish** (the word, ἀνάγκαις, is plural; Paul uses it, e.g. at Rom. xiii. 5, in its common meaning, 'necessity'; the context here and in xii. 10 requires the not uncommon sense of suffering; quite possible is 'tortures'—see the good parallel in Diodorus Siculus iv. 43. 5, τοὺς μὲν ἐν ταῖς ἀνάγκαις ὄντας, those who were suffering these tortures), **in distresses** (cf. xii. 10; Rom. viii. 35; see also iv. 8, with which there is a formal contradiction—but Paul is applying no rigid definition to the word:

he knows what it is to fare ill, but has never been crushed out of existence). The English construction in the translation now changes, though Paul continues to use the same Greek preposition
5 (ἐν). **Beaten** (cf. xi. 23), **imprisoned** (cf. xi. 23), **mobbed** (literally, in (violent) disorders; the word is used in a different sense at 1 Cor. xiv. 33; on xii. 20 see the note), **labouring** (literally, in labours; cf. xi. 23, 27; it was Paul's custom to work for his living, and especially in Corinth, where he had made a special point of imposing no financial burden on the church—xi. 7, 9, 10; 1 Cor. ix. 12, 15), **sleepless, hungry** (literally, in watchings, in fastings; cf. xi. 27; lack of sleep and food was due apparently to physical necessity, not to voluntarily undertaken spiritual discipline).

Up to this point we have an account of the external circumstances of Paul's life. The next verse appears to describe (with the possible exception of one term) the moral characteristics of Paul's be-
6 haviour. He has acted **in purity** (perhaps, in innocence; see the use of the cognate adjective, ἁγνός, at vii. 11; but cf. xi. 3 for a possible use of the noun; also for the adjective xi. 2; Phil. iv. 8), **in knowledge** (ἐν γνώσει). The usage and meaning of this word are complicated and diverse; see the notes on 1 Cor. i. 5; vi. 12 f.; viii. 1; x. 23. It has already been used at 2 Cor. ii. 14; iv. 6 in a sense equivalent or at least related to the Gospel Paul preaches. It is conceivable but unlikely that it should have this meaning, or one more closely related to gnosticism (as a distinct kind of religious thought), here. The closest parallel is 1 Peter iii. 7, where Christian husbands are urged to live with their wives 'according to knowledge' (κατὰ γνῶσιν), and by knowledge 'is meant Christian insight and tact, a conscience sensitive to God's will' (J. N. D. Kelly, ad loc.). In his treatment of the church at Corinth Paul claims to have shown (and it would be hard to dispute the claim) understanding of this kind. For a different view see Windisch: it is *in knowledge* that 'the inspired charismatic (*Pneumatiker*) speaks to the church'. Compare xi. 6, where Paul claims not to be surpassed *in knowledge* (τῇ γνώσει). But the next two words are against Windisch's view; Paul manifests his understanding by acting **in patience, in kindness.** The next phrase is ambiguous: **in a holy spirit** (ἐν πνεύματι ἁγίῳ). Identically the same expression occurs at Rom. ix. 1; xiv. 17; xv. 16; 1 Cor. xii. 3; 1 Thess. i. 5. In each of these passages it must be understood as a reference to

the Spirit of God. In seven other passages Paul speaks of a holy spirit: Rom. i. 4 (but here the Greek is different—see the note); v. 5; xv. 13, (19); 1 Cor. vi. 19; 2 Cor. xiii. 13; 1 Thess. i. 6; iv. 8. In these too the Holy Spirit is the Spirit of God; they are however only a very small number out of all the Pauline references to the Spirit, which is more often described in other terms (e.g. of God, of Christ). Paul also uses the word (πνεῦμα) to describe an element in human make-up, or behaviour; see Rom. i. 9; viii. 16; xi. 8; 1 Cor. ii. 11; iv. 21; v. 4, 5; vii. 34; xiv. 14, 32; xvi. 18; 2 Cor. ii. 13; vii. 1, 13; xii. 18; Gal. vi. 1, 18; Phil. iv. 23; 1 Thess. v. 23; Phm. 25. Of these, two in the present epistle (vii. 1; xii. 18) are particularly important because they are related to moral characteristics (defilement; the upright spirit shared by Titus and Paul in their work at Corinth), and most important of all is 1 Cor. vii. 34, where it is said that 'the unmarried woman . . . is anxious about the things of the Lord, in order that she may be holy (ἁγία) both in body and in spirit'. Now it is certainly unlikely that Paul should simply throw in a reference to the Third Person of the Trinity in the midst of a series of human ethical qualities ('knowledge, patience, kindness, the Holy Spirit, love, . . .'); and the evidence adduced from his usage elsewhere seems to give adequate support to the view that in this verse *spirit* (πνεῦμα) means the human spirit, and that *holy* is a description of its ethical quality.

There is one more term in the description of Paul's behaviour as an apostle: **in undissembled** (ἀνυποκρίτῳ) **love.** The same words are used at Rom. xii. 9. He then turns to his work as a
preacher: **in** (that is, he has been occupied in proclaiming) **the** 7
word of truth. Compare iv. 2, with the note; also Gal. ii. 5, 14; Col. i. 5 (the truth of, consisting in, the Gospel; 'the truth' stands alone in this sense at 2 Thess. ii. 12). *The word of truth* is a more general, and therefore in this setting a more suitable, term than, for example, the word of reconciliation (v. 19); and *truth* is not without a polemical glance at his opponents. That what he preaches is true appears from the manifestation of divine power that accompanies the preaching—**in the power of God.** For such manifestations of power (δύναμις) see Rom. i. 16 (the Gospel itself, as preached, is the power of God); xv. 19; 1 Cor. i. 18; ii. 4 f.; 2 Cor. iv. 7; 1 Thess. i. 5. It was not Paul's eloquence but the powerful operation of the Spirit of God that convicted his hearers. It was in this sense that he was equipped **with the armour**

of righteousness to right and left. The metaphor is common; see x. 4; also Rom. vi. 13; xiii. 12, with the notes. It is not clear in what sense Paul uses the word *righteousness* here. It may look back to his reference to the Gospel (*the word of truth*); the Gospel is a manifestation of the righteousness of God (Rom. i. 16 f.), so that when Paul acts as a preacher of the Gospel he is like a soldier whose weapons are righteousness. Or, perhaps in the Corinthian situation rather more probably, the word may look forward to the description of the sort of reputation Paul acquires. He is 'armed so strong in honesty' that the opinions of men pass him by as 'the idle wind'. Gnilka (*P. & Q.*, p. 57) refers to the practical righteousness of Qumran, for example, 1 QS i. 4 f.; Testament of Dan vi. 10; but though there may be a measure of similarity it does not demonstrate direct relationship. With this clause the preposition changes. After using 'in' (ἐν) eighteen times, Paul changes to 'through' (διά, here translated *with*), which he uses three times. Lietzmann notes, 'On the left is the shield, on the right the sword'; this is substantially correct, though for sword, spear or javelin might stand. Probably Paul means to convey only the completeness of the equipment provided by God. Allo thinks one may add the thought that both prosperity and adversity can be used by the apostles; but this is doubtful.

The description of Paul's life and work as an apostle now moves into a different phase. Verses 4, 5 described external circumstances, verse 6 the moral and spiritual characteristics of Paul's behaviour, verse 7 the work he does as a preacher of the Gospel. Now a sequence of double terms depicts first the twofold response that his ministry encounters, and then, by a natural transition, its paradoxical character. The terms cannot all be interpreted in the same way; to some extent Paul is carried away by his rhetoric, and his words are not to be treated as a matter-of-fact account of his work.

8 The opening words, however, are easy. Paul moves **through**, experiences, **glory and disgrace.** Sometimes he was accepted with every mark of honour, for example, Gal. iv. 14. He also knew what it was to be rejected, for example, 1 Thess. ii. 2; see also 2 Cor. xi. 23-33. The next phrase restates substantially the same fact: **through good report and ill.** Compare 1 Cor. iv. 13: it is clear that Paul was evil spoken of within as well as outside the churches. See also Rom. iii. 8. The next phrase, **as deceivers yet** (adversative καί) **true men,** may again be repetition in different

language: some people regard us as deceivers, others think that we are speaking truth. It is perhaps more probable that Paul is moving towards the phrases that occur in the next two verses, in which each of the two descriptions that stand together in pairs may in a paradoxical sense be said to be true. Not of course that Paul would for a moment allow that he was a deceiver; he was a bearer of the truth; but he recognizes an impression he had given in a charge that had been brought against him—in the crudest form at xii. 16 ff., possibly at 1 Cor. xv. 15 (cf. also the passages where Paul passionately affirms that he is not lying, Rom. ix. 1; 2 Cor. xi. 31; Gal. i. 20—had some people said he was?). See also Schoeps, *T.G.J.*, pp. 128, 431; if in the Pseudo-Clementines the figure of Simon Magus stands for Paul he had certainly then become the Deceiver. In the nature of things Paul could only rebut this charge; he could not prove it false.

The next phrase is literally translated 'as unknown yet well
known'; the sense is, **as unrecognized** and **yet recognized.** 9
Even Paul's adversaries could scarcely say that he was one 'of whom nothing was known' (Lietzmann); the point rather is that he was not recognized as an apostle—see 1 Cor. ix. 1; xv. 8 f., with the notes. It is clear that, especially in chapters x–xiii, Paul was dealing with a situation in which a rival apostolate refused to recognize his apostleship, and that his rivals seemed likely to convince the church in Corinth of their view. Yet he was *recognized.* By whom? By God, from whom alone his apostleship came (Gal. i. 1), but also in fact by the so-called Pillars in Jerusalem (Gal. ii. 7, 9; cf. Schoeps, *Paulus*, p. 46; E.T., p. 68); and surely (Paul could still hope) by the Corinthians themselves (v. 11). Here however the paradox runs deeper. Externally, as Paul could not fail to see, there was little to commend him. He had been a persecutor; he had not seen the risen Christ at the same time as the other apostles (1 Cor. xv. 5-8); his version of the Gospel was at least widely criticized. Against this he could point only to his own awareness of God's call at the time when he revealed his Son (Gal. i. 12, 16), to the intrinsic truth of his message, and to the fruit of his ministry.

Paul is now fully launched upon his paradoxical rhetoric; yet it is meaningful rhetoric. **As dying, yet see—we are alive.** As an apostle, he was like a man under sentence of death (i. 9; 1 Cor. iv. 9); he carried with him the killing of Jesus, death was at work in

him (iv. 10, 12). These were at the same time theological and historical truths. The 'old man' was continually assailed in the last throes of eschatological travail, and the death Paul had died by faith was worked out on the plane of history. Yet if he died it was that the life of Jesus might be manifested in him (iv. 10 f.). Again, the thought is both theological and practical. Paul lives now in and for the age to come; and repeatedly (see xi. 23-33) he escapes from dangers and sufferings that must ordinarily have proved fatal. **As undergoing punishment yet not put to death** emphasizes the practical side of the preceding clause; God disciplines his servant
10 for his servant's good. Compare 1 Cor. v. 5; xi. 32. **As sorrowing**
but always rejoicing: sorrow (λύπη, λυπεῖσθαι) has already been mentioned in the epistle—ii. 1, 3, 7; see also vii. 10; ix. 7; Rom. ix. 2; Phil. ii. 27. The Corinthians themselves were responsible for a good deal of Paul's suffering, but other personal events grieved him, as well as the thought of the unbelief of Israel. But in spite of this joy is an inalienable feature of Paul's life as a Christian: see ii. 3; vii. 4, 7, 9, 13; xiii. 9; Rom. xii. 12, 15; xiv. 17; xv. 13, 32; xvi. 19; 1 Cor. xvi. 17; Gal. v. 22; Phil. i. 4, 18; etc. xiii. 9 is specially to be noted here: sorrow and weakness can be a cause of joy if they help to manifest the Gospel and build up the church. The same may be said of **as poor yet making many rich;** Paul will gladly choose poverty if it will enrich his people. So for example in Corinth he renounces his apostolic rights and takes no pay for preaching the Gospel because he judges that this will be for the good of the church (xi. 7-10; xii. 13; 1 Cor. ix. 12, 15, 18). For the wealth of the Corinthians see ix. 11; 1 Cor. i. 5; and for the theological fact behind Paul's own practice see viii. 9, with the note.

Finally, Paul describes himself **as having** (ἔχοντες) **nothing yet possessing** (κατέχοντες) **all things.** The latter verb is used at 1 Cor. vii. 30, but there the context gives it a different turn. Those who buy in this age do not really possess what they pay for; the coming of the future age will put an end to all such things. This is, at least in part, what Paul means here by *having nothing*; but the man who in this age has nothing, and knows he has nothing, possesses an inheritance in the age to come; compare Luke vi. 20; Matt. v. 3. See also 1 Cor. iii. 22 ('All things are yours'), and the note. 'It is in Christ, and in the community that is in Christ, that humanity recovers its lost lordship, and because Christ is the Lord over the world, over life and death (through his crucifixion and resurrection), and over both this age and the age to come, that his people are no longer the servants of destiny and corruption, but free lords over all things' (*1 Corinthians*, pp. 95 f.). But Paul continues (in 1 Cor. iii. 23), 'You belong to Christ'. This is the equivalent in the present passage of *having nothing*. It is precisely in the recognition that he is not his own but Christ's, that he is not an independent free man but his Master's slave, that whatever he has he has only by faith and not at all in his own right, that the Christian may be described as *possessing all things*.

This is an exalted passage, not without parallels in Hellenistic and Jewish-Hellenistic rhetoric of the period. Lietzmann cites Epictetus, II xix. 24; Show me someone who is sick and happy, in danger (cf. xi. 26) and happy, dying (ἀποθνήσκοντα) and happy, exiled and happy, disgraced (ἀδοξοῦντα) and happy. Show me; by the gods, I want to see a Stoic. The content as well as the form of this is important; the parallel and difference between the Stoic missionary and Paul were noted above, p. 185. Lietzmann's quotation from Philo (*Quod Det. Pot.* 34) is less valuable, for it represents lovers of virtue as humble and suffering, while the fortunate are 'those who look after themselves'.

Paul is aware that he has digressed far from the point he was
making at the beginning of the paragraph. The very fact however
that he had the freedom to do so is significant. **Corinthians** (cf. 11
Gal. iii. 1; Phil. iv. 15; the only places where Paul uses such a vocative; it is always a sign of strong feeling), **I have let my tongue run away with me**; literally, Our mouth is open (perfect intransitive, ἀνέῳγεν; has opened, stands open) to you; that is, I have spoken to you in complete freedom (cf. vii. 4). The usage is Greek—see Aeschylus, *Prometheus Vinctus* 609 ff., I will speak . . . not twisting up riddles, but in straightforward speech, as it is right to open (οἴγειν) one's mouth to friends; compare Ezek. xvi. 63; xxix. 21; also Eph. vi. 19. Paul's freedom of speech reflects an inward attitude: **my heart is wide open to you.** There are no secrets in it; there is room for you in it, and I long to have you there; compare iii. 2; vii. 3; Phil. i. 7 (I have you in my heart—Beare). There is room for you in my heart, that is, in my affection. The language of Ps. cxix (cxviii). 32 is similar, the
sense different. **If there is any lack of space it is not on my** 12
side, but in your own feelings. It is impossible to find a render-

ing of this sentence that is both idiomatic and near the Greek. You are not squeezed for space: the verb is that translated at iv. 8 'crushed'; the idea is that of being forced into too narrow a space. Here the point of the metaphor is different. Paul is not shutting the Corinthians out, or confining them to a narrow, inadequate corner of his affection. No, if there is any shortage of space it is on their side, literally, in their bowels, but the word is used, as often in Biblical Greek (cf. vii. 15), as we use 'heart'—'the self as moved by love' (Bultmann, *Theol.*, p. 218; E.T., i. 221 f.). Paul means that any narrowness lies not in his approach to them but in their response to him.

13 Hence his appeal to them: **As a recompense of like kind** (in the accusative, which is a kind of appositional accusative to that implied in the main clause—Show as a recompense the same openness; see Robertson, p. 486; Moule, *Idiom*, pp. 34 ff., 160 f.; B.D. §154; M. iii. 245)—**I am speaking as to my children** (*my* is not expressed in Greek, and Paul may mean simply that he is speaking as he would to children; but cf. 1 Cor. iv. 14 f.; and especially Gal. iv. 19)—**do you be wide open** (cf. verse 11) **to me.** Paul appeals for a response; there is no apostolic authority by which he can compel it.

The appeal is continued, in similar but not identical language, at vii. 2. On the question whether the intervening paragraph (vi. 14–vii. 1) is to be regarded as an interpolation, whether from another epistle or from a non-Pauline source, see pp. 193 ff., also Introduction, pp. 11 f., 14, 21-5. The present verse itself provides no ground for a decision.

12. vi. 14–vii. 4. RESPONSE TO GOD IS EXCLUSIVE

(14) You must not get into double harness with unbelievers. For what partnership have righteousness and iniquity? or what association has light with darkness? (15) What harmony is there between Christ and Beliar,[1] or what common lot

[1] *Beliar* is the original text; Belian (presumably an accusative), Beliab, and Belial (the reading of the Vulgate, conformed to the Hebrew *b*ᵉ*liyya'al*—see below, p. 198) also occur.

has a believer with an unbeliever? (16) What agreement can God's temple have with idols? For we are[1] the temple of the living God; as God said, I will dwell in the midst of them, and walk among them, and I will be their God, and they shall be my people. (17) So come out of the midst of them, and be separate, says the Lord, and touch nothing unclean. Then I will receive you, (18) and I will be a father to you, and you shall be sons and daughters to me, says the Lord, the Almighty. (1) Since then, my dear friends, we have these promises, let us cleanse ourselves from every defilement of flesh and spirit, perfecting our holiness in the fear[2] of God. (2) Take us into your hearts! We wronged no one, we ruined no one, we defrauded no one. (3) I do not say this by way of condemnation; for I have told you before that you are in our hearts, bound up with us in death and in life. (4) I can use great freedom of speech towards you, I can boast freely about you. I am full of comfort, I am overflowing with joy in all our affliction.

The view has long been current that vi. 14–vii. 1 is an intrusion in the text of 2 Corinthians. It has been supported by a twofold argument. (a) There is no connection between vi. 13 and vi. 14, and between vii. 1 and vii. 2. In vi. 13 Paul begs his readers to make room for him in their hearts; in vi. 14 he tells them sharply to have nothing to do with unbelievers. In vii. 1, after quoting Scripture, he urges them to take thought for holiness of life in the fear of God; in vii. 2 he returns to self-defence, and a renewed personal appeal. (b) Not only is vi. 14–vii. 1 without direct connection with what precedes and what follows; if it is removed, vi. 13 and vii. 2 are found to connect admirably. (11) My heart is wide open to you . . . (13) As a recompense of like kind—I am speaking as to my children—do you be wide open to me . . . (2) Take us into your hearts! These observations are valid, and the argument must seem a cogent one, unless it proves possible to trace Paul's thought through without more deviation than can always be expected in a writer of his sort. The transitions (from vi. 13 to 14 and from vii. 1 to 2) will be examined with care; see also Introduction,

[1] 𝔓⁴⁶ C G and the majority of MSS have 'you are'; this is due to assimilation to 1 Cor. iii. 16; cf. vi. 19.

[2] 𝔓⁴⁶ alone has 'in the love of God'—an interesting but mistaken reading; cf. Jude 21.

pp. 11 f., 14, 21-5. Those who deem vi. 14–vii. 1 to be an intrusion have in the past most often supposed it to have been drawn from another Pauline epistle, probably from the so-called 'Previous Letter'; see 1 Cor. v. 9, with the notes, and *1 Corinthians*, pp. 12-17. More recently however it has also been suggested that the material is not Pauline, in particular that it is related to the Qumran literature; on this see the literature cited in note 2 on p. 14; also Schweizer, *Beiträge*, p. 98; and *T.W.N.T.* vii. 125; also the long note by Braun, ad loc. The hypothesis can only be tested by verse-by-verse examination of the thought of the paragraph and of the language in which the thought is expressed.

In order to assess the connection between this paragraph and the preceding one it is necessary to go back over the whole of vi. 1-13; Paul not infrequently allows himself to wander from his point, and then brings himself back to it with something of a jerk. At vi. 1, having spoken of the content of the Gospel of divine reconciliation that he preaches, he begs the Corinthians not to receive God's grace in vain. This leads him to an account of his own apostolic ministry, with its paradox of glory and dishonour, and so to an appeal that the Corinthians will recognize his love for them, and respond with a similar attitude to him. This (he says) is my message, this is the kind of messenger I have been. Will you not accept both me and him whose messenger I am? The Corinthians would not have said no; but at the same time they were having dealings with other apostles (who would have excluded Paul), and a different Gospel in which a different Jesus was proclaimed (xi. 4). This was an intolerable position; and it seems not unreasonable that Paul should have turned aside to indicate the fact. 'I am showing my love to you, and I ask your love in return; but do not suppose that I can afford to be soft about this. If you turn to God and to me his messenger, it means a break with the world.' 'He who has become righteousness (v. 21) can have nothing more to do with unrighteousness' (Wendland). Calvin puts the same point in a more personal way: 'He has exhorted them to show themselves amenable to him as to a father, and now with the right of a father he reproves the fault into which they have fallen'. The transition from vi. 13 to 14 is more abrupt than most, even in Paul's writing; but it seems by no means impossible. Collange's suggestion (p. 283), based on the observation that vi. 3-13 and vi. 14–vii. 4 are parallel, that the middle part of the epistle was current in two forms, ii. 14–vi. 13 and ii. 14–vi. 2; vi. 14–vii. 4, is not convincing.

To make his point Paul uses a metaphor that was probably
strange to his Gentile readers in Corinth. **You must not get into** 14
(B.D. §354) **double harness** (a double yoke; see the note on verse 15) **with unbelievers** (ἄπιστοι, non-Christians; see 1 Cor. xiv. 22 f., and the notes). The metaphor looks back to the Old Testament prohibition of 'mixtures' (Lev. xix. 19, where a related word for double harness is used; Deut. xxii. 9 ff., especially xxii. 10: Thou shalt not plough with an ox and an ass together), developed in the Mishnah tractate Kilạim. Just as 'one kind of cattle with another, one kind of wild animal with another, wild animals with cattle, one kind of unclean beast with another, one kind of clean beast with another, an unclean beast with a clean, a clean beast with an unclean—it is forbidden to plough with them, draw with them, or drive them' (Kilaim viii. 2), so Corinthian Christians must not unite themselves with unbelievers. Is this consistent with what Paul says about unbelievers elsewhere? Is it perhaps rather a Qumran attitude? The relevant material in 1 Corinthians is as follows: v. 9 f. (I wrote to you in my letter that you should not mix with people guilty of fornication—not in the absolute sense that you should avoid contact with the fornicators of this world, or the rapacious and thieves, or idolaters, since then you would have to come out of the world); vi. 1-6 (Does any of you dare, when he has a suit against his fellow, to go to law before the unrighteous, and not before the saints? . . . Has it come to this, that there cannot be found among you one wise man, who can decide between his brothers, but brother goes to law with brother, and that before unbelievers?); vii. 12-16 (If a Christian brother has an unbelieving wife (and vice versa), and she is content to live with him, let him not divorce her . . . the unbelieving wife has been sanctified through the Christian brother . . .), 39 (. . . if her husband falls asleep she is free to marry anyone she chooses—remembering only that she is a Christian); viii. 10 f. (If someone sees you, who have knowledge, sitting at table in an idol-shrine . . .); ix. 21 f. (To those who were outside the law I became as if I were outside the law . . . in order that I might win those who are outside the law . . . I have become all things to all men); x. 21 (You cannot drink the cup of the Lord, and the cup of demons; you cannot partake of the table of the Lord, and of the table of demons),

27 (If any unbeliever invites you, and you wish to go, eat everything set in front of you, and make no inquiries based on conscientious scruples), 32 (Be men who lay no stumbling-block before Jews, or Greeks, or the church of God); xiv. 23 ff. (If then the whole church assembles together, and all its members are speaking with tongues, and unbelieving outsiders come in . . .). It is not easy to summarize this material. Paul did not ask his converts to come out of the world; he did not even ask them to abstain from non-Christian dinner parties, though he was aware that these could constitute a problem. He did not expect marriages to be broken up on the ground that only one of the partners had become a Christian; Christian and non-Christian (unless the latter took the initiative) should continue to live together. A widow, remarrying, should, however, exercise a Christian choice. Paul could, in the interests of the Gospel, live like a Gentile, and it was possible for unbelievers to find their way into the Christian assembly. On the other hand, Paul warned his readers against the practice of taking part in meals in idol-shrines, and expected them to settle their own disputes without making use of non-Christian courts; and one must remember the moral break made by conversion (1 Cor. vi. 9 ff.), and the separate existence of the church as the community of God's elect (1 Cor. i. 1-9). The position was anything but simple. The Christian was in the world, but must remember that the outward shape of this world is passing away (1 Cor. vii. 29 ff.). He could not but live in the midst of unbelievers, and must live in contact with them since in this way he might hope to save them (see 1 Cor. vii. 16 for a special case); but he himself was a member of the holy people, who would judge the world (1 Cor. vi. 2 f.).

Does *You must not get into double harness with unbelievers* express this, or a different view? At first sight it appears to forbid any kind of relation with unbelievers, and it is not surprising that it has been regarded as part of the letter misunderstood by the Corinthians (1 Cor. v. 9) to mean that, in effect, they must withdraw from the world. Nor is it surprising that it should be held to reflect (though, as Gnilka insists, with Christian revision) the Qumran requirement of separation not only from the world but from the unbelieving and disobedient in Israel. In fact, what the paragraph requires is that those addressed should avoid idolatry and moral defilement. This is no more than Paul requires in 1 Corinthians; it may suffice to quote 1 Cor. vi. 18 (Flee from fornication) and x. 14 (Flee from idolatry). It remains possible that it was an interpolated fragment, and that the Corinthians had misunderstood it—some people will misunderstand anything; but it does not express an unpauline view. Schlatter aptly entitles the paragraph vi. 11–vii. 1, 'The church's obligation to make up its mind' (Die Verpflichtung der Gemeinde zur Entschiedenheit).

Philo (*Spec. Leg.* iv. 203-18) has a detailed moralizing allegory of the Kilaim law; Paul applies it in a sequence of rhetorical questions. **For what partnership have righteousness and iniquity? Or what association has light with darkness?** *Partnership* (μετοχή) and *association* (κοινωνία) are, as near as may be, synonyms. Both have a legal usage (joint ownership), but both can be used in general contexts, for example, Euripides, *Iphigeneia in Tauris* 254 (τίς θαλάσσης βουκόλοις κοινωνία; What have herdsmen to do with the sea?). *Iniquity* (ἀνομία) is sufficiently a Pauline word (Rom. iv. 7; vi. 19; 2 Thess. ii. 3, 7), and the ethical use of *righteousness* (δικαιοσύνη), though not the most characteristically Pauline usage, is not unpauline; see especially (in view of the reference to iniquity) Rom. vi. 19: Just as in the past you offered your members to uncleanness and iniquity as their slaves (with the result of producing iniquity), so now offer your members to righteousness as its slaves (the result of this will be sanctification). It is true that this ethical use of *righteousness* appears in the Qumran literature too, but this means no more than that both Paul and the Qumran writers were influenced by the Old Testament. Thus we cannot from this verse conclude (with Schlatter) that not legalism but iniquity (ἀνομία) was the peril Paul had to face in Corinth, and that there were therefore no Judaizers there.

Light and *darkness* also are Qumran metaphors; it suffices to refer to the so-called War Scroll (the war of the sons of light against the sons of darkness). But Paul too uses the metaphor (e.g. Rom. xiii. 12; 2 Cor. iv. 6; xi. 14; 1 Thess. v. 5), and there is no reason to suspect here a different kind of dualism from that of Rom. xiii. To describe the church and the world pictorially as *light* and *darkness* can hardly be said to go much further than to speak of 'those who are on the way to salvation and those who are on the way to destruction' (ii. 15). More rhetorical questions follow.

What harmony (συμφώνησις is not a musical term, and could be 15 translated simply 'agreement' if this word were not needed in the next verse) **is there between Christ and Beliar, or what common lot** (or 'share'—μέρις) **has a believer with an unbeliever?** There is nothing surprising in the contrast between Christ and the devil, or an Anti-Christ figure; the name *Beliar* (on the variant forms see note 1 on p. 192) however is significant. It occurs nowhere else in the New Testament, and (in the form Belial) in the LXX only at Judges xx. 13 (A) (cf. Judges xix. 22, Theodotion), where it is used in translation of the Hebrew *b^ene b^eliyya'al*, 'sons of worthlessness', that is, evil men, a not uncommon Hebrew phrase, usually translated rather than transliterated. *Beliar* (with the variant forms) developed as a personal name in post-biblical Judaism; for the evidence as far as it was known (in 1933) see the article by W. Förster in *T.W.N.T.* i. 606. It is certainly true that the Dead Sea Scrolls have produced a large number of further occurrences of the word *Beliar* as the name of the prince of evil; see the full discussion by G. R. Driver, in *The Judaean Scrolls* (1965), pp. 486-91. 'Belial or Beliar were [*sic*] eventually identified with Satan, and the two names could be used interchangeably in a late apocalypse [Ascension of Isaiah]; hence Beliar came to be nothing but a synonym of Satan in the New Testament' (op. cit., p. 488). This however proves nothing more than that Beliar(-l) was a vogue word in the first century; it certainly does not prove any relation between 2 Corinthians and Qumran. 'The first two of these myths, those of Belial or Beliar and of the anti-Messiah or anti-Christ seem to have been merged in one another by *c.* A.D. 30–60 and both to have been independently fused with the third, the Neronic myth, at some time during the last quarter of the first century A.D. The development of ideas in these myths appears to have proceeded *pari passu* in the inter-testamental literature and the New Testament and in the Scrolls' (op. cit., pp. 490 f.). In the light of Paul's metaphor in verse 14 it is worth noting that the word *b^eliyya'al* was sometimes (see Sifre Deut. 117 (on xv. 7 ff.) (98b); Sanhedrin 111b) interpreted as *b^eli 'ol*, 'having no yoke', that is, as one who has thrown off (God's) yoke.

The answer to Paul's rhetorical question is self-evident: there is no harmony between Christ and Satan. Since believers are believers in Christ, the next proposition follows: *believer* and *unbeliever* have nothing in common. *Unbeliever* (ἄπιστος) is frequently used by Paul for one who is not a Christian (e.g. ii. 14); but *believer* (πιστός) is not used by him in an absolute way to denote one who believes. The adjective is used of God (meaning 'faithful', 1 Cor. i. 9; x. 13; 2 Cor. i. 18; 1 Thess. v. 24; 2 Thess. iii. 3), and of men, predicatively, or qualifying a noun (1 Cor. iv. 2, 17; vii. 25; Gal. iii. 9; Col. i. 2, 7; iv. 7, 9), but not alone, in the sense of 'believer'. The usage does occur in deuteropauline literature, for example 1 Tim. iv. 10, 12; v. 16; and this fact has been taken to point to the deuteropauline origin of vi. 14–vii. 1 (see Gnilka, op. cit., pp. 57 f.). There is some substance in the argument, but it is, in itself, anything but conclusive; the semi-technical use of *believer* was bound to develop sooner or later out of the description of Christians as faithful, and there is no reason why Paul should not himself have been responsible for the development. The Christian faith is exclusive, and the question is intended rather to make the point that one cannot be a believer and an unbeliever at the same time than that Christians and non-Christians may have no contact with each other.

Paul's last question takes up a special metaphor for the Christian
society. **What agreement can God's temple have with idols?** 16
For we are the temple of the living God. For the church as God's temple (ναός) see 1 Cor. iii. 16; vi. 19, with the notes, especially the latter passage, since there Paul thinks of a corporate rather than an individual indwelling, though 'God can only dwell in the midst by dwelling in each one' (Calvin). To men who considered themselves to be the legitimate heirs of the Old Testament this was a natural development, and there is no need to see in it the influence of Qumran imagery and theology, though it is true that the image of the temple was current at Qumran (see Gnilka, op. cit., pp. 61 f.). Paul borrowed it (so far as it was not a fresh Christian usage) from the Old Testament, from the familiar institution of Jewish religion, and also to some extent from Greek religious symbolism (for this see *1 Corinthians*, pp. 90, 151). And it is impossible to mistake Paul's horror of idolatry; see 1 Cor. v. 10, 11; vi. 9; viii passim; x. 7, 14, 19; xii. 2; Gal. v. 20; Col. iii. 5; 1 Thess. i. 9. 'Fornication and idolatry are both impossible for a Christian because of his exclusive relationship with Christ' (*1 Corinthians*, p. 238; see 1 Cor. vi. 18; x. 14).

Paul has now used a sequence of rhetorical questions to drive home his point, *You must not get into double harness with un-*

believers. He underlines it by means of a series of Old Testament quotations; these are not given exactly, and it is not always easy to know what Old Testament passage Paul has in mind.

As God said: this is not Paul's usual citation formula. He more often says, 'As it is written', or the like (see iv. 13, and the note). Gnilka (op. cit., p. 58) notes that 'God said' is used in the Damascus Document (CD vi. 13; viii. 9; xix. 22). In the other Pauline writings however we may note Rom. ix. 15, 25; 2 Cor. vi. 2; (Gal. iii. 16); 2 Cor. iv. 6. The formula is not frequent, but occurs often enough to leave no doubt that Paul *could* have used it here, especially as it introduces the direct speech of God himself.

I will dwell (*ἐνοικήσω*; this verb does not appear to be used of God in the LXX) **in the midst of them, and walk among them, and I will be their God, and they shall be my people.** These words recall a number of Old Testament passages, such as Lev. xxvi. 12 (I will walk among you, and I will be your God, and you shall be my people); Ezek. xxxvii. 27 (My dwelling—*κατασκήνωσις*—shall be among them, and I will be God for them, and they shall be my people); compare Exod. xxv. 8; xxix. 43 ff.; 2 Sam. vii. 14, 27; Isa. lii. 4, 11; Ezek. xx. 34. Philo too quotes Lev. xxvi. 12, and brings out the implication that God's people must be pure (*De Somniis* i. 148; ii. 248; see Knox, *P.G.*, p. 164). It is God's promise, made, and renewed for the time to come, that he will be immediately present with his people. The Old Testament represents his presence sometimes as effected by the institution of the temple, sometimes as given independently of any instrumental mediation; he is present in his word and his act. By identifying the Christian society with the temple Paul virtually excludes any dependence of God's presence upon any kind of institution, and is in agreement with the tradition of the sayings of Jesus (Matt. xviii. 20).

The presence of God requires the purity of his people; 'from the promise there follows for Paul the necessity of sanctification'
17 (Wendland). **So come out of the midst of them, and be separate, says the Lord, and touch nothing unclean.** This is closest to Isa. lii. 11: Depart, depart, go out from there and touch nothing unclean, go out of the midst of her, be separate, you who bear the Lord's vessels. Compare Jer. li. 45; several Old Testament texts seem to have been combined (J. Bonsirven, *Exégèse rabbinique et Exégèse paulinienne* (1938), p. 316). In Isaiah the people are

ordered to go away from Babylon, leaving the city to its fate, separating themselves from the uncleanness of pagan life. They must be clean in virtue of their cultic responsibilities. There is some evidence for messianic interpretation of this prophecy (see E. E. Ellis, *Paul's Use of the Old Testament* (1957), p. 57, referring to Exod. Rabbah xv. 18), but it seems probable that it has been taken freshly (from memory) from the Old Testament, and given a new, non-cultic interpretation. Contact with God in the new Christian way involves a new kind of purity, which is to be described at vii. 1; touch (ἅπτεσθαι) has now lost its cultic connotation (Betz, *Lukian*, p. 32). If the people of God cease to be separate in moral holiness from the rest of mankind they cease to be the people of God; but on what this separateness means, see above, pp. 195 ff.

After these imperatives follows an 'and' (καί) and a future tense; the construction is not, as has been supposed, a Semitism, but has Greek parallels (Beyer, p. 253). **Then** (translating the Greek καί)
I will receive (εἰσδέξομαι) **you, and I will be a father to you,** 18
and you shall be sons and daughters to me, says the Lord, the Almighty (or All-Sovereign, παντοκράτωρ—elsewhere in the New Testament only in Revelation, nine times). Compare Ezek. xx. 34: I will bring you out of the peoples, and receive (εἰσδέξομαι) you out of the countries, in which you were scattered; 2 Sam. vii. 14: I shall be a father to him, and he shall be a son to me (quoted, but not in the Pauline reformulation, at 4 Qflor. i. 11); vii. 27: Lord almighty (παντοκράτωρ), king of Israel . . . . Paul puts singular into plural, and adds a reference to *daughters*, possibly (e.g. Schlatter; Bonsirven, op. cit., p. 333) recalling Isa. xliii. 6 (Bring my sons from a far land, and my daughters from the ends of the earth). Dodd, *A.S.*, pp. 45 f., 105 sees references here to Jer. xxxi. 9, 31 ff. To Paul it was an essential feature of Christian existence that by faith and in Christ men became sons of God (Gal. iii. 26; cf. iv. 6; Rom. viii. 15 f.), and the statement in the same context in Galatians (iii. 28) that in Christ there could be neither male nor female could be otherwise expressed by speaking of daughters as well as of sons of God. It is significant that Paul, whose attitude to women has often been misrepresented, should modify his Old Testament quotation so as to include God's daughters as well as his sons. The promise of 2 Sam. vii. 14 was originally addressed to the king; the king is Jesus, and in him men and women participate in his status before God.

It has now been demonstrated from Scripture that the Christians, as the people of God, are, like a temple, the place of God's habitation, the sons and daughters of God among whom he dwells. This fact must have its consequence in holiness of life. Compare *1 Corinthians*, p. 90, and the quotation from Epictetus (II viii. 14): If an image of God were present you would not dare to do any of the things you do. But when God himself is present within, and sees and hears all things, are you not ashamed to be
1 pondering and doing these things . . . ? **Since then, my dear friends, we have these promises** (*these* is in an emphatic position: these promises that God himself will be in our midst), **let us** (Hughes rightly notes the remarkable fact that Paul classes himself with the Corinthians) **cleanse ourselves from** (Paul is still using cultic language—on *καθαρίζειν ἀπό* see G. A. Deissmann, *Bible Studies* (1901), p. 216 and Robertson, p. 576—in a non-cultic setting) **every defilement** (Paul does not use this noun elsewhere, but uses the cognate verb at 1 Cor. viii. 7) **of flesh and spirit.** It has been argued (Gnilka, op. cit., pp. 58 f.; on the other side see Schlatter, pp. 580 f. and Windisch) that this use of *flesh and spirit* is not Pauline, but recalls Qumran. For Paul (it is said) the *flesh* is intrinsically evil, so that it is impossible to cleanse it (Braun lays much stress on this point), and the *spirit* is intrinsically good, so that it is impossible that it should be defiled—it was probably with this thought in mind that Marcion (see Tertullian, *Adv. Marcionem* v. 12) substituted blood for *spirit.* At Qumran, on the other hand, both flesh and spirit had to be cleansed (e.g. 1QM vii. 5 f.: They must all be men ready for war, and perfect in spirit and flesh, *t[e]mime ruaḥ ubasar*). But it is quite mistaken to suppose that Paul was incapable of using *flesh* and *spirit* without giving them their full theological meaning. Both are used in a loose popular way in this epistle. At vii. 5 Paul says 'Our flesh found no relief', meaning exactly what he had said at ii. 13, 'I got no relief for my spirit'. In each case, he means, 'I got no relief', both *flesh* and *spirit* standing for the self. In the present verse, since they can hardly be identical, they will refer to the inner and outer aspects of the self. Compare 1 Cor. vii. 34, '. . . that she may be holy both in body and in spirit', outwardly and inwardly; that this is a quotation from a Corinthian opinion does not abate its relevance. Compare 1 Thess. v. 23.

A people among whom God dwells must be holy as he is holy

(cf. Lev. xix. 2; 1 Peter i. 16), cleansing themselves from every kind of defilement, **perfecting our holiness in the fear of God.** Again Paul uses cultic language; the temple is a holy place. *To perfect* (ἐπιτελεῖν) has various meanings, but these include 'to discharge religious duties' (L.S., s.v. II). For Paul, however, religious duties are not cultic but ethical (cf. above, pp. 27, 100). *The fear of God* is, as in the Old Testament (cf. v. 11, and the note), practical, not speculative, piety.

If *holiness* is not cultic but practical, how is it to be expressed? This question is the key to the problem of the transition from vii. 1 to vii. 2. It is only a matter of seconds (as Paul talks the epistle through) since he was begging his readers not to receive God's grace in vain (vi. 1), and to express their appropriation of grace in their attitude to the messenger of God's grace, Paul himself. This was the true response to grace, and Paul, after developing the theme of Christian obligation, comes back with renewed vigour
to the appeal of vi. 11 ff. **Take us into your hearts!** This 2
rendering (of χωρήσατε ἡμᾶς) was not made up to fit the connection between vi. 11 ff. and vii. 2; see L.S. (s.v. χωρεῖν; Allo and Héring take this to mean 'understand' (cf. Matt. xix. 11 f.), but this is only part of the sense). You are in our heart—now make a reciprocal gesture; that is, love us as we love you. Paul adds that on his side at least there is no impediment; he has done nothing to diminish the Corinthians' confidence in him. **We wronged no one** (the word, ἀδικεῖν, is that of vii. 12; 1 Cor. vi. 7 f.; Gal. iv. 12; Philemon 18), **we ruined no one** (financially; so Bauer, but φθείρειν can be used of many sorts of damage and destruction), **we defrauded no one** (the word, πλεονεκτεῖν, is used at ii. 11 of Satan's activities, but the parallel with xii. 17 f. is decisive here). Paul refers to his visits to Corinth. It is a reasonable inference that he had been accused of doing such things as he here repudiates and that the charge had poisoned relations between him and the church. If it is right to think that chapters x–xiii were written a little later than chapters i–ix (see Introduction, pp. 9 ff.), what began as a whispering campaign later developed into open attack. The charges are not true (cf. 1 Cor. iv. 4); but Paul is not going to retort them upon his accusers (though he may have been
tempted to do so). **I do not say this by way of condemnation.** 3
Compare 1 Cor. iv. 14, and contrast 1 Cor. vi. 5; xv. 34. I am clearing myself, not accusing you. **For I have told you before**

(προείρηκα, evidently not in the same sense as at xiii. 2; it will refer to vi. ii; possibly to i. 6; iii. 2; iv. 12) **that you are in our hearts, bound up with us in death and in life** (literally, to die together and to live together). Paul is not making the theological point of Rom. xiv. 7, but simply expressing his affection for the Corinthians. As a pastor he gives himself to his people, grateful or ungrateful, without reserve. For the language, compare Horace, *Carmina* III ix. 24: Tecum vivere amem, tecum obeam libens.

It is in this relationship, not because he has been credibly informed that the Corinthians are models of Christian virtue, that
4 Paul writes the next verse. **I can use great freedom of speech** (παρρησία; cf. iii. 12, and see the literature cited on that verse) **towards you** (cf. vi. 11), **I can boast freely about you**. That is, when Paul speaks to the Corinthians he can say all that is in his heart, because there is in his heart nothing but good will towards them. When he speaks about the Corinthians to others he can and does speak freely of their merits; for examples, see vii. 14; ix. 2—unfortunately in the latter case there was some reason to fear that the Corinthians might let him down. This however is a possibility Paul does not contemplate here. **I am full of comfort** (cf. i. 4-7), **I am overflowing with** (for the dative see B.D. §195. 2) **joy in all our affliction.** Some see here a sign that we have before us part of Paul's last letter to Corinth, written after the troubles reflected in chapters x-xiii had been assuaged (see Introduction, pp. 12 ff.). This view cannot be held by those who see in ii. 14-vii. 4 a further part of the 'severe letter' (in addition to x-xiii), and indeed is not suggested by the wording itself. Paul's confidence and joy, the comfort that he experiences, are experienced not after but *in all our affliction*. The troubles are not over; they have not reached their peak. He is still (as he will be throughout his life) 'carrying about in the body the killing of Jesus' (iv. 10), and the life of Jesus, which is manifested in consolation and joy, is life in and through death. This does not mean, however, that it is not evoked by specific causes on particular occasions. An example follows.

D. PAUL'S PLANS FOR CORINTH, AND THEIR WORKING OUT IN THE FUTURE vii.5–ix.15

13. vii. 5-16. NARRATIVE RESUMED (cf. 4); PENITENCE OPENS THE DOOR TO THE FUTURE

(5) For even when we came into Macedonia our flesh found no relief, but we suffered every kind of affliction—fights without, fears within. (6) But he who comforts the downcast, God himself, comforted us by the arrival of Titus, (7) and not only by his arrival, but by the comfort he had enjoyed among you. He reported to us your longing for us, your lamentation, your zeal on our behalf, so that I rejoiced the more. (8) For though I hurt you by my letter, I do not regret it; though I did regret my letter, I now see that the hurt it caused was only temporary (9) and led to repentance, and seeing this I now rejoice, not that you were hurt, but that the hurt led to repentance; for you were hurt in the way of God's will, in order that you might suffer no kind of damage because of us. (10) For a hurt in the way of God's will effects repentance, which leads to salvation—and that is not a thing to be regretted. A worldly hurt, on the other hand, effects death. (11) For look! this being hurt in the way of God's will, what earnestness it has produced in you—and a defence, and indignation, and fearful respect, and longing, and zeal, and a desire for vengeance. In every respect you showed that you were innocent in the matter. (12) So, though I wrote to you, it was not on account of him who committed the wrong, nor on account of him who was wronged, but in order that your earnestness on our behalf might be manifested to yourselves before God. (13) For this reason we have been comforted. And in our comfort we rejoiced the more especially at the joy of Titus, for his spirit has been refreshed by you all. (14) For in any boasts I had made to

him about you, I was not disgraced, but as all the things we said to you were said in truth, so also our boasting before Titus proved to be the truth. (15) And his affections turn especially to you, as he remembers the obedience of you all, how you received him with fear and trembling. (16) I am glad that I have every confidence in you.

Between vii. 4 and vii. 5 there is an abrupt transition, akin to that between ii. 13 and ii. 14; moreover, vii. 5 takes up the story of Paul's anxious wait for Titus where this was left off at ii. 13. These facts have led to the view that ii. 14–vii. 4 (or, omitting vi. 14–vii. 1, ii. 14–vi. 13; vii. 2-4) is an interpolated fragment of the 'severe letter', which deals with Paul's apostolic office; see the notes on ii. 13, and Introduction, pp. 11 f., 14. The validity of this hypothesis turns upon the question whether an adequate explanation can be given for the dropping and resumption of the story about Titus. That the transitions are abrupt is beyond dispute; that Paul was not the smoothest of writers, but capable of rapid movement and of digression, is equally beyond dispute. In fact, if the explanation offered for the transition from ii. 13 to ii. 14 can be accepted, that for vii. 4 to vii. 5 should offer little difficulty. Paul has been writing (in a way which it is difficult to harmonize with the view that vii. 2-4 belongs to the 'severe letter') of his consolation and joy, and of the confidence he feels in the Corinthians. He proceeds to give, in vii. 5, an outstanding example at once of the power and willingness of God to comfort him in his afflictions, and of the good reports that fill him with confidence (misplaced confidence, perhaps) in the Corinthians. The opening words of the new paragraph (*καὶ γάρ*) are consistent with this view, and indeed almost demand it, though it is of course possible to attribute them to an editor who wished to make the transition more tolerable. There is also a little too much repetition and variation (to which attention will be called in the notes) to make it plausible that vii. 5 should be a direct continuation of ii. 13.

5 **For even when we came** (at ii. 13 Paul was using the first person singular; here too he is referring to himself, not to a plurality, but, as often in this epistle, he uses the plural; it is not likely that in a continuous narrative Paul would have changed his mode of expression in this way) **into Macedonia.** It was pointed out on p. 95 that, starting from Troas, Paul might have

travelled into Macedonia by sea or by land, and that, unless he had concerted a plan with Titus, he must have run the risk of missing him. The trouble that beset Paul in Troas accompanied him to Macedonia. **Our flesh found** (ἔσχηκεν; on the use of the perfect see the note on i. 9; here however 𝔓[46] B G K have the aorist ἔσχεν, perhaps rightly) **no relief.** Compare ii. 13, I got no relief for my spirit. Neither *flesh* nor *spirit* is used in its profound Pauline theological sense. Compare vii. 1, with the note. Here *my flesh* is simply 'I'; see Bultmann, *E. & F.*, p. 156. In view of *fears within* it cannot be said that Paul chooses the word *flesh* because he is thinking of external troubles. There was *no relief*; on the contrary, **we suffered** (Paul uses the participle, not the finite verb; after *our flesh found no relief* the masculine plural participle is strictly speaking in anacolouthon, but there is an easy *ad sensum* connection not only with *our* but also with *we came*; cf. v. 12, and see B.D. §468; M. iii. 343; Robertson, pp. 439, 1135) **every kind of** (rendering ἐν παντί) **affliction.** Compare i. 4. The *affliction* is further, but still not very precisely, specified. **Fights without,** presumably against adversaries, whether Christian or non-Christian—Paul had many; **fears within,** for the safety of Titus, who might have been carrying a large sum of money (see p. 95 above), and was seriously overdue, and for the success of the work in Corinth. For the use of the plural compare Xenophon, *Hiero* vi. 5. Windisch, citing other passages, shows that it is classical.

There was no need to describe the affliction more precisely, for it
was now ended. **He who comforts** (ὁ παρακαλῶν, precisely as at 6
i. 4) **the downcast** (τοὺς ταπεινούς; Paul often—xi. 7; xii. 21; Rom. xii. 16; Phil. iii. 21—reflects the Greek use of this word and its cognates not for the Christian virtue of humility but for 'humiliatedness'; cf. Isa. xlix. 13), **God himself** (included as an appositional subject, almost as an afterthought, to make the point quite clear), **comforted us by** (or 'at', but Paul's thought includes instrumentality) **the arrival of Titus.** This was what Paul longed for; he now had his colleague with him, and nearly first-hand contact with the Corinthian church. This double point is brought
out in the next verse. Paul was comforted **not only by his arrival,** 7
which gave back to Paul one colleague, safe and sound, **but by the comfort he had enjoyed among you.** Titus had no doubt shared Paul's anxiety about the church at Corinth, and must, notwithstanding Paul's boasts (verse 14), have wondered what he would

find there and how he would be received. He had been comforted (perhaps to some extent because he misread the situation—see Introduction, pp. 8 f.); things were not as bad, and the Corinthians not as formidable, as he feared. This, reported to Paul, naturally comforted him too. Titus had been better treated, and the Corinthians must therefore be better Christians, than there had seemed reason to think. Exactly what Paul and Titus had feared, and how Titus had been comforted, must be inferred from the following clauses. **He reported** (not a finite verb but the participle ἀναγγέλλων; cf. v. 12; ix. 11) **to us your longing for us** (the last two words are added to the Greek, since without them the English would scarcely be tolerable; see below), **your lamentation, your zeal on our behalf, so that I rejoiced the more.** In the context, *longing* can only mean that the Corinthians longed to see Paul in person. He had refrained from visiting Corinth when he might have done so (ii. 1), and had sent Titus. They now hoped to see Paul himself. *Lamentation* is less clear, but probably includes regret not only that Paul had not come but also that he had felt it better to stay away; it does not necessarily include lamentation of past sin—see below. He had forborne to come (see i. 23) because of an unfortunate incident that took place on his second visit. Another visiting missionary had attacked him and the Corinthians had not taken, or had not appeared to take, his part. They now showed (so Titus reported) *zeal on our behalf*. This meant that Paul could forget the unhappy past, and, with the Corinthians no longer lukewarm but firmly on his side, could look forward to the future with confidence (cf. verse 16)—*so that I rejoiced the more*; perhaps, I rejoiced rather—rather than mourning for Corinthian failure; so Goudge and Windisch.

The rejoicing was the greater because Paul had not been sure that he had taken the right steps to deal with a difficult situation. He had written a letter (which perhaps Titus had delivered; see 'Titus', p. 10; then he regretted sending it; it hurt the Corinthians when they read it, but the hurt was only temporary, and did good, so that in the end Paul ceased to regret that he had written. So much is reasonably clear, but the language of verse 8b is very confused; the confusion probably reflects Paul's embarrassment.
8 The first sentence is structurally straightforward. **For though I hurt you by my letter, I do not regret it**—as will appear, because the ultimate effect was good. But what was the letter?

Some think that it was 1 Corinthians, but this is difficult to square with the few facts we have. Would 1 Corinthians have hurt the Corinthians? Possibly, but one would not have thought it would do so to such an extent as to make this hurtfulness its main feature. Paul wrote (verse 12) not on account of him who committed the wrong, nor on account of him who was wronged. This has been taken to be an allusion to 1 Cor. v. 1; but this is improbable (see below). If (as is probable) the same letter is referred to in ii. 4, Paul wrote 'out of much affliction and distress of heart, with many tears'; this does not seem a probable description of 1 Corinthians. *My letter*, then, was probably not 1 Corinthians. It is usually described as the 'severe letter'. For the view, not adopted in this Commentary, that parts of it are to be found in 2 Cor. ii. 14–vi. 13; vii. 2-4; x–xiii, see Introduction, pp. 11 f., 14. More probably, this letter has been lost. It is not surprising that the Corinthians, who were hurt by it, should lose it. Paul wrote, then, and in the end did not regret that he had done so. He continues in a sentence which can be translated literally as follows: Though I did regret it, I see that that letter, though only for a moment, hurt you, I now rejoice, not because you were hurt, but because you were hurt in a way that led to repentance. This quite impossible sentence is perhaps best regarded as a compound of a number of sentences, each of which represents part of what Paul wished to say. (a) Though I did regret sending it, I see that it was only for a moment that the letter hurt you. (b) Though I did regret sending it, I see that the letter hurt you in a way that led to repentance. (c) Though I did regret sending it, I now rejoice, because you were hurt only for a moment. (d) Though I did regret sending it, I now rejoice, not because you were hurt, but because you were hurt in a way that led to repentance. It will be seen that all these sentences have a common protasis: Though I regretted. (a) and (b) share a common apodosis, I see; (c) and (d) share a common apodosis, I now rejoice. It is now possible to understand how the sentence built up in Paul's mind. He starts from his regret at having written—a regret, as he has already said, that he no longer feels. Now that he has met Titus he sees what the effect of the letter has been—a temporary hurt, which has led to repentance. Seeing this, he now rejoices, not in the immediate but in the ultimate effect of his letter. With this in mind, and considering Paul's intention as well as his language, we may offer as repre-

senting what he *meant* to say: **Though I did regret my letter,**
9 **I now see that the hurt it caused was only temporary, and led to repentance, and seeing this I now rejoice, not that you were hurt, but that the hurt led to repentance.** It should be added that the addition of one Greek letter would mend this grammatically intolerable sentence. If instead of the first person singular indicative active *I see* (βλέπω) we were to read the present participle active *seeing* (βλέπων) the sentence, though clumsy, would be possible: Though I did regret it, seeing, as I do, that that letter, though only for a moment, hurt you, I now rejoice, not because you were hurt, but because you were hurt in a way that led to repentance. The participle is read by 𝔓[46] (the only Greek witness to do so), and is presupposed by the Vulgate ('et si paeniteret videns quod epistula illa et si ad horam vos contristavit nunc gaudeo non quia contristati estis sed quia contristati estis ad paenitentiam'), supported by the Old Latin MS *c*. It is tempting to suppose (with e.g. Westcott and Hort, and Moffatt) that this was the original text; that the *I see* (βλέπω) of B D* Ambrosiaster was an accidental corruption; and that the *for I see* (βλέπω γάρ) of the majority of MSS was an attempt to mend a muddle. But Paul did sometimes mix up his sentences, and the most difficult reading, that of B D*, is probably right. On this point see more detail in Windisch.

Fortunately, as has been pointed out, there is no serious doubt about what Paul meant (for a discussion of the thought of verses 8-11, see Barth, *C.D.* IV i. 361 f.). The hurt lasted only for a moment (πρὸς ὥραν, as at Gal. ii. 5; Philemon 15; cf. 1 Thess. ii. 17); so, it may be feared, did the repentance, but that is another story; see Introduction, pp. 9 f. How the repentance expressed itself is shown in verses 11 f. Another way of describing the salutary kind of hurt that leads to repentance is to say that it was *in the way of God's will* (κατὰ θεόν; cf. Rom. viii. 27; Gal. i. 4). So Paul proceeds: **for you were hurt in the way of God's will, in order that you might suffer no kind of damage because of** (causal ἐξ; M. iii. 260) **us.** Lietzmann thinks the dependent clause to be consecutive: with the result that you suffered .... But the reference to *God's will* makes it possible to treat it as final: it was God's purpose that you should not suffer .... Paul is still thinking of his letter; it could have injured the Corinthians if its effect had been to make them angry, bitter, or despondent. But this was not
10 so. The result was good, **for a hurt in the way of God's will**

effects repentance, which leads to salvation—and that is not a thing to be regretted. *Not to be regretted* (ἀμεταμέλητον) could be applied either to *repentance* (Lietzmann and Héring), or to *salvation* (Schlatter); probably it applies to both, or rather to the compound thought, repentance-unto-salvation. Bultmann (*Exeg.*, p. 402) points out that only here, and perhaps at xii. 21, does Paul speak of the penitence of Christians, and Kümmel observes that repentance does not play a large part in Paul's thought; here it is not a fundamental element in the way of salvation so much as a return to the way after deviation from it. Windisch discusses the question why Paul has so little to say about repentance, answering, perhaps rightly, that the notion smacked of Hellenistic intellectualism, and did not give as much weight as Paul desired to the action of God in salvation. For *salvation* see Rom. xiii. 11, and the note; Paul does not develop the theme here, but, before bringing out the practical effects of the Corinthian's repentance, notes its opposite: **A worldly hurt** (cf. verse 9b—a hurt that leads to damage)**, on the other hand, effects death,** by fostering resentment, and the like; for the wage paid by sin is death (Rom. vi. 23).

The *For* (γάρ) with which verse 11 begins looks back to the godly
hurt of verse 10a. **For look!** (ἰδού to emphasize what is being said; 11
cf. v. 17; vi. 2, 9; xii. 14) **this being hurt in the way of God's will, what earnestness it has produced in you** (they are now taking the matter seriously)**—and a defence** (against an accusation; ἀπολογίαν, a forensic term)**, and indignation** (presumably with the person who attacked Paul)**, and fearful respect** (for me)**, and longing** (to see me; cf. verse 7)**, and zeal** (cf. verse 7)**, and a desire for vengeance** (on the assailant). This rendering perhaps under-translates the rhetorical force of the verse. The word *but* (ἀλλά; for the intensifying effect of this word cf. 1 Cor. iii. 2, and see Robertson, p. 1185; B.D. §448.6), standing for *not only but also* is repeated before each noun after the first: 'What earnestness, yes, and defence, yes, and indignation, . . . ' might perhaps over-translate. There are parallels, much less extensive, in Epictetus III ix. 10; IV xi. 19 (Lietzmann). *Earnestness* (σπουδή) might have been translated *zeal* had this word not occurred (with a perhaps more personal flavour) later in the verse. It suggests that, until they read Paul's letter, the Corinthians had not grasped the seriousness of the matter. They now defended themselves (against Paul's charge that they had not shown a proper regard for him?),

and showed a *desire for vengeance* (ἐκδίκησις); this begins with a desire to clear themselves of a charge, but almost amounts to a counter-charge. The Corinthians thus had set out to prove their innocence; moreover, they had succeeded: **In every respect you showed that you were** (εἶναι; Bachmann and Allo take this as a real present: You are now, as you were not) **innocent in the matter.** *Showed* is the verb which in this epistle often means 'to commend' (iii. 1; iv. 2; v. 12; vi. 4; x. 12, 18; xii. 11); but it can also mean 'prove' (Rom. iii. 5; v. 8; Gal. ii. 18), and it is clear from the context that the Corinthians had at least convinced Titus that in respect of the trouble that had taken place they were *innocent* (ἁγνοί; cf. xi. 2, where the word is used of a *pure* virgin). See 'The Injury', pp. 153 f. This shows that the Corinthians' repentance (verses 9 f.) was not for a wrong they had themselves committed, but for their negligence in dealing with a wrong committed by another. This point is made positively in the next verse. 'The Corinthians gave clear and genuine evidence that they were in no way involved in the crime in which their connivance seemed to implicate them' (Calvin).

12 **So, though I wrote to you, it was not on account of him who committed the wrong, nor on account of him who was wronged.** Neither person is named, nor is the wrong itself defined. For a detailed discussion of this problem see 'The Injury'. It may be set out paradoxically in two double propositions.

1 (a) The offender was closely related to the Corinthian church, and is indeed usually supposed to have been a member of it (so e.g. Kümmel, *Introduction*, p. 208).
(b) The Corinthians were *innocent in the matter* (verse 11).
2 (a) Paul's 'severe letter' evoked *repentance* (verse 9).
(b) The Corinthians were *innocent in the matter* (verse 11).

'There seems to be only one solution of this problem: the man who committed the wrong was closely associated with the Corinthian church but was not himself a Corinthian. As a visitor to Corinth, claiming superior rights for himself, he had challenged the apostle's position, belittled his authority, and had thus both injured and insulted his person. He was not strictly a Corinthian, so that the Corinthians might be innocent while he was not; they were innocent, yet they had not taken Paul's part with that zeal, that earnestness, they should have shown, and of this they repented'

('The Injury', p. 155, except that I have omitted or translated Greek words used there). This conclusion fits the evidence of both chapters ii and vii about the 'severe letter'. Paul wrote (ii. 3), 'confident in respect of all of you that my joy was the joy of all of you'. He wrote with tears, but only 'that you might know the love that I have specially for you' (ii. 4). Hurt that Paul has received matters little (he says); the danger is that the church, or a substantial part of it, may be damaged (ii. 5). Chapter vii suggests that 'Paul had probably been uncertain how far the Corinthians had themselves been implicated in the action of the intruder; had he written too strongly? Would they be further estranged from him in injured innocence? No; they had taken the letter in the right way, and his confidence had been made good (verse 14). The letter had hurt them, but it had hurt them to good effect; they repented that they had ever listened to the anti-Pauline intruder. They now manifested *zeal on my behalf* (verse 7) . . . Verse 12 comes into clearer focus when it is grasped that neither *he who committed the wrong* (the intruder) nor *he who was wronged* (Paul) was in the ordinary sense a member of the Corinthian church. Inevitably they had played a large part in the letter, which might on that account have been misunderstood. Paul's real purpose was not with these wanderers, himself and another, but with the local church, of which he had made his boast to Titus' ('The Injury', p. 156, with translation of Greek quoted there).

The *wrong*, and the incident in which it was committed, cannot be more precisely described. It was once widely held that Paul was referring again to the 'fornication' mentioned in 1 Cor. v. 1. This view is now almost universally abandoned; it is hard to think that, after writing 1 Cor. v. 2-5, Paul would be content to have the incident simply washed out. Another suggestion is that the verb *to do wrong* (ἀδικεῖν) should be given full legal force: in disregard of the teaching of 1 Cor. vi. a Christian had taken legal action against a fellow-member of the church—so, for example, Windisch. But an incident of this kind would hardly suffice to explain Paul's strong language and change of plan. It is best to suppose that Paul had been attacked, either face to face, on his second visit, or in his absence, through disobedience and revolt, or in the person of one of his assistants, such as Timothy. References to the sorrow caused by his second visit (ii. 1; see the note) suggests that a face-to-face attack probably took place. Paul hoped that the problem had now been solved; chapters x–xiii show that his hopes were disappointed. See Introduction, pp. 9 f.

Paul had not written to attack *him who committed the wrong*, or to defend *him who was wronged* (probably himself, though conceivably Timothy), **but in order that your earnestness** (as in verse 11) **on our behalf** (Schlatter accepts a variant reading that reverses the pronouns—'our earnestness on your behalf') **might be manifested.** This virtually final clause (Moule, *Idiom*, p. 83) is expressed in an unusual way (ἕνεκεν, followed by the genitive of the articular infinitive); it is formed by analogy—not for the sake of X, not for the sake of Y, but for the sake of there being shown . . . (B.D. §403; M. iii. 144). It is significant that Paul wishes the Corinthians' *earnestness* to *be manifested* **to yourselves**; some such stimulus as his letter was needed in order to enable them to see their indebtedness to and fundamental loyalty towards the apostle. Not that this was simply a psychological reaction; their *earnestness* was to *be manifested* **before God**, who alone was the proper judge of it. 'This verse of course describes, not S. Paul's purpose in writing his severe letter, but the purpose which the letter had actually served, and which God had intended it to serve' (Goudge).

With this (to us, enigmatic) glance at the past Paul returns to the
13 present: **For this reason we have been comforted**—have been,
and still are, comforted (this is the force of the Greek perfect). In this Paul is anxious to associate Titus with himself. **And in our comfort we rejoiced the more especially** (Paul heaps up words which demand a somewhat clumsy English equivalent: περισσοτέρως μᾶλλον; see B.D. §246; M. iii. 29) **at the joy of Titus,** who evidently had been most favourably impressed by the attitude of the Corinthians. **His spirit** (for this 'untheological' use of *spirit* cf. ii. 13; vii. 1, and the notes) **has been refreshed** (cf. 1 Cor. xvi. 18, where also *spirit* is used; Philemon 7, where without change of meaning 'bowels' is used) **by you all.** Later developments suggest that Titus may have misread the situation (see below, pp. 243 f.), but he had found his visit to Corinth an encouraging and hopeful experience.

This experience of Titus's reflected back upon Paul, for it
14 verified what he had predicted to Titus. **For in any boasts I had
made to him about you** (literally, If I had made any boasts to him about you—a good Greek construction; Beyer, p. 81)**, I was not disgraced,** by their being proved false. **But as all the things**

we said to you were said in truth (literally, as we spoke all things to you in truth), **so also our boasting before Titus proved to be the truth.** As at i. 17-20, Paul connects the sincerity and accuracy of his plans and judgements with the truth and faithfulness of the Gospel he preaches; not that the latter stands or falls with the former, but because one who is committed to the Gospel, as *the* truth, is unlikely to be careless of fact. It is to be noted that Paul sent Titus to Corinth (which apparently he had not visited before) with boasts about the Corinthian Christians. 1 Corinthians shows that he must have been aware of their limitations; but on the whole he had confidence in them, and therefore told Titus that they were fundamentally sound. 'Boasting' indeed suggests a good deal more than this somewhat faint praise; it cannot possibly mean less. This observation suffices to disprove the common opinion that Titus (armed perhaps with the 'severe letter') was sent by Paul to subdue a situation of revolt which he himself had been unable to control. The main purpose of Titus's visit was to organize the collection (viii. 6). See 'Titus' passim.

Nevertheless, Paul was glad to hear such good news from Titus
—for his own sake, for the Corinthians' sake, and for Titus's sake.
His affections (or, feelings; literally, bowels; see vi. 12 and the 15
note) **turn especially to you, as he remembers the obedience
of you all** (there was no recalcitrant minority), **how you received
him with fear and trembling.** Titus did not quell a riot; he was
received with great respect, and Paul does not claim that the
Corinthians had to be reduced to obedience. They were obedient.
Hence **I am glad that I have every confidence** (θαρρῶ, as at 16
v. 6, 8; it is also used, in a somewhat different, though closely
related sense, at x. 1, 2, which may look back to the present passage;
for ἐν, cf. Gal. i. 24; iv. 20; Phil. i. 30) **in you.** Paul is satisfied, on
the evidence of Titus, that the Corinthians understand the apostolic
message and mission in the same way that he does himself. There
is nothing to fear from a rival apostolate (though it is always
necessary to warn the church against perversions of Christian faith
and behaviour). The Corinthians are obedient, and earnest on
his behalf. On this basis Christian activity, such as the Collection,
may proceed.

14. viii. 1-24. THE COLLECTION (1)

(1) We draw your attention, brothers, to the grace of God that has been given to the churches of Macedonia; (2) I mean, that, though they were sorely tried by affliction, the overflowing of their joy and their rock-bottom poverty overflowed in the wealth of their simple-hearted goodness. (3) For they acted up to their power, as I can bear witness, and beyond their power, of their own accord (4) asking us with earnest request that they might share in the generosity and fellowship of the service to the saints. (5) And this they did, not as we hoped, but first of all they gave themselves to the Lord, and to us, through God's will, (6) so that we asked Titus that, as he had already previously made a beginning, so he would also complete for you this grace too. (7) Only, as you abound in every sort of gift, in faith and speech and knowledge and every kind of zeal, and in the love that reaches you from us,[1] see that you abound in this grace too. (8) I am not saying this by way of command; I am using the zeal of others to test the genuineness of your love. (9) For you know the grace of our Lord Jesus Christ, that, for your sake, though he was rich he became poor, in order that by his poverty you might become rich. (10) In this I am giving you my advice, for such participation is expedient for you, people who last year were beforehand not only in action but also in your determination. (11) Now finish off the action, in order that as there was readiness of will so there may be also readiness to bring to completion, as far as your resources permit. (12) For if the readiness is present, the acceptability of the gift is judged on the basis of what one has, not on the basis of what he does not have. (13) For the intention is not that there should be relief for others, affliction for you, but that, as a matter of equality, (14) at the present time your abundance may be matched

[1] This is the reading of $\mathfrak{P}^{46}$ B and a few other witnesses. Most MSS, including ℵ C D G and the Latin, reverse the pronouns: 'your love to us'. This is the easier, more obvious reading; the more unusual should, as in the translation, be adopted.

against their want, in order that in turn their abundance may come to be matched against your want, in order that there may be equality—(15) as it is written: He who had much did not have more, and he who had little did not have less.

(16) But thanks be to God, who is kindling[1] the same zeal on your behalf in the heart of Titus, (17) for he has accepted our request, and being more zealous has set off to you of his own accord. (18) We have sent with him the brother whose praise in the Gospel is current in all the churches, (19) who moreover was appointed by the churches to act as our travelling companion in dealing with this grace, to the glory of the Lord himself,[2] and at our suggestion; (20) for we seek to avoid the possibility that anyone should blame us in respect of this large sum that is being administered by us. (21) For we are concerned to have a good reputation, not only with the Lord but with men. (22) We have sent with them our brother, whom we have in many matters and on many occasions tested and proved to be zealous, and now the more zealous in view of his great confidence in you. (23) If there is any inquiry about Titus—he is my partner and fellow-worker in relation to you; if there is any inquiry about our brothers—they are the envoys of the churches, the glory of Christ. (24) So show them a proof of your love, and of the truth of the boast about you that we made to them, so that all the churches can see.

Paul's collection for the poor saints in Jerusalem was undoubtedly one of his major activities in the middle fifties. It is referred to in Rom. xv. 25-32; 1 Cor. xvi. 1-4; on both passages see the notes. Compare Gal. ii. 10. Surprisingly, it receives only incidental mention in Acts (xxiv. 17), unless xi. 27-30 is regarded as a misplaced reference. On the general question see D. Georgi, *Die*

[1] This translates the present participle, διδόντι; the aorist, δόντι, 'who kindled', is read by 𝔓⁴⁶ D G L. This makes sense, and could be right; cf. vii. 7 for the good impression the Corinthians had made on Titus. But vii. 7 may well have suggested this reading instead of the less obvious present.

[2] *Himself* is omitted by B C D* G L, giving an easier text, which is to be rejected. It is quite possible that Paul wrote (dictated) αὐτοῦ, noticed that this would not be clear, and added τοῦ κυρίου to bring out his meaning, so that we should translate not *of the Lord himself*, but 'his—I mean, the Lord's'.

Geschichte der Kollekte des Paulus für Jerusalem (1965) and K. F. Nickle, *The Collection* (1966); also Bornkamm, *Paulus* (1969), pp. 61 f., 107. Detailed observations will be made in the commentary on chapters viii and ix, and are summed up in the Introduction, pp. 25-8.

A fresh subject of this kind could hardly be introduced without a break in the flow of the epistle, though it could reasonably be said that the last verses of chapter vii, in which Paul expresses his confidence in the Corinthians, prepare well for an appeal for the collection (so Allo). Notwithstanding a measure of abruptness, which shows 'how hard it was for the apostle to "beg" in this church' (Lietzmann), the transition from vii. 16 to viii. 1 is not such as to suggest that two different letters have been put together.

1 Paul begins, **We draw your attention** (γνωρίζομεν, translated as at 1 Cor. xv. 1; the fundamental sense is, We cause to know), **brothers** (cf. i. 8; xiii. 11; see the note on 1 Cor. i. 1), **to the grace** (χάρις; this word is used in these chapters in a bewildering variety of ways—see viii. 1, 4, 6, 7, 9, (16), 19; ix. 8, 14, (15); it is always translated *grace* where it relates to God) **of God that has been given to** (possibly 'in'; M. iii. 264) **the churches of Macedonia.** 'The Macedonians had no need of commendation whereas the Corinthians had every need of stimulation' (Calvin). Since 148 B.C. Macedonia had been a Roman province, from 27 B.C. to A.D. 15, and again from A.D. 44 onwards a senatorial province, situated north of Achaea and stretching from Apollonia in the west to Philippi in the east. For its share in Paul's collection see Rom. xv. 26; for other references, i. 16; ii. 13; vii. 5; xi. 9; Phil. iv. 15; 1 Thess. i. 7, 8; iv. 10. Philippi and Thessalonica (also Beroea, Acts xvii. 10) were Pauline towns in Macedonia. We know from the following verses that notwithstanding their poverty the Macedonian churches had given generously; it is to this that Paul refers when he speaks of the *grace of God* given to them. *Grace* itself means generosity (see *Romans*, p. 76; *1 Corinthians*, pp. 35 f.); theologically, the generosity of God in giving freely to those who as sinners deserve nothing except punishment (see verse 9). Paul may mean (a) that the generosity of the Macedonians is the generosity of God himself, or (b) that God has given grace to the Macedonians (cf. 1 Cor. i. 4 for grace in this sense) with the result of making them generous; perhaps he would not have wished to distinguish too nicely between the two possibilities.

Paul proceeds to explain (though still somewhat obscurely)
what he means by the grace of God given in Macedonia. **I mean** 2
(these words are not in the Greek but are needed after the English *draw attention to*), **that** (ὅτι; this could be rendered 'for') **though they were sorely tried** (δοκιμῇ, more or less as at xiii. 3; not as at ii. 9; ix. 13; Rom. v. 4; Phil. ii. 22) **by affliction** (Barth, *C.D.* II ii. 637 sees here 'vindication resulting from affliction'), **the overflowing of their joy** (Schlatter notes that joy arises as the consequence of liberality, rather than from Corinthian self-importance) **and their rock-bottom** (κατὰ βάθους, literally, down to depth; cf. Strabo, ix. 419) **poverty overflowed** (in Greek, the verb cognate with the noun rendered *overflowing*) **in** (or into; but εἰς with the accusative was sometimes used to mean *in* in Hellenistic Greek) **the wealth of their simple-hearted goodness** (ἁπλότης, as at Rom. xii. 8 (see the note); also 2 Cor. ix. 11, 13; xi. 3; Col. iii. 22). *Affliction* in the Macedonian churches is attested by Phil. i. 29 f.; 1 Thess. i. 6; ii. 14; iii. 3 f.; 2 Thess. i. 4-10. *Poverty* was probably to a great extent a Christian phenomenon and the result of persecution, for Macedonia seems on the whole to have been a prosperous province, with flourishing agriculture and mining and lumbering industries (*C.A.H.* x. 403; xi. 568), though Plummer (p. 233) writes, 'The Romans . . . had taken possession of the gold and silver mines which were rich sources of revenue, and had taxed the right of smelting copper and iron; they had also reserved to themselves the importation of salt and the felling of timber for building ships. The Macedonians said that their nation was like a lacerated and disjointed animal (Livy, xlv. 30).' It should be noted however that this passage in Livy relates to the period just after the battle of Pydna, in 168 B.C. Héring's suggestion of earthquakes is, as he recognizes, unsupported by evidence. *Affliction* and *poverty*, however caused, have not suppressed but rather quickened the Macedonians' generosity. They may have felt that they understood the situation in Jerusalem (1 Thess. ii. 14). In Philippians, Paul thanks his readers for their generosity to him (Phil. iv. 10-20), and to the Thessalonians he says that he has no need to write to them about brotherly love (1 Thess. iv. 9 f.). Of *simple-hearted goodness*, Bousset-Gressmann, p. 419, say that it is 'a fundamental concept of Jewish ethics', quoting from the Testaments of the Twelve Patriarchs, Reuben iv. 1; Walk in singleness (ἁπλότητι) of heart, in the fear of the

Lord; Levi xiii. 1: Fear the Lord your God with all your heart, and walk in integrity (ἁπλότητι) according to all his law; Simeon iv. 5: Walk in singleness (ἁπλότητι) of heart, that God may give you grace and glory and blessing; Issachar iv. 1; v. 1. See also Reicke, *Diakonie*, p. 204. The word tends, as here, in the direction of 'liberality'; Hughes cites Josephus, *Antiquities* vii. 332; Tacitus, *Hist.* iii. 86 (*simplicitas*).

In the translation of verse 2 adopted here the verb *overflowed*, though singular (ἐπερίσσευσεν), has been given a double subject: *the overflowing of their joy* and *their rock-bottom poverty*. There is no difficulty in this: 'In concord with several words connected with *and* [καί] the same free rules apply for the New Testament as in the classical language' (B.D. §135). It is however possible to construe the sentence differently: The overflowing of their joy was in deep trial of affliction, and their rock-bottom poverty abounded in .... But it is the Macedonian contribution to his collection that (at least for the moment) interests Paul, and it is to this that the sentence leads up.

3 The Macedonians' generosity is described: **They acted** (this
verb is a supplement, not strictly necessary, for a finite main verb
is to be found in verse 5, *they gave themselves*, but undoubtedly
desirable in the interests of clarity) **up to their power, as I can**
bear witness (an easy parenthesis—B.D. §465.2), **and beyond**
their power (that is, doing more than could in the circumstances
be expected of them), **of their own accord** (that is, without any
prompting from Paul; cf. verse 17, where the same word is used
4 of Titus) **asking us** (cf. v. 12) **with earnest request that they**
might share in (another supplement; literally, asking for ...)
the generosity (χάρις; here a human act of love, distinct from,
but comparable with and prompted by, God's; the Hebrew *ḥesed*
develops in a similar way—cf. *g^e^miluth ḥ^a^sadim* in the famous saying
of R. Simeon the Just (Aboth i. 2)) **and fellowship** (or sharing,
κοινωνία; cf. ix. 13; Rom. xv. 26) **of the service** (διακονία; like
κοινωνία, one of Paul's distinctive words for the collection; cf.
Rom. xv. 31 and the note; 2 Cor. ix. 1, 12, 13; Reicke, *Diakonie*,
p. 25, puts the two words together as 'beneficence in service'
(*dienende Wohltätigkeit*)) **to the saints** (not Christians in general,
as at i. 1, but the poor saints at Jerusalem, as at Rom. xv. 25, 26,
5 31; 1 Cor. xvi. 1; 2 Cor. ix. 1, 12—see the notes). **And this they**
did (another supplement, picking up *they acted* in verse 3, and

pointing to *they gave* in verse 5b), **not as we hoped** (that is, not simply as we hoped; Paul hoped that they would give to the collection, and this they did), **but first of all** (before giving to the collection; Robertson, p. 1152—καὶ ἡμῖν coordinates) **they gave themselves to the Lord, and to us, through God's will.** Thus a gesture of economic relief was made an act of Christian devotion. This is the converse of the point made above (see p. 100), that when Paul uses the language of cultus he applies it to Christian service in the affairs of everyday life. The first step in their ministering to the saints was the offering of themselves to Christ (*the Lord*; 𝔓[46] has God). They also offered themselves to the apostle—and it was God's will that they should. Paul's position as an apostle was a paradoxical one; see above, pp. 32 f., 48 f.; below, e.g. pp. 247 f.; and *Signs*, pp. 41-4. He would only present himself to his people, not as a lord over their faith (i. 24) but rather as their slave (iv. 5). Yet God had given him authority (for building up, not casting down; x. 8; xiii. 10), and he could offer himself as an example (1 Cor. iv. 16; xi. 1). There could be no question of his right to be taken as an example in the sphere of service to fellow-Christians.

Here then were the Macedonians clamouring to be allowed a
share in the collection, which had been introduced to the Corinthians some time previously (1 Cor. xvi. 1-4; see the note). The
result was **that** (εἰς τό is used, exceptionally, to introduce a 6
consecutive clause; see Robertson, p. 1003; Moule, *Idiom*, p. 141) **we asked** (in Hellenistic Greek the verb παρακαλεῖν often has no stronger meaning than this; note the use of the same verb at xii. 18, and the cognate noun at viii. 17) **Titus that** (ἵνα introduces the content of the request), **as he had already previously made a beginning** (in Corinth, we must suppose; the same word is used at verse 10, with the same meaning but with reference to a different time; see the note), **so he would also complete for you this grace** (χάρις; see the note on verse 1) **too** (the last word, translating καί, seems unnecessary, unless we are to think that Titus had completed some other task in the Corinthian church). Titus, who had probably conveyed the 'severe letter' (see p. 8), had at the same time been charged with a task in relation to the collection; see 'Titus', p. 10.

Here Paul abandons for the moment his account of the arrangements he is making in order to exhort the Corinthians to participate in them whole-heartedly. **Only, as you abound** (the word 7

translated *overflow* in verse 2) **in every sort of gift** (literally, in everything, or in every way; the meaning is the same as in 1 Cor. i. 5), **in faith** (for faith as a gift see 1 Cor. xii. 9; xiii. 2, 13, with the notes) **and speech and knowledge** (see the notes on 1 Cor. i. 5) **and every kind of zeal** (cf. Betz, *Lukian*, p. 9; I now use the English word that had to be avoided at vii. 11), **and in the love that reaches you from us** (literally, the love from us to you——cf. ix. 2, and see M. iii. 259; for the text see note 1 on p. 216; Héring: the love that is in you, and which I have inspired), **see that** (imperatival ἵνα, sometimes found where it does not exist, is certain here; see Moule, *Idiom*, p. 144; Robertson, p. 994; M. i. 179; iii. 95; Turner, *Insights*, p. 147; B.D. §387; the last rightly point out that the present imperative, περισσεύετε, would be ambiguous here, since it could equally be indicative) **you abound in this grace** (this translation is preferable here to such a word as 'generosity', because it makes clear that, whether the Corinthians saw it in this way or not, this kind of service was as much a divine gift as *gnosis* or tongues) **too.**

This may sound like an order, but it is not to be understood in
8 this way. **I am not saying this by way of command** (cf. 1 Cor.
vii. 6, and see the note on verse 5; Paul respects the independence of the church—Bachmann); **I am using the zeal of others** (the Macedonians) **to test the genuineness** (for the abstract noun Paul uses the neuter of the adjective; cf. 1 Cor. i. 25, with the note, and see B.D. §263.2; M. iii. 14; G. A. Deissmann, *Bible Studies* (1901), p. 250) **of your love** (your love for me, expressed in doing what I ask, but also your Christian love more generally—do you love in deed or in word?).

The Macedonians will provide a useful measuring rod by which
the Corinthians may estimate their achievement in the realm of
9 Christian love; there is however a better. **For you know** (indi-
cative, not imperative; if you are Christians at all you must know this) **the grace** (once more, χάρις; 'generosity' would be a good 'non-theological' translation) **of our Lord Jesus Christ, that** (that is to say, this is what you know about him, and it is in this that grace consists), **for your sake** (not 'on your behalf', ὑπὲρ ὑμῶν, as at v. 21, but the less theologically precise δι' ὑμᾶς, on your account), **though he was rich he became poor** (ingressive aorist), **in order that by his poverty you might become rich.** The sense is similar to that of Rom. xv. 3, and here, as there, the

story of Christ is used as in the first instance an example. If the Corinthians are being asked to impoverish themselves for the benefit of others, this is no more than the Lord himself did—though 'being rich' (πλούσιος ὤν) could be taken to mean that even when he became poor he was still in a sense rich; compare the 'being in the form of God' (ἐν μορφῇ θεοῦ ὑπάρχων) of Phil. ii. 7. Bachmann, however, rightly objects to this that it was precisely by Christ's *giving up* heavenly riches that the Corinthians *became* rich. Here even less than in the Christological passage in Phil. ii. 6-11 can a kenotic Christology in the modern sense be drawn from Paul's words. Before the incarnation, the eternal son of God lived the life of heaven, which, to Paul, must have been desirable in every way, and could be anthropomorphically depicted in terms of wealth. To be born of a woman, born under the law (Gal. iv. 4) was, in every possible sense, a step down. Jesus was not bereft of all divine power; Paul never explicitly credits him with miracles, but since he believed that he himself worked such signs (xii. 12) it is unlikely that he would suppose that Jesus could not do so. His earthly life, however, was by definition without the circumstances of heaven; and it ended in the absolute naked poverty of crucifixion. It is rightly observed that Paul is not here concerned to convey information about the sort of life Jesus lived on earth, with less comfort than birds and foxes (Matt. viii. 20; Luke ix. 58); it may however justly be added that Paul could not have written as he did had it been known that Jesus lived a kind of life radically different from that depicted in the gospels. Paul 'never appeals to incidents, not because he does not know them, or because he despises them, but because it is far more potent and effectual to appeal to Christ' (Denney). His voluntary poverty was assumed in order that *you might become rich*; compare v. 21, for the interchange of righteousness and sin, but the theology is not worked out here as it is in chapter v. Lietzmann quotes a hymn of Luther's (which Bach uses with equal appropriateness in the Christmas Oratorio):

> Er ist auf Erden kommen arm,
> Dass er unser sich erbarm
> Und in dem Himmel machet reich
> Und seinen lieben Engeln gleich.

Luther of course was using Paul's thought; Christians are rich (see 1 Cor. i. 5, but also iv. 8—like Paul, Luther dreaded a false *theologia gloriae*), and will be richer. For reference to Irenaeus and Cyril of Alexandria, see Cerfaux, *Christ*, p. 133; E.T., pp. 169 f. See also the Acts of Philip 141; He was great (μέγας) and for our sake became small (μικρός).

There seems no good reason to suppose that Paul is here quoting a Christological hymn (as he appears to do at Phil. ii. 6-11), though equally there is no reason why the theme of wealth and poverty should not have been applied to Christ and Christians by some earlier writer. It is characteristic of Paul to introduce a theological proposition in the midst of a practical exhortation (he does so in both Rom. xv and Phil. ii). It is more important to inquire how Paul's thought in this verse is related to the gnostic theme of the descending and ascending Redeemer (cf. Bultmann, *Theol.*, p. 174; E.T., i. 175; *E. & F.*, p. 149). The problem is more complicated than the form of this question may suggest, for, as is well known, there is no clear evidence that this myth existed in pre-Christian times, though it would be fallacious to conclude from this lack of evidence that it did not so exist. It is best to see passages of this kind as Paul's contribution to a developing picture which was not to be complete until primitive Christian conviction about Jesus (which as early as Paul included the notion of pre-existence) had combined with Jewish and non-Jewish speculation to produce the developed mythologies of the second and later centuries. It should be noted that Paul insists that what he is describing happened in history.

After this reminder of fundamental Christian doctrine and the
10 fundamental Christian example, Paul can proceed. **In this I am giving you my advice** (cf. 1 Cor. vii. 25), **for such participation** (Greek, this; Lietzmann takes the meaning to be 'this advising, not commanding') **is expedient for you** (cf. 1 Cor. vii. 35; and note the sequence of parallels in this chapter—*command* (6, 25), *advice* (25), *expedient* (35)), **people who** (if, with Moule, *Idiom*, p. 124, we are to see more in οἵτινες than in the simple relative οἵ) **last year** (this need not mean 'a year ago'—see below) **were beforehand** (the same word as was used in verse 6 of Titus) **not only in action but also in your determination** (literally, not only to do but also to will). Compare ix. 2, with the note. Whole-hearted participation is called for by the need of the poor saints, by the example of the Macedonians, by the example of Christ, and also by the fact that the Corinthians had themselves embarked upon

the project before the Macedonians had done so, and before Titus had reached them (see 1 Cor. xvi. 1-4; this seems to be the force of προενήρξασθε). This was *last year*, an expression that can only begin to become precise if we know what calendar the author is using. There are three main possibilities (longer lists will be found in Windisch and in Allo): (a) the Roman calendar, beginning on January 1; (b) the Jewish calendar, beginning in the Autumn; (c) the oriental-Julian calendar, also beginning in the Autumn. (b) and (c), between which we need not for this purpose distinguish, are more probable than (a). 1 Corinthians was written probably early in 54 (*1 Corinthians*, p. 5); 2 Corinthians (or, more precisely, this part of it) will therefore have been written some time after October 54. To observe that 'beginning beforehand' means something different for the Corinthians from what it meant for Titus is to explain a feature of this verse that commentators have always found difficult. 'Not only to do but also to will' seems to be an inversion (not a violent one, according to Robertson, p. 425, yet surprising); surely common sense demands 'Not only to will but also to do'. Lietzmann can only suggest that Paul wrote or spoke carelessly, but 'all is clear if, as seems reasonable, we can take the meaning to be, "You not only began (under the guidance of Titus) to make the collection; you had already last year, and without prompting, formed the intention of joining in the collection"' ('Titus', p. 11). 1 Cor. xvi. 1-4 suggests that the Corinthians had heard about the collection and had taken the initiative in asking Paul what they should do; see the notes. Calvin speaks of their 'spontaneous enthusiasm'.

Now finish off (the same word as is used in verse 6) **the action,** 11
in order that as there was readiness of will so there may be also readiness to bring to completion, as far as your resources permit (ἐκ as at Xenophon, *Anabasis* IV ii. 23, but ἐκ τοῦ ἔχειν is an unusual expression; according to B.D. §403 it is probably equivalent to καθὸ ἐὰν ἔχῃ in verse 12; see also Robertson, pp.
1073 f.). **For if the readiness is present, the acceptability of** 12
the gift is judged on the basis of what one has, not on the basis of what he does not have. Literally the last sentence runs, ... it (that is, the gift, or the giver, or the readiness) is acceptable according to whatever he has (καθὸ ἐὰν ἔχῃ), not according to what he has not (οὐ καθὸ οὐκ ἔχει—note the distinction between subjunctive and indicative; see Robertson, p. 967). For the principle,

compare Luke xii. 47 f.; also Menahoth xiii. 11: It is all one whether a man offers much or little [in the first instance, with reference to sacrifices], if only he directs his mind toward Heaven.

13 'Having' and 'not having' suggests a further thought. **The intention is not that there should be** (giving the ἵνα final sense; some would make it imperatival—let there not be; see Moule, *Idiom*, p. 145) **relief** (the word used at ii. 13; vii. 5) **for others, affliction for you.** So far (apart from the different ways of taking ἵνα) the sentence is clear. The idea is not that the Corinthians and the poor saints in Jerusalem shall change places—poverty in Corinth and luxury in Jerusalem. Paul develops this theme, but it is not certain how his words should be punctuated. There are two possibilities. (a) A stop should be put at the end of verse 13 (after ἐξ ἰσότητος). If this is done a number of words have to be supplied: *The intention is not* . . . but that matters should be regulated on the basis of equality. This is a fairly considerable ellipsis, but it is not too great for Paul; it means however that the new sentence in verse 14 begins without any connecting particle, and this must swing the balance in favour of the alternative punctuation and translation, (b) *the intention is not that there should be relief for others, affliction for you*; **but that, as a matter of equality,**
14 **at the present time your abundance may be matched against their want, in order that in turn** (καί) **their abundance may come to be matched against your want, in order that** (having used ἵνα several times Paul now uses ὅπως, without change of meaning) **there may be equality.** The second occurrence of *equality* is clumsy, but by no means impossible. Paul does not here develop the argument of Rom. xv. 27 (If they shared their spiritual things with the Gentiles, the Gentiles ought to minister to them in the things of flesh and blood); he appears to mean only that if in the future there is need in Corinth the Jerusalem Christians, if they are better off, will share with their Gentile brothers. 'Paul would never think of wishing the Corinthians spiritual food from Jerusalem, of all places!' (Lietzmann).

A completely different interpretation of what Paul says about equality (ἰσότης) is given by Georgi, *Kollekte*, pp. 62-6. Noting Philo's discussion of the word in *Quis Rer. Div. Her.* 141-206 (to which Windisch also refers; see in addition the article by G. Stählin in *T.W.N.T.* iii. 343-56, especially 355 f.), he argues that equality was not merely a familiar term in Hellenistic philosophy but a divine power, so that Paul's *as a matter of equality* (ἐξ ἰσότητος) is virtually equivalent to 'from God' (ἐκ θεοῦ), or 'of grace' (ἐκ χάριτος). This, he holds, clears up the difficulties in what are certainly two apparently clumsy and repetitive verses. In addition to these cosmic and charismatic-mystical features (which this understanding of *equality* introduces) there is also a relation to righteousness (δικαιοσύνη), to which Paul subordinates the cosmic and mystical elements. This is quite unconvincing. *Equality* was, as it remains, a fundamentally moral concept. Thinkers such as Philo were apt to personify it in cosmic and mystical directions; but Paul was not such a thinker, and in these verses is concerned with fair dealing.

What Paul asks is in fact common sense and Christian charity; in addition, the course he suggests is indicated by Scripture.
As it is written, He who had (supplying ἔχων, 'according to a 15
common Greek idiom' (Robertson, p. 1202), 'in accordance with the Pauline connection' (Lietzmann)) **much did not have more, and he who had little did not have less.** Paul quotes the LXX of Exod. xvi. 18 (quoted also by Philo, in *Quis Rer. Div. Her.* 191), with a change in the order of words. Whereas, however, the story of the manna appears to mean that there was a miraculous equalization of the amounts collected, Paul means that there is, or ought to be, equality of supply (verses 13 f.) because the more fortunate give away their surplus, and the less fortunate receive it. He uses the Old Testament here rather to illustrate than to authorize his advice (verse 8), but the illustration has an authority of its own.

From exhortation Paul returns to the arrangements he had begun to suggest in verse 6, and in particular to the role of Titus,
who had proved an enthusiastic volunteer. **But thanks** (another 16
use of the word χάρις—see the note on verse 1; but this is so idiomatic with Paul as to have no special significance here) **be to God, who is kindling** (for the text see note 1 on p. 217) **the same zeal** (σπουδή; cf. verse 8; that is, the same zeal that I have myself, and have now described) **on your behalf in the heart of Titus;** that is, according to verse 6 Paul asked Titus to deal with the collection at Corinth, but as time went on he proved to need
no asking. **For he has accepted the request** (the noun cognate 17
with *ask* in verse 6), **and being more zealous** (σπουδαιότερος; according to B.D. §244.2; M. iii. 30, elative comparative; or possibly comparative for positive; or perhaps simply, 'more

zealous than I had allowed myself to hope') **has set off to you of his own accord** (as the Macedonians had acted, verse 3), to complete the work of the collection. Strictly speaking, Titus cannot have acted both on a request and of his own accord. Presumably Paul means that he made the request and found it unnecessary—Titus was already anxious to go. Paul requests; he does not order. 'Even in his dealings with those who travelled with him he was not a master; a leader indeed, but a leader of free men' (Schlatter).

18 **We have sent with him** (almost an epistolary aorist, 'We are now sending'; the past tense is used from the point of view of the recipients of the letter) **the brother** (that is, the brother Christian; see 1 Cor. i. 1, and the note) **whose praise in the Gospel is current in all the churches;** that is, he is widely reported for his service in the Gospel, not only as an evangelist, or preacher of the Gospel, but as one who carries out such Christian services as the making of the collection. Lietzmann (cf. Windisch) argues strongly that the original letter must have included the brother's name, 'for it is absolutely obvious, not merely polite, that one does not introduce and commend unnamed people'. This is quite possible, but leaves out of account that Titus would probably read the epistle aloud to the assembled church, and would at the appropriate point present *the brother* to the company. This is more probable than that the three were already at work in Corinth, introduced by a separate letter (Allo). The difficulty is removed if (see Robertson, p. 770) we take the article with *brother* to be equivalent to the possessive pronoun: Titus was accompanied by his own brother. But *brother* is too common a word for 'Christian' for this to be convincing. There seems to be no good reason for the name to have been omitted if it originally stood in the text. Long lists of suggested identifications are given by Allo, Héring, Hughes, and others.

The brother not only has a good reputation in general terms.
19 He **moreover was** (paraphrasing 'not only', which related to what precedes) **appointed** (aorist participle passive, *χειροτονηθείς*, where the finite verb would have been expected; cf. v. 12; vii. 7; see Radermacher, p. 167; B.D. §468.1) **by the churches** (not by Paul) **to act as our travelling-companion in dealing with this grace** (*χάρις* once more, as at verse 1). This man was probably appointed as their representative by the churches of Macedonia;

he may have been one of the group mentioned in Acts xx. 4:
Sopater of Beroea, Aristarchus and Secundus of Thessalonica.
Appointed refers to appointment by show of hands; the word
(χειροτονεῖν) has nothing to do with the laying on of hands.
The appointment was made **to the glory of the Lord himself**
(whom the brother would serve; on the text and translation see
note 2 on p. 217), **and at our suggestion,** in agreement with
our own eager will. (Kümmel thinks this translation scarcely
possible; the appointment was for the glory of the Lord, and
increased our readiness). It was in fact one of the steps taken by
Paul (verse 20) to ensure that no accusation could be levelled
against his handling of the financial side of the collection. His
care was of no avail (see xii. 16 ff.); but he was doing his best. **For** 20
we seek to avoid (unless we take it back to συνεπέμψαμεν in
verse 18, the participle στελλόμενοι is in anacolouthon; Robertson,
pp. 431, 1134; B.D. §468.1; M. iii. 343) **the possibility that**
anyone should blame us in respect of this large sum that is
being administered by us. Paul could hardly hope to avoid the
charge that he was enriching himself by his missionary work; few
evangelists have avoided it. Again, as at verse 15, he turns to
Scripture to confirm his action. **For we are concerned to have a** 21
good reputation (for the verb cf. Xenophon, *Cyropaedia* IV i. 6),
not only with the Lord but with men. Paul does not claim this
as a quotation, but is evidently using Prov. iii. 4 (LXX), Provide
for a good reputation with the Lord and with men; compare Rom.
xii. 17. It is true that it is only the Lord's judgement that counts
(1 Cor. iv. 4), but a reputation for dishonesty would hinder the
work of the Gospel; compare 1 Cor. x. 32. See Calvin's remarks
on the practical and theological importance of this.

Paul has digressed once more, and now returns again (cf. verses
16, 18) to practical arrangements. **We have sent** (as at verse 18) 22
with them (Titus and the brother) **our brother** (again unnamed;
cf. the note on verse 18), **whom we have in many matters and**
on many occasions tested and proved (ἐδοκιμάσαμεν; cf. e.g.
Rom. xii. 2; 1 Cor. xvi. 3) **to be zealous, and now the more**
zealous in view of his great confidence in you. It would be
possible (since the Greek has no possessive pronoun) to read the
last eight words as, 'in view of my great confidence in you'. They
would then have to be taken as an adverbial phrase with *we have*
sent.

23 All Paul's colleagues will stand up to any test. **If there is any inquiry about Titus** (literally, If about—ὑπέρ in the sense of περί, B.D. §231.1—Titus)**—he is my partner and fellow-worker in relation to you; if there is any inquiry about our brothers** (but Paul has forgotten the preposition, ὑπέρ, and the genitive case it governs, and simply writes the nominative; it would be possible to translate, If our brothers are inquired about, but it is not necessary to write such offensive English)**—they are envoys of the churches** (ἐκκλησιῶν lacks the article because this is necessarily wanting with ἀπόστολοι)**, the glory of Christ.** We do not know which churches are referred to, but may make guesses similar to those above in the note on verse 19. Titus and the brothers do not stand on the same level. He is one of the small group, including Timothy and Silvanus, who are partners in the mission led by Paul, and associated with him in letter-writing. The *brothers* are *envoys of churches*—apostles (ἀπόστολοι), but in a sense different from that in which Paul was an apostle. He was appointed by no human agency whatever, but was 'an apostle of Christ Jesus by the will of God' (i. 1; cf. Gal. i. 1). The word however was not in Paul's time the technical term it has since become; its ordinary meaning was *agent*, and it was Paul himself more than anyone else who gave it the meaning of 'missionary'. The *brothers* had been appointed by churches, not as missionaries or as ministers in the modern sense of the term but to act as collectors. As such they enjoyed the authority their principals committed to them. On the primitive Christian apostolate see *Signs*, pp. 23-81, and the literature there referred to. These men are subordinate apostles, local agents helping to supervise a financial operation, but they are *the glory of Christ*, because they are carrying out faithfully the work of love and service that has been assigned to them.

24 **So show them a proof of your love, and of the truth** (these three words must be added to make a clear English sentence) **of the boast about you that we made to them, so that all the churches can see** (literally, in the face of the churches). The last clause could be attached to *the boast that we made*, but in Greek it immediately follows *show*, and should probably be attached to this word. *Show* in Greek is not an imperative but a participle (ἐνδεικνύμενοι; many MSS have ἐνδείξασθε, but the harder reading should be adopted). On the imperatival use of the participle see *Romans*, pp. 239 ff. The present passage however cannot

easily be brought under the account there given, for it is not in a code but in a straight command: *Show them a proof*, that is, Treat them with affection and respect on the occasion of their visit. D. Daube, in his appended note in E. G. Selwyn, *The First Epistle of St Peter* (1946), expresses doubt regarding the reading, and adds that, if the participle is read, 'it is best explained as loosely connected with the εἰς ὑμᾶς [in you] of verse 22' (p. 481). It is hard to find a better explanation, especially in view of the discordant participles in verses 19, 20.

For Paul's boasting about the Corinthians see vii. 14; ix. 3. He uses *the churches* (plural) at Rom. xvi. 4, 16; 1 Cor. (iv. 17); vii. 17; xi. 16; xiv. 33; 2 Cor. viii. 18, 24; xi. 28; 2 Thess. i. 4, to denote the universal church (or something approaching this). It is very seldom in the genuine epistles that the singular is used for this purpose. Paul does not forget that the totality is the sum of local units.

15. ix. 1-15. THE COLLECTION (2)

(1) For concerning the service to the saints, it is superfluous for me to go on writing to you like this. (2) For I know your readiness; I am boasting about it on your behalf to the Macedonians, telling them that Achaea has been prepared since last year, and your zeal has stirred up the majority of them to emulation. (3) But I have sent the brothers, in order that the boasts we have uttered on your behalf may not in this respect be proved empty, in order that (as I was saying) you may be ready, (4) lest if Macedonians should come with me and find you unprepared we—not to say you—may be put to shame in this confidence of ours. (5) So I thought it necessary to ask the brothers to go on ahead to you, and prepare that gift of yours, which had been promised in advance, that it might thus be ready as a gift and not as something wrung from you. (6) But, you know, this is true: He who sows sparingly will also reap sparingly, and he who sows bountifully will also reap bountifully. (7) Let each man give as he has decided in his heart, not as if it hurt him, or out of necessity; for God loves a cheerful giver. (8) God is able to make all his grace abound to you, so that

in all ways, at all times, you may have all sufficiency, and enough to spare for all kinds of good work, (9) as it is written, He scattered abroad, he gave to the poor, his righteousness abides for ever. (10) He who provides seed for the sower and bread for eating shall supply and multiply your seed, and shall make[1] the fruits of your righteousness grow. (11) In every way you are enriched, with a view to your perfect integrity, which, working through us, produces thanksgiving to God; (12) for the execution of this act of public service not only supplies the wants of the saints, but also overflows in many thanksgivings to God; (13) they glorify God for the obedience shown in your confession of faith in the Gospel of Christ, proved as it is by this service, and for the integrity of your fellowship with them and with all; (14) and in their prayer for you[2] they long for you on account of the surpassing grace of God bestowed upon you. (15) Thanks be to God for his unspeakable gift.

At this point the discussion of the collection for the poor saints in Jerusalem takes a new turn—so sharply that some have seen here the beginning not of a new paragraph but of a part of a different letter from that contained in chapter viii. See Introduction, p. 12; some think that the letter was sent to Corinth at a different time from chapter viii, others that it was sent at about the same time but to the other churches of Achaea. There is a careful discussion in Windisch, pp. 286 ff. It will appear however from the exegesis that the transition is not as sharp as is sometimes supposed, and that chapter ix deals with the same situation as chapter viii, yet does not repeat its contents; it is therefore best to treat it as a continuation of chapter viii, and as belonging to the same letter as chapters i–viii.

1 **For** (*γάρ*; this links with the *boasts* of viii. 24—I can make confident boasts about you, for . . .; alternatively, with Goudge, I have been speaking about the commissioners, for it is unneces-

[1] The majority of MSS put this and the preceding two verbs into the optative: May he supply and multiply . . . and make grow. $\mathfrak{P}^{46}$ has two optatives and an indicative: May he supply and multiply . . .; and he will make grow. These represent the final and an intermediate stage in the weakening of Paul's confident assertion.

[2] Instead of *for you*, B ℵ* and a few others have 'for us'—an easier reading, which is to be rejected.

sary to speak about the collection itself) **concerning the service to the saints** (the same words as at viii. 4; cf. ix. 12, 13), **it is superfluous for me to go on writing to you like this.** The last two words represent Paul's use of the article with the infinitive (τὸ γράφειν). Similar expressions but without the article occur at Phil. iii. 1; 1 Thess. iv. 9; v. 1. The use of the article ('This writing to you') is strong ground for the view that chapters viii and ix belong together; Denney translates, 'to be writing to you as I do'. The sentence includes a particle (μέν) which looks forward to verse 3 (ἔπεμψα δέ) in a way that suggests some limitation of the thought ('I know you need no reminder . . . but all the same I am sending . . .').

In the meantime, the confidence of verse 1 is given its ground
in the opening of verse 2. Further exhortation is superfluous, **for I** 2
know your readiness. This restates viii. 10 ff., using the same word (προθυμία). Knowing it, **I am boasting about it on your behalf to the Macedonians.** Paul is presumably in Macedonia (vii. 5); if the Corinthians had been there they might well have found the opportunity of boasting on their own account. Paul boasts, **telling them** (these two words, not in the Greek and not strictly necessary in English, help out the following ὅτι, *that*) **that Achaea** (Corinth was not the whole of Achaea, or the only church in Achaea—see Rom. xvi. 1; but it was the largest town and probably the biggest church; see i. 1 and the note) **has been prepared since last year** (the same expression—ἀπὸ πέρυσι—as at viii. 10; see the note). It is true that there is a good deal of difference between readiness (in the sense of willingness), making a beginning (viii. 10), and being prepared (in the sense of having completed the task); this does not mean that Paul was writing chapter ix at a later date than chapter viii, but that he had used the forwardness of the Corinthians to encourage the Macedonians, as he was now using the generosity of the Macedonians to encourage the Corinthians (viii. 1, 8). The context (verses 3 f.) shows that Paul was already somewhat embarrassed, and feared further embarrassment; an unkind judgement might say that Paul had exaggerated if he had not actually twisted the truth. There is a careful discussion of this question in Windisch, pp. 270 f. The fact is that, notwithstanding all the problems they caused, he was in the habit of seeing the best in his people and presenting them in this light to others. The Corinthians had begun so well—surely

they must be well on the way to completion! It was probably a greater shock to Paul than to anyone else to find that they were not. But, perhaps too optimistically, he had boasted about the Corinthians, **and your zeal has stirred up the majority of them** (cf. ii. 6, and see Moule, *Idiom*, p. 108) **to emulation.** The last word is used in a good sense; the result is to be seen in the sacrificial giving described in chapter viii. It is clear however that the situation would become intolerable, and the Macedonians might do more than change their minds, if it appeared that the Corinthians, however keen at the outset, had abandoned the project. It was vital that Paul should ensure that they were doing their best.
3 **But** (δέ, answering the μέν of verse 1, on which see the note: I am
confident about you, but . . .) **I have sent** (see viii. 17, 18, 22; the
persons are being sent now, perhaps as bearers of the letter) **the**
brothers. The reference is clearly to viii. 6, 17-24, but since names
and numbers are not given it is not clear whether *the brothers* are
Titus and the two unnamed brothers, or some two out of these
three. Probably all three are intended here (for Titus as a *brother*
see ii. 13); Titus and the other two can be distinguished in the
sense that Titus was Paul's representative while they were independent witnesses intended to serve as a check on the integrity of
the proceedings, but they would all serve the same purpose of
stimulating the Corinthians to action. Thus Paul sends the
brothers **in order that the boasts** (singular in Greek) **we have**
uttered on your behalf (cf. verse 2) **may not in this respect**
(Paul had made other boasts about the Corinthians; vii. 14) **be**
proved empty (for this term see 1 Cor. ix. 15), **in order that**
(this second *in order that*, ἵνα, is, like the first, dependent on
4 *I have sent*) **you may be ready, lest, if Macedonians should**
come with me (Paul is thinking of a third visit, but thinking of it
in terms different from those of xii. 14; xiii. 1, a hint that chapters
x–xiii are later than chapters i–ix; see Introduction, pp. 10, 21)
and find you unprepared, we—not to say you (see B.D. §495
for a sensitive note on Paul's delicacy here)—**may be put to**
shame in this confidence (cf. xi. 17; Hatch, *Essays*, pp. 88 f.)
of ours.
5 **So** (to sum up and repeat, but also to take the argument a stage
farther) **I thought it necessary to ask** (for the weak sense of
this verb cf. viii. 6) **the brothers** (see verse 3) **to go on ahead**
(evidently Paul expects to follow at no long interval; see verse 4)

to you, and prepare (*προκαταρτίσωσιν*; it is necessary to stress the pre- in *prepare*; it is undesirable to use 'in advance' twice in one English sentence) **that gift of yours, which had been promised in advance.** *Gift* translates a word (*εὐλογία*) not commonly used in this sense (L.S. quote only biblical passages—Josh. xv. 19; 4 Kdms v. 15 in addition to 2 Corinthians); Windisch suggests that it may have occurred to Paul as an expression alternative to 'collection' (*λογία*); see also G. A. Deissmann, *Bible Studies* (1901), p. 144.

All this is to be done **so that it** (the gift) **may thus be** (taking the accusative and infinitive, *ταύτην ἑτοίμην εἶναι*, as final, though according to Moule, *Idiom*, p. 141, it might be consecutive) **ready as a gift**—a real gift—**and not as something wrung from you.** The last four words translate a word (*πλεονεξία*), which Paul uses elsewhere at Rom. i. 29 (translated 'covetousness'; see the note); Col. iii. 5 (where it is said to be equivalent to idolatry); 1 Thess. ii. 5. It means avarice, rapacity. The cognate *nomen agentis* (*πλεονέκτης*) occurs at 1 Cor. v. 10, 11; vi. 10 ('rapacious men'); the verb (*πλεονεκτεῖν*) has already occurred at ii. 11; vii. 2; but decisive for the sense here is the occurrence at xii. 17, 18, where it appears that Paul had been accused of using the collection as a means of taking money from the Corinthians. The gift which Paul hopes to get from the Corinthians for his collection may be either a genuine gift, or something extracted from them, by force, deceit, or some kind of moral blackmail ('You surely won't let the Macedonians please me more than you do!'). This takes the 'desire to have' as existing essentially on the side of the collector; this seems better than transforming avarice into 'stinginess', though this is accepted by a number of commentators.

The rest of the chapter consists of an exhortation to liberality
cast in more general terms. **But, you know, this is true** (an 6
expanded translation of *τοῦτο δέ*—Paul is about to set forth a proposition which he is sure will be accepted by his readers and should determine their attitude; for the ellipsis see B.D. §481, and cf. 1 Cor. vii. 29; xv. 50): **He who sows sparingly will also reap sparingly, and he who sows bountifully** (an adverbial phrase based upon the noun, *εὐλογία*, translated *gift* in verse 5) **will also reap bountifully.** *Sparingly* is an adverb developed out of a participle; for this see Radermacher, p. 54 (and cf. Plutarch, *Alexander* 25) The saying has the appearance of a

proverb, but there does not appear to be any precise parallel. Paul himself uses the image of sowing and reaping at Gal. vi. 7, and to this more general use of the figure there are numerous parallels (see Schlier, ad loc.). See for example Aristotle, *Rhetoric* III 3. 4: You sowed these things shamefully (αἰσχρῶς), but you reaped them in evil (κακῶς); Cicero, *De Oratore* ii. 65 (261): Ut sementem feceris, ita metes; 3 Baruch xv. 2 f.; As for the angels which brought the baskets which were full, he [Michael] filled them with oil, saying, Take it away, reward our friends an hundredfold, and those who have laboriously wrought good works. For those who sowed virtuously, also reap virtuously. And he said also to those bringing the half-empty baskets. Come hither ye also; take away the reward according as ye brought, and deliver it to the sons of men. The image of sowing and reaping is so self-evident that it must have been used at all times and places; and the thought that the quantity of the harvest is (other things being equal) proportionate to the quantity of seed sown is scarcely abstruse.

The appeal to harvest implies that it is for each man to sow as (in the light of the principle stated) he sees fit. This conclusion is
7 explicitly stated. **Let each man give** (this word has to be supplied) **as he has decided in his heart** (his outward act expressing inward conviction rather than desire for praise or fear of censure)**, not as if it hurt him** (that is, in a grudging spirit)**, or out of necessity** (through moral or other pressure)**; for God loves** (gnomic present; Moule, *Idiom*, p. 8) **a cheerful giver.** Here Paul has adopted the words of Prov. xxii. 8(9)a (LXX: God blesses a cheerful and liberal man; Hebrew: He that hath a bountiful eye shall be blessed). Compare Rom. xii. 8, with the note, including the reference to Leviticus Rabbah xxxiv. 9 (131 b): When a man gives alms he should do it with a joyful heart; also Sirach xxxv. 11. As Windisch says, 'The thought is thoroughly Old-Testament and Jewish'. The saying recurs in the Martyrdom of Peter 9: Hilarem datorem diligit Deus. *Loves* is of course used here in the sense of 'approves', 'values'; it would be absurd to see a contradiction of the belief, held by no one more strongly than by Paul, that God loves the sinner, the man who will not give at all, cheerfully or otherwise.

That God *loves* the *cheerful giver* in this way implies that he
8 rewards him. **God is able to make all his grace** (or 'generosity' —χάρις; see viii. 1, and the note) **abound** (here the verb,

περισσεύειν, is used transitively, as at iv. 15; 1 Thess. iii. 12) **to you** (cf. Phil. iv. 19), **so that** (ἵνα is here on the boundary between final and consecutive senses) **in all ways, at all times, you may have all sufficiency, and enough to spare** (here the verb περισσεύειν is used intransitively, as at viii. 7; ix. 12) **for all kinds of good work.** At the end of the sentence 'every kind' would be a better rendering (of πᾶν ἔργον ἀγαθόν); I have used *all kinds* in order to represent in English the heaping up of the word *all* (πᾶς occurs four times, the related πάντοτε once). The sense of the verse seems to be that if men are willing to give, God will always make it possible for them to give. *Sufficiency* (αὐτάρκεια; cf. Phil. iv. 11) is a Stoic word (see Sevenster, *Seneca*, p. 113). 'In the Cynic-Stoic philosophy it denotes the man who in terms of his own inward potentiality practises ἀρκεῖσθαι [contentment] and thereby becomes an independent person, who is complete in himself (in sich selbst ruht) and in need of no other' (G. Kittel, *T.W.N.T.* i. 466). Of 'contentment' (he is discussing the Greek verb ἀρκεῖσθαι, to be content) the same writer says, 'Let a man be content with the natural good things appointed him by fate or by God; let him practise ἀρκεῖσθαι τοῖς παροῦσι [contentment with what he has], let him desire nothing more than what is given him' (p. 464). It will be clear that this is not exactly what Paul means, though it is related to it. The Stoic's sufficiency is from himself, whereas Paul's sufficiency is the gift of God, the result of his grace (χάρις). The Stoic's sufficiency is sufficiency for himself—necessarily, for it springs not from the quantity of external goods but from within, since it means contentment with whatever external goods are available, many or few; whereas Paul is thinking of such a supply of external goods as will permit the Christian to give some of them to others in good works. There is a relation, however, between Paul's thought and that of the Stoics, for Paul is certainly not so crude a thinker as to mean that the Christian is always assured of such a material standard of living that he will be able to act charitably towards others—he knew in his own experience (xi. 23-33; cf. Phil. iv. 12) that this was not true; Schweitzer, *Mysticism of Paul the Apostle* 1931), p. 313, exaggerates the difference between Jesus and Paul in this respect. But because the Christian is supplied not from within but by the grace of God there will always be some kind of good work that he can do. The last phrase should be noted; no one opposed more vigorously than Paul the notion that man could be justified on the basis of works done in obedience to the law (see e.g. Rom. iii. 20), but this opposition is completely misunderstood if it is not seen to be accompanied by the strictest requirement that man shall, in obedience to God, do works that are good in God's sight (see e.g. Rom. ii. 7). These are not done in order that the doer may be justified, but as a consequence of the fact that he has been justified.

9 This view Paul supports from the Old Testament: **as it is written, He scattered abroad, he gave to the poor, his righteousness abides for ever.** It would be possible to take the aorists *scattered, gave* (διεσκόρπισεν, ἔδωκεν) as gnomic, proverb-like, and virtually equivalent to presents—this is what the man in question habitually does. The quotation is from Ps. cxii. 9, in agreement with the LXX (cxi. 9). According to Lietzmann, Paul takes *righteousness* in the sense it has in Matt. vi. 1, by which he presumably means almsgiving. It is true that in late Hebrew *ṣ*[e]*daqah* (cf. the Aramaic *ṣidqatha*) came to mean almsgiving, and that late rabbinic interpretation of Ps. cxii. 9 (see S.B. iii. 525) adopts this meaning; it is however far from certain that this is the meaning of righteousness in Matt. vi. 1; it is also doubtful whether this is the sense in which Paul uses the word here, even though (according to Windisch) Chrysostom understood it in the sense of charitableness (φιλανθρωπία). It is more likely that the word is used in the general moral sense (as at vi. 14); and not impossible that it has its characteristic forensic sense. The man who thus obeys God's will in caring for the poor maintains his justified relation with God. For development of this theme, see Georgi, *Kollekte*, pp. 69-72; the collection is a sign to the Jews of the justification of the heathen.

Paul continues to use the Old Testament, but not to quote it
10 exactly. **He who provides seed for the sower and bread for eating shall supply and multiply your seed** (that is, shall make you prosper, with 'increasing surplus for service' Goudge; similarly Bachmann—the metaphor of seed runs through the context, and no special meaning should be sought in it here)**, and shall make the fruits of your righteousness grow.** On the text of this verse see note 1 on p. 232. Compare Isa. lv. 10: For as the rain or snow comes down from heaven and does not return, until it waters the earth, and makes it grow and sprout, and gives

seed to the sower and bread for eating, so shall be my word . . .; Hos. x. 12: Sow for yourselves in righteousness (εἰς δικαιοσύνην), harvest for the fruit of life, shine on yourselves with the light of knowledge, seek the Lord until the fruits of righteousness come for you. It is unnecessary to point out in detail how Paul has combined words and phrases from these passages; there is no citation formula, and no appeal to scriptural authority. God is the supplier of all good things; he will prosper your work and thereby make it possible for you to express your right status before God (see the note on *righteousness* in verse 9). The Old Testament passages, under Christian reflection, are sufficient to account for Paul's words; but compare *Corpus Hermeticum* xiii. 22a, which speaks of 'immortal fruit' (Knox, *H.E.*, p. 94).

Paul's appeal for Corinthian participation in the collection thus contemplates the benefit (in different ways) of both the Corinthians and the poor saints in Jerusalem; this however is not the end of the story, for beyond these human goods is thanksgiving to God and the consequent increase of his glory (see Kümmel, also Georgi, *Kollekte*, pp. 74-7, with the reference each makes to G. H. Boobyer, *Thanksgiving and the Glory of God* (1929); and the notes on verse 12, 13).

In every way you are enriched (the English finite verb 11
translates a Greek participle, πλουτιζόμενοι, which, like the participle in verse 13, is in anacolouthon; this probably means no more than that Paul has forgotten how the sentence is going, and loses control of it; see B.D. §468.2; Turner, *Insights*, p. 166; cf. v. 12). For the sense, compare 1 Cor. i. 5. The enrichment however is not for your benefit, save in so far as it is **with a view to your perfect integrity** (for the word ἁπλότης see the note on viii. 2), and this **working through us produces thanksgiving to God.** The single-minded devotion to Christian duty shown by the Corinthians works *through* us because Paul's collection provides a suitable outlet for it, and it *produces thanksgiving* primarily in those whose benefit from it is most obvious. For *thanksgiving* (εὐχαριστία) see the notes on verses 12 and 13.

For the execution (διακονία; this would usually be trans- 12
lated 'service', as at viii. 4, but this before the next noun is impossible; the word is sometimes used rather of administration than of ministry, or ministration; cf. Georgi, *Kollekte*, p. 74, *Durchführung*) **of this act of public service** (λειτουργία, Phil.

ii. 17, 30; the cognate verb is used by Paul at Rom. xv. 27, the *nomen agentis* at Rom. xiii. 6; xv. 16; Phil. ii. 25) **not only supplies** (a periphrastic present, possibly with the meaning, . . . is to supply; cf. Col. i. 24; *Corpus Hermeticum* xiii. 1; Knox, *H.E.*, p. 92) **the wants of the saints** (as at viii. 4), **but also overflows** (cf. viii. 2) **in** (or through) **many thanksgivings to God.** *Execution* (διακονία) and *public service* (λειτουργία; cf. G. A. Deissmann, *Bible Studies* (1901), p. 144) could be nearly synonymous, but even when used separately they are not identical. The latter throws some additional light on the way Paul regarded the collection. It was not a tax, which the Corinthians and other Gentile Christians were under obligation to pay, but voluntary service; it was undertaken for the benefit of the 'city'—that is, of the church—as a whole. The word is sometimes used in a religious sense, of the service of the gods; so far as this is suggested, Paul sees divine service in the care of the needy; see p. 100 above. There is no ground for seeing here the allusion to the gifts or offertory of the eucharist suggested by Richardson, *Theology*, p. 297. More directly 'liturgical' action comes from the beneficiaries, from whom proceed *many thanksgivings to God.* At no stage does Paul allow the caritative action of his churches to escape from the theological context which supplies its meaning, any more than he allows his theology to be without practical expression. This becomes apparent in the alternation that continues through the remaining verses of the chapter.

The generosity of the Gentile churches issues in *thanksgivings*
to God, but the *thanksgivings* are not simply (though doubtless
13 they are in part) for cash received. **They**, the poor saints who
receive the benefits, **glorify** (a participle in anacolouthon; cf. verse 11 and the note) **God for the obedience** (ὑποταγή, subordination of yourselves to. . . ; Schlatter properly compares 'the obedience of faith', Rom. i. 5; xvi. 26) **shown in your confession of faith** (for the noun ὁμολογία as a technical term see 1 Tim. vi. 12, 13, with my note; Heb. iii. 1; iv. 14; x. 23; Paul uses the cognate verb at Rom. x. 9, 10; Héring translates 'religion') **in the Gospel of Christ, proved as it is** (literally, through the proof, or on account of the proof; for διά and the genitive in causal sense see Radermacher, p. 118, and cf. Rom. viii. 3) **by this service** (here Paul returns to the word διακονία in a more common sense; see viii. 4). The service of the Gentile churches to the poor saints is a part,

or aspect, of their confession of faith in the Gospel, and shows this confession to be not a matter of words only but genuine obedience to God who is the author of the Gospel. This is why the saints glorify God: they do so in response to a different way in which others have already given glory to God. Equally they glorify God **for the integrity** (on ἁπλότης see viii. 2) **of your fellowship** (or, your participation (in the collection); Paul uses this word, *κοινωνία*, in speaking of the collection at viii. 4; Rom. xv. 26) **with them, and with all** (that is, with all Christians; Paul is not here thinking of charity beyond the bounds of the Christian society, within which there is a special mutuality of love; cf. Gal. vi. 10). That is, they glorify God not simply for a share (this is behind the word *fellowship*) in the Corinthians' resources, but for the quality of Christian life exemplified in it; not only because the Corinthians show this quality to them, but because they manifest it universally (though not in all cases in the same way, that is, by a gift of money). There is no hint here, as there is in Rom. xv. 30 f., of the possibility of an unfavourable reception; Paul would not mention it here because it would discourage Corinthian generosity (Windisch).

The saints give thanks; they also pray. **And in their prayer** 14
for you, they long (the same verb as at v. 2; Rom. i. 11; the cognate noun is used at vii. 7, 11; here, as in the last verse, we have not a finite verb but a participle, this time in the genitive) **for you,** to have direct fellowship with you—a human enough desire; they long to see their benefactors. But the motivation is theological: **on account of the surpassing** (this word was used with 'glory' at iii. 10) **grace** (or generosity, *χάρις*; see the note on viii. 1) **of God bestowed upon you.** The real significance of the Corinthians as benefactors is not in themselves but in God; their generosity is a sign of the grace of God. Hence the conclusion, with which
Paul winds up his treatment of the whole matter: **Thanks** (*χάρις*; 15
note the final play on this word) **be to God for his unspeakable gift!** This gift refers back in the first instance to the grace of verse 14, but, standing as it does in this summarizing position, it can hardly fail to refer also to viii. 9, and the primary gift of God which has established the whole framework of Christian life and fellowship within which Paul's preaching and collection alike stand. Georgi, *Kollekte*, pp. 78 f., sees an allusion to 1 Chron. xxix; this is doubtful, but his conclusion (p. 79) may be quoted:

'As its history unfolded, the collection became for Paul a model (*Modellfall*) of his theology, a fact that shows, conversely, that Pauline theology, including the doctrine of justification, is directed towards living history, and is as far removed from mystical as from apocalyptic speculation'. Paul's thought is certainly not a matter of apocalyptic speculation; yet justification, a fundamentally forensic concept, owes not a little to a framework of ideas originally formulated in the realm of apocalyptic.

From this point we are about to move to a part of the epistle which strikes a different note; see pp. 243 f., and Introduction, pp. 10, 12. There is an unmistakable difference between the end of chapter ix and the beginning of chapter x, but it is well not to exaggerate the difference either by heightening the colours of i–ix or darkening those of x–xiii. In chapter ix Paul has been describing not what is actually happening in Corinth and Jerusalem, but what he hopes will happen. 'The impression, which is not to be wiped out, that Paul is here praising the Corinthians in an exaggerated way . . . is lessened if it is borne in mind that in verses 12-15 he is painting a picture of the future, as it will be if the Corinthians come up to his expectations' (Lietzmann). Paul writes under the influence of the report brought by Titus. All will surely now be well; and this will include Corinthian participation in the collection. Let there be rivalry between Achaea and Macedonia! Each can provoke the other to more generous action. But there is nothing to suggest that Paul has yet received a penny piece to transmit from Corinth to Jerusalem. Perhaps it will turn out that Corinthian expressions of loyalty had no greater reality or permanency in them than the fast-fading enthusiasm for the collection. It is needless to add that Paul's observations about the interrelation of divine grace and human generosity are confirmed rather than disproved by the Corinthians' failure to receive the one and to manifest the other.

E. THE FUTURE THREATENED

x. 1–xiii. 10

16. x. 1-6. AN APPEAL FOR COMPLETE OBEDIENCE

(1) I, Paul, I myself urge you, by the meekness and gentleness of Christ, I who in person go humbly among you, but when absent am bold towards you; (2) I ask you not to compel me when present to show that confident boldness which I think I shall dare to use against certain people who think of us as if we conducted ourselves according to the flesh. (3) For though we conduct our life in the flesh we do not make war according to the flesh, (4) for the weapons with which we go to war are not fleshly but powerful on God's side for the pulling down of strongholds, as we pull down thoughts (5) and every exalted thing that lifts itself up against the knowledge of God, lead every design into captivity and obedience to Christ, (6) and are ready to punish every disobedience when your own obedience is perfect.

That we enter here upon a new division of the epistle is unmistakable, and underlined by the fact that the two preceding chapters have dealt, in hopeful terms, with the collection Paul is organizing. In chapters x–xiii there is no word of the collection (apart from the negative allusion in xii. 16 f.). If we go back to the earlier chapters of the epistle, the distinction, though it exists, is less emphatic. In chapters i–vii we find allusions to those who commend themselves, flashes of self-defence against accusations which it is not hard to reconstruct, and above all an exposition of what Paul understands by the office of an apostle. These themes recur in chapters x–xiii; their recurrence has given rise to the belief that ii. 14–vii. 4 was originally part of the same letter as x–xiii, but is in fact a refutation of this view, for it is scarcely thinkable that Paul should in the same letter go over more or less the same ground, first in a frame of mind that suggests that he expected that he would only have to remind his readers of the truth to ensure their acceptance of it, and then in such a way as to suggest his belief that the cause was as good as lost, and that little remained for him but to make a desperate counter-attack. There is a unity of subject-matter in 2 Corinthians, and a unity of treatment; but there is a change in atmosphere, a change in the mood of Paul's response, and also a change in the response that he appears to expect from his readers. It is these changes that make it difficult to accept the literary unity of the epistle. Lietzmann thinks that a sleepless night would account for the difference between i–ix and x–xiii, and Denney puts the matter even more strongly: the break could be explained 'if Paul stopped dictating for the day at the end of chapter ix—if he even stopped for a few moments in doubt how to proceed . . .'. Such delays might possibly cause a change of mood; they might even give rise to the change from a 'We-epistle' to an 'I-epistle' (Bachmann), but they could not give rise to a new reaction, or change a hopeful to a despairing attitude. The only adequate explanation of the new tone in x–xiii is that Paul had heard further news from Corinth—not that the situation had changed completely but that it had developed. Such news could have arrived while he was writing; he could have decided to let what he had written stand and simply add a supplement. It is hard, however, to think that he would have been content with such a proceeding, and it is more likely that he had already sent i–ix. He could not call these chapters back —perhaps would not have done so if he could; but a new letter was called for. The main difference, as will appear in detailed comment, is not in theme, but in the fact that, whereas in i–ix Paul had warned the Corinthians against certain errors and certain persons, with some confidence that the Corinthians would heed his advice, in x–xiii he finds that the Corinthians have rejected him and his Gospel in favour of the pseudo-apostles and their pseudo-gospel. This change of tone is against W. H. Bates's view that x–xiii is a 'recapitulation' (*N.T.S.* xii. 56-69—an otherwise persuasive discussion).

The view suggested here involves the consequence that the letter contained in i–ix has lost its end, that in x–xiii its beginning. There is no difficulty in this. It would be quite natural to put together, in proper chronological sequence, two letters written with only a short interval between them; a grace could follow immediately after ix. 15, and x. 1 need have been preceded by no more than the customary epistolary formula, 'Paul, an apostle of Christ Jesus, to the church of God in Corinth, etc.'. This is a much easier process than that presupposed by the common view that x–xiii (perhaps together with ii. 14–vii. 4) is part of the severe letter, written before i–ix (or some part or parts of this). For this alternative see the Introduction, pp. 12 ff.

For the understanding of x–xiii, and of the historical situation that these chapters imply, it is of fundamental importance to distinguish between three groups: (a) the Corinthians themselves, over whom Paul grieves, because they have been led astray; occasionally anger breaks out, but Paul seldom forgets that they are not the prime movers, and that their ingratitude and disloyalty are not entirely their own fault; (b) false apostles, who have invaded his mission-field and, with their 'other Jesus', their 'different Gospel', their new conception of what apostolic ministry is, have seduced the Corinthians, destroying the relation between them and Paul, and threatening their Christian existence; (c) apostles of recognized eminence, who, notwithstanding the fact that there is, or appears to be, some kind of relation between them and the false apostles, must be accepted as apostles of Christ, though Paul insists that he is in no way inferior to them. The existence of these three groups, one of which he (not uncritically) defends, one of which he attacks, and one of which he deals with on equal terms, is evidently an embarrassment to Paul, and the cause of a good deal of obscurity in his writing. Their existence (against for example Bultmann, who—*Probleme*, pp. 23-30—identifies (b) and (c), and thinks that the false apostles represent a 'hellenistic-gnostic Jewish Christianity') will be brought out in the course of the commentary. Its effect is that the 'Pauline apostolate is to be recognized as the real theme of debate [*Kampfobjekt*] in 2 Cor. x–xiii' (Käsemann, *Legitimität*, p. 49/31). It is not adequate (with Allo) to describe these chapters as Paul's 'apology', for this implies a personal defence. Personalities do play some part, but it is the nature of the apostolic Gospel, and the apostolic authority behind it, that are at stake (see also Käsemann, *Legitimität*, p. 50/33, with the quotation from F. C. Baur).

The new paragraph begins abruptly, but the whole is abrupt and forceful writing; there is no need to suppose that anything
has been lost before the opening words. **I, Paul, I myself urge** 1

(at viii. 6 παρακαλεῖν was translated 'ask', but the word is one that takes force and colour from the context, and a stronger equivalent is needed here) **you.** The content of Paul's request will not appear till verse 2, but his vehemence is already manifest. Paul uses his own name in this kind of address to his readers only at Gal. v. 2; 1 Thess. ii. 18; each time he is writing with intense conviction. Here he underlines his name with two emphatic pronouns (αὐτὸς δὲ ἐγὼ Παῦλος). Some have seen in this an indication that at this point in the letter Paul began to write with his own hand (as at Gal. vi. 11); but the comparison with Galatians is sufficient to show that this is not necessarily so. There is no attempt to use an autograph for authentication (cf. 1 Cor. xvi. 21; Col. iv. 18; 2 Thess. iii. 17).

Paul *urges* his readers **by** (διά) **the meekness and gentleness of Christ.** Compare Rom. xii. 1: 'I exhort you, brothers, by (also διά) God's mercies'. The parallel (strengthened by recollection of viii. 9, and the fact that Paul says *Christ*, not Jesus) has suggested that Paul refers here not to the characteristics of the earthly life of Jesus, but to his meekness and humility in accepting the conditions of earthly life at all; compare Phil. ii. 6 ff. There is something to be said for this view, but it would have been impossible as theology had it been known that the behaviour of Jesus had been marked by arrogance and violence, and frigid if there had not been a tradition that depicted him as meek and gentle. Kümmel (also Windisch) sees no reason why there should not be a reference here to Matt. xi. 29. Paul occasionally presents material (e.g. Rom. xiii. 1-7, 8 ff.) that closely recalls the gospel tradition, but without any indication that he is aware of the fact. His interest here is not in the communication of information about the earthly life of Jesus but in the parallel between Jesus' behaviour and his own. The existence of Christians is determined both theologically and ethically by Jesus. It may become necessary for his apostle to behave with an energy and strictness (cf. 1 Cor. iv. 21) not compatible with *meekness and gentleness*; but if this happens it is a clear sign that something is wrong. Hence Paul is already taking action in order to ensure, if possible, that it shall not happen. *Meekness* (πραΰ(ό)της; cf. Aristotle, *Nicomachean Ethics* IV v (11) 1125b) and *gentleness* (ἐπιείκεια; cf. Betz, *Lukian*, p. 209) were probably a recognized pair in Hellenistic ethical thought; they occur side by side in Plutarch, *Pericles* 39; *Sertorius* 25; *Caesar* 57;

compare Paul's use of the adjective 'gentle' (ἐπιεικής) at Phil. iv. 5. *Meekness* he sees as a characteristic Christian virtue, or gift: Gal. v. 23; vi. 1; Col. iii. 12. Taken together the two words suggest a tolerant attitude towards others; the man who has these virtues will not lose his temper or grow impatient. This is consistent with verse 2.

Meekness and gentleness may unfortunately be misunderstood; the next words can hardly be marked as a quotation because Paul uses the first person singular, but it is very probable that he echoes the language of opponents who claimed that Paul's behaviour when he was in Corinth, and the letters he wrote to the church, were inconsistent, and no doubt drew the inference that he was a coward who dared to speak his mind only when at a safe distance. *I urge you,* **I who in person** (κατὰ πρόσωπον is not a Semitism—B.D.§ 217.1) **go humbly among you, but when absent am bold towards you.** For *humbly* (τάπεινος) compare vii. 6; xi. 7; xii. 21; the word has not yet been fully accepted as descriptive of a Christian virtue. Here (and it must be remembered that Paul is taking up the language of others, so that Betz's interesting note (especially p. 51) on its revaluing by the Cynics is not strictly relevant) it has the same sense as in Xenophon, *Memorabilia* III x. 5, where (as neuter adjective used for abstract noun) it forms a pair with servility (ἀνελεύθερον) over against nobility (μεγαλοπρεπές) and dignity (ἐλευθέριον). When face to face with those who are prepared to stand up to him, Paul (it is alleged) adopts a cringing attitude (cf. 1 Cor. ii. 3): to such an extent can *meekness and gentleness* be misunderstood. Absent, however, that is, when writing letters or sending messages through his assistants, he shows (they say) a bold confidence (cf. v. 6, 8; vii. 16—see the notes). To what letter or message can this refer? There is a threat of sorts in 1 Cor. iv. 19 ff., but these verses can hardly be said to be characteristic of the letter as a whole. It is more probable that the reference is to the 'severe letter', which we know cost Paul tears in the writing, and hurt the Corinthians when they read it (ii. 4; vii. 8), and perhaps to the attitude that Titus had been charged to adopt. If this is so, it will follow that x–xiii is not the 'severe letter', or part of it.

Güttgemans (pp. 135-41) has made the paradoxical observation that in this verse the clause introduced by the relative (ὅς) has the form of a Christological confession (cf. Phil. ii. 6; Col. i. 15;

1 Tim. iii. 16), though evidently it relates directly not to Christ but to Paul. Yet the immediately preceding words refer to the *meekness and gentleness of Christ*, and in fact Güttgemans is not far wide of the mark, though it would be possible to find fault with the way he expresses his point, when he says, 'Because the apostolic "weakness" is thus christological *proclamation*, Paul can directly admonish the Corinthians *by* (*durch*) his apostolic "weakness", for this is the mark of the presence of the Crucified' (p. 141). Paul's behaviour in Corinth, as elsewhere, is part of his preaching of the cross (cf. 1 Thess. ii. 1-12); hence he can invite his converts, 'Be imitators of me—as I am of Christ' (1 Cor. xi. 1; see the note); hence also the misunderstanding to which an apostolic ministry on the lines described in 1 Cor. iv. 9-13; 2 Cor. iv. 7-10; vi. 4-10 is inevitably exposed. This verse does not bear the marks of a highly wrought, precise style, and was probably flung off in hot blood; but it is inadequately described as 'savage irony'. Paul's humbleness is not servility but part, a necessary part, of his service of the humble Christ; thus it is precisely *by the meekness and gentleness of Christ* that he begs his readers not to force him to adopt a different attitude, which may become necessary, and yet at the same time will obscure the Gospel. Paul is in a cleft stick; this fact determines, and thus goes far to explain, chapters x–xiii as a whole.

2 **I ask you** (the new verb, δέομαι, is here taken as resumptive of the verb—*urge*—in verse 1; it would be possible, since *you* is not expressed in the Greek, to take it to mean 'ask in prayer'—'I pray that I may not show . . .'; so Bachmann) **not to compel me** (the last three words are not in the Greek but bring out the force of Paul's request to the Corinthians; a literal rendering would be, I ask not when present to be bold . . .; for the construction cf. B.D. §399.3) **when present to show that confident boldness which** (literally, 'to be bold (as in verse 1) with that confidence with which . . .') **I think I shall dare** (cf. 1 Cor. vi. 1, with the note) **to use against certain people who think of us as if we conducted ourselves according to the flesh** (cf. 1 Cor. iii. 3, where similar words are used; for *according to the flesh* see the next verse). The context suggests an appeal to the Corinthians rather than a prayer. There is a point at which *meekness and gentleness* cease to be recognizable as the characteristics of Christ; and this corresponds to the fact, which Paul does not mention, that the historical tradition about Jesus, though it refers to his

meekness (e.g. at Matt. xi. 29), also represents him as moved with anger (e.g. Mark iii. 5). In Jesus himself, and in the apostle, both attitudes are exposed to misunderstanding; but it is better (if need be) to be misunderstood in *meekness* than in anger, and Paul hopes that *boldness* will not become necessary, though he is prepared to use it, and is thinking of it, considering (λογίζεσθαι) it.

He is prepared to show *boldness* against those who misunderstand, falsely evaluate (again the word is λογίζεσθαι) his behaviour, mistaking *meekness* either for weakness or for cunning. It is not until the last verse of this paragraph that we find a clear clue to the identity of these persons (see the note on verse 6); but it is to be noted that Paul proposes to show *confident boldness against certain persons*; he does not say (though it would have been easy to do so), I ask *you* to repent, that I may not have to show this bold front against *you*. The sentence takes a turn in the middle. *Certain persons* could be 'some of you'; do you *as a whole* so act that I may not have to deal firmly with a minority, but again Paul does not say this, though had he intended this it could easily have been done (cf., in the view of some, ii. 6). His language does not demand but is certainly consistent with the view that the persons in question are to be distinguished from the Corinthians; see above, p. 245, and compare Goudge: '(a) The indefinite "some" (better "certain people") suggests that he is not referring to the Corinthians. (b) On the other hand, the appeal of the verse presupposes that it depends upon the action of the Corinthians whether S. Paul has to act sternly or not'. That there is a close relation between the various persons in question is shown by Paul's request; the Corinthians can (or Paul's request is futile) act in such a way as to make it unnecessary for Paul to take a firm line. This they could do, presumably, by withdrawing support, or credence. But support and credence had already gone far (xi. 20); Titus had perhaps underestimated the degree to which the Pauline church had been eroded (vii. 11).

Paul was bound (in view of passages such as Rom. viii. 4-8) to disagree with those who considered his behaviour to be *according to the flesh*; but it is probable that what they meant by this phrase (κατὰ σάρκα) was not Paul's meaning. For Paul, to 'live according to the flesh' means (see above, p. 170) to have an egocentric, or at least anthropocentric, existence, to be so absorbed in that which is not God as to relegate God to a subordinate place, if to any place at all. It appears from the context of x–xiii as a whole that for his adversaries to 'live according to the flesh' meant not to have visions and ecstatic experiences; perhaps, even, not to behave in an authoritarian, self-assertive way that could be ascribed to spiritual authority and superiority. Further description of these men must follow where Paul provides the material for it; see for example pp. 261, 274–7, 285 ff., 291 f.; also Introduction, pp. 28 ff.; and 'Paul's Opponents'. The difference in usage calls for some explanation, which unfortunately (from our point of view) Paul does not give systematically. It is clear, however, that we have to deal with two fundamentally different ways of understanding *flesh* and *spirit*. Calvin adopts a similar but not identical view: *flesh* means 'external pomp or show, the only standards by which the false apostles usually commend themselves'.

3 **For though we conduct our life** (περιπατεῖν, as in verse 2) **in the flesh we do not make war according to the flesh.** Paul changes his preposition from *in* (ἐν) to *according to* (κατά); for this reason it seems wise not to attempt here to paraphrase 'according to the flesh' as has been done from time to time in *Romans* and *1 Corinthians*. Paul is not consistent in his use of *in the flesh* (see *Romans*, p. 158). At Rom. viii. 9 he declares that Christians are not in the flesh; at Gal. ii. 20 he speaks of the life he lives in the flesh, meaning undoubtedly his life as a Christian, since it is lived by faith. The present passage is akin to that in Galatians. According to Schlatter *in* (ἐν) is causal: Paul means that he needs the service of his body; it is more probable that by *in the flesh* Paul means 'in the world' (cf. 1 Cor. v. 10), in the ordinary circumstances of human existence. Though he may on occasion have been caught up to the third heaven or paradise (xii. 2, 4) this is not his normal experience. This is constantly repeated in chapters x–xiii, and is indeed one of the fundamental themes of the *theologia crucis* (see Introduction, pp. 42 f., 48 ff., and *Signs*, pp. 41-4, 80 f.; cf. 104 f.) which 2 Corinthians more clearly than any other letter proclaims; Paul knows no kind of Christian existence that is not a matter of 'dying, yet see—we are alive' (vi. 9). *In the flesh* means dying; but this is not the last word. Here Paul does not say simply, We now live according to the Spirit (κατὰ πνεῦμα), because he is dealing with a particular aspect of his apostolic life: he has to wage war upon an enemy. To do this *not according to the flesh* means (in the light of what was said above) neither with self-centred motives,

that is, to establish one's own position and increase one's own power, nor on the basis of one's own resources. The positive side of this is stated in verses 4, 5.

The weapons with which we go to war (Paul has no interest 4
here in specifying and allegorizing particular weapons as he does at 1 Thess. v. 8; cf. Eph. vi. 14-17) **are not fleshly** (that is, *we do not make war according to the flesh*—repeating verse 3b) **but powerful on God's side** (literally, powerful to, or for, God, δυνατὰ τῷ θεῷ). It is not certain how *God* (in the dative case) is to be understood. It may be simply a kind of superlative, based on a Hebrew construction (as at Gen. x. 9; Jonah iii. 3; cf. Acts vii. 20). Moule, *Idiom*, p. 184 (cf. M. ii. 443) appears to favour this view; it is supported by the fact that Modern Greek has many words compounded with God (θεο-) which are simply superlatives (e.g., θεόγυμνος, stark naked; θεόκωφος, completely deaf; θεότυφλος, quite blind). On this view we should translate 'extremely powerful'. The alternative is to take the word as a *dativus commodi*, 'for God', employed on God's behalf (cf. xi. 2). This is more probable; Paul could not have expected the Corinthians to understand a Septuagintal barbarism, and it is very unlikely that he would have absent-mindedly employed the word *God* without thinking what it meant. The weapons are not fleshly; that is, they are spiritual; therefore they are powerful (Lietzmann). Paul omits the middle term.

He is in fact hurrying on to say what the weapons achieve. They are *powerful* **for the pulling down of strongholds** (on the form of this word, ὀχύρωμα, see M. ii. 71). There is a probable allusion to Prov. xxi. 22: The wise man attacks strong (ὀχυράς) cities, and destroys the stronghold (ὀχύρωμα) in which the ungodly trusted (I take the LXX's aorists to be gnomic). Windisch compares Philo, *De Conf. Linguarum* 129-31, where a similar figure is used in an attack on sophistic; he thinks Paul is attacking Corinthian gnosis. Betz, pp. 68, 140 f., underlines the theme of an attack upon sophists. In fact we have so far no ground for identifying the object of Paul's attack; this must be discovered as he proceeds.

The construction shifts sharply, and the sentence is carried on with a series of nominative plural participles (masculine, and therefore not in agreement with *weapons*, ὅπλα, which is neuter). Compare ix. 11. The participles must be put into finite verbs in English.

We pull down (the verb, καθαιροῦντες, is taken out of the noun, καθαίρεσις, in the preceding clause) **thoughts** (or plans, λογισμοί, but there is a play on the verb λογίζεσθαι in verse 2)
5 **and every exalted thing that lifts itself up against the knowledge of God, lead every design into captivity and obedience to Christ.** The suggestion (Lietzmann) is probably correct that Paul is thinking of characteristics of his adversaries, the intruding apostles. This is fairly clear for *thoughts*; the only other occurrence of this noun is at Rom. ii. 15, where it is of neutral meaning, but it is probably used here in the sense of a compound noun (διαλογισμός) found at Rom. i. 21; 1 Cor. iii. 20; Phil. ii. 14 in a bad sense. *Design* (νόημα) is used in a good sense at Phil. iv. 7; but in 2 Corinthians it is either bad or potentially bad: ii. 11; iii. 14; iv. 4; xi. 3. Both words thus suggest the supposed cleverness of human wisdom, which is so satisfied with itself that it has no need of God, or evolves its own god, made in its own image. It is not so easy to deal with *exalted thing* (ὕψωμα, which occurs in a different sense at Rom. viii. 39). Chrysostom (for the evidence see Lietzmann) explained it as a 'high tower', but this meaning cannot be found for the word in Greek usage. Probably no further interpretation is required than is provided by the participle attached to the noun and indicating the setting in which it exalts itself. It is the highmindedness (cf. Rom. xii. 16) which thinks itself superior not only to fellow-men but also (in this instance) to God. This is precisely a definition of sin (see Rom. i. 18-23, with the notes), and there is no room for it in the Pauline view of Christianity (cf. xii. 7), though it is essentially a religious attitude. Paul however speaks of that which exalts itself not simply against God but *against the knowledge of God.* It is unlikely that he means more than he does at Rom. i. 28, They did not see fit to take cognizance of God (τὸν θεὸν ἔχειν ἐν ἐπιγνώσει); that is, they would rather exalt themselves than recognize God (which can be done only in self-abasement); but the word *knowledge* (γνῶσις; see *1 Corinthians*, pp. 189 ff.) was current in Corinth, and it may have suggested one or both of two further points. (a) Paul has made it clear that the true Christian knowledge of God is found only in Christ crucified (*1 Corinthians*, pp. 17 f.); it is precisely against this knowledge that men exalt themselves, because it offends their sense both of reason and of propriety (1 Cor. i. 23). They reject the truth that we know about God. (b) It may be that Paul

uses the word *knowledge* because his opponents used it; they rejected what he understood by knowledge of God (*gnosis*) in the interests of their own *gnosis*. For *gnosis* at Corinth see further 'Christianity at Corinth' (pp. 275-86), and Introduction, pp. 37 f. To *lead into captivity and obedience* is a translation that slightly expands 'take as prisoner of war into obedience', and takes the 'obedience of Christ' as an objective genitive. Men's designs are captured and transferred to a new authority; instead of serving other interests they will henceforth be obedient only to Christ. A different translation would be necessary if we were to accept Barth's view (*C.D.* IV i. 194) that the genitive is both objective and subjective (cf. Rom. v. 19, and the description of Jesus as the 'servant of God', that is, one who renders obedience to God). What Barth says about the obedience shown by Christ in his earthly life is true and important, but the present context, which speaks of taking designs into *captivity to Christ*, does not suggest it. Instead of thinking and planning in a self-regarding way, men shall henceforth think and plan in *obedience to Christ*. It is worth noting that Paul describes his objective in this way. He is ready enough to fight if that be necessary, but he is not fighting on his own account, that men may recognize what an important apostle he is and render obedience to him (contrast xi. 20). The centre of the stage belongs no more to him than to his rivals, but to Christ only.

A further part of Paul's controversy is that we **are ready to** 6
punish (ἐκδικεῖν; for the meaning see Schrenk in *T.W.N.T.* ii. 441) **every disobedience** (that is, to Christ; this confirms the view of verse 5b taken above) **when your own obedience is perfect** (has reached completion, πληρωθῇ; see Delling in *T.W.N.T.* vi. 296). It is hardly credible that Paul should mean: When you Corinthians have become perfectly obedient I will proceed to punish all your past disobedience. This would be the moment for remitting punishment. If however this is not Paul's meaning, he must mean, When you are completely obedient, I will proceed, on that basis, to punish the disobedience of someone else (see 'Paul's Opponents', p. 239; Héring, who, unlike some commentators, does see that there is a problem here, takes πληρωθῇ as inchoative). These disobedient persons (*every disobedience* is too general for us to confine Paul's reference to a single person, notwithstanding x. 7-11, on which see the notes), since

they are not Corinthians, will have come into Corinth and the Corinthian church from outside, and it is natural, and almost certainly right, to explain them in the light of x. 12-18; that is, they are persons who have invaded Paul's mission field, in which they had no rights, in disobedience to the arrangement for a division of apostolic work agreed upon in Jerusalem (Gal. ii. 9). *Obedience* and *disobedience* are related to belief and unbelief (Bornkamm, *Paulus*, p. 154), but are here not quite synonymous with them, for all the persons concerned are Christians (though in Paul's view some of them are very unsatisfactory Christians). *Obedience* includes loyalty to Paul (such as apparently had not been shown on the occasion of Paul's unhappy visit to Corinth; see pp. 7 f., 89, 93, 212 f.), and *disobedience*, which on the part of non-Pauline Christians cannot mean disloyalty to Paul, means disregard of an agreement to which Paul was a party—though in all probability he used the word partly because it formed a convenient pair with *obedience*. If the 'disobedient' were not Corinthians, and were at fault because they had infringed the agreement of Gal. ii. 9 (or at least some such agreement), the probability is that they were in some sense based upon, and took their orders from, Jerusalem.

It would be wrong at this stage to argue ahead of the evidence, but we may look back to the distinction made on p. 245 between three groups of persons. Paul now recognizes more clearly and definitely than he had done in chapters i–ix that the Corinthians were not completely on his side; he can still aim, however, at perfect obedience on their part as a goal. When he has achieved this goal, his next step will be to punish the intruders, whose presence has come near to ruining his work.

17. x. 7-18. A DECLARATION OF WAR ON THE COUNTER-MISSION

(7) Look at the things immediately before you. If anyone is confident with regard to himself that he belongs to Christ,[1] let him consider again by himself that as he belongs

[1] The Western Text (D* G Ambrosiaster) has '. . . that he is the slave of Christ'; a secondary expansion, but one that gives the right sense. Compare xi. 23.

to Christ, so also do we. (8) For if[1] I make a further boast about our authority, which the Lord gave for building you up, and not for pulling you down, I shall not be put to shame. (9) I forbear to do this lest I should seem as if I were frightening you to death by my letters. (10) For 'His letters', he says,[2] 'are weighty and powerful, but his bodily presence is weak and his speech excites contempt.' (11) Let the man who says that kind of thing bear this in mind, that when present we shall be in action just the same that we are in word through our letters when absent. (12) For we do not dare to class or compare ourselves with some of those who commend themselves; but they, measuring themselves by themselves, and comparing themselves with themselves, are without understanding. (13) We however[3] shall boast in no unmeasured way, but only according to the measure of the province God dealt out to us as our measure, that we might reach as far as you. (14) For we are not overstretching ourselves, as if we did not reach as far as you, for in the Gospel of Christ we got to you first, (15) and do not boast in an unmeasured way in other men's labours, but have the hope that, as your faith increases, we may grow in your estimation according to our province, and in such overflowing measure (16) that we may preach the Gospel in the areas beyond you, and not boast in ready-made achievements in someone else's province. (17) If anyone is to boast, let him boast in the Lord. (18) For it is not the man who commends himself who can be accepted as approved, but the man whom the Lord commends.

Paul now makes clear—as far as the very difficult Greek of an
extremely complicated passage can do so—what has been happening in Corinth and caused the trouble which he is writing to
assuage. He invites his readers to observe what is going on under
their own noses. **Look at the things immediately before you.** 7

[1] Paul seems to have written ἐάν τε γάρ, though τε is omitted by 𝔓[46] B and others, who may have felt (with M. iii. 339) that it was a 'superfluous affectation'. See further however Radermacher, p. 5, and especially B.D. §443.3 and Thrall, pp. 96 f., with the quotation from Aristotle, *Politics* 1318b 33.

[2] Some authorities have 'they say'. See the commentary.

[3] The last words of verse 12 and the first of verse 13 are omitted by some MSS; see the commentary, pp. 263 f.

It would be possible to translate, You look at the things immediately before you (since βλέπετε may be either imperative or indicative—only the context and sense can decide). If the latter rendering is adopted (J. A. T. Robinson, *The Body* (1952), p. 26) the sense will be, You look at things from a human, fleshly (x. 2 f.) point of view—you are 'content with outward show' (Calvin); you have therefore misunderstood the situation. It is against this that *the things immediately before you* (*τὰ κατὰ πρόσωπον*) means simply what it says, and to look at what is immediately before you does not necessarily imply that you look at and estimate it from a fleshly point of view. It is by no means decisive, but is a fact worth bearing in mind, that the verb form in question (βλέπετε) is often, and indeed characteristically, used by Paul as an imperative (1 Cor. viii. 9; x. 18; xvi. 10; Gal. v. 15; Phil. iii. 2; Col. ii. 8; iv. 17; cf. Eph. v. 15; 1 Cor. i. 26 is probably not to be included —see the note).

There was at Corinth, as Betz, pp. 132-7, ably brings out, a 'problem of evidence' (*Evidenzproblem*). If the Corinthians will open their eyes and look, they will see that the situation is not as one-sided as they may have supposed. **If anyone** (it is not clear whether this is a generalization or refers obscurely to a particular person; see verses 10, 11, with the notes, which suggest the latter possibility) **is confident with regard to himself** (or possibly, in himself—ἑαυτῷ) **that he belongs to Christ, let him consider again by himself** (ἐφ' ἑαυτοῦ; cf. Herodotus iii. 71 for a good parallel (ἐπ' ὑμέων αὐτῶν βαλόμενοι); *again* probably refers to the reflexive pronoun—let him have another look at himself) **that as he belongs to Christ, so also do we.** The meaning of 'belonging to Christ' (Χριστοῦ εἶναι) is disputed. Windisch distinguishes four possible ways in which the phrase may be taken: (a) It may mean simply 'being a Christian'; (b) it may refer to a special historical relation with Jesus of Nazareth; (c) it may refer to the status of an apostle; (d) it may refer to a mystic-gnostic relation with the heavenly Christ—cf. Schmithals, who (pp. 162 ff.) takes 'I belong to Christ' to be equivalent, on the lips of a Corinthian gnostic, to 'I am a spiritual man (πνευματικός)'. Windisch himself prefers (c), possibly in combination with (b). The question is far from simple. All Christians belong to Christ, and there is no doubt therefore that (a) is a possible meaning: if anyone is confident that he is a Christian, let him bear in mind that I am too.

Negatively, this implies a serious accusation: Paul is not a Christian. Positively, however, it is so tame (the intruder is only making the modest claim, I am a Christian) that it is very unlikely that this can be more than a part (at most) of the meaning. The man must be claiming to belong to Christ in some special sense. This recalls xi. 23: 'Are they servants of Christ?' And this may in turn point to xi. 15, where behind both 'servants of Satan' and 'servants of righteousness' may lie the same claim to be in a special sense a servant of Christ (and apostle—xi. 13). This probably points to the claim that had been made in Corinth, and had impressed the Corinthians. Possibly no negative implications were explicitly drawn, but hearers of the claim, I am Christ's man, would be left to make their own inferences: This man, not Paul, is the accredited and authoritative apostle. From this it would not be a long step to add, Since Paul claims (wrongly) to be an apostle he must be a false apostle, and if he is a false apostle he is not a Christian at all. Thus Käsemann (*Legitimität*, p. 36/11; not convincingly answered by Kümmel) is at least not far wrong in seeing here an attack on Paul's standing not only as an apostle but as a Christian. It is less probable that there is any connection between this passage and the group referred to in 1 Cor. i. 12, whose watchword was, I belong to Christ. It is far from clear who the so-called 'Christ-party' were, and how they were distinguished from the other groups in Corinth (see *1 Corinthians*, pp. 43-6); but they belong to a set of divisions, or incipient divisions, in the Corinthian church as a whole, whereas we seem here to be dealing with one or more persons who had come to Corinth from without and had laid claim to the church's adherence on the ground of his, or their, special qualifications. Besides, Paul claims that he too belongs to Christ, and can hardly mean that he is a member of the Christ-party. The claim to a special relation with Christ may have meant no more than the claim to be pre-eminent servants of Christ (see above); it may also have included a claim to acquaintance, which Paul did not have, with the historical Jesus; see also v. 16, with the notes. He could and did claim to be equally 'Christ's' (Χριστοῦ); compare 1 Cor. vii. 40. This relationship was dependent not on the chances of history, but on faith and the Spirit; compare Gal. ii. 20; Rom. viii. 9; John xx. 22.

Pressed to the limit, the question raised here is whether Paul is or is not a Christian; it is not this, however, but the question

whether he is or is not an apostle, with an apostle's authority (whatever that may turn out to mean) that is explicitly taken up in
8 the next verse. **For if** (on the text see note 1 on p. 255) **I make a further boast** (that is, beyond that of being, equally with my assailant, 'Christ's') **about our authority, which the Lord gave for building you up, and not for pulling you down** (practically the same words are used at xiii. 10; cf. Jer. i. 10; xxiv. 6)**, I shall not be put to shame.** The same expression is used, in the past tense, at vii. 14 (cf. ix. 3). The boast will prove to be no more than the truth. *Pulling down* recalls x. 4; it applies to that which opposes God, not to the church. The metaphor of *building* is common in Paul; see xii. 19; xiii. 10; 1 Cor. x. 23; xiv. 4, 17; Gal. ii. 18; 1 Thess. v. 11. At v. 1 the word *building* (οἰκοδομή) was used in the sense of that which is built; here it refers to the process, which is described in other terms at i. 24, and indeed runs throughout the epistles. Paul as an apostle has authority, but it is authority to proclaim the Gospel and thus call churches into being, and to watch over their growth once they exist. He has no authority to destroy the work of God; it is implied that when a man so acts as to endanger or damage the church, whatever status he may claim he has no authority and is no apostle. 'If anyone destroys God's temple, God will destroy him' (1 Cor. iii. 17, in a context that uses the figure of building).

It is possible to take the opening words of verse 8 differently: If I boast somewhat excessively about our authority . . . But the words 'somewhat excessively' (περισσότερόν τι) in Paul's usage suggest a real comparison (1 Cor. xii. 23, 24; xv. 10; 2 Cor. i. 12; ii. 4; vii. 13, 15; xi. 23; xii. 15; Gal. i. 14; Phil. i. 14; 1 Thess. ii. 17), and if a comparison is to be found here, it must be in the sense: I can boast of being Christ's (a very paradoxical kind of boasting), and I can boast of more than that, namely, of my authority . . .

The connection of thought with the next verse is very difficult to follow. Literally it begins, ' . . . that I may (might) not seem . . . ', or ' . . . lest I should seem . . . '; but it is not clear whether 'that . . . not' or 'lest' is to be connected with *If I boast*, with *gave*, or with *I shall not be put to shame*. None of these makes very good sense: 'If I boast . . . that I may not seem to frighten'; 'The Lord gave . . . that I might not seem to frighten'; 'I shall not be put to shame lest I should seem to frighten'. It is perhaps a little more

promising to connect verse 9 with *gave not for pulling down*: 'My authority was given not for pulling down lest I should seem to frighten'. But this is by no means satisfactory. The problem may be resolved by taking the opening word (*ἵνα*) of verse 9 as an imperatival particle (Moule, *Idiom*, p. 145): Let me not seem to frighten you! This could be understood as ironical, but the connection would still be poor. Lietzmann supposes in effect that Paul has left out (what would really have been the essential thought) the statement that he would not appeal to his authority. 'I belong to Christ just as much as other people do (verse 7); if I wished to go beyond this claim to equality with my adversaries and boast yet more about myself, namely that I have received from the Lord a special authority, that of an apostle, I should not be put to shame (because it would in fact be true—xii. 6); but he gave me this authority for building you up and not for throwing you down (xiii. 10). I will therefore not bring this authority into play, that I may not come under suspicion of wishing to intimidate you by my letters.' This is probably the best suggestion; Paul was not the most careful of writers, especially when writing, as here, under
emotional stress. We thus translate: **I forbear to do this** (these 9
words are not in the Greek, but make the connection as explained above; some connect verse 9 with verse 11, treating verse 10 as a parenthesis) **lest I should seem as if I were frightening you to death** (Paul uses not the simple verb, *φοβεῖν*, 'to frighten', but the intensive compound, *ἐκφοβεῖν*) **by my letters.** Again, the construction is not clear, though the translation is probably correct. Paul could have written simply '. . . seem to be frightening . . .', but adds a particle, or, as otherwise written, a pair of particles (*ὡσάν*, or *ὡς ἄν*) between *seem* and the infinitive. This is almost but not quite a classical construction (*ἄν* with the infinitive); see Robertson, p. 1095; also pp. 969, 1040. Moule, *Idiom*, p. 152, is probably right in saying that the construction looks like a conflation of 'lest I should seem to frighten you' (*ἵνα μὴ δόξω ἐκφοβεῖν ὑμᾶς*) and 'lest I should seem as if I wished to frighten you' (*ἵνα μὴ δόξω ὡς ἐὰν ἐκφοβεῖν ὑμᾶς βούλωμαι*).

This remark (however we may explain its construction) was not made in the air. As the next verse shows, comment had already been made on Paul's letters. It is not easy to account for this unless the 'severe letter' had been sent and read in Corinth; but if this was so, chapters x–xiii were not the 'severe letter', or part of it.

Plummer sees this difficulty in the common identification of these chapters with the 'severe letter' (see Introduction, pp. 12 ff.), but suggests (unconvincingly) that 1 Cor. v may supply a sufficient explanation.

It was not everyone in Corinth who had made this adverse comment on Paul's letters; the account of the reception of the 'severe letter' given in vii. 9 ff. (though Titus may have exaggerated its good effect) was not altogether false. The adverse comment began, it seems, from a particular person, alluded to but not named in this passage. This is a probable, but not certain,
10 interpretation. **For 'His letters', he says, 'are weighty and powerful'.** *He says* translates a Greek word (*φησίν*; the plural, *φασίν*, 'they say', though read by B, is a simplification which arose mainly in translation—it appears in the Latin and Syriac versions) which is sometimes used in a general sense to mean 'it is said', 'the saying goes'. It is possible that it is so used here: this is what is being said in Corinth. It is however probably incorrect to say (as Lietzmann does) that there is a similar use of the verb at 1 Cor. vi. 16; here we should probably supply as subject 'Scripture' (or 'God'); the words cited are not common opinion but a text of the Old Testament. Moule, *Idiom*, p. 29, quoting B.D. §130.3, thinks of the style of the diatribe: Someone will say . . . But this does not fit the context well; Paul is not speaking of a possible reaction, but of one that has taken place, and to which he is now in turn reacting. M. iii. 293, also referring to the diatribe, renders, 'says my opponent'; compare Robertson, p. 392, 'of his opponent'; similarly Denney and Goudge. This view, that Paul is quoting the words of a specific person, receives a good deal of confirmation from verses 7, 11. No one is named; the words used are capable of generalization; but the multiplication of references (see also xi. 4) adds to the probability that Paul has in mind a leader of the opposition, though verses 12 f.; xi. 12-15 show that others were associated with him. Betz (p. 8 and passim) sees here part of a 'formal pronouncement' (*Gutachten*) of Paul's opponents.

Paul's letters (he had already written at least four to Corinth, but no doubt the 'severe letter' is specially in mind), it is allowed, are weighty and powerful; hence Paul's sensitiveness to the charge, implied by verse 9, that he sets out to terrify people by writing to them. But the opponent makes this point only in order to underline the sneer that follows: **his bodily presence** (what he is when he arrives—the word *παρουσία* is used—in the body) **is weak and his speech** (in the sense both of what he says and how he says it) **excites contempt.** Paul was probably hampered by ill health—see the note on xii. 7; the meaning of *weak* here, however, is 'unimpressive'. Unlike his rivals (see x–xiii passim) he did not know how to impose himself on the churches by violence of action or of speech—or, if he knew, did not choose to use his skill. This lowered his credibility with those who believed that the signs of the Spirit and of apostleship (cf. Wilckens, *Weisheit*, pp. 46 f., 218; also Schmithals, pp. 142-5) were to be seen in inspired and impressive speech, in the aura of a visionary, and in the imposition of the apostle's will on others. Paul represented himself as a slave (iv. 5), asked for and would receive no pay (xi. 7-11; xii. 13; cf. 1 Cor. ix. 12, 18), and had long ago renounced the arts of the sophist (1 Cor. ii. 1-5). Respect for an imposing personality and impressive speech would be common ground to the Corinthians and the rival apostles who were infiltrating into Paul's church (see p. 245; Introduction, pp. 28 ff.; 'Paul's Opponents', pp. 250-3). For Paul as a speaker compare xi. 6, and the note there. It may be that Paul was apt, when speaking excitedly, to tie himself in grammatical knots—as he does in this paragraph.

Paul judges that the time has come to reply. The reader may
wonder if this was a mistake, if Paul would not have done better
to go on being weak in Christ (xiii. 4), and to suffer all the conse-
quential abuse and scorn. There is, however, if we are to believe
Paul, a time when being a fool for Christ's sake (1 Cor. iv. 10)
involves being the kind of fool who speaks in x–xiii, answering
other fools according to their folly; a time when continuing
weakness and meekness are even more exposed to misunderstanding than vigorous defence and counter-attack. **Let the man who** 11
says that kind of thing (literally, such a man, referring back to
verse 10) **bear this in mind** (the word of verse 7, *λογίζεσθαι*,
is repeated), **that when present** (Paul is now looking forward to
a third visit; see xii. 14; xiii. 1, and cf. i. 23; ii. 1) **we shall be in
action just the same** (*τοιοῦτοι—οἷοι*) **that we are in word
through our letters when absent.** In a word, Paul is, and means
to be, consistent. If his letters, and one of them in particular,
seemed severe, this was not because he was unwilling, or afraid,
to say hard things face to face. When he was absent a letter must
serve; but now he means to be present, and will act in terms of

what he has written. There is only one Paul; and when plain speech is called for he will give it, whether on paper or face to face.

He moves on to ironical counter-attack; he has no high opinion of those who have invaded his church and perverted the loyalty
12 of his people. **For we do not dare to class or compare ourselves** (it does not seem possible to represent Paul's word-play in English: to judge ourselves among, *ἐγκρῖναι*, a word used by Josephus, *War* ii. 138 for enrolment in the Essene society, or to judge ourselves with, *συγκρῖναι*) **with some** (*τισιν*, certain people—the Corinthians would know that he was referring to rival apostles, probably the false apostles of xi. 13 ff.) **of those who commend themselves.** Paul has no time for self-commendation (see iii. 1; v. 12, and the notes), and little for the commendation of others (though he is glad to be commended by his own churches, whose very existence commends him: iii. 2; 1 Cor. ix. 2); he is no apostle of men (Gal. i. 1), and Christ's commendation (whose apostle he is) is of the paradoxical kind described in iv. 8 ff.; vi. 8 ff.; 1 Cor. iv. 10–13. It is however the clear implication of Paul's ironical words that the rival apostles made much of the business of commendation. Paul does not count himself in their number, nor will he compare himself with them—the Corinthians had been making comparisons, but he will not join them in the game.

Self-commendation robs those who practise it of any objective standard of judgement, and thus of any means of understanding themselves or their environment. **They, measuring themselves by themselves, and comparing themselves with themselves, are without understanding** (*οὐ συνιᾶσιν*; this verb can be used without an object—Schlatter compares Matt. xiii. 19, 23). This difficult sentence can be differently construed: M. iii. 160 takes the participles (*measuring*, *μετροῦντες*, and *comparing*, *συγκρίνοντες*) to be dependent on *do not understand* (as a verb of perceiving), and translates, 'they do not realise that they are measuring themselves by their own standards'. This is a possible view, and though it inverts the relation of the participles to the main verb ('because they act thus they do not understand'; 'they do not understand that they are acting thus'), it gives a substantially similar overall meaning to the verse, namely, that which was outlined above: their behaviour goes with their failure to understand, whether as cause or as consequence—indeed the use of present participles means that we need not distinguish too nicely between the two. It is however fair to say that the rivals had no intention of measuring themselves by Paul's apostolic standard, and the rendering adopted in the text may for this reason be preferred—they knew quite well that they were using their own standards, and did not mean to use any others. What they failed to understand was that measurement by their own standards meant in effect the use of no standards at all. This leads to the thought of the next verse. For the textual problem involved in the step from verse 12 to verse 13, see below.

It is implied by the next words that Paul's rivals have boasted of their apostolic status. Since, when one measures himself by himself, it is hardly possible to achieve less than complete success,
their boasting had had no measure or limit. **We however shall** 13
boast in no unmeasured way, or, to no unmeasured degree. Since the only measurement, or limit, or standard, of Paul's apostolic life and ministry was Jesus Christ (e.g. iv. 10; Gal. ii. 20; 1 Cor. xi. 1, with the important limiting clause) there was no possibility of his running past the scale by which they were measured. His use however of *in no unmeasured way* (especially in Greek, εἰς τὰ ἄμετρα; for this Moule, *Idiom*, p. 71, suggests: by reference to a standard which we have no right to use, but it is not clear how this rendering is reached, or what exactly it means) suggests a new idea which considerably complicates both the thought and language of the rest of the paragraph. Before proceeding with this, we must note a variant reading which gives a different turn to the argument. The last words of verse 12 and the first of verse 13, *are without understanding. We however* (οὐ συνιᾶσιν. ἡμεῖς δέ) are omitted by D* G, a few other Greek MSS, by the Old Latin and in part by the Vulgate. The short text has received strong support (e.g. B.D. §416.2; Windisch; Käsemann; Bultmann; Héring). If it is accepted, the translation must be: But we ourselves, measuring ourselves by ourselves and comparing ourselves with ourselves (or, though we measure ourselves by ourselves and compare ourselves with ourselves), shall boast in no unmeasured way. Reference (unless by allusion; see below) to Paul's rivals now falls away, and measurement and comparison by one's own standard have to be given a different sense—since they are done by Paul they must be understood to be (in his view) good. Presumably they will mean that since his

standard is what it is (namely, the objective one of Jesus) there is no fear that he (perhaps he hints—as some do) will boast without measure. But this is forced; it is not easy to find a good sense for 'measuring ourselves by ourselves', even by reference to 1 Cor. ii. 15 f. (Kümmel against Käsemann). This argument however could be reversed: Why should the Western Text introduce the difficulty? The answer to this question probably lies in the observation that all the witnesses for the short text are either Latin or Graeco-Latin. In Hellenistic (not classical) Greek, the plural reflexive pronoun (ἑαυτούς) was common to all persons: in Latin the persons were distinguished. A translator would be obliged in the middle of verse 12 to choose what person of the pronoun he intended to use. A short-sighted translator could have chosen, wrongly, the first person, and written 'sed ipsi in nobis nosmet ipsos metientes et comparantes nosmet ipsos nobis'; he would now find the third person, *they are without understanding* (οὐ συνιᾶσιν) unintelligible, and would drop it. The next two words, We however (ἡμεῖς δέ), though superfluous would not be meaningless; some Latin witnesses retain them (nos autem), others do not. It is not claimed that this explanation of the textual history of these verses is completely convincing, but it is perhaps as convincing as any (few commentators attempt one); and the strongest argument in favour of the long text remains the drift of the passage. 'Paul objects to his opponents that they commend themselves, measure themselves by themselves instead of by a divine measuring-rod independent of themselves, and through this unmeasured glorying prove themselves to be without understanding; Paul himself does not measure himself by himself, but by the measuring-rod given him by God (verse 13)' (Kümmel). Compare Bachmann's argument that the short text is to be rejected because (a) it makes the pronoun (αὐτοί) in verse 12 superfluous, and (b) to measure oneself by oneself is not the way to avoid unmeasured boasting.

The clue to the very difficult sentences that follow is to be found in the observation made above on *We shall boast in no unmeasured way*. This means in the first place, We shall not boast excessively; but the notion of measurement (involved in εἰς τὰ ἄμετρα) carries the mind further. Measurement implies an instrument of measurement, such as a measuring-rod (in Greek, κανών), and Paul proceeds to use this word in verses 13, 15, 16 (cf. Gal. vi. 16, the only other use in the New Testament). This word, in its ordinary usage (cf. e.g. Aristophanes, *Birds* 992-1021, where Meton, equipped with various κανόνες, proceeds to measure, μετρεῖν, Cloudcuckooland), suggests the measurement of lengths and areas. It was frequently used in a variety of senses (Hughes thinks of the 'course or lane' which 'was measured out for each of the runners' in a race; see also Schweizer, *C.O.N.T.*, n. 779, and H. W. Beyer in *T.W.N.T.* iii. 603 f.), but Paul (as various words in the context, suggesting stretch, extent, and the like, show) was aware of and did not forget this primary meaning, which appears quite clearly in verse 16. God had provided a standard of apostolic behaviour and of apostolic preaching; he had moreover assigned to the various apostles their appropriate fields of work (Gal. ii. 9; this does not necessarily refer to geographical areas—the agreement probably contained an unfortunate ambiguity), and here too the notion of measurement was appropriate. It is perhaps impossible to find a single English word that will serve the various purposes to which Paul applies his Greek word in these few verses; I have adopted *province* (*Shorter Oxford English Dictionary*, s.v., II: 'The sphere of action of a person or body of persons; duty, office, business, function, department') as possibly the least unsatisfactory.

We shall boast in no unmeasured way, **but only** (for ἀλλά in this sense see L.S. s.v. I 3, and s.v. ἀλλ' ἤ; M. i. 241; B.D. §448.8; M.M. s.v.) **according to the measure of the province God dealt out to us as our measure, that we might reach as far as you.** The way in which the two words *measure* and *province* are used in this sentence shows that Schlatter (p. 624) can hardly be right when he says 'The measure, μέτρον, is measured by the measuring-rod, κανών'; nor is Bachmann convincing in the view that the latter is simply a more precise definition of the former. If Paul is going to boast at all, he will do so not in terms of what he himself has done, but of what God has done through him in the evangelization of hitherto untouched territory: 'Here then is the glorying [or boasting; καύχησις] I have in Christ Jesus, in things relating to God; for I will not dare to say anything of the things which Christ did not carry out through me for the obedience of the Gentiles . . . so that from Jerusalem and round about as far as Illyricum I have completed the Gospel of Christ, being in this way ambitious to preach the Gospel not where Christ had been named, lest I should build upon someone else's foundation' (Rom.

xv. 17-20). In fulfilling this divine assignment Paul had reached Corinth, and the success there of his missionary work in calling a church into being was proof that he had rightly understood his commission and that God had approved of his work. It is thus right to say with Käsemann (*Legitimität*, pp. 60/49 f.; Kümmel agrees), 'Since the existence of the Corinthians as Christians arose out of his apostolic ministry, they, if they wished to contest his legitimacy, would have to admit that they were not Christians. The apostle has become the measure assigned to them, just as they are his'. It is not right however to exclude reference to the appointed areas of apostolic work, which were to Paul a matter of considerable importance. The last words in the verse, *that we might reach* (ἐφικέσθαι, an infinitive loosely attached to *dealt out*, ἐμέρισεν) *as far as you*, relate in the first instance to Paul's itinerancy. Verse 16 puts this beyond question.

The Greek of this verse is made no simpler by some rather irregular attraction (the antecedent of the relative οὗ is μέτρον but it is attracted into the case of κανόνος; μέτρου then necessarily follows—see M. iii. 324; Robertson, p. 719; B.D. §294.5).

14 **For** (in making the claim at the end of verse 13) **we are not overstretching ourselves, as if we did not reach as far as you, for in the Gospel of Christ** (that is, in preaching the Gospel, as its ministers and envoys) **we got to you first** (that is, before any of our rivals). It is implied that, in the claims they make, Paul's rivals are *overstretching* themselves. Allo's note is worth quoting: 'In order to depict the claims of these people Paul evokes a picture which is really comical (and very little understood); with all their letters of commendation, their self-praise, their intrigues designed to capture the minds of the Corinthians, with whom, though they reside among them, they still do not seem to feel that they are really in contact, they look like little men who are standing on their toes and stretching their arms as high as they can, in order to touch the desired object, which is still too high for them.' Allo's picture is correct, but not his inference; the little men had made a very deep impression on the Corinthians. What they failed to do was to establish any foundation for their claims. In this sense Paul still *reached* as far as Corinth (and this will be the force of the present participle ἐφικνούμενοι).

It can hardly be accidental that in the second part of the verse (*we got to you first*) Paul uses a different verb (φθάνειν) from that which he used in verses 13, 14a (ἐφικνεῖσθαι). It is true that Paul sometimes (Rom. ix. 31; Phil. iii. 16; 1 Thess. ii. 16) uses this verb to mean simply arrival, without any sense of anticipation; but this sense, which properly belongs to the verb in Greek usage generally, appears in 1 Thess. iv. 15, and should be understood here. It is impossible to deny that the rivals did get to Corinth—they are there at the time of writing. But Paul got there first. This was not simply a distinction that no subsequent event could obliterate; it meant that Corinth was part of the virgin territory that Paul claimed as his special mission field (see Rom. xv. 17-20, quoted above). He has staked a claim, not for himself but for the Gospel, and the intruders, with their strange Gospel (xi. 4), have no right to interfere. This vital point is missed by both Käsemann (*Legitimität*, pp. 56/43 ff.) and Bultmann (*Probleme*, pp. 20-23) in their dispute about the meaning of verses 12 ff. See however Betz, pp. 130 ff.

In the opening words of the next verse Paul restates the position.
We **do not boast in an unmeasured way** (cf. verse 13) **in other** 15
men's labours. Compare Rom. xv. 20. *In an unmeasured way* has now moved into the sense, 'in respect of work done outside the area of evangelism measured out to us by God'. If there is to be any sort of expansion it will not be by an inflated estimate of his own past or by poaching on other men's preserves, but by the increasing faith of those whom Paul has already won as converts, and by the spread of the mission into new and hitherto untouched areas. This is rather obscurely expressed in verses 15b, 16. We **have the hope** (Allo remarks that Paul is still fundamentally hopeful about the Corinthian situation) **that, as your faith increases** (a genitive absolute)**, we may grow in your estimation** (ἐν ὑμῖν, which could be connected with the preceding clause but would there be tautologous—Kümmel) **according to our**
province, and in such overflowing measure that we may 16
preach the Gospel in (εἰς with the accusative for ἐν with the dative) **the areas beyond you, and not boast** (as some do) **in ready-made achievements in someone else's province.** There can be little doubt that this translation (which has been helped out by the provision of conjunctions and the conversion of participles and infinitives into finite verbs) gives the sense that Paul meant to convey; several details however are uncertain, and call for discussion.

As your faith increases may reflect a claim that, since Paul's time in Corinth, the Corinthians' faith had moved on to a higher level—he must not expect to find them, now that they have had the advantage of instruction by better qualified teachers, as he had left them. Well; we will hope that your faith does increase (cf. 1 Cor. iv. 8), but that we may grow with it. Paul's word may mean 'to be magnified' in the sense of 'praised', 'glorified' (as at Phil. i. 20), or actually 'to become larger'; the translation inclines to the latter but preserves something of both senses. This growth, since it would be in Corinth, would be in relation to *our province*—the unevangelized Gentile world assigned by God to Paul as the area, the circumstances, in which his apostleship is to be exercised. This, Paul hopes, will happen to excess (εἰς περισσείαν; see viii. 2; Rom. v. 17—the only other Pauline occurrences of the word), not in the sense that he himself will be valued and praised beyond his deserts (cf. xii. 6; xiii. 7), but in that his influence, or rather the influence of the Gospel, may spread beyond the Corinthian sector of his apostolic province. This Paul proceeds to state explicitly; and the best comment on verse 16a is provided by Rom. xv. 23 f., written, in all probability, either at or near Corinth (see *Romans*, pp. 3 f.). What Paul has in mind is an evangelistic journey leading on from his present Aegean field to Rome, and further to Spain. The geographical reference here confirms the view of *measure* and *province* (μέτρον and κανών) taken above against Käsemann (*Legitimität*, pp. 56-61/43-51), though he may well be right in thinking that it was Paul's adversaries who first employed these words; and they may have used them in a different way. It is fruitless to draw lines on the map from Rome or Spain to Corinth and produce them eastward in the hope of finding whether this verse was written in Ephesus (as the 'severe letter' probably was), or, like chapters i–ix, in Macedonia. *The regions beyond you* were conceived not in terms of geometry but of missionary strategy—'the next places on the list'.

By proceeding in this way, though Rome would constitute a possibly embarrassing exception, Paul would be able to avoid the province of others (such as Peter, his Jerusalem colleagues, and their dependants), and so far from boasting in *ready-made achievements* (εἰς τὰ ἕτοιμα, things one would find ready to hand) would have to begin again from scratch. It is implied (and as we have seen the theme runs through the paragraph as a whole) that the rival apostles are content to work in another man's (notably Paul's) province, to appropriate (and spoil) his results, and to boast of their second-hand achievements. See Introduction, pp. 28 ff.

Paul drives home the point with a biblical quotation and a
summary. **If anyone is to boast** (or glory), **let him boast** (or 17
glory) **in the Lord.** Paul uses the same words (apart from the particle δέ) in 1 Cor. i. 31 (see the note; the recurrence of the quotation here must weaken the view that in 1 Corinthians Paul was quoting from—even preaching on—the Haphtorah for Ab 9; the verse sums up what he has learnt from the Old Testament). Jer. ix. 22 f. (LXX) runs: Let not the wise man boast in his wisdom, and let not the strong man boast in his strength, and let not the wealthy man boast in his wealth, but let him who boasts boast in this, that he understands and knows that I am the Lord, who do mercy and judgement and righteousness on the earth. The passage quoted makes a positive point, which is admirably taken up by Betz, p. 96; there is a proper 'boasting', which should not be omitted because boasting can be misapplied (see p. 70). It is however with the implied negatives that Paul is concerned here, though they are not so clearly apt in this chapter as they are at 1 Cor. i. 31, since those who are unjustifiably boasting are not men of wisdom, power (in the ordinary sense), or wealth, but the intruding apostles, who commend themselves to the Corinthians as servants of Christ and authorized representatives of the true church. The passage nevertheless does apply to them (since, as Calvin notes, it means that it is by the Lord's judgement alone
that we stand or fall), **for it is not the man who commends** 18
himself (cf. iii. 1; v. 12) **who can be accepted as approved** (δόκιμος, tested and approved; cf. xiii. 7; also Rom. xiv. 18; xvi. 10; 1 Cor. xi. 19, with the notes), **but the man whom the Lord commends.** Self-commendation may produce an impressive personality, but this is not synonymous with apostleship. If it is asked how it may be known whom the Lord (here undoubtedly Jesus Christ—significant in view of the use of an Old Testament passage where 'the Lord' meant God; see Bousset, *Kyrios Christos* (1913), p. 122) commends, Paul has no answer to give, save that the true apostle bears the true Gospel (xi. 4; cf. Gal. i. 8 f.), and in life as well as teaching is conformed to the image of the Lord's death (iv. 10; xiii. 4; Phil. iii. 10). But his discussion of the matter has scarcely begun.

18 xi. 1-15. THE CHURCH AT CORINTH ENDANGERED BY RIVAL APOSTLES

(1) I wish you would put up with me in a little foolishness; yes, do put up with me; (2) for I am jealous for you, with God's own jealousy, for I betrothed you to one man, with a view to presenting you as a pure virgin to Christ; (3) and I am afraid lest, as the snake in his craftiness deceived Eve, your minds should be corrupted from the sincerity[1] of their attachment to Christ. (4) For if your visitor proclaims another Jesus, whom we did not proclaim, or you receive a different Spirit, which you did not receive, or a different Gospel, which you did not accept, then you put up[2] with him all right! (5) For I consider that I come behind the super-apostles in no way at all. (6) I may be unskilled in speech, but I am not unskilled in knowledge; on the contrary, in every way we have revealed it[3] to you in all things. (7) Or did I commit a sin in humbling myself that you might be exalted, by preaching the Gospel of God to you for nothing? (8) I robbed other churches by taking pay from them in order that I might be able to serve you, (9) and when I was present with you and fell into want I made myself a burden to no one, for the brothers who came from Macedonia supplied my need, and in every way I kept, and I will keep, myself from being burdensome to you. (10) As Christ's truth is in me, I shall not be silenced in this boasting in the whole province of Achaea. (11) Why? Because I do not love you? God knows the truth about that. (12) But what I am doing, that I will also continue to do, in order to cut off opportunity from those who would like to have an

[1] Many of the best and oldest MSS (including 𝔓[46] B ℵ D G it) add 'and purity' (or have 'purity and sincerity'). They may be right, but the addition was probably suggested by *pure* in verse 2 (Lietzmann). The variable position of 'purity' confirms its inauthenticity.

[2] The text translated (ἀνέχεσθε) is that of 𝔓[46] B D* 33 sa; the majority of MSS, including ℵ G vg, have ἀνείχεσθε, which, notwithstanding the absence of ἄν, is presumably intended potentially: if he comes, you would ... This is a weakening of what Paul wrote; the Corinthians had already been taken in.

[3] For the text see the commentary.

opportunity to become, in their boasting, just what we are. (13) For such men are false apostles, deceitful workmen, disguising themselves as apostles of Christ. (14) And no wonder; for Satan himself disguises himself as an angel of light. (15) It is no great thing therefore if his servants too disguise themselves as servants of righteousness. Their end will correspond to their deeds.

x. 12-18 is a digression, though, like most of Paul's digressions, it is related to the main theme, since it deals with boasting and counter-boasting, self-commendation and commendation by God. In x. 11 Paul gave notice that he would make a vigorous personal response to those who challenged his position; he is now preparing for personal encounter by bringing the Corinthians, who will witness rather than take part in the encounter, into the right frame of mind. He is concerned for them, and angry with those who are imperilling their position as Christians.

I wish (the construction, with ὄφελον, is the same as at 1 Cor. 1
iv. 8; Gal. v. 12; see B.D. §359.1) **you would put up with me** (ἀνέχεσθαι takes the genitive—μου—as at xi. 19; Col. iii. 13) **in a little** (μικρόν τι is accusative of respect; Robertson, p. 486) **foolishness.** Paul's argument in chapters xi and xii is all brought under the heading of *foolishness*, a fact of which he constantly reminds his readers; see xi. 1, 16, 17, 19, 21; xii. 6, 11. There is no escape from it: the Corinthians compelled Paul to it (xii. 11)—that is, he saw it as the only way to make them see the truth, to look at what was immediately before them (x. 7). This kind of folly, like church order (which is in fact a part of it), is a function of the church's life in the world. Christians have not always been as successful as Paul in distinguishing between regrettable and unnecessary folly, regrettable but necessary folly, and divine wisdom. In the next clause it is impossible to be certain whether the verb (ἀνέχεσθε) is indicative or imperative. If the latter, the conjunction (*but*, ἀλλά) is copulative: I wish you would . . . yes, do; if the former, it is adversative: I wish you would . . . but in truth you already do. Notwithstanding Lietzmann, who thinks it impossible, the imperative may be chosen as making a better connection with what follows (B.D. §448.6; Robertson, p. 1186).
**Yes, do put up with me; for I am jealous for you, with God's 2
own jealousy.** Paul has serious fears that the Corinthians may

have abandoned not him only but the Christian faith he had taught them. He is jealous for them, over against the intruders, but not on his own account. *With God's own jealousy* could be little more than a superlative (cf. x. 4, and the note), but here the context requires the full force of the words; it is God's jealousy that lies behind Paul's (so, e.g., Goudge).

Jealousy is naturally taken up in a metaphor drawn from marriage. **For I betrothed** (Paul uses the middle, instead of the more usual active voice, of ἁρμόζειν, perhaps because of his personal concern in the matter, M. i. 160—he was, as it were, the bride's father (xii. 14; 1 Cor. iv. 15); but Philo uses the middle: *Leg. Alleg.* ii. 67; *De Abr.* 100) **you** (collectively—the whole church of Corinth is the bride; 'non singulatim, sed conjunctim' (Bengel)) **to one man** (the emphasis is on the fact that there is one person, and one only, to whom the Corinthians owe their allegiance)**, with a view to presenting you as a pure virgin** (bride—cf. 1 Cor. vii. 36 and the note) **to Christ**—the one to whom faithfulness is due. The presentation to Christ will presumably take place at his coming; the betrothal correspondingly refers to the conversion of the Corinthians and the establishing of their church. In the meantime, during the period of the engagement, it is the duty of the Corinthians to keep themselves completely loyal to the one to whom they are to be united—within Paul's metaphor, to preserve their virgin status. It is because Paul doubts their will, or ability, to do this that he writes. It is not his intention to produce a new allegorical interpretation of the marriage figure (already familiar in the Old Testament), or of the story of Adam, Eve, and the snake; these are introduced as incidental illustrations, and it is for this reason that the imagery of verse 3 is confused—for this reason also that the best approach to verse 3 is recollection of the historical circumstances, in which (as Paul sees them) Christians who, with all their faults, had received from him the Gospel of Christ in its purity are being won over to a radically different (even if superficially similar) Gospel by men whom he can only regard as being, like the snake in Eden, servants or impersonations of Satan (verses 13 ff.).

The Eden story recounts the loss of man's innocence, and had already (it seems) been elaborated in the sense that the snake was believed actually to have seduced Eve, who was thus not merely tempted into disobedience but lost her virginity in unfaithfulness to the man whose partner she had been created to be. This development of the story (see in addition to the commentaries Bousset-Gressmann, p. 408; Schoeps, *Paulus*, p. 29, E.T. p. 39; W. D. Davies, p. 32; E. E. Ellis, *Paul's Use of the Old Testament* (1957), p. 129; E. Brandenburger, *Adam und Christus* (1962), pp. 45, 50) is rabbinic (Yebamoth 103b; Abodah Zarah 22b; Shabbath 146a), but is alluded to also in earlier apocalypses: 1 Enoch lxix. 6, Gadreel . . . led astray Eve (this may but need not mean seduction); 2 Enoch xxxi. 6, He enticed and seduced Eve, but did not touch Adam; Apoc. of Abraham 23, Now look again in the picture, who it is who seduced Eve and what is the fruit of the tree. There may be an allusion in 1 Tim. ii. 14, where the same word for deceived (*ἐξαπατᾶν*) is used as in verse 3. The image of Israel as God's bride occurs at Hos. i–iii; Ezek. xvi; Isa. l. 1; liv. 1-6; compare Eph. v. 22-33; Rev. xix. 7; xxi. 2, 9; xxii. 17; see C. Chavasse, *The Bride of Christ* (1940), and Windisch's long note on the church as the bride of Christ (pp. 320 ff.). There is no uniformity in detail; various authors use, and may use independently, a sufficiently obvious image to bring out God's election of and love for Israel, and the obligation upon Israel to have no dealings with strange gods. For the language compare Sotah iii. 3, where the wife suspected of adultery may confess, 'I am unclean'.

I am afraid: this is part of the pastoral care referred to in xi. 28, 3
and is the motive for writing. To judge from the tone of x–xiii as a whole, and indeed of the next few verses, Paul says less than he feels. At least he recognizes a real danger that his work in Corinth may be lost, and that the church there may perish (see however on this Barth, *C.D.* III ii. 302-5). As 1 Cor. ix. 27; x. 1-13 show, he did not believe that either he or his fellow Christians enjoyed any security before God. Neither their participation in baptism and the Lord's Supper, nor the original purity and innocence of their faith, could act as a safeguard to prevent corruption. 'Ecclesia semper reformanda': because the church is always exposed to corruption it must always give heed to the apostolic admonition. Paul is afraid **lest, as the snake in his craftiness deceived** (*ἐξηπάτησεν*; cf. Gen. iii. 13; Philo, *Leg. Alleg.* iii. 59; also Rom. vii. 11) **Eve, your minds** (*νοήματα*, as at iii. 14; iv. 4; not as at ii. 11; x. 5) **should be corrupted** and so seduced **from the sincerity** (*ἁπλότης*; see viii. 2, and the note; on the text here see note 1 on p. 270) **of their attachment to Christ** (literally, from

their sincerity to Christ, εἰς Χριστόν). It is not certain that Paul says that the snake seduced Eve. His word, a compound form of that used at Gen. iii. 13, can bear this meaning (as e.g. at Herodotus ii. 114), but need not do so; it may mean simply 'to lead astray', that is, into disobedience to God's command. There is no need for Paul to develop this point, for in the situation he is dealing with disobedience to God and unfaithfulness to the bridegroom (Christ) are one and the same thing. The snake as the representative of Satan (or possibly as Satan in disguise; see verse 14, and cf. Wisd. ii. 24) is the supreme exponent of *craftiness*; compare iv. 2; 1 Cor. iii. 19; and see especially Betz, pp. 104 ff.—'The passages cited justify the conclusion that the abusive word πανοῦργος [crafty] was used especially in antisophistic polemic and in polemic against religious superstition' (p. 105). It is thus, in Betz's view, especially appropriate in Paul's apology. In xii. 16 Paul is accused of craftiness in cheating the Corinthians of their money; it is the sort of charge that can easily be flung from side to side, and as the next few verses show, Paul saw the snake's *craftiness* in the behaviour of his rivals (see especially verse 13; also 'False Apostles'). The result of their work, if successful, as Paul fears it may be—perhaps that it has been—would be to corrupt not the Corinthians' morals (it is noteworthy that Paul expresses no fears on this count; this is consistent with the view that the intruders were a strict Judaizing rather than a gnostic party—see Introduction, pp. 28 ff.) but their thinking, that is, their understanding of the Gospel. That Paul does not take this in a purely intellectual way is shown by the last phrase, a pregnant one, in the verse. What is at stake is not in the modern sense orthodoxy but sincerity of attachment to Christ. This is a different form of the test of 1 Cor. xii. 3 (cf. Rom. x. 9). Sincerely to say, Jesus is Lord, is an adequate sign of Christian faith; the role of the intellect is to examine the question whether the Jesus of whom lordship is predicated, is the real Jesus of the authentic apostolic proclamation (cf. 1 Cor. xv. 3 f.), or another Jesus.

With the next verse we come to a 'key-point for the understanding of the opponents who appeared in Corinth' (Käsemann,
4 *Legitimität*, p. 38/14). **For** (γάρ; this gives a double connection,
grounding both the fear expressed in verse 3, and the appeal—*Put up with me*—in verse 1; Paul prefixes the particle μέν; there is no answering δέ (though B supplies one in verse 5), but Paul

implies: You put up with him, but you do not put up with me—with one who merely *comes*, as against one who is *sent*, an apostle) **if your visitor** (literally, he who comes, ὁ ἐρχόμενος) **proclaims another** (ἄλλον) **Jesus, whom we did not proclaim, or you receive a different** (ἕτερον) **Spirit, which you did not** formerly **receive** (ἐλάβετε), **or a different** (ἕτερον) **Gospel, which you did not** formerly **accept** (marking a different, though probably a synonymous verb, ἐδέξασθε), **then you put up** (on the text see note 2 on p. 270) **with him all right** (καλῶς; cf. Mark vii. 9 for the ironical use of this word)! This verse raises a number of questions in itself; on its relation with the following verses, see below, pp. 277 f.; also 'Paul's Opponents', pp. 242 ff. Schoeps, *Paulus*, p. 74, E.T. p. 79, may well be right in the view that Paul had himself been accused of preaching another Jesus and a different Gospel.

Your visitor may be a pure generalization—any one who comes with a new Gospel (see Allo: le premier venu); compare Gal. v. 10, anyone who troubles you. This interpretation however is not entirely satisfactory. There is in our passage no equivalent to the 'whoever he may be' (ὅστις ἐὰν ᾖ) of Gal. v. 10, and the singulars of x. 7 (τις), 10 (φησίν), 11 (ὁ τοιοῦτος) must not be forgotten. It is certain that Paul was faced in Corinth by a plurality of opponents; there is at least some reason to suspect (see in addition to the above passages ii. 5-8; vii. 12, with the notes) that they had a ringleader. Schlatter's view that the visitor was a 'judge' from Jerusalem, and that Paul is not writing ironically ('You may indeed put up with the intruders if the one who comes—Peter, perhaps—decides in their favour'), has little to commend it.

That Paul could distinguish between *other* and *different* is shown by Gal. i. 6 f.; it does not however appear that he does so here. So, rightly, M. iii. 197 ('found together for variety'); Robertson, p. 747 ('It may be that variety . . . is all that induces the change here. But it is also possible that Paul stigmatizes the gospel of the Judaizers as ἕτερον (cf. Gal. i. 6) and the Spirit preached by them, while he is unwilling to admit another (ἄλλον) Jesus even of the same type as preached by him') is not convincing. It might be nearer to the truth (though it cannot be claimed that this is required by Paul's language) that Paul's rivals preach the same Jesus differently (that is, according to the flesh; v. 16) apprehended, and that this results in a different Gospel and a different religious experience. Compare Schmithals, p. 54. Calvin's attempt to distinguish this passage from Gal. i. 8, and his argument that Paul is here dealing not with a false Gospel but only with the Gospel preached by other preachers, are unconvincing.

The *different Gospel* of Gal. i. 6, though at that point in the epistle stated in quite general terms, suggests the errors of the Judaizers, and it is natural to think that the same meaning will apply in 2 Corinthians. This harmonizes with the view that the intruders were Judaizing envoys of the Jerusalem church, but not with other views about them (for a good summary of different views of the *different Gospel* see Goppelt, p. 128). A decision about the identity of the opponents cannot be reached on the basis of this verse alone (see Introduction, pp. 28 ff., and 'Paul's Opponents'). It is right to note that along with the *different Gospel* stand *another Jesus* and a *different Spirit*. According to Georgi, *Gegner*, these additional terms show what distinguishes the new Gospel from Paul's. 'Above all, the difference lies in Christology' (p. 285). The use of the simple name Jesus points, he thinks, not to a gnostic Christology but to an interpretation of the earthly Jesus, and the clue is given by iv. 5. It is the humble behaviour of Paul that marks him out, over against his adversaries, as a true witness to the lordship of Christ. Thus the interpretation of the earthly Jesus that Paul rejects here is one that is bound up with the tradition used by his adversaries and with their own consciousness of spiritual authority. 'Precisely this last observation leads to the suggestion that the adversaries maintained a Christology in which Jesus appeared as an outstanding spiritual man [*Pneumatiker*], as a θεῖος ἀνήρ ['divine man']' (p. 286). Lütgert reached a somewhat similar view of the intruders on the basis of the *different Spirit* (see Käsemann, *Legitimität*, pp. 39 f./17).

Georgi's argument falls short of proof. (a) It does not give due weight to the fact that Paul mentions not only *another Jesus* but also a *different Spirit*. (b) It is not quite correct to say that in Paul the simple name Jesus must point to the earthly Jesus. (c) It is a disputable question (see Introduction, pp. 29 f.) whether the adversaries thought of themselves as being in the class of 'divine men'. Georgi is however right in seeing a close connection between the different Gospel and its understanding of Jesus on the one hand, and on the other the moral characteristics of the apostles who maintained it, and of this iv. 5 is a good indication; the ultimate question is whether the interpretation of Jesus provided by Paul's apostolic preaching and practice is correct (see *Signs*, pp. 77-81). If it is, it is reasonable to infer that an interpretation of Jesus as a 'divine man', maintained by apostles who regarded themselves as 'divine men', would be mistaken; but it is a further inference, with no basis in the present passage, that the Corinthian opposition so regarded themselves, and Jesus. Paul's only test of the Spirit is that of 1 Cor. xii. 3; and his complaint against the preachers of the *different Gospel* appears to be that they do not treat Jesus crucified as Lord—even though they may profess to regard him in this way.

A different Gospel, another Jesus, a *different Spirit*, and another apostle thus go together. And if a *visitor* appears who is such an apostle and preaches such a Gospel, the Corinthians receive him and bear with him. It is not a hypothetical question of what in certain circumstances they might do, but a matter of what they are in fact doing. The visitor is there, and the Corinthians are listening to him. Paul does not tell them that they must not do this, or that they should excommunicate his rival, even though he uses plenty of hard words. At this point, all Paul asks is that the same measure of toleration should be granted to him as is accorded a teacher of error. Paul hardly knows a heretic 'in the sense of a fellow-Christian, concerning whose divergent belief one is convinced that it excludes him from salvation' (W. Bauer, *Rechtgläubigkeit und Ketzerei* (1934), p. 236). He does however ask to
be tolerated, **for** (γάρ) **I consider that I come behind the super-** 5
apostles in no way at all (μηδέν is emphatic). A first impression of this verse is that Paul asks to be treated as well as the *visitor* (verse 4), because he is not his inferior; that is to say, the *visitor* (and this may be a general term, concealing a plural) is identified with the *super-apostles*. Since we hear later that the *visitor* and his like are servants of Satan (verses 13 ff.) it is impossible to identify the *super-apostles* with the Jerusalem apostles, Peter and his colleagues. This view is held by many, but not in this commentary. The evidence, of which some has appeared in chapter x, multiplies from this point onward; in the commentary it will be discussed as it comes. See also Introduction, pp. 28-32, and 'Paul's Opponents'.

'The transition from verse 4 to verses 5 f. (γάρ) seems far from clear' (Windisch); certainly much less clear than might at first appear, for the *for* with which verse 5 opens gives the third of three grounds for the appeal of verse 1, which is the real point of connection. I ask you to put up with me: (a) for I am, and have reason to be, really concerned about you; (b) for you put up with a false apostle who preaches a false Gospel; (c) for I am equal to the highest apostles of all. This gives a reasonable and intelligible progression of thought; and to it may be added the argument that Paul is unlikely to have made the modest claim that he was not excelled by those whom in the context (verses 13 ff.) he was to describe as the servants of Satan. 'That cannot be explained, even as mockery. There is no sort of comparison with servants of Satan' (Käsemann, *Legitimität*, p. 42/21). Bultmann (*Probleme*, pp. 26 f.; see also Schmithals, p. 53, note 1) replies against Käsemann that comparison with the false apostles is understandable if done in a sharp attempt to open the eyes of the Corinthians to the truth, and argues that the reference in verse 6 to *speech* and *knowledge* shows that Paul is comparing himself with someone who is known to the Corinthians because he is already on the spot (note the similar comparison at xii. 11 f.). But *speech* and *knowledge* are best taken not as a reference to claims made by Paul's rivals, but as criteria employed by the Corinthians; hence their use by Paul here. The balance of probability lies with Käsemann's view; compare Héring: 'The super-apostles . . . can hardly be other than those of Jerusalem'.

Super-apostles is an ironical expression (interesting parallels are given by Betz, p. 121), and recalls the irony with which Paul writes of the so-called 'pillars' in Jerusalem (see *Studia Paulina*, pp. 1-19). Goppelt, p. 126, may be right in thinking that the irony is directed not against the Jerusalem apostles themselves but against the appeal made to them and their authority; but that there is at least some connection with Jerusalem is very probable. Galatians in fact reveals precisely the same attitudes as appear in 2 Corinthians: a vigorous attack upon false apostles (verse 13), or false brothers (Gal. ii. 4), and an ironical but unaggressive attitude to another group, clearly defined in Galatians as the 'pillars', and named as James, Cephas, and John. There is some probability that, as the attitudes are the same, so too are the persons concerned. In 1 Cor. xv. 9 Paul declared himself to be the least of the apostles; but this (see *1 Corinthians* ad loc.) was not said from the standpoint of his critics. He had been a persecutor, an enemy of Christ himself; it was the grace of God alone that changed the antagonist into an apostle; but 'the grace which he bestowed upon me did not prove vain, for I laboured more abundantly than all of them.' It is in this sense that Paul does not come behind even the super-apostles.

Here too Paul manifests the same desire not to claim too much
that appears in 1 Cor. xv. 9. **I may be unskilled in speech, but** 6
I am not unskilled in knowledge. *Unskilled* is not an adjective but a noun (ἰδιώτης), denoting 'one who stands outside a particular activity or office' (see 1 Cor. xiv. 16, 22, 23, with the notes, especially on xiv. 16), and therefore is untrained in the skills proper to that activity or office. Paul disclaims ability in the art of speaking; see x. 1, 10; also 1 Cor. ii. 3 f., and the note; and compare Plato, *Ion* 532D, You rhapsodes and actors, and the poets whose verses you sing, are wise; and I am a common man (ἰδιώτην ἄνθρωπον), who only speak the truth (Pauline and Socratic irony have something in common). Paul's writing so strongly resembles speech, and in its own way very eloquent speech, that there is much force in the conclusion that either Paul suffered from an impediment in his speech (which could have been the physical weakness he appears to refer to in xii. 7—see the notes), or that he writes with undue modesty. More probably Paul is admitting (and in the admission continues his ironical vein) a judgement of his eloquence based upon presuppositions he did not himself share. According to Käsemann (*Legitimität*, p. 35/9) he was judged deficient in ecstatic speech, and for this reason his possession of the Spirit was called in question; compare Reicke, *Diakonie*, p. 278, who thinks that the judges who pronounced the unfavourable verdict were the Christ-party of 1 Cor. i. 12. Betz, especially p. 59, thinks that the preferred alternative to Paul's kind of speech was that of the Sophists. Paul replies in the manner of the Cynics by distinguishing between form (*speech*) and content (*knowledge*): these two are, according to Betz, but different sides of the same matter. The Corinthians would understand Paul's point. 'With his "admission" (xi. 6) he places himself automatically on the side of the "philosophers", while those who take this to be a deficiency just as automatically come to stand on the side of the "sophists". We may suppose that Paul could reckon on being understood by the Corinthians, since the arguments and topoi of the Cynic street-preachers were probably widely known. He could also expect that the church would receive this argument with sympathy, since "cynicizing" features, or features related to Cynicism,

were characteristic of Corinthian church life, as we know from 1 Corinthians and 1 Clement' (Betz, p. 66).

It is doubtful whether Paul would use the word *knowledge* (γνῶσις) simply to mean content over against form; it was not without connotations. Yet the word must not be given too precise a meaning. See x. 5, with the notes and the references. Its use here is often taken to show that Paul's rivals rated knowledge (together with speech) as their most valuable possession and highest qualification; that is, they were gnostics of a sort. But the word is more common in 1 Corinthians (ten times) than in 2 Corinthians (six times); the native Corinthians were at least as interested in knowledge as any of their visitors, and it is probable that Paul's reference here reflects a Corinthian criterion for judging apostles (cf. xiii. 3) rather than a characteristic of the opponents. Corinthian gnosis provided a speculative and rational basis for considerable freedom of action; see 1 Cor. viii. 1, and the note. It is quite unjustified to conclude from the present verse that gnostic principles played a significant role in Paul's theology. The opposite conclusion is equally unjustified. We have no material here for reconstructing either Paul's theology or that of the Corinthian church. We conclude only that the word *gnosis* was being bandied about; this however is a not insignificant fact, and must be borne in mind as we follow Paul further.

The next words are practically untranslatable, and may well be corrupt. A word-by-word rendering is: But in everything having manifested in all things to you. We have observed (see v. 12, and cf. Moule, *Idiom*, p. 180) that Paul sometimes uses a participle where a finite verb would be correct; but even if we allow for this, In everything we manifested in all things to you, remains unintelligible. Several textual variants improve the sentence: having manifested ourselves (0121); having been manifested (plural: the majority of MSS); having been manifested (singular: D* Ambrosiaster). These all amount to: You know what I am like, what sort of person I am. They do not however say it very clearly, and must be dismissed as attempts to mend a difficult text. The simplest and possibly the best expedient is to suppose that something has dropped out of the text, either by accident in transmission, or perhaps because Paul omitted to write it: an 'it' (αὐτήν), referring back to *knowledge*; 'the truth' (τὴν ἀλήθειαν); or 'ourselves' (ἑαυτούς). Of these the first is simplest and best, and we may write out the verse: *I may be unskilled in speech, but I am not unskilled in knowledge*; **on the contrary, in every way we** (this must be epistolary and refer to the writer alone—Moule, *Idiom*, p. 119) **have revealed it to you in all things.** Even this suggestion, however, does not remove the repetition (which the translation alleviates) of *in every way . . . in all things*, and it may be that one of these phrases (ἐν παντί or ἐν πᾶσι, probably the former) is a corruption of an object 'all things' (τὰ πάντα, or πάντα): In all ways we have revealed all things to you. Alternatively, Paul is doubly (and somewhat clumsily) underlining that the knowledge he is communicating is not partial but complete.

The Corinthians may not think much of Paul as a speaker (and, unless we are to blame the copyists, they certainly had something to complain of in his writing), but they cannot, he says, complain of his lack of knowledge. Perhaps there is another cause of complaint. **Or did I commit a sin in humbling myself that you** 7
might be exalted, by preaching the Gospel (in that I preached, ὅτι . . . εὐηγγελισάμην) **of God to you for nothing?** Paul's irony is here at its most bitter. In the first epistle (see *1 Corinthians*, pp. 200-210) he had made it clear both that he believed that apostles had a right to expect support from the churches which they founded and in which they ministered, and that he had no intention of availing himself of this right; see 1 Cor. ix. 4-18; 2 Cor. xii. 13. We do not know why Paul adopted this course in Achaea and not—it seems (see the specific reference to Achaea in verse 10, and to the 'other churches' in xii. 13)—elsewhere. The reasons given in 1 Cor. ix. 16 ff. would apply equally in all mission fields. One can only conclude that Paul judged the situation in Corinth and the surrounding area to be such that it would be better for the progress of the Gospel if he were under no financial obligation to the church; his grounds for this judgement are not stated. Goudge suggests that he wished to distinguish himself from 'professional sophists and rhetoricians'—a partial anticipation of Betz's view of chapters x–xiii, not noted by him. The present verse suggests that Paul's judgement in this matter may have been—at least on a superficial level—mistaken. The Corinthians, it seems, thought less of him because he refused to be a burden. Greek teachers in general would not work with their hands, and the Corinthians may well have thought of Paul as Antiphon did of Socrates: If you set any value on your society, you would insist on getting the

proper price for that too. It may well be that you are a just man because you do not cheat people through avarice (πλεονεξία); but wise you cannot be, since your knowledge is not worth anything (Xenophon, *Memorabilia* I vi. 12). Other apostles (see especially xi. 20) behaved differently, and were so much the more impressive; Paul, who made no claims for himself, must be, if an apostle at all, an apostle of inferior rank and qualification, whose presentation of Christian truth could accordingly not be trusted. Paul was not in error, however, even if he was misunderstood. For him to be brought low and his converts to be lifted up (both verbs, ταπεινοῦν and ὑψοῦν, retain something of their literal sense; for Greek usage of the former root see vii. 6; x. 1, and the notes) was the pattern of the Gospel (see e.g. iv. 12), and nothing could make it clearer than this kind of behaviour. Paul lives in physical poverty, that his hearers may become spiritually rich (cf. vi. 10; ix. 11; 1 Cor. i. 5); there is no respect in which Paul could be more like the Lord himself (viii. 9). The true nature of the apostolic life and the apostolic message are disclosed, and with them the meaning of apostolicity (see *Signs*, pp. 85-92). The doctrine of the church and Christology are brought into close connection. As Cerfaux says, 'The christological theme is playing on muted strings' (*Christ*, p. 295; E.T., p. 393). By his manner of life as well as by his preaching Paul proclaims *the Gospel of God*; for this phrase see Rom. i. 1 (with the note); xv. 16; 1 Thess. ii. 2, 8, 9. If *the Gospel of God* proved offensive, this was no more than might be expected (1 Cor. i. 18, 23).

The principle has been stated; Paul proceeds to describe how
8 he had carried it out. **I robbed** (ἐσύλησα; cf. the compounds ἱεροσυλεῖν, ἱερόσυλος, at Rom. ii. 22; Acts xix. 37 respectively; the simple form does not in itself suggest sacrilege, but provides a purely secular—and mainly military—metaphor) **other churches** (to which he was at the time rendering no service) **by taking pay** (the word, ὀψώνιον, is used, in accordance with common Greek usage, of the soldier's pay at 1 Cor. ix. 7; Denney pursues the metaphor—'he devoted the spoils of his earlier victims for Christ to a new campaign in Achaia') **from them** (these two words are not in the Greek) **in order that I might be able to serve you** (literally, for your service, that is, for the service of you—objective
9 genitive)**, and when I was present with you and fell into want** (aorist participle, ὑστερηθείς) **I made myself a burden to no**

one (Paul uses the verb, καταναρκᾶν, only in this setting; see xii. 13, 14; L.S. seem to prefer 'to be slothful towards', but see Hesychius, who identifies with κατεβάρησα, and Bauer, s.v., and note the Vulgate, 'nulli onerosus fui'—and Jerome, *Epistle* CXXI. x. 4). According to Acts xviii. 3 Paul had worked at his trade in order to maintain himself. One must suppose that this did not suffice; either trade was bad, or he gave so much time to evangelism that he could not earn enough. On these lines, perhaps, the question (raised by Windisch) why Paul makes no reference to his wage-earning activity may be answered. In these circumstances the churches he had recently founded came to his aid, and he allowed himself to take from them money they could ill spare (*robbed* suggests this). But he continued to make no claims on, and (if they were offered) to accept no gifts from the Corinthians. **For the brothers who came from Macedonia** (see ii. 13; vii. 5; viii. 1; ix. 2, 4) **supplied my need** (there may be a reference to this operation in Phil. iv. 15—in Thessalonica (iv. 16) Paul was still in Macedonia), **and in every way I kept, and I will keep, myself from being burdensome** (not the word καταναρκᾶν discussed above; what Paul says here however reinforces the interpretation given to that word) **to you.**

The Corinthians might regard Paul's independence as a sin
(verse 7); to him it was a matter for boasting—the only sort of
boasting he would allow himself, because it was boasting in
weakness, and thus a sort of boasting in the Lord (xii. 9; x. 17;
cf. Gal. vi. 14). There can have been few things about which he
felt more strongly, and he winds up his treatment of the matter
with passionate words. **As Christ's truth is in me. . . .** Bultmann 10
(*Exeg.*, p. 138; with many others) is probably right in seeing here
an oath formula. In the light of Matt. v. 34, 37 this raises a problem,
hardly disposed of by Calvin's reference to 'legitimate and holy
oaths'. Moule, *Idiom*, p. 112, suggests 'I am speaking Christian
truth when I say that . . .', but rightly adds that if this is the
meaning, 'it is a much smaller and particularized sense of ἀλήθεια
[truth] as associated with Christ'. Compare i. 17-22 for Paul's
association of his own integrity with the truth of the Gospel.
I shall not be silenced in this boasting (literally, this boasting
shall not be stopped up for me; the verb, φράσσειν, is that used
in Rom. iii. 19, that every mouth may be shut) **in the whole
province** (see Bauer, s.v. κλίμα) **of Achaea.** The reason for

Paul's behaviour has already been given in verse 7; it is a manifestation of the Gospel itself, because it reflects the voluntary poverty of Christ which makes others rich. But of course it will be misunderstood; humility and self-sacrifice often are, especially by those who do not themselves frequently practise them. The
11 next words reflect Corinthian misunderstanding. **Why? Because I do not love you?** The Corinthians had no doubt said that his actions showed that he did not love them. But **God knows the truth about that** (literally, God knows). On the whole question of the apostle's financial support see now Betz, pp. 100–117. He concludes: 'To sum up, one may say that Paul did not reject financial support from the Corinthians because he maintained on principle an ascetic ideal of poverty. Originally concrete reasons, no longer accessible to us, must have existed which decided him to renounce his right to maintenance. In 2 Cor. x–xiii this situation is presupposed. It immediately gives Paul the opportunity to use an anti-sophist topos, which disembarrasses him and puts his adversaries into the role of avaricious deceivers' (p. 117).

Up to this point however Paul has treated his financial independence as a question between himself and the Corinthians alone. There were others (as is already noted in the quotation from Betz) who were involved in the situation (see above, pp. 274-9, and Introduction, pp. 28 ff.); this group provided the strongest
12 motivation for Paul's attitude. **What I am doing, that I will also continue to do, in order** (or, with a different punctuation, What I am doing and will continue to do, is in order . . .; Allo prefers this because of the parallel in verse 9; there is little difference in sense) **to cut off opportunity** (*ἀφορμή*, translated 'occasion' at v. 12; see also Rom. vii. 8 (with the note), 11) **from those who would like to have an opportunity to become** (literally, to be found; taking the second *ἵνα* to be dependent on the second *ἀφορμήν*; as Windisch observes, to attach it to *ποιήσω* practically reverses the sense), **in their boasting, just what we are.** This involved sentence is best approached from its end. What Paul, in his boasting, is, is an apostle, who disinterestedly serves the Gospel and his people (iv. 5) without any recompense. His rivals would like to boast of being, equally with him, apostles; but as long as he maintains the practice he has described they have no opportunity of putting themselves in the same disinterested

category—unless of course they should adopt his practice of preaching for nothing. It is a morally effective argument—one hopes it was effective in Corinth; but it is not logically effective, for the intruders could claim that they were following the example of Cephas and other apostles (1 Cor. ix. 5 f.), and that this put them on at least as high a level as Paul. Even so, however, they could never claim to be his kind of apostle; and it may not unreasonably be observed that the church owes more to Paul's kind of ministry than to the other.

It must not be forgotten that Paul himself argued in 1 Cor. ix
for the principle that the apostle was entitled to support. The real
point is that the requirement of self-sacrifice (which Cephas
doubtless would have made in circumstances that he thought called
for it) marks out the true apostle from the false. It is so here, **for** 13
such men as those referred to **are false apostles** (ψευδαπόστολοι, pseudo-apostles, perhaps a word of Paul's coinage; for detailed discussion of the word and the context see 'False Apostles'), **deceitful workmen** (ἐργάται; the only other Pauline use of this word, at Phil. iii. 2, is also in a bad sense; this may be pure coincidence, for Paul speaks of those who do the work—ἔργον—of the Lord, as he does himself—e.g. 1 Cor. xvi. 10; see Georgi, *Gegner*, pp. 49 ff.), **disguising themselves** (for this verb, μετασχηματίζειν, see 1 Cor. iv. 6, with the note; in the active, as at Phil. iii. 21, it means 'to transform', in the middle, as here and in the following verses, 'to transform oneself', hence 'to disguise') **as apostles of Christ.** Both the background of the word, and *disguising themselves*, indicate that the primary sense of *false apostles* is, 'men who claim to be apostles but are not', but (as verse 3 is in itself sufficient to show) Paul quickly moves on to the thought that they are apostles, envoys, who speak what is false—a *different Gospel.* The results of an examination of background and context are as follows ('False Apostles', pp. 395 f.—translating Greek words): '(1) It would be understandable if the accusation of falsehood were first thrown at Paul; by his life and doctrine he was playing false to the ancestral religion. Once the charge was made it would be both natural and easy, and almost inevitable, to return it; it was not Paul, but his opponents who were resisting the destiny appointed by God for his people. But only Jews, and in particular Jewish Christians, would be open to this kind of accusation . . . The real question is the fulfilment of Judaism . . .

(2) This means that the *false apostles* of 2 Cor. xi. 13 are Judaizers; it follows that the trouble in Corinth was a Judaizing trouble. This in turn means that Judaizing is not a matter of circumcision only, and that there is a close relation between 2 Corinthians and Galatians. The dispute between Paul and the Judaizers . . . touched the roots of both religions. (3) Paul viewed the *false apostles*, and Jewish perversion of the Gospel as well as Jewish rejection of the Gospel, as an eschatological phenomenon. It would be difficult to account otherwise for the passionate feelings that evidently were evoked on each side.'

In this setting *apostle* is used in a wide sense. It could hardly have been profitable to pretend to be one of the Twelve—disproof would have been too easy; but the apostles (cf. 1 Cor. xv. 7, with the note) were a larger group. For the different sorts of persons who seem to have borne the title see *Signs*, pp. 71 ff. Paul calls the apostolic claimants *deceitful* (δόλιοι); it is worth noting that in xii. 16 he is accused of deceit (δόλος).

There is precedent for the deception and disguise practised by
these men in Corinth; they are only following the example of their
14 master, the Arch-Deceiver. **And no wonder** that they should so
behave, **for Satan himself** (see ii. 11; xii. 7) **disguises himself**
as an angel of light. The thought was connected with the
deception of Eve, and the reference to this in verse 3 was no doubt still in the back of Paul's mind. In the Apocalypse of Moses xvii. 1 Eve herself recalls the event: 'When the angels ascended to worship God, then Satan appeared in the form of an angel and sang hymns like the angels. And I bent over the wall and saw him, like an angel.' In the related Life of Adam and Eve ix. 1, Satan was wroth and transformed himself into the brightness of angels, and went away to the River Tigris, to Eve. The Slavonic text, xxxviii. 1, has: 'The devil came to me, wearing the form and brightness of an angel.' Further illustrations of the myth are given by Windisch. More important than the details of the Satan myth is the fact that Paul regarded the opposition to his work as of Satanic origin, that is, he considered it to be directly opposed to God. This coincides with Gal. iv. 9: for the Gentiles to judaize meant a relapse into heathenism, a falling under the power of the elements; and with v. 4: to seek justification through Jewish ordinances was to finish with Christ and with grace.

15 Paul moves back from Satan to his servants. **It is no great thing**

therefore if his servants too disguise themselves as servants of righteousness. *Of righteousness* is probably (like *of light* in verse 14) a descriptive genitive; it is not necessary to regard either as in any direct sense a Semitism. Although *deceitful* (and because deceitful) they make themselves out to be upright servants of Christ. It has been suggested that the genitive is objective: they serve, or profess to serve, righteousness, that is, by insisting upon obedience to the law; but this would not make Paul's point; the Judaizers (if such the intruders are) do not disguise themselves as *servants of righteousness* in this sense; they *are* servants of legal righteousness, and it is precisely this that Paul objects to. It is mistaken to read too much theology out of these verses; Paul is speaking in moral terms, and alleges that his rivals are deceivers. They are not the upright, honest men they profess to be, any more than Satan is an angel of light. Theologically Paul cannot parley with them at all. If he is right, they are diabolically wrong. And for such men there can be only one fate: **Their end will correspond to their deeds.** Compare v. 10: men are rewarded at the judgement according to what they have done; see also Rom. iii. 8; Phil. iii. 19. Paul does not elaborate this theme; but he does not conceal the fact that *their deeds* threaten the destruction of the work of God (cf. 1 Cor. iii. 17) in the Corinthian church.

The persons described in verses 13 ff. had been, probably still were, at work in Corinth, and claimed the titles apostle and servant of righteousness, probably also (Käsemann, *Legitimität*, p. 37/13) mission-worker and servant of Christ (cf. xi. 23). They are to be distinguished from the *super-apostles* who are treated with gentle irony and not subjected to the bitter attack of these verses. They are not the Jerusalem apostles, but they are Judaizers (see above), and may well have appealed to the authority of the Jerusalem church, and of its highest officials. How far they were justified in making this appeal we can hardly hope now to determine (see 'Paul's Opponents', pp. 252 f.). 'Judaizing' was of more than one kind; this kind may have appeared the more dangerous to Paul because it did not make (as Galatian Judaizing did) the blatantly Jewish demand that all Gentile Christians should be circumcised, and was prepared to accommodate itself to the criteria of apostleship proposed in Corinth.

19. xi. 16-33. ANSWERING FOOLS ACCORDING TO THEIR FOLLY: (a) QUALIFICATIONS

(16) I say again, let no one think me a fool. And even if you do, then accept me as the fool you take me to be, that I too may boast for a little while. (17) What I am saying now, I am not saying as a servant of the Lord, but as it were in my own folly, in this boastful confidence. (18) Since many boast according to the flesh, I too will boast. (19) For you who are so sensible gladly put up with the foolish. (20) If anyone enslaves you, if anyone eats you out of house and home, if anyone gets you in his power, if anyone exalts himself over you, if anyone strikes you on the face, you put up with him. (21) I say it to my shame: We have been weak! Yet (I am speaking foolishly) any bold claim that anyone else can make, I can make too. (22) Are they Hebrews? So am I. Are they Israelites? So am I. Are they the seed of Abraham? So am I. (23) Are they servants of Christ? I am really going out of my wits when I say it, I am even more a servant of Christ. I have toiled harder, I have been in prison more frequently, I have been beaten beyond measure, often exposed to death. (24) Five times the Jews have given me 'forty stripes save one'; (25) three times I have been beaten with rods; once I have been stoned; three times I have been shipwrecked, I have spent a day and a night out in the deep. (26) Often I have been on my travels, exposed to dangers from rivers, dangers from bandits, dangers from my own people, dangers from the Gentiles, dangers in the crowded city, dangers in the lonely country, dangers on the sea, dangers among false brethren; (27) I have lived in the midst of labour and toil, often in wakefulness, hungry and thirsty, often fasting, in cold and nakedness. (28) Apart from such external matters, there is that which presses upon me every day,[1] the care of all the churches. (29) Who is weak, and I am not weak too? Who is offended, and I do

[1] On the text here see the commentary.

not burn too? (30) If I must boast, I will boast of what belongs to my weakness. (31) The God and Father of the Lord Jesus, he who is blessed for ever—he knows that I am not lying. (32) Why, the ethnarch of King Aretas was guarding the city of the Damascenes in order to arrest me, (33) and I was let down through a window in a basket, by the wall, and so I escaped out of his hands.

I say again. Paul had not previously said, in this or any other 16
extant epistle to Corinth, the words that follow in the next clause. He is however taking up the thought of xi. 1, from which various considerations had deflected him. He is asking, ironically, that he too may boast a little; others have boasted of their qualifications, which, we may deduce from the letter as a whole, consisted of commendation from high authority, impressive speech and behaviour, and manifestations of the Spirit, and Paul, seeing the peril of the Corinthian church, decides, against his will, to beat them at their own game—to answer them according to their folly. His difficulty is that he recognizes, as they do not, that viewed from a Christian standpoint he is making himself a fool. Christians, except under duress, do not act or speak in this way. It is however sometimes necessary to argue *ad hominem*, and if the man in question is a fool this means that it is necessary to argue *ad insipientem* (the word used here by the Vulgate). But **let no one think me a fool.** There is a sense in which a man must be ready to recognize that he is a fool—without true wisdom—if he is to be wise in God's sight (1 Cor. iii. 18); here Paul means that no one should think him a fool in the sense of the self-opinionated man who believes that he can demonstrate his own wisdom and authority. But perhaps the Corinthians will be glad to take up the word (Robertson, p. 853, rightly says that the tense of δόξῃ implies 'no one did, of course'; the new clause represents Paul's second thoughts). **And even if you do** ('otherwise', εἰ δὲ μή γε, a classical construction, here only in Paul), **then accept me as the fool you take me to be** (expanding the translation in Moule, *Idiom*, p. 151, where the use of κἄν is rightly explained), **that I too** (like the false apostles in their way) **may boast for a little while** (or, a little, taking μικρόν τι as at xi. 1: but Paul does not mean to boast only to a small extent; he will boast as much as he can—but only for so long as he allows himself to do so). Schoeps

(*Paulus*, p. 74; E.T., p. 79) thinks that foolishness (ἀφροσύνη) was a charge brought by the Corinthians against Paul, and verse 19 adds weight to this view. v. 13, however, suggests that the Corinthians were prepared to use any weapon that came to hand: Paul might be too ecstatic, or too rational, but never what they thought right. He makes here the point that boastfulness (such as the Corinthians gladly take from his rivals) is the real folly, and invites them to take some of it from him for a change. It is to be noted that he does not immediately speak about ecstatic phenomena; these come later, in chapter xii. The ironical vein, and the safeguarding of his position as strictly temporary and *ad hominem*, continue for several verses. Plato, *Symposium* 212, adduced here by some, is at best an extremely remote parallel.

17 **What I am saying now, I am not saying as a servant of the Lord** (literally, according to the Lord, that is, at his command and with his authority; cf. 1 Cor. vii. 12; Paul might mean, In imitation of the Lord's meek behaviour, but there is nothing to indicate that this was in his mind), **but as it were** (ὡς; cf. verse 21; Paul does not find it easy to make clear how far he is serious, how far ironical) **in my own folly, in this boastful confidence** (taking 'of boasting', τῆς καυχήσεως, as an adjectival genitive). The word rendered *confidence* is that which occurs at ix. 4 (ὑπόστασις; see the note); in the present passage it would be possible to translate 'in this matter of boasting', but the two verses should probably be taken in the same way (Paul does not use the word elsewhere;
18 cf. Heb. xi. 1). **Since many boast according to the flesh,** that is, on a scale of values that leaves God out of account (see above,
19 p. 170), **I too will boast. For you who are so sensible gladly put up with the foolish** (after *sensible* it is tempting to translate 'senseless', since the Greek words are etymologically related; on the whole, however, it seems better to retain the English word used elsewhere). Compare 1 Cor. iv. 10, We are fools (a different word) for Christ's sake, you are sensible in Christ, where the irony is similar. From their position of supposed superiority the Corinthians look down upon apostles who are foolish enough to allow themselves to be made to look ridiculous, and worse, for Christ's sake, and tolerate them if they feel inclined to do so. From Paul's point of view it is intolerable that Christians should adopt such an attitude of superiority to their fellow Christians and judge them as they see fit (cf. Rom. xiv. 4); yet he proceeds to tolerate it, and

even to ask for his converts' tolerance. The mixture of humility and of bitter retaliatory irony is both subtle and striking.

Paul proceeds now to introduce a new theme. You suppose yourselves to be superior, and in a position to pass judgement on others; the result of your attitude is that you make yourselves inferior to the unworthy. I can say that you put up with fools, for
if anyone enslaves you (cf. Gal. ii. 4), **if anyone eats you out of** 20
house and home (interpreting κατεσθίει on the basis of 1 Cor. ix. 4 ff. (cf. Mark xii. 40)—unlike Paul, this person takes advantage of the privilege of receiving maintenance, perhaps for his wife as well as himself, from the church; Reicke, *Diakonie*, p. 280, thinks that he 'eats your food' at the Supper; alternatively, the word could be interpreted in terms of Gal. v. 15, of aggressive and quarrelsome behaviour), **if anyone gets you in his power** (λαμβάνει, 'to take', or 'to receive', is used in a wide variety of senses; cf. Rom. vii. 8, 11; 1 Cor. x. 13, all metaphorical; 2 Cor. xii. 16 is similar; C. Lattey, *J.T.S.* xliv. 148 thinks that the word implies violence—'lays hands on you'), **if anyone exalts himself over you** (ἐπαίρεται, used with a similar meaning at x. 5; cf. Betz, *Lukian*, p. 129), **if anyone strikes you on** (εἰς for ἐπί; see M. iii. 256) **the face** (for a similar expression used metaphorically cf. 1 Cor. ix. 27), **you put up with him.** Some of the words in this verse are not easy to translate with confidence, and it is difficult to give any of them a precise connotation. It is hardly possible to give to *anyone* (τις) the singular interpretation that seems to be required by x. 7, 10, 11; xi. 4. Paul is writing in general terms, though there is no reason why there should not have been a ringleader among the persons whose behaviour he describes (cf. pp. 260, 275). *If anyone enslaves you* suggests most naturally 'enslaves you to himself', and an attitude the opposite of iv. 5 is no doubt in mind. The theological enslavement behind this kind of behaviour is that of Gal. ii. 4; iv. 9; to accept the Judaizers' 'Gospel' is to fall back into the bondage of heathenism. The other verbs, more or less clearly, elaborate the meaning of enslavement. The master will batten upon the slave's property, at the slave's expense; he has him in his power, he imposes his will on him; and if he sees fit he beats him. How far the last verb has to be taken metaphorically is not clear; probably not wholly so. In verse 26 (see the note) Paul puts perils experienced among *false brothers* in the same category with perils experienced among robbers and

perils caused by falling into rivers, and the Corinthian intruders, whether or not we identify them with the *false brothers*, were probably not averse to violence if it suited their purpose; compare Acts xxiii. 2. If anyone treats you like this, *you put up with him*—feeling, apparently, that here is one whose conduct proves his status, and justifies his exploitation of apostolic rights. The Corinthians were not the last Christians to find ecclesiastical pomp and circumstance impressive. Grovelling submission to it is hardly less evil than the original arrogance.

In the competition for apostolicity Paul comes off badly. So he
21 admits, ironically. **I say it to my** (this pronoun is not in the
Greek; it would be possible to supply 'your', but the irony of *my* suits the context) **shame: We have been weak!** For the construction (ὡς ὅτι), introducing a statement Paul does not mean seriously to make (though there was a sense in which it was true), see the notes on v. 19; and compare 2 Thess. ii. 2. In comparison with these dignified and energetic persons who assert themselves at the expense of their congregations, he has been weak; that is, he has not been strong in the way in which they have been strong. It was a genuine weakness, not a crafty yieldingness adopted as a means of acquiring and exercising power; but as a genuine human weakness it had been the scene on which divine power was displayed; compare xii. 9 f., with the notes. Human strength is known by its fruit: the acquisition of dignity and influence by those who possess and use it. Divine power also is known by its fruit: the conversion of men and their building up into the new Christian society.

We have been weak; but now, to bring the Corinthians to their senses, a change of method: **Yet (I am speaking foolishly) any bold claim that anyone else can make, I can make too** (literally, wherein anyone is bold, I too am bold; the word *claim*, not in the Greek, is suggested by the context). With *anyone else* Paul's thought has moved beyond his immediate rivals, the intruders who have been exalting themselves in Corinth and intimidating (and thereby, so perverse is human nature, gratifying) the Corinthians, to those who stand behind them and whose authority (rightly or wrongly) they appear to have claimed. This was not the time to bargain with subordinates; Paul had no need to fear comparison with the principals, though he continues to insist that to make such comparisons is foolish. Who these persons were is fairly clearly indicated in the next verse and a half.

Are they Hebrews? So am I. In the New Testament, the 22
adjective Hebrew (Ἑβραῖος) occurs only here, at Acts vi. 1, and at Phil. iii. 5, where Paul claims to be a 'Hebrew born of Hebrew parents' (Beare's translation; Ἑβραῖος ἐξ Ἑβραίων). It has been shown conclusively by, for example, Bauer, s.v., Lietzmann-Kümmel, and von Rad–Kuhn–Gutbrod (*T.W.N.T.* iii. 356-94), that the word is used in two senses. The primary one (clearly used in Phil. iii. 5), is that of pure-blooded Jew; only secondarily, and in contexts where the *Hebrew* is contrasted with other Jews (as at Acts vi. 1), do considerations such as language (Hebrew-speaking over against Greek-speaking) arise. There is in any case a probability that one who is in the primary sense a Hebrew will be acquainted with Hebrew and Aramaic, even if circumstances force him to use other languages through the greater part of his life, and that he will have at least contacts with Palestine (as Paul, if we may trust Acts, had; see W. C. van Unnik, *Tarsus of Jerusalem* (1952; E.T., 1962)). But that *Hebrew* was used to mean simply Jew, without any necessary linguistic connection, is shown most neatly by the Greek synagogue inscription found at Corinth, 'Synagogue of the Hebrews' (Συναγωγὴ Ἑβραίων; see Introduction, p. 2). Paul thus claims himself to be a full Jew by descent, and does not dispute the claim when it is made for those with whom he is comparing himself.

Are they Israelites? So am I. An *Israelite* is a member of Israel, the people of God. It is hard to understand how Lietzmann can claim that this word has the same meaning as *Hebrew*, when he proceeds immediately to quote an inscription from a Jewish catacomb (H. W. Beyer and H. Lietzmann, *Jüdische Denkmäler 1: Die jüdische Katakombe der Villa Torlonia in Rom* (1930), p. 37), in which a proselytess describes herself as 'a Jewess, an Israelite' (or 'a Jewish Israelite', Εἰουδέα Ἰσδραηλίτης). From Paul's point of view the word may be said to describe the same fact from a new angle; *Hebrew* deals with it from the racial, *Israelite* from the social and religious angle.

Are they the seed of Abraham? So am I. The persons in question are Jews, and it would be natural, and correct, to say that *seed of Abraham*, like *Hebrew*, describes them from the racial point of view. The phrase certainly denotes the descendants of Abraham.

The word *seed* (σπέρμα, *zera'*), however, is a collective term, and connotes the people of God in a collective sense, as those who come into existence as a body on the basis of God's call and promise (cf. 1QM xiii. 7; 1QH xvii. 14; but neither in these nor in other passages cited by S. Schulz, *T.W.N.T.* vii. 544, is Abraham mentioned, and there is no close parallel to Paul's usage, which appears to be based directly on the Old Testament); it may thus be said to describe Jews from a theological point of view. Precisely for this reason Paul takes up the phrase and uses it of Christ (Gal. iii. 16, 19) and of the Christian church (e.g. Gal. iii. 29), denying that the principle of physical descent is constitutive of the people of God (Rom. ix. 6-13). In fact, in this verse as a whole he says little more than, Are they Jews? So am I. But he says this with every possible emphasis, bringing out the fact that there is no conceivable Jewish qualification that he does not share on equal terms with the Jerusalem apostles. All this is too biblically determined and motivated for there to be more than a distant connection with the 'enconium topos' that stresses the subject's noble birth (Betz, p. 97). Georgi's detailed discussion of the opponents (*Gegner*, pp. 51-82) is valuable, but his conclusion that they are Hellenistic Jews must be corrected by Kümmel's argument. It results from the meaning of *Hebrew* 'that Paul's opponents in Corinth were Palestinian Jews, who objected to Paul that he lacked personal knowledge of the earthly Jesus (v. 16) . . . that these opponents when in Corinth attached themselves to the "pneumatic" gnosis that Paul attacks in 1 Corinthians is shown by 2 Cor. xi. 6; xii. 1 ff., so that in 2 Corinthians, in contrast with 1 Corinthians, Paul had to fight on a double front.' Apart from the fact that Kümmel does not distinguish between the false apostles and the super-apostles this seems to be a correct conclusion.

23 Paul moves from Jewish to Christian qualifications. **Are they servants** (διάκονοι) **of Christ?** Paul does not deny this; and the consequence of his admission, not perceived by, for example, Lietzmann and Kümmel, is that the persons referred to here cannot be identified with those of xi. 13 ff. It is probably wrong to stress the fact that they describe themselves not as apostles but as *servants*; the two words are used in very close connection in xi. 13 ff., and verses 23-30 describe experiences which Paul saw as essentially part of his apostolic life; compare also vi. 4, where he uses the word servant of himself. Col. i. 7 is the only other possibly

relevant Pauline passage for 'servant of Christ'. There is nothing in the word itself to suggest that it applies especially to those who were disciples of Jesus during his earthly ministry, though it may well be that Paul's lack of this privilege was in some quarters held against him. Schmithals (pp. 172 ff.) attempts to show that this verse relates to gnostics. That it is expressed in an 'ungnostic' manner is due to the fact that it was formulated by Paul himself, who introduced the word servants, though he should simply have said (cf. x. 7), 'Do they belong to Christ? I do so even more.' This is too far-fetched to be taken very seriously. More to the point is Georgi's discussion (*Gegner*, pp. 31-8), in which he recalls that in Cynic usage 'service' (διακονία) is close to what Paul meant by apostleship. See especially Epictetus III xxii. 69; III xxiv. 64 ff.

But above all service means service, and if the word *servant* is taken in this sense Paul's answer is clear. If they are *servants of Christ*, and I do not deny it, then, though **I am really going out of my wits** (a word different from but related to that of verse 21, probably intended to be stronger) **when I say it, I am even more** (adverbial use of ὑπέρ; see B.D. §230; M. iii. 250) **a servant of Christ.** Compare 1 Cor. xv. 10: it was by the grace of God that Paul was able to serve Christ. What Paul means by his claim he brings out more fully in the following verses, which give the most vivid picture of his life. They also show clearly that he understood his apostolic vocation in terms of pioneer missionary work. This was perhaps not the only legitimate understanding of the word apostle (ἀπόστολος, *shaliaḥ*); see p. 230; *Signs*, pp. 32 f., 68 f., 77. But it was the one that was most in harmony with the work of Jesus himself. Acts provides very few parallels to the biographical details referred to here; its account of Paul (though invaluable) is meagre and impressionistic, and quite inadequate for the reconstruction of a 'life'. For the relation between Paul's account of his labours and sufferings and the Cynic diatribe, see Betz, p. 99.

I have toiled harder: this only repeats the main proposition, but does so in characteristically Pauline language. The word he uses (a noun, κόπος, here paraphrased in the verb) often means specifically Christian work (1 Cor. xv. 58; 2 Cor. vi. 5; x. 15; 1 Thess. i. 3; ii. 9; iii. 5; (2 Thess. iii. 8)); so does the cognate verb (κοπιᾶν; Rom. xvi. 6, 12; 1 Cor. (iv. 12); xv. 10; xvi. 16; Gal. iv. 11; Phil. ii. 16; Col. i. 29; 1 Thess. v. 12). **I have been in prison more frequently.** Up to this point, Acts has described half a night's imprisonment at Philippi (xvi. 23-30); not even the wildest exaggeration could spin Paul's statement out of this. Imprisonment may but certainly need not be implied by 1 Cor. xv. 32; 2 Cor. i. 8 f. Even the elaborate (and very questionable) account of Paul's misfortunes in Ephesus in G. S. Duncan's *St Paul's Ephesian Ministry* (1929) is hardly sufficient to provide the evidence for 'in prisons more abundantly'. Compare however 1 Clement v. 6, according to which Paul was imprisoned seven times. **I have been beaten beyond measure.** This statement is expanded below. **I** have been **often exposed to death,** literally, often in deaths, the word death (*θάνατος*) being used to mean 'situations in which I was in danger of death'. Compare i. 9 f.

24 **Five times the Jews have given me** (literally, From the Jews I received—the verb corresponds to rabbinic usage; see S.B. iii. 527) **'forty stripes save one'.** According to Deut. xxv. 2 f. the maximum punishment of this sort was forty stripes. This is developed in Makkoth iii. 10: How many stripes do they inflict on a man? Forty save one, for it is written, By number forty [*bᵉmispar 'arba'im*]; that is to say, a number near to forty. The same variation on the biblical text appears in Josephus, *Antiquities* iv. 238, 248; there can be no doubt that it represents common practice in the first century. Synagogue flogging was inflicted for a variety of offences, which are listed in Makkoth iii. 1-9. Many of these are offences of which it is unlikely that Paul could have been held to be guilty, such as illegal sexual connections, the making of the sacred anointing oil or incense, or tattooing. In view of Acts xxi. 28 (which of course falls at a period later than the writing of 2 Corinthians) it is worth noting that one punishable offence was entering the Temple in a state of uncleanness (Makkoth iii. 2). In the third century (see S.B. iv. 318 ff.) it became customary to inflict flogging (as the less degrading punishment) upon a scholar who had deserved the synagogue bann. It is possible that this may have happened earlier in isolated cases. It can hardly be doubted that Paul refers to floggings he had received (broadly speaking) for being a Christian (Schürer II ii. 262), though it would be more accurate to speak of specific offences, such as consorting with Gentiles and eating forbidden food (cf. e.g. 1 Cor. x. 25, 27) which Paul had committed because he was a Christian. The floggings will probably go back (Goppelt, *Christentum und Judentum*, p. 87; *Apostolic and Post-Apostolic Times* (1970), p. 74;

Goppelt also points out that Paul must have been expelled from the synagogue, though wishing to remain within it) to the earliest period of his apostolic work, but the fact that he endured a formidable punishment (for details see Makkoth iii. 12 ff. . . . If he dies under his hand, the scourger is not culpable . . .) five times shows that he did not lightly give up his Jewish status and connection (cf. Rom. ix. 1-5; x. 1). Acts recounts none of these beatings.

Three times I have been beaten with rods. This was a 25
Roman punishment; see Acts xvi. 22. As this chapter (xvi. 37) testifies, it was one that should not have been inflicted (at least, in the circumstances described) upon a Roman citizen; compare Acts xxii. 25, 29, and Cicero, *In Verrem* v. 66 (170): Facinus est vincire civem Romanum, scelus verberare, prope parricidium necare. As Haenchen (on Acts xvi. 37; the reference to Cicero should be corrected) remarks, however, this formulation betrays the eloquence of the orator, and Roman governors will not always have been too deeply concerned about the letter of the law. The same oration of Cicero's may be cited (62 (162)): 'Caedabatur virgis in medio foro Messanae civis Romanus, iudices, cum interea nullus gemitus, nulla vox alia illius miseri inter dolorem crepitumque plagarum audiebatur nisi haec, "Civis Romanus sum". See also Josephus, *War* ii. 308: Florus ventured that day to do what none had ever done before, namely, to scourge before his tribunal and nail to the cross men of equestrian rank, men who, if Jews by birth, were at least invested with that Roman dignity. On the legal question see (in addition to the commentaries of Haenchen, Conzelmann, and Bruce on Acts xvi and xxii) H. J. Cadbury's extended note in *Beginnings V*, pp. 297-338; A. N. Sherwin-White, *Roman Society and Roman law in the New Testament* (1963), especially pp. 48-98. The fundamental law is the Lex Porcia: Porcia tamen lex sola pro tergo civium lata videtur: quod gravi poena, si quis verberasset necassetve civem Romanum, sanxit (Livy, x. 9). The fact that Paul was *three times beaten with rods* does not disprove the claim of Acts (xvi. 37; xxii. 25; xxv. 10) that he was a Roman citizen; it shows Roman magistrates exercising (perhaps at times without due consideration) their power of *coercitio*. His crime was probably that of creating a public disturbance. Roman flogging, like Jewish, could cause death.

Once I have been stoned. It is natural, and probably correct, to recall Acts xiv. 19, though this does not (any more than the narrative of Acts vii. 57-60) resemble an official Jewish stoning (for which see Sanhedrin vi. 1-6). The difference creates no difficulty. Paul was writing Greek, and *stoned* (ἐλιθάσθην) means to have stones thrown at one (cf. 2 Kdms. xvi. 6). Presumably the attempt described in Acts xiv. 5 came to nothing.

Three times I have been shipwrecked. A shipwreck is described in some detail in Acts xxvii. 14-44; this had not taken place when 2 Corinthians was written. Up to this point, Acts has mentioned the following voyages: Seleucia to Cyprus (xiii. 4); Paphos to Perga (Attalia) (xiii. 13); Attalia to Antioch (xiv. 26); Troas to Samothrace (xvi. 11); Beroea to Athens (xvii. 15); Corinth to Syria, calling at Ephesus (xviii. 18); in addition, the journeys of ix. 30; xi. 26 could have been made partly by sea. To these we may perhaps add the sorrowful second visit to Corinth (ii. 1) and the journey from Troas to Macedonia (ii. 13; vii. 5, with the notes). For the 'shipwreck theme' in Hellenistic literature see Knox, *H.E.*, p. 13; but (whatever may be said of Acts xxvii) Paul's references are history, not fiction. None of our sources gives any hint of a wreck on any of the voyages mentioned: we know very little even of outstanding events in Paul's life. One wreck at least was a very serious matter: **I have spent** (for a not very successful attempt to explain the perfect πεποίηκα, see M. i. 144) **a day and a night out in the deep**—waiting, presumably, for rescue.

The shipwrecks suggest travelling in general, which Paul now mentions, going on to list some of the dangers it involved. Books on New Testament history often refer to the facilities for the spread of the Gospel afforded by Roman Peace and the Roman system of roads. If such remarks are taken in a comparative sense, in relation to the centuries that preceded and those that followed the early Empire, they are true enough; but Paul does not exaggerate the perils of his day, nor have they altogether ceased. 'The neighbourhood of Miletus one evening in April, 1906, when we had lost our way and were riding after sunset through the swamps of the Maeander, and next day when we were at Didyma in the house of a Greek, who had just been shot dead by robbers, afforded us a drastic commentary on the "perils of rivers, perils of robbers," 2 Cor. xi. 26' (A. Deissmann, *St Paul in the Light of Social and Religious History* (n.d.), p. 37); and the solitary traveller sixty-five

years later has not always escaped without encountering brickbats
on the old roads of Asia Minor. **Often I have been on my travels** 26
(journeys by road, ὁδοιπορίαι, distinguished from voyages where the danger was from shipwreck), **exposed to dangers from rivers** (some difficult to cross at any time, some changing in a moment from half-dry river beds to rushing torrents), **dangers from bandits** (especially when funds were being conveyed; see above, p. 94). M. iii. 212 suggests that the genitives (ποτάμων, λῃστῶν) are genitives of place: in rivers, among robbers; it is better, perhaps, with B.D. §166, to see them as genitives of origin: dangers arising from . . . When later in the verse Paul wishes to refer to place he uses *in* (ἐν).

A different pair of dangers follows: **dangers from my own people** (ἐκ γένους), **dangers from the Gentiles.** Clearly these refer to personal attacks; the former kind must have been particularly hard for Paul to bear. For Jewish attacks on Paul see Acts ix. 23, 29; xiii. 8, 45; xiv. 2, 19; xvii. 5; xviii. 6, 12; xx. 3, 19; xxi. 11, 27. In Acts, Gentile attacks are much less frequent; see xvi. 20; xix. 23. This relative infrequency may be due to Luke's intention to represent the Jews as the enemies of the Gospel and to show that Roman officials looked upon it with some favour; Paul's words, however, show that there were Gentile attacks, and serious ones; the Christian mission was less pleasing to official eyes than Acts suggests. In the context, *danger* must almost certainly mean danger to life; by legal process and by mob violence Jews and Gentiles alike had sought to end Paul's work by ending his life.

Dangers in the crowded city, dangers in the lonely country (the adjectives *crowded* and *lonely*, not in the Greek, are added to bring out Paul's point: city and country would afford different kinds of opportunity to Paul's enemies); **dangers on the sea**—presumably from shipwreck; see above. **Dangers among false brethren** is probably intended as a climax, and as particularly relevant to the context, in which Paul is dealing with his Corinthian rivals (*false apostles*, xi. 13—these are still in mind, though not the persons directly referred to in verse 22), and their backers. For *false brethren* compare Gal. ii. 4. The word *brethren* is in itself almost enough to prove that they were, or at least claimed to be, Christians, and this is confirmed by the fact that Paul has already spoken of his *own nation* and of *Gentiles*; only Christians are left.

Certainly in Galatians, and probably here, they are distinguished from the Jerusalem apostles; to judge from the context in both epistles they are Judaizing Christians, whom Paul is unwilling to think of as Christians at all. They form the climax of a list of dangers, and in particular of physical dangers. Allo and Héring suggest that they might have betrayed Paul to hostile authorities; physical danger and the bitterness of treachery would then be combined. Direct physical violence cannot be ruled out. It is in these circumstances (not in the enjoyment of mystical vision) that Paul's union with Christ is expressed (Dibelius, p. 96).

Apart from attacks made by his enemies and the instant dangers
of storm and flood, Paul's life was not a comfortable one (cf. iv.
27 8 ff.; vi. 8 ff.; 1 Cor. iv. 9-13). **I have lived** (the Greek proceeds
without a verb, but English cannot dispense with one indefinitely) **in the midst of labour** (this repeats the noun, κόπος, of verse 23) **and toil** (Paul uses this pair, *labour and toil*, at 1 Thess. ii. 9; 2 Thess. iii. 8; both words suggest not only hard work but the resulting hardship and fatigue), **often in wakefulness** (because sleep was impossible, not because it was deliberately shunned), **hungry and thirsty, often fasting** (after *hungry* this must refer, as the usage of the word suggests, to voluntary fasts, though why they were undertaken is not stated; cf. vi. 5; it is possible that Paul refers to abstinence he underwent on account of his determination to take no money from the Corinthians), **in cold and nakedness** (these certainly would be caused by lack of money). Kümmel notes the paradoxical resemblance between this list (verses 23-7) and the lists of achievements that appear 'in the inscriptions of oriental kings, in the *res gestae* of Roman emperors, and in Greek novels'.

Conditions such as these would have killed most men; they
28 formed the smaller part of Paul's burden. **Apart from such
external matters** (χωρὶς τῶν παρεκτός; Windisch translates, 'Apart from the things I leave out'—which seems hardly worth saying), **there is that which presses upon me every day, the care of all the churches,** or, perhaps, anxiety about all the churches. Some of them, not least Corinth, gave Paul abundant cause for anxiety. This is the only place where Paul uses the noun (μέριμνα); the cognate verb (μεριμνᾶν) is used at 1 Cor. vii. 32, 33, 34; xii. 25; Phil. ii. 20; iv. 6. 1 Cor. xii. 25 and Phil. ii. 20 are the closest parallels. From this verse, from the epistles in

general, and from the narrative in Acts, it is clear that Paul felt responsible for the continuing Christian existence of the churches that had come into being through his preaching: 'Now we are alive, if you are standing firm in the Lord!' (1 Thess. iii. 8). It is however of anxious concern that Paul speaks; he is still no lord over his people's faith (i. 24). H. Conzelmann (*Geschichte des Urchristentums* (1969), p. 76) sees in our passage an 'indication of the busy activity in his organizing headquarters (des Betriebs in seinem Organisationszentrum)'; but this paints the wrong picture. The Pauline mission was not run like a business organization; all the Christians, even the most troublesome, were Paul's brothers, 'for whom Christ died' (1 Cor. viii. 11), and the pressure they put upon him (ἡ ἐπίστασίς μοι) was the pressure of love. True, there was organization, and it involved a good deal of anxious work and travelling (the mission of Titus to Corinth, ii. 13; vii. 5, may be recalled), but this energetic activity was the outward sign of inward pastoral care. Paul refers to the 'pressure on me', which in itself might refer to the pressure of persons, or of things and duties. Many MSS have a different (though related) noun (ἐπισύστασις) which suggests more specifically aggressive pressure; there is also a variant pronoun (μου, genitive, instead of μοι, dative), which might justify the translation 'my oversight', that is, the 'pressure' I exert on others. But the text explained above is almost certainly what Paul wrote. He refers here to *all the churches*, meaning something like the totality of Christian churches, that is, the church as the whole people of God. He uses the plural *churches* in this way at Rom. xvi. 4, 16; 1 Cor. (iv. 17); vii. 17; xi. 16; xiv. 33, (34); 2 Cor. viii. 18, (19, 23, 24); 2 Thess. i. 4. 'The church' is a sum of local churches.

Pastoral care is relatively easy (even though it involves endless hard work) when it is done for those who love their pastor and value his ministry. It was by no means always so with Paul. This
explains the transition to the next verse. **Who is weak, and I am** 29
not weak too? Who is offended, and I do not burn too? *To be weak* (ἀσθενεῖν) is used by Paul in two main senses, (a) of the man who is weak in faith, conscience-ridden, dependent on laws and regulations (Rom. iv. 19; xiv. 1 f.; 1 Cor. viii. 11, 12), and (b) of infirmity, lack of strength in any respect (Rom. viii. 3; 2 Cor. xi. 21; xii. 10; xiii. 3, 4, 9; Phil. ii. 26 f.). Either of these uses would give a good sense here. (a) To the weak in his churches Paul

himself becomes weak (1 Cor. ix. 22), though he himself is one of the strong (*Romans*, pp. 263, 269; *1 Corinthians*, pp. 215, 240-4). This is what *the care of all the churches* means. (b) Repeatedly in this and the following paragraphs Paul declares that he is weak, and that it is in his weakness—his humble and humiliated behaviour, his poverty, his unimpressive appearance—that the power of Christ is made known. If anyone can call himself weak, I am yet weaker! The second part of the verse suggests that (b) is more nearly correct than (a). To be *offended* could also fit into the context of pastoral care (see e.g. Rom. xiv. 13); if any of his people is made to stumble and so to lose his faith (Rom. xiv. 1–xv. 6; 1 Cor. viii), Paul burns with anger—his own work, and, more important, the Lord's work is being destroyed. But more probably Paul means that he too knows what it is so to be offended as to burn with anger.

Paul has now (for the moment; see xii. 1, 11) worked off his fit of folly and has returned to his normal sound mind. He has worked through the qualifications of which he thought he might boast, and the list changed its character as he did so. He as much as anyone was a *Hebrew*, an *Israelite*, a *servant of Christ*. But in the end he is speaking of qualifications no man would wish to share with him as he makes his perilous way by land and sea. This development is
30 crystallized in the words: **If I must boast** (and it may perhaps be necessary), **I will boast of what belongs to my weakness.** Paul takes up the Corinthian requirement ('one must boast') ironically (Betz, pp. 72 ff., 90). Compare xii. 5, and the reason given in xii. 9. Doubtless the Corinthians will continue to misunderstand; that is a risk he must take. This is the only kind of boasting tolerable for one who understands apostleship in Paul's sense. This verse fixes the meaning of *weakness* in the sense adopted in verse 29.

Is it possible that a man can say this kind of thing and mean it? Is it possible that the same man can claim all the qualifications described in verses 22-7? that is, that he can share the dignities of the chief apostles, and yet also suffer like a slave? This was perhaps not easy to believe, even in the apostolic age, and Paul vehemently asserts his truthfulness (cf. Rom. ix. 1; Gal. i. 20).
31 **The God and Father of the Lord Jesus, he who is blessed for ever—he knows that I am not lying.** Schoeps, *Paulus*, p. 156 (E.T., p. 152), argues that the clause of blessing, which recalls the

extremely common Rabbinic expression, 'The Holy One, blessed be he' (*ha-qodesh baruk hu'*), applies to the Lord Jesus. This is grammatically impossible, since *the Lord Jesus* (τοῦ κυρίου Ἰησοῦ) is in the genitive, and *he who is* . . . (ὁ ὢν . . .) in the nominative. If some strong theological reason for reversing the plain construction of the sentence could be adduced the change of subject might possibly be defended, but there is in fact no good reason why Paul should not have invoked blessing upon God. Compare Rom. ix. 5, where the problem is much more complex; also Rom. i. 25. For the description of God as the one who is the Father of Jesus see i. 3 and the note.

Paul's asseveration of truthfulness both winds up the main part of the paragraph and also introduces a fresh point. The connection of verses 32 f. with what precedes has given rise to much difficulty. Some have proposed their deletion as no original part of the epistle (this does not solve, but sharpens the problem, for who would have inserted them at this point?); some suggest that the story had been told to ridicule Paul, or to represent him as a coward, so that he now feels obliged to give his own version of what took place. In fact the verses are a crowning illustration of the weakness and humiliation of which Paul speaks and boasts. Do you doubt either the depth of the humiliation I have experienced or my willingness
to accept it? **Why, in Damascus the ethnarch of King Aretas** 32
was guarding the city of the Damascenes in order to arrest
(πιάσαι, infinitive of purpose) **me, and I was let down through** 33
a window in a basket, by (διά) **the wall** (Schlatter wonders if
Paul was thinking of Josh. ii. 15), **and so I escaped out of his
hands.** Aretas ('Ḥarithath, lover of his people', according to the inscriptions—S.B. iii. 530) was king of the Nabataean Arabs from about 9 B.C. to A.D. 39; the incident therefore fell early in Paul's career. Damascus was brought under Roman rule by Pompey the Great (Josephus, *Antiquities* xiv. 29; *War* i. 127). Coins of the Emperors Augustus, Tiberius, and Nero have been found there, but not of Caligula (37-41) or Claudius (41-54); this may mean that during this interval Damascus fell under the control of the Nabataeans, and from 37 to 39 was ruled by Aretas. This however is far from certain; the absence of coins of Caligula and Claudius may be due to chance, and there may have been a dual sovereignty in Damascus, Aretas governing as a vassal-prince of Rome (so T. Mommsen, *The Provinces of the Roman Empire* II (1886), pp. 148 ff.).

Moreover, the meaning of *ethnarch* (ἐθνάρχης) is uncertain. Josephus uses it of Simon (*Antiquities* xiii. 214), and of Hyrcanus (xiv. 151, 191). The ethnarch who sought to arrest Paul may have been Aretas's governor, or, if the Romans were still in sole authority, his chargé d'affaires in the city, dealing with the business of resident Arabs; or, possibly, a sheikh operating outside the city; this last is supported by *was guarding the city*, which suggests a watch on the gates from without rather than from within. Even if the watch was within there is no need to suppose that the ethnarch was military ruler of the city; a few Arab guerillas could keep watch both effectively and unobtrusively. Not, however, effectively enough; Paul escaped as described in verse 33.

A very similar narrative is recounted in Acts ix. 24 f. Here it is the Jews who plotted against Paul. They watched (παρατηρεῖν, not φρουρεῖν) the gates (not the city) to kill (not to arrest) Paul. His disciples took the initiative in arranging his escape. It is not said that they used a window (though this is obvious enough), and a different word for basket (σπυρίς, not σαργάνη) is used. Otherwise even the wording is almost identical. Since it can hardly be doubted that Paul's version is correct, discussion of the differences is more profitable in the study of Acts than of 2 Corinthians. It is however worthwhile to note the difference in atmosphere between the two passages (see *New Testament Essays*, pp. 95 ff.). Acts provides at this point the first example of the way in which God delivers Paul out of the hand of his enemies. He is God's chosen vessel, and God will always see him through his adventures; he triumphantly thwarts the plot of the Jews. In 2 Corinthians however we have an outstanding example of the humiliation and weakness to which Paul is exposed. To say that Luke writes in terms of a *theologia gloriae*, Paul of a *theologia crucis* (see *Signs*, pp. 41-4, 104 f.) is a generalization unfair to Luke; but it throws some light on Paul.

20. xii. 1–10. ANSWERING FOOLS ACCORDING TO THEIR FOLLY: (b) REVELATIONS

(1) I must boast; it is not expedient, but I will come[1] to visions and revelations of the Lord. (2) I know a man in Christ, fourteen years ago (whether he was in the body, or out of the body, I do not know—God knows), I know that a man like that was caught up as far as the third heaven. (3) And I know that a man like that—whether in the body or apart from the body God knows—(4) I know that he was caught up into Paradise and heard unutterable words, which it is not permitted a man to speak. (5) On behalf of a man like that I will boast, but on my own behalf I will boast only in my weaknesses. (6) For if I choose to boast I shall not turn out to be a fool, for I shall speak the truth; but I am trying to spare you, lest anyone should reckon to my account more than he sees in me, or hears of me. (7) And because the revelations were so marvellous,[2] that I might not be unduly exalted there was given me a thorn in my flesh, an angel of Satan sent to beat me, that I might not be unduly exalted. (8) Concerning this angel I asked the Lord three times that he might go away from me, (9) and he has said to me, My grace is enough for you; for power comes to perfection in weak-

[1] The translation renders the following text: *καυχᾶσθαι δεῖ· οὐ συμφέρον μέν, ἐλεύσομαι δέ* . . . There are many variations, of which the most important are the following. (a) H vg and a few other authorities place *εἰ* before *καυχᾶσθαι*: If it is necessary to boast, it is not expedient but I will come . . . (b) instead of *δεῖ*, ℵ D* have *δέ*, and many MSS, mostly late, have *δή*. It is then necessary (see however Robertson, p. 1092) to join *καυχᾶσθαι* with the next verb: To boast is not expedient . . . (c) Many of the same MSS as in (b) connect the next clause not by means of *but* (*δέ*) but by *for* (*γάρ*). These variations are certainly not older than the text translated, and on the whole seem to have originated as attempts to remove difficulties. The same may be said of conjectural emendations (for which see Windisch), notably (d) Boasting is not expedient for me, but I will come . . . (*καυχᾶσθαι δὴ οὐ συμφέρει μοι, ἐλεύσομαι δέ* . . .; and (e) To boast is not expedient, but I will come . . . (*καυχᾶσθαι οὐ συμφέρον μέν, ἐλεύσομαι δέ* . . .).

[2] The textual problem here is discussed in the commentary. *Wherefore* (*διό*; see p. 313) is omitted by 𝔓[46] D lat syr Irenaeus Origen and the majority of MSS. The second *that I might not be unduly exalted* is omitted by ℵ* A D G lat Irenaeus and a few other witnesses.

ness. Therefore will I most gladly boast rather in my weaknesses, in order that Christ's power may rest upon me. (10) So I am well content in weaknesses, in insults, in anguish, in persecutions and distresses, endured on behalf of Christ; for when I am weak, then am I strong.

There is no escape from this theme of boasting, which runs throughout chapters x, xi, and xii (x. 8, 13, 15, 16, 17; xi. 10, 12, 16, 17, 18, 30; xii. 1, 5, 6, 9—but even these verbal statistics do not give an adequate account of the theme). *One must boast* may have been a Corinthian watchword, but the necessity arises out of the circumstances too. It is not expedient to boast, but it might be even more inexpedient not to boast. This is the cleft stick in which apostles, and the church after them, find themselves. Paul deals with the problem by boasting in the way his opponents do, showing this to be folly (but a folly that is forced upon him; xii. 11), and then boasting in the only fully legitimate way open to a Christian—that is, in weakness that discloses the Lord's power, and thus is
1 in effect boasting in the Lord (x. 17). **I must boast** (on the text see note 1 on p. 305). The intruders had apparently boasted of themselves as apostles of Christ (xi. 13) who had come to take over the Corinthian church in the name of Jerusalem (x. 12-16; see the notes), and of the supreme qualification of those from whom they claimed to have received commendation and authority. Paul had answered with equal and even superior qualifications, though the paragraph (xi. 16-33) in which he did so took a surprising turn, and ended with a refugee apostle climbing out of Damascus. It seems that his rivals also boasted of ecstatic and visionary experiences in which the Lord himself appeared to them; Betz, p. 73, compares *Corpus Hermeticum* i. 30. Again, Paul can follow suit, though again his boasting reverts to the old theme (cf. xi. 30) of weakness. **It is not expedient, but I will come** (this suggests turning to a specific point, possibly raised by others) **to visions and revelations of the Lord.** The sentence (on the text see note 1 on p. 305) is usually taken differently, with *it is not expedient* as a parenthesis between *I must boast* and *I will come . . .* The construction adopted here seems however to be demanded by the two particles (μέν and δέ) which bind together the second and third clauses in the verse as opposite members of a pair: It is indeed not expedient, yet I will come. *Expedient* (συμφέρον,

participle, accusative absolute, for συμφέρει; Robertson, p. 1130) is a word that in Paul's usage points to the welfare not of the individual but of the Christian society: viii. 10; 1 Cor. vi. 12; x. 23; xii. 7. This boasting is not really the way to build up the church; it may nevertheless clear the ground for building if it permits Paul to work in Corinth without disturbance from outside. Kümmel argues that the genitive *of the Lord* is a genitive of the author, not of the object; the distinction may not be a real one. The genitive applies to both *visions* and *revelations*, and these two words cannot be nicely distinguished. The appearance of Christ to Paul at his conversion is described in Acts xxvi. 19 as a *vision* (ὀπτασία); Paul does not use this word elsewhere, and *revelation* (ἀποκάλυψις) he uses most often in eschatological contexts (Rom. ii. 5; viii. 19; 1 Cor. i. 7; 2 Thess. i. 7). He uses it also however in relation to his conversion (Gal. i. 12; cf. the use of the cognate verb at Gal. i. 16). A special *revelation* sent him to Jerusalem (Gal. ii. 2), and *revelations*, apocalypses, enlivened the meetings of the Corinthian church (1 Cor. xiv. 6, 26). It could be argued that *vision* points directly to the thing seen, or the experience of seeing it, *revelation* to its intelligible content and its communication, but it would be unwise to build on this, and unnecessary, since Paul goes on to speak of one experience without further defining it (see however verse 7). For the polemical reference to *visions and revelations* in the Clementine Homilies see Schoeps, *T.G.J.*, pp. 130, 425.

The translation of the next few verses imitates to some extent the involved and tortuous style of the original. Even when boasting of his own visions Paul is unwilling to do so directly, and tells his story as if it related to someone else, of whom he speaks in the third person. We may compare the occasional rabbinic use of 'this man' for 'I' (S.B. iii. 531): but Wendland is not far wrong in saying that Paul distinguishes two men within himself. There is *a man* who is a visionary, and this man is in fact Paul; but Paul would rather be thought of as the weak man, who has nothing to boast of but his weakness. Betz's account (pp. 84-92) of verses 2-4 as a parody of an ascension narrative (of which there were not a few in the ancient world) is full of useful parallels and of suggestion; it seems to me, however, that the passage has an inner motivation that makes it essentially independent of the parallels. Paul is not writing a literary exercise in a given style. Betz does not suggest

that he is, and his discussion is illuminating, but misses some of
2 the raw force of Paul's writing. Note verse 6. **I know a man in Christ** (that is, a Christian), **fourteen years ago.** So Paul must go back fourteen years (that is, to about A.D. 40, long before any date that can be assigned to the foundation of the Corinthian church; see Introduction, p. 4) for a suitable example of *visions and revelations of the Lord.* He was thus ordinarily anything but a visionary, though it is no doubt true that he picked out the most striking, and not the only, visionary experience that he could claim. Wendland asks why Paul does not refer to the Damascus road experience; the answer is that Paul did not regard this as a vision. He then saw Jesus our Lord objectively.

It is an easy and probably correct guess that those in Corinth who interested themselves in visions would discuss their mechanism, and the relation of the mystics to common life. Paul has no pronouncement to make on this question: **Whether he was in the body, or out of the body** (curiously, in this verse and the next, *body*, σῶμα, has the article at the second occurrence, not at the first; see Moule, *Idiom*, pp. 114, 203—the explanation may be that *out of* and *apart from* are 'improper' prepositions), **I do not know—God knows.** It is true that Paul here 'reckons ... with the possibility that the self may in the present life be separated from the σῶμα [body], and this σῶμα [body] can only be the physical body' (Bultmann, *Theol.*, p. 199; E.T., i. 202). It is however also clear that Paul was unable to distinguish between the two states, *in the body* and *out of the body*, or rather that he thought the distinction irrelevant, or inapplicable. He did not know whether on this occasion he had been *in the body* or *out of the body.* Many details of various kinds of rapture are given by Windisch, pp. 374 ff. Philo knew that contact with heaven meant being *out of the body*: 'To such strains [of heavenly music] it is said that Moses was listening, when, having laid aside his body (ἀσώματον γενόμενον), for forty days and as many nights he touched neither bread nor water at all' (*De Somniis* i. 36; see Knox, *P.G.*, p. 102, and cf. also Josephus, *War* vii. 349, cited by Schlatter). This is not Paul's view; indeed Paul was probably deliberately refraining from expressing a view, that is, from adopting either a Corinthian-Gnostic view, that religious experience to be valid must be *out of the body*, or the direct negative of this. He will not affirm, or imply, that the body is necessarily evil; equally he does not deny the possibility that the soul may leave the body and have dealings with spiritual, non-corporeal beings. *God knows* has the effect of underlining *I do not know*; but this is not to say that Paul did not seriously mean it. The mechanism of man's communion with God may be safely left to God.

I know (the verb is not repeated in Greek, but even in English that imitates Paul's Greek it must be added in the interests of intelligibility) **that** (supplying *I know* we may best take the sentence as an accusative and participle construction) **a man like that** (literally, such a man) **was caught up as far as the third heaven.** Paul's only other use of *caught up* (ἁρπάζειν) is 1 Thess. iv. 17, where Christians who survive till the Lord's coming are caught up to join him, and the dead, who have already been raised up, in the air. The experience described in our passage may be thought of as an anticipation of the final transference of believers to heaven, or Paradise. Mystical and apocalyptic-eschatological religion are not as far apart as is sometimes supposed. Apocalyptists describe the future on the basis of insight granted them in the present into what already is in heaven (see *S.J.T.* vi. 138 f.). Parallels to Paul's experience can be cited from many fields. From apocalyptic the following examples may be quoted: In those days a whirlwind carried me off from the earth, and set me down at the end of the heavens. And there I saw another vision . . . (1 Enoch xxxix. 3 f.; cf. lii. 1); And these men took me and led me up on to the second heaven, and showed me darkness, greater than earthly darkness . . . (2 Enoch vii. 1; in viii Enoch proceeds to the third, in xi to the fourth heaven, in xviii to the fifth, and so on to the tenth); And he took me and led me to the first heaven, and showed me . . . (3 Baruch ii. 2; and so on to the fifth heaven). Mystical speculation was by no means unknown among the rabbis. The best known single passage is Hagigah 14b: There are four who entered into Paradise; these are Ben 'Azzai and Ben Zoma, Aher, and R. Aqiba. Compare Megillah iv. 10 and Hagigah ii. 1, which forbid the reading of and discourage speculation upon the chapter of the Chariot (Merkabah; Ezek. i). Ecstasy is a familiar phenomenon in Hellenistic mysticism, and it sometimes takes the form of a journey into other worlds; so for example the Myth of Er in Plato, *Republic* x (614-21; 'He said that when he left the body his soul went on a journey . . . He was to be the messenger who would carry the report of the other world to men . . .'), especially as interpreted by Proclus. Philo can speak of his ecstatic experiences both as a descent of divine influence upon him (e.g. *De Migr. Abr.* 34 f.), and as an ascent: 'I had no base or abject thoughts nor grovelled in search of reputation or of wealth or bodily comforts, but seemed always to be borne aloft into the heights with a soul possessed by some God-sent inspiration, a fellow-traveller with the sun and moon and the whole heaven and universe. Ah then I gazed down from the upper air . . .' (*Spec. Leg.* iii. 1 f.).

There was a great deal of contemporary precedent for Paul's experience of rapture into heaven (for much more evidence see e.g. Lietzmann; also Betz, *Lukian*, pp. 38, 142, 169), and the striking thing is not that Paul should have experienced such a rapture but that he should go back fourteen years to find an example, and then depreciate its significance.

It is evident that Paul believed in a plurality of heavens (presumably spherical, or hemispherical, shells); it cannot be inferred from his reference to a *third* that he believed in only three (as against five, seven, ten, or any other number), though three seems to have been the number commonly accepted in his time (S.B. iii. 531 ff.). See below on Paradise. Calvin's view, that 'the number three is used as a perfect number to indicate what is highest and most complete', may be correct.

3 In very hesitant and repetitive style Paul proceeds, **And I know**
that a man like that (Paul appears to resume the accusative and
participle construction used in the preceding verse, but after the
parenthesis this breaks down)**—whether in the body or apart**
from (a different word, χωρίς, not ἐκτός, is used, but probably
without change of meaning) **the body God knows** (Paul implies
but this time does not say, I do not know—many MSS include
4 οὐκ οἶδα, but probably by assimilation)**—I know** (not in the
Greek, which continues καὶ ὅτι, 'and that'; Paul should have
written the participle, ἁρπαγέντα) **that he was caught up into**
Paradise. For the most part Paul here repeats the language of
verse 2, but for *the third heaven* he substitutes *Paradise*. There is
no difference in meaning; this is not a second rapture but the
same which is given, with its date, in verse 2. 2 Enoch viii places
Paradise in the third heaven; in the Apocalypse of Moses xxxvii. 5
God says to Michael, Lift him [the dead Adam] up into Paradise
unto the third heaven, and leave him there unto that fearful day
of my reckoning, which I will make in the world. For many

references to Paradise, see Windisch. The word (παράδεισος), originally a Persian nobleman's park, was adopted into Greek, used of the Garden of Eden, and thus (in the realm of thought where it was believed that the last days would be like the first) came to be used of the abode of the blessed, after death or after the final judgement. In Paradise he **heard unutterable** (ἄρρητα; not the word of Rom. viii. 26) **words, which it is not permitted a man to speak;** that is, they were *unutterable* in the sense that they conveyed divine secrets which were not to be communicated to men at large. The language is that of mystery religions: see for example Apuleius, *Metamorphoses* xi. 23: 'Perhaps, diligent reader, you desire with some solicitude to know what then was said, what done; I would tell you, if it were permitted to tell (si dicere liceret), you should hear it, if it were permitted to hear (si liceret audire). But both your ears and my tongue would bear the like pain, my tongue for impious loquacity, your ears for rash curiosity.' Previously the priest in charge of Apuleius's initiation had committed to him certain precepts 'which surpass human speech' (quae voce meliora sunt). It would be wrong, however, to suppose that Paul was directly dependent on the mysteries. Not only had Philo already appropriated such language (e.g. *Leg. Alleg.* ii. 57, Not to all must leave be given to contemplate the secret things (ἀπόρρητα) of God, but only to those who are able to hide and guard them; cf. *Quod Det. Pot.* 175), and not only was the notion of secret revelation current in rabbinic Judaism (see J. Jeremias, *Jerusalem in the Time of Jesus* (1969), pp. 237-41); the idea of sealed revelation was already to be found in the Old Testament (Isa. viii. 16; Dan. xii. 4; cf. also 2 Enoch xvii; Rev. xiv. 3). Paul's revelation thus falls into a familiar form—familiar no doubt at Corinth as a boast of Paul's rivals. Of this he too can boast; but, as throughout these chapters, his boasting is twisted into an unusual form.

On behalf of a man like that (or, taking τοιούτου to be neuter, 5
'of an experience like that'; but τοιούτου must be masculine because of the previous occurrence of the word and the following *on my own behalf*—so, rightly, Bachmann) **I will boast, but on my own behalf I will boast only in my weaknesses.** The strange, third person, reference to the recipient of the revelation continues, and is underlined by the first person that follows. According to Lietzmann (cf. Wendland, referred to on verse 1),

the text distinguishes between 'Paul the apocalyptist' and 'Paul the man and apostle'. This is true as far as it goes. Käsemann (*Legitimität*, pp. 63-71/54-66), followed by Kümmel, makes the point that Paul evaluates his experience of exaltation into heaven, as he does his speaking with tongues (1 Cor. xiv. 19) and his ecstasy (2 Cor. v. 13), in relation to his service to the church. Details of his rapture to the third heaven, which concern only his personal relation with God, have no value for the church; he therefore sees no point in boasting about them, and suppresses them. This also is a correct observation, but (as the next verse makes clear) Paul is also concerned not only that he should be rightly evaluated but that he should be evaluated by the right criteria. It is often deduced (see Introduction, pp. 29 f.) from these verses that Paul's opponents, the Corinthian intruders, were men who boasted of great 'spiritual' gifts and prided themselves on their visions and raptures. It is more probably true (see 'Paul's Opponents', pp. 251 f.) that the insistence on 'spiritual' and ecstatic phenomena as the marks of apostleship originated in Corinth, though the visiting apostles, seeing that these marks were demanded, proceeded to produce them. But for Paul the only valid and visible sign of apostolicity was the *weakness* the apostle was prepared to accept that the power of Christ might be manifested in him. The theme of *weakness* is developed through the next few verses. The choice of this theme is deliberate and not forced upon Paul by
6 lack of other material, **for if I choose** (θελήσω; this verb properly carries with it an element of deliberate preference) **to boast** (i.e., about things other than my weaknesses) **I shall not turn out to be a fool** (caught out in false claims)**, for I shall speak the truth.** There may be a hit here at those who, spurred on by Corinthian requirements, boasted about visions they had not had. It is not only common honesty on Paul's part that he should speak the truth; that men should see his weakness was part of the manifestation of the apostolic Gospel. If he speaks about visions and the like he will speak the truth; **but I am trying** (taking the present tense as conative—the Corinthians have only themselves to blame that they have brought upon themselves the story of Paul's rapture) **to spare you** (φείδομαι; this is usually taken to mean, 'I spare myself'; but cf. i. 23; xiii. 2; also Rom. viii. 32; xi. 21; 1 Cor. vii. 28)**, lest anyone should reckon to my account** (a commercial expression; see examples in Lietzmann) **more than**

he sees in me (literally, more than he sees me—an accusative of respect?), **or hears of me** (or, from me, ἐξ ἐμοῦ). Paul does not wish too high an opinion of him to become current; it would obscure the fact that it is to his Gospel, and not himself, that men should attend, and that he is a more effective witness to Christ crucified if he endures suffering and disgrace. 'That means that he intends to be understood simply on the basis of his service (diakonia)' (Käsemann, *Legitimität*, p. 69/64; cf. p. 70/65, with the reference to Rengstorf; Paul refuses an 'enthusiastic' foundation for apostleship).

The next verse can hardly be in the form that Paul intended it to have, though it may possibly be in the form in which he wrote, or dictated, it. For the textual variants see note 2 on p. 305. The view taken here is that, difficult as the text is, the many conjectures that have been offered do not make it substantially easier, and that the first five words of the Greek (*καὶ τῇ ὑπερβολῇ τῶν ἀποκαλύψεων*, literally, and by the pre-eminence (cf. iv. 7) of the revelations) should not be attached to the end of verse 6. A literal rendering of the whole verse will now run as follows: And by (reason of) the pre-eminence of the revelations, wherefore, in order that I might not be unduly exalted, there was given me a thorn in my flesh, an angel of Satan, (sent) to beat me, in order that I might not be unduly exalted. The general meaning of this is clear. God gave (the passive voice implies divine action) Paul a thorn in his flesh, or, in other words, sent an angel of Satan to beat him, in order that he might not become unduly exalted through receiving such outstanding revelations. The thorn, or angel, would keep him humble. That this is what Paul meant is hardly open to doubt, but it cannot be got out of the text by the application of the ordinary rules of syntax. Either the text has been badly corrupted in transmission, or Paul made more than one attempt at the sentence. He began to write: Because the revelations were so marvellous, God took steps to see that I should not be unduly exalted. But he got to the purpose of God's action before he described the action itself. *Wherefore* (διό), though unnecessary, is not difficult, since it simply anticipates the final clause (for which reason, namely, in order to . . .); the reason and purpose of God's action are simply stated: *Because* the revelations were so marvellous, *in order that* I might not be unduly exalted . . . It is perhaps the use of the passive, and the addition of the *angel* after the *thorn*, that led Paul

to forget that he had stated the purpose of God's action early in the sentence, and so to repeat it: That I might not be unduly exalted there was given me a thorn . . . an angel . . . that I might not be unduly exalted. Thus we arrive at what it is perhaps hardly fair to call a translation, but does represent Paul's meaning and
7 uses his words as far as possible: **And because the revelations were so marvellous, that I might not be unduly exalted there was given me a thorn in my flesh** (for the dative *τῇ σαρκί* see Radermacher, p. 106; Robertson, p. 538), **an angel of Satan sent to beat me, that I might not be unduly exalted** (taking the second *ἵνα* to be dependent on the first, in order to give some justification for the final clause).

God allowed Paul astounding revelations of heavenly truth, which could not be communicated, but he did not intend that these should go to the apostle's head—the duplicated clause, though it may have been written through an oversight, underlines this, perhaps with reference to others, whose heads had been turned by flattery, with the result that they had got above themselves (*ὑπεραίρονται*). Paul was to be kept humble, and aware of his weakness. The meaning of *a thorn in my flesh* has been disputed at great length. Among many accounts of the history of interpretation see Hughes and Windisch ad loc., Allo's Excursus (pp. 313-23), H. Clavier (*Studia Paulina*, p. 66; Clavier says that his list reads like a medical dictionary), and P. H. Menoud (also in *Studia Paulina*, pp. 163-71). There is no unanimity about even the kind of suffering or disability Paul was alluding to. Calvin notes that flesh is the 'part of the soul that is not regenerate', and so paraphrases, 'To me has been given a goad to jab at my flesh for I am not yet so spiritual as to be exempt from temptation according to the flesh'. Few if any modern writers adopt this view. Many but not all see a reference to physical sickness. J. J. Thierry (*Nov. T.* v. 301-10) takes Paul to mean 'An angel of Satan was given me as a thorn in the flesh', so that there is no need to see any reference to physical disorder. Menoud (op. cit. p. 168) observes that 'the great suffering that befell Paul was that he was unable to win the Jews for the Gospel'. E. Kamlah (*Z.N.T.W.* liv. 219) thinks of the temptation to hate fellow-Christians. Clavier (op. cit. p. 79) comes nearer to the purely physical realm with 'morbid conditions that followed upon the visions and revelations'. It is almost certainly wrong to suppose (see the notes on iv. 10) that Paul had literally been crucified; there is more in Schlatter's observation that *thorn* (σκόλοψ, which could be equivalent to σταυρός) could mean *cross*, and his reference based on this observation to Gal. v. 24. Gal. iv. 13 ff. is often invoked, and sometimes taken to mean that Paul suffered from a disease of the eyes; but, as Lietzmann says, Gal. iv. 15 means only 'You would have sacrificed your most precious organ to help me'. *In my flesh* does not necessarily refer to physical trouble (cf. Num. xxxiii. 55, Then shall those which ye let remain of them be as pricks in your eyes, and as thorns in your sides; cf. also Ezek. xxviii. 24—Héring), nor does the *angel of Satan sent to beat me* (strictly, about the head) necessarily imply that Paul was beaten to the ground in attacks of epilepsy (see however Schoeps, *T.G.J.*, p. 433, referring to *Clementine Homilies* xx. 19 = *Recognitions* x. 64 (61 seems to be intended)). The plain fact is that Paul's physical health (which must on the whole have been very good, or he could never have survived the hardships and perils described in xi. 23-33; see Introduction, p. 33), and the precise meaning of *thorn* and *angel*, are anyone's guess. If a specific physical defect is to be looked for, possibly as good a suggestion as any is that Paul suffered from an impediment in his speech. This would allow for the fact that he could make a very bad first impression (Gal. iv. 13 ff.) and be judged poor in presence and in speech, but impressive in his letters (x. 1, 9, 10, 11; xi. 6). The letters are so eloquent (*1 Corinthians*, p. 64) that it is hard to believe that Paul was a bad speaker unless he suffered from a speech defect. But this too is a guess and nothing more; see W. K. Lowther Clarke, *New Testament Problems* (1929), pp. 136-40. Acts xiv. 12 speaks against the suggestion, but (a) Luke may be mistaken, and (b) the thorn in the flesh was given (aorist, ἐδόθη; this is emphasized by Bachmann) to Paul on a specific occasion, possibly after the visit to Lystra.

Thorn (σκόλοψ) could be a stake, including a stake used for torture or execution. At Num. xxxiii. 55 (quoted above), however, it translates *sek*, which appears to mean thorn, but is a hapax legomenon, and open to some doubt. For *angels of Satan* see Matt. xxv. 41; Rev. xii. 7, 9; and S.B. i. 136, 983 f. 'Expressions such as "angels of Satan", "angels" or "spirits of the devil" occur seldom in ancient Jewish literature' (p. 983). They are, however, occasionally mentioned, and to the material known to Billerbeck we may now add CD xvi. 5 (*mal'ak ha-masṭema*, angel of Mastema). Moreover it must be remembered that *angel* (ἄγγελος) means 'messenger', and need not be a fully technical term. This makes it the more striking that Paul should imply (he does not actually say) that the messenger of Satan was sent by God. Satan has only limited freedom of action; God remains in control.

8 **Concerning** (ὑπέρ for περί, as at i. 8) **this angel** (the Greek could mean 'this matter'—τούτου neuter—but the next clause, of which the angel must be the subject, determines the application of *this*) **I asked** (it is tempting to translate παρεκάλεσα more strongly—I begged; but see viii. 6; ix. 5; and for the wording as a whole cf. *Sylloge* 804. 30 f. (in the third edition, 1170. 31 f.), καὶ περὶ τούτου παρεκάλεσα τὸν θεόν, cited by Bachmann) **the Lord three times** (this probably should be taken to signify earnest and repeated prayer, but Windisch and others take the number literally; cf. the prayers of Jesus in Gethsemane, Mark xiv. 35-41) **that he**
9 **might go away from me. And he has said** ('The perfect stands for a decision valid once and for all'—Bachmann; cf. Moule, *Idiom*, p. 15) **to me, My grace is enough for you; for power comes to perfection in weakness.** 'Benignissima repulsa', says Bengel, who goes on to observe that the Lord as it were put these words in Paul's mouth, so that he might subsequently say, 'Sufficit mihi, Domine, gratia tua.' Calvin points out that there are two kinds of answer to prayer, and that we must distinguish between ends and means: the Lord may grant an end that we properly seek, but not by the means we desired. *Grace* has been so frequently and so widely used in the epistle (e.g. i. 2, 12; iv. 15; viii passim; ix. 8, 14) that it is unlikely that it here means the special grace that makes Paul an apostle. It may be added, however, that it is grace by which any man becomes the sort of Christian that he is and does the sort of service that he does (vi. 1; Rom. xii. 6; 1 Cor. i. 4); in Paul's case this means being an apostle and doing the work of an apostle (Rom. i. 5; xii. 3; 1 Cor. xv. 10). *Grace* however is also, and more fundamentally, the movement in love of God to man that takes effect in Christ (viii. 9); through it, man is assured of his standing with God, and that nothing in life or death, in the present or the future, can separate him from God's love in Christ (Rom. viii. 38 f.). This makes the sharpest suffering and the lowest humiliation tolerable, and enables Paul to continue his apostolic ministry. Not only so, it means that one can rejoice in tribulation (Rom. v. 2 ff.), because a scene

of human weakness is the best possible stage for the display of divine power. So far from *coming to perfection*, divine power is scarcely perceptible in the impressive activities of the ecclesiastical potentates with whom Paul has to contend. It is when he is weak, really weak—poor, sick, humiliated, despised, unloved by his own spiritual children as well as scorned by the world—that God's power comes into view. For 'God's foolishness is wiser than men, and God's weakness is stronger than men' (1 Cor. i. 25).

This is the final demonstration that Paul's attitude to the question of boasting has been right. **Therefore will I most gladly boast rather in my weaknesses** (rather, that is, in them than in anything else—as Robertson, p. 664; B.D. §246 observe, *μᾶλλον* is not to be taken with *ἥδιστα*, but it is awkward that no comparison is expressed)**, in order that Christ's power may rest upon me.** For the preference, compare Sifre Deuteronomy 32 (on vi. 5) (73 b) (S.B. iii. 798): Let a man rejoice in sufferings more than over good. The reason given in Sifre, however, is that suffering leads to repentance, whereas Paul means to boast in weakness rather than strength in order that *the power of Christ may rest upon him.* The verb (*ἐπισκηνοῦν*) is used only here in the New Testament (but cf. the use of *σκῆνος*, tent, in v. 1 ff.), and suggests the overshadowing of Israel by the divine presence (Schlatter).
So I am well content in weaknesses, in insults (cf. 1 Thess. 10
ii. 2)**, in anguish** (cf. vi. 4)**, in persecutions and distresses** (cf. vi. 4)**, endured on behalf of Christ; for when I am weak** (by human standards)**, then am I strong** (not in myself but in that *Christ's power rests upon me*)**.** This is the picture of apostolic life that has been repeated again and again in this letter; see for example iv. 10 ff., and *Signs*, pp. 41-4. This is the meaning of living by faith, not by sight. The power of Christ may become visible, for example, in the conversion of unlikely sinners (1 Cor. vi. 9 ff.); but it is not under man's control, and therefore never the theme of man's boasting. Philo, at *Vit. Mos.* i. 69, uses similar language (Your weakness is your strength, *τὸ ἀσθενὲς ὑμῶν δύναμίς ἐστιν*), but the sense is different. Betz, pp. 92 f., finds here another parody (see the note on verses 2-4 above); Paul offers his version of the marvellous cures performed by the gods for their petitioners. He prayed for relief in due form, but the answer he received was both less and greater than those of the advertised cures. There is force, as in verses 2-4, in the parallels adduced, but

again there is so much theological drive and coherence in what Paul says that the element of parody cannot be judged to be more than peripheral and incidental.

There is a short but perceptive exegesis of verses 1-10 in Barth, *C.D.* I ii. 332.

21. xii. 11-18. ANSWERING OBJECTIONS

(11) I have become a fool;[1] you compelled me to it. For I ought to be commended by you; for I came behind the super-apostles in no way at all—even though I am 'nothing'. (12) At least, the 'signs of an apostle' were performed among you, as I endured every kind of suffering and abuse. My endurance was accompanied by signs and portents and mighty works. (13) In what respect were you put lower than the other churches, except that I myself did not make myself a burden to you? Forgive me this injury. (14) Look! this is the third time I am ready to come to you, and I will not make myself a burden to you; for I seek not your property, but you. For children ought not to save up for their parents, but parents for their children. (15) And for my part I will most gladly spend and be spent up in the interests of your souls. If I love[2] you more abundantly, am I loved the less? (16) All right; I laid no burden on you, but confidence trickster as I was I caught you by craftiness. (17) Any of those whom I have sent to you—did I defraud you through him? (18) I asked Titus to visit you, and with him I sent

[1] Many MSS add καυχώμενος: I have become a fool with this glorying. The interpretation is correct, the text secondary.

[2] *If* (εἰ) is read by 𝔓46 B ℵ; *although* (εἰ καί) by the majority of MSS; the word is omitted by D it Ambrosiaster. *I love* (ἀγαπῶ) is the reading of a few MSS only, notably ℵ* A. The rest (including 𝔓46 B D G and the Latin) have the participle, ἀγαπῶν. These variants require different punctuations of the verse, and give rise to the following three ways of taking it, in addition to that given in the text. (a) Loving you more abundantly, am I loved the less? This is indistinguishable in meaning from the translation in the text. (b) Loving you more abundantly, I am loved the less—a statement of fact. (c) I will most gladly spend and be spent up in the interests of your souls, even though, loving you more abundantly, I am loved the less. (c) is a late form of the text, unlikely to be original. (a) could be what Paul wrote, but the reading adopted in the text is livelier and more 'Pauline'. See also the commentary.

the brother. Did Titus defraud you? Did we not behave in the same spirit, walk in the same footsteps?

There is to be no more boasting. Reluctantly, self-consciously, paradoxically, Paul has indulged in it (x. 8; xi. 16, 17, 18; xii. 5, 6, 9), caught in the dilemma in which it is necessary to defend the Gospel, only with the result of proving that to defend the Gospel is to destroy it. It is necessary, and at the same time inexpedient (xii. 1); here above all is the point at which the church is broken (see the Preface, pp. viii f.). Put in personal terms, this necessity
of inexpedient and ultimately un-Christian boasting means, **I have** 11
become a fool (on the text, see note 1 on p. 318); **you compelled me to it.** *I have become a fool* because I have joined in the activity I have condemned in others, arguing myself to be a better Jew, a more devoted servant of Christ, than they, then driven to the paradox of boasting in weakness. *You compelled me* (as the following words show) by not speaking on my behalf and doing the boasting for me (cf. vii. 11). This is a key-verse for understanding the Corinthian situation (see Introduction, pp. 28 ff.). Paul's foes are neither the Jerusalem apostles (see below, and verse 12) nor the Corinthians, but the pseudo-apostles (xi. 13); the fault of the Corinthians had been their silence. They had not actively taken the part of those who opposed Paul (see vii. 11, and the notes), but neither had they stood up for him, commended him, as they should have done. Hence Paul had had to speak for himself, and thereby (in his own estimation) prove himself a fool. He was obliged to do this, **for I ought to be commended by you;** but the Corinthians had failed in their duty. No amount of commendation from the Corinthians could make Paul an apostle (cf. iii. 1; but Paul is not contradicting himself by asking for the same sort of commendation that the Corinthians had given to his rivals); his apostleship was of no human origin (Gal. i. 1), and was exposed to no human judgement, even his own (1 Cor. iv. 3 f.). Yet the Corinthians were the seal of his apostleship (1 Cor. ix. 2) in that their very existence as Christians validated Paul's apostolic mission, through which they had been converted (1 Cor. iii. 6, 10; iv. 15). It was necessary only that they should have acknowledged that they were what they were; this would have commended Paul as an apostle; but they had failed to do this, ashamed of their cheap (xi. 7-11; xii. 13 ff.) and tongue-tied (x. 1, 10; xi. 6) apostle as they compared him with his

domineering rivals (xi. 20). In fact, Paul had every right to be commended, **for I came behind the super-apostles in no way at all.** For the identification of the *super-apostles* see xi. 5 and the note (also Introduction, pp. 30 ff. and *Signs*, pp. 37-40). In xi. 5 *to come short* (ὑστερεῖν) is expressed in the perfect, but here in the aorist (ὑστέρησα); this has been taken to imply that Paul is here referring to a specific occasion in Corinth when the Corinthians had had the opportunity of comparing Paul and his rivals. This, if true, would prove that the *super-apostles* had been in Corinth and were thus to be identified not with the Jerusalem apostles but with the *pseudo-apostles* (xi. 13). The conclusion is however by no means necessary; the aorist is constative, and sums up in a single point the substance of Paul's dealings with Corinth. If he is equal to the super-apostles he is not inferior to the intruders.

There is still irony in Paul's mind, and he takes the language of others—rivals and Corinthians—on his pen. He is not inferior to the super-apostles, **even though I am 'nothing'.** The punctuation adopted here implies that others described Paul as a *nothing*—unworthy of consideration. This is not a stronger expression than those of x. 1, 10 (ταπεινός, ἀσθενής, ἐξουθενημένος) and 1 Cor. xv. 8, 9 (ἔκτρωμα, ἐλάχιστος τῶν ἀποστόλων). Compare Plato, *Phaedrus* 234 CDE (including the strange expression, τῆς ἐμῆς οὐδενίας—Betz, p. 122); Epictetus, III ix. 14 (οὐδὲν ἦν ὁ Ἐπίκτητος); IV viii. 25. Paul was human enough for the word to rankle, though there was a sense in which he could gladly claim it to be true; he was well pleased to be *nothing* that Christ might appear to be the more, and his people advantaged (cf. e.g. xii. 9; xiii. 7, 9).

The main point at the moment, however, is that Paul is no less
12 than the super-apostles. **At least** (this is probably the 'restrictive force' of μέν solitarium—Robertson, p. 1151; alternatively (Allo), The signs were indeed there [but you did not recognize them]), **the 'signs of an** (in Greek, the generic use of the definite article; Robertson, p. 757) **apostle'** (there is a wide-ranging discussion in Betz, pp. 70-100) **were performed** (he does not say, I performed them; cf. Mark xvi. 17, 20) **among you, as I endured every kind of suffering and abuse** (literally, in all endurance; but it is clear from the epistle as a whole what it was that Paul had to endure). It is probable that in *the signs of an apostle*, that is, the signs that mark out an apostle, Paul borrows words that others had used. It

has often been suggested that they were the words of his rivals in Corinth, who claimed to be able to show (and perhaps that Paul could not show) signs that demonstrated their apostolic status; it is however perhaps more probable that Paul was using words not of his adversaries but of the Corinthians, who looked for appropriate signs in those who approached them as missionaries. 'In an apostle the Corinthians wished to see a special bearer of the Spirit [*Pneumaträger*], who by "signs and wonders" confirmed the power of the Spirit-Revealer, which he would have to have at his disposal in unlimited degree' (Wilckens, *Weisheit*, p. 218). They were the judges, who put others to the test (cf. xiii. 3, 5, with the notes); and the test included the requirement of miracle-working. Paul's rivals, originally standing on a Jewish-Christian platform, had no difficulty in accommodating themselves to the requirement (and thus in some respects give the impression of claiming to be 'divine men', θεῖοι ἄνδρες; see Introduction, pp. 29 f.; also 'Paul's Opponents', pp. 251 f.); he himself elsewhere speaks of miracle-working (Rom. xv. 19; Gal. iii. 5), and there is no doubt that, whether or not other explanations of the phenomena in question may seem desirable to us, it was believed in the primitive church that miracles took place. Paul, who like most of his contemporaries had no difficulty in accepting the miraculous, made his contribution to the matter in hand not by a claim that miracles had been wrought but by adding *in all endurance.* Miracles were no contradiction of the *theologia crucis* he proclaimed and practised, since they were performed not in a context of triumphant success and prosperity, but in the midst of the distress and vilification he was obliged to endure. The miracle the Lord did not perform was that of removing the angel of Satan sent to buffet Paul (xii. 8 f.); Käsemann, *Legitimität*, p. 63/53, rightly refers also to xi. 23 ff. But both sides of the picture are important and valid, and if the signs were performed in a context of endurance **my endurance was accompanied by** (these five words are not in the Greek but seem to be implied by the dative case in which the three nouns following stand) **signs and portents and mighty works.** For this compound expression compare Acts ii. 22; 2 Thess. ii. 9. The pair *signs and portents* is much commoner. *Portent* (τέρας) is used in Acts nine times; elsewhere in the New Testament seven times; *mighty work* (δύναμις) is the usual synoptic word for the miracles of Jesus. We cannot infer from the epistles what miracles were performed by Paul; see Acts xiii. 11; xiv. 10; xv. 12; xvi. 18; xix. 11 f.; xx. 10 ff.; xxviii. 3-6, 8.

The Corinthians had had their share of miracles, and from Paul too. What then was their complaint? Paul returns to the question that re-echoes through the Corinthian letters (xi. 7-11; 1 Cor. ix. 4-18), his refusal to accept payment from the church. It seems that the point was one on which both he and the Corinthians were exceptionally sensitive. It is clear (verse 15) that Paul felt that his motives had been misunderstood, and it is not impossible that the Corinthians felt the same; they wished to be allowed to contribute to the apostle's expenses as the other churches did (xi. 8 f.; Georgi, *Gegner*, p. 238, makes the good point that Paul accepted support only when it was understood not as the reward of an inspired man [*Pneumatiker*] but as a mark of personal fellowship), and saw no reason why they should be singled out for treatment that seemed to stamp them as less responsible and trustworthy than, say, the Macedonian churches. There is however no reason to suppose that Paul, who knew the situation at first hand, was fundamentally wrong in judging that the Corinthian attitude arose out of a false understanding of apostleship. An apostle, they thought, must be (not necessarily a 'divine man'—see above—but certainly) a powerful and imposing person, standing out for all the rights he could possibly claim, performing miracles, and accepting the adulation and support of those whom he was able to impress. That such persons arose within the church at an early date is proved by xi. 20; that they continued into the second century is illustrated by such figures (Lucianic caricatures though they may be) as Peregrinus and Alexander the false prophet; that the *theologia gloriae* (see e.g. p. 304; also *Signs*, pp. 104 f.) they represent is a permanent threat to Christianity is written on every page of church history and is in itself a sufficient reason for the continued
13 study of 2 Corinthians. **In what respect** (γάρ in this sentence
cannot be translated; the word is used 'in abrupt questions'—
L.S., s.v., I 4) **were you put lower** (for the verb ἡσσώθητε, with
variants ἡττήθητε, ἐλαττώθητε, compare the use of the cognate
noun ἥττημα in Rom. xi. 12, with the note) **than the other**
churches (which Paul had allowed to contribute to his keep),
except that I myself (emphatic, αὐτὸς ἐγώ; perhaps 'I at any
rate, whatever others may do') **did not make myself a burden**

(κατενάρκησα; for the word see xi. 9) **to you?** Paul adds, with cutting sarcasm, **Forgive** (χαρίζεσθαι, not a theological word with Paul; cf. ii. 7, 10) **me this injury** (cf. ii. 10; vii. 12; the person concerned in these passages had injured Paul; see also vii. 2)—the omission of the one missing 'sign of an apostle'.

They must be prepared to forgive, to indulge him in this incomprehensible behaviour, for he does not propose to change his ways.
Look! this is the third time I am ready to come to you. 14
The Greek construction, like the English, is ambiguous (Beyer, p. 280, sees here a Semitic clause: Though I am ready . . . I will not . . .; his view is not convincing). It might mean, I am now for a third time ready to come, or, I am now ready to come for a third time. xiii. 1 makes it virtually certain that the latter is what Paul intended. Earlier he had forborne to pay this third visit (see i. 23; ii. 1), but he is now on the point of making it; the Corinthian problem must be settled once for all. There will be no change of policy: **I will not make myself a burden** (the same word as in verse 13) **to you.** The reason is clear: **I seek not your property, but you.** Compare Cicero, *De Finibus* II 26, 85 (Me igitur ipsum ames oportet non mea, si veri amici futuri sumus); other passages are cited in Windisch. Paul's motives in refusing payment had been questioned; but the minister who receives payment must always expect that his motives (which may be faultless) will be questioned. Perhaps he is aiming at his converts' pockets. No one could say that of Paul in relation to Corinth (and it may well be that to take money from, say, Philippi for use in Corinth was less open to objection). He sought them partly in the sense of desiring an answering affection from them (not only verse 15, but also vi. 13; vii. 2), but primarily in the sense of gaining them for Christ (1 Cor. ix. 19-22, with the use of the verb κερδαίνειν; see *1 Corinthians*, p. 211). A simple human analogy confirms Paul's principle: **For children ought not** (that is, children are not under obligation) **to save up for their parents, but parents for their children.** For the father–child relation between the evangelist and his converts see 1 Cor. iv. 15 and the note. Through the Gospel, Paul had begotten (cf. Philemon 10) them as Christians, and was therefore responsible for, and for maintaining, their Christian existence; they were in no sense responsible for him. What then are we to say of the relation between Paul and Philippi? and of other apostles, who received support from the churches? It would

be mistaken to draw negative implications from Paul's dealings with Corinth. 'What he did, he did as a father, but if he had done otherwise, he would not have ceased to be a father' (Calvin). There are no detailed regulations for the relations between father and child.

Paul was prepared to accept parental responsibility to the full.
15 **And for my part** (the sentence begins with an emphatic ἐγὼ δέ) **I will most gladly spend** (not only money, of which Paul had little, but time, energy, and love) **and be spent up** (not this time the simple verb, δαπανᾶν, but the compound ἐκδαπανᾶν; on the perfective force of ἐκ in this verb see Robertson, p. 596, and cf. iv. 8) **in the interests of your souls,** that is, in your interests; for *your soul* in the sense of *you* compare i. 23, and see Conzelmann, *Theologie*, p. 201. There are no lengths to which Paul will not go for the salvation (the highest interest) of the Corinthians. This is the result of his love for them, and should evoke response (see above, pp. 319 f.; also vi. 11 ff.). **If I** thus **love you more abundantly, am I loved the less?** Compare xi. 11; the Corinthians took Paul's apostolic independence as a sign that he did not love them. On the text, see note 2 on p. 318; Allo prefers the participle (ἀγαπῶν), and translates, . . . even if the more I love you, I have to be loved the less.

This was a serious charge; but a worse had been made, and in the
next verse Paul states not what he admits as truth, but an accusa-
16 tion that some at least in Corinth were making. **All right** (ἔστω δέ, literally, Let it be so; as Robertson, p. 392, says, the subject of this verb is the preceding sentence); **I laid no burden** (κατεβάρησα, not the word of verses 13, 14; but cf. xi. 9, ἀβαρής) **on you, but confidence trickster** (cf. the use of the cognate qualitative noun at iv. 2; xi. 3; πανοῦργος is common in the Wisdom literature; for the Cynic background see Betz, p. 105) **as I was** (causal use of the participle ὑπάρχων; Moule, *Idiom*, p. 103) **I caught** (ἔλαβον; cf. xi. 20) **you by craftiness** (δόλῳ; the cognate verb occurs at iv. 2). The next two verses show that the allegation was: Paul has made a great show of asking for no money, but he has instituted what purports to be a collection for the poor saints in Jerusalem, and has pocketed the proceeds himself. Note that the absence of any reference to this accusation in chapters viii, ix makes it very difficult to believe that these chapters were written after chapters x–xiii; see also below, and Introduction, pp. 12–17.

It was not the smallest part of the hurtfulness of this charge that it touched Paul's assistants as well as himself; but he can defend the
integrity of all. **Any of those whom I have sent** (the perfect 17
tense—ἀπέσταλκα—implies 'those whom I have from time to time sent'; see M. i. 144; iii. 70; Robertson, pp. 893, 896) **to you —did I defraud** (cf. ii. 11; vii. 2) **you through him?** The broken English construction imitates the anacolouthon in the Greek; see B.D. §466 and Robertson, p. 436—also Moule, *Idiom*, p. 176, though the emotion with which Paul is writing is perhaps a more probable explanation of the anacolouthon than a Semitic way of handling pronouns. The record is available to the Corinthians; let them examine it, and bring a precise charge instead of generalizations which can be neither proved nor easily disproved.

Take Titus in particular. **I asked** (παρεκάλεσα; cf. viii. 6, 17) 18
Titus to visit you (the last three words are not in but are implied by the Greek), **and with him I sent the brother** (cf. viii. 18, 22 f., with the notes; Lietzmann thinks a name—'Brother Y'—must have fallen out of the text). The coincidence in wording as as well as substance makes it virtually certain that Paul is here looking back not, as for example Lietzmann and Schlatter suggest, upon an earlier visit but upon the mission planned in chapter viii, which must therefore have been written before chapter xii (and therefore before the unit made up of chapters x–xiii; thus Windisch takes x–xiii to be Paul's fifth letter to Corinth—see his concluding note at the end of chapter xiii). The only difference is that in chapter viii two brothers are sent with Titus. The reason for this (see 'Titus', p. 12) is probably that only one of the two was Paul's nominee; the other was 'appointed by the churches' (viii. 19), and his integrity would not be impugned—and if it were would not affect the point at issue here. In any case, attention focuses on Titus, who of the three stood closest to Paul. **Did Titus defraud you?** The question (with μήτι) expects the answer No—you know perfectly well that he did no such thing. **Did we not behave** (literally, walk) **in the same spirit, walk in the same footsteps?** In this rhetorical question, as elsewhere in the epistle, *we* can be taken in different ways: (a) Did not I, for my part, behave in the same way that, as you must acknowledge, Titus behaved? and (b) Did we not, Titus and I, behave in the same way? The sense is little affected. Paul associates himself with Titus, and claims not only that both he and his colleague acted

with complete integrity, but also that the Corinthians, if they are honest, must acknowledge this fact. *Spirit* could here refer to the Holy Spirit: Were not our actions motivated and directed by the same Spirit of God? But the parallel with *footsteps* suggests the non-theological use (cf. vi. 6; vii. 1) of the word: Each manifested the same spirit of integrity.

There is no more to say on this issue. If the Corinthians believe Paul to have been capable of stealing the collection (and there could be no conclusive means of disproving the suspicion) confidence and pastoral relationship are at an end. This Paul cannot accept, and therefore continues.

Timothy is not mentioned here; from this Plummer infers that that he had not reached Corinth (1 Cor. xvi. 10). The argument is by no means compelling.

22. xii. 19–xiii. 10. THE APOSTLE AND THE CHURCH: THE TRUTH

(19) You have been thinking for a long time now[1] that we are making a defence before you. You are wrong; it is before God, in Christ, that we are speaking; and all that we are doing, my dear friends, is for the purpose of building you up. (20) For I am afraid lest, when I come, I should find you not such men as I desire, and that you may find me not the sort of man you desire. I am afraid lest there should be among you quarrelling,[2] envying,[3] outbursts of anger, intrigues, evil-speaking, whisperings, inflated opinions, disorders; (21) lest, when I come, my God should humiliate me again in your presence, and I should mourn for many of those who sinned previously and did not repent of the uncleanness, fornication, and lasciviousness they had committed.

[1] Instead of πάλαι (*for a long time now*) 𝔓[46] has οὐ πάλαι (presumably asking a question—'You have been thinking, haven't you . . . ?'), and the majority of MSS, including D, have πάλιν, 'again'. The latter variant is probably an assimilation to iii. 1; v. 12; the οὐ in 𝔓[46] may have come from v. 12.

[2] B D G and the majority of MSS have the plural ἔρεις, quarrels, or outbreaks of quarrelling. This is probably due to assimilation to the other plurals in the list.

[3] ℵ and the majority of MSS have the plural ζῆλοι, particular instances of envy. This is probably due to assimilation to the other plurals in the list.

(1) This is the third time I am coming to you. 'At the mouth of two or three witnesses shall every matter be established.' (2) Those who have sinned previously, and all the rest, I have warned and do now warn, when I was present the second time and now that I am absent, that if I come for another visit I shall not spare them—(3) since you seek proof that it is Christ who speaks in me, Christ who is not weak towards you, but mighty in your midst. (4) For[1] indeed he was crucified because of his weakness, but he lives because of God's power. For indeed we are weak in[2] him, but we shall live with[3] him because of God's power—and that in relation to you. (5) Examine yourselves, to see whether you are in the faith, test yourselves. Or do you not recognize that Jesus Christ is in you? Unless indeed you fail to stand the test. (6) But I hope you will recognize that we do not fail to stand the test. (7) We pray to God that you may do no evil thing, not that we may appear when tested to be in the right, but that you may do what is good, though we should appear to be in the wrong. (8) For we can do nothing against the truth, but only for the truth. (9) For we rejoice when we are weak, but you are strong; this is what we pray for, your restoration. (10) The reason why, in my absence from you, I am writing these things is that I may not, when present, exercise severity, in accordance with the authority which the Lord gave me for building you up and not for pulling you down.

What has Paul been doing in the epistle, and especially in
chapters x, xi, xii? What he had written was to some extent open
to misunderstanding, and Paul was under no illusion about the
ability of the Corinthians to mistake what he had written. **You** 19
have been thinking for a long time now (on the text see note 1
on p. 326) **that we are making a defence before you.** M. i. 119
(cf. Robertson, p. 879) notes that the construction (πάλαι with a

[1] Most Greek MSS, the Vulgate, and Marcion have καὶ γὰρ εἰ: For if he was crucified . . . yet he lives . . . This variant lacks the vigour of the text translated (without εἰ, *if*), which insists with equal emphasis upon both the weakness and the power manifested in Christ crucified and risen, and is less Pauline.

[2] ℵ A G it pesh have *with* (σύν), by assimilation to *We shall live with him.*

[3] 𝔓[46] D* have *in* (ἐν); but Paul's usage confirms *with* for union with Christ in glory; see p. 337.

progressive present) is equivalent to an English perfect, but takes it as a question: Have you been thinking all this time? This may well be right; but Paul knew his Corinthians. Their view would not be entirely without ground. In 1 Cor. ix. 3 Paul speaks of a defence (ἀπολογία) he is prepared to make against his critics, and even though (by his own standards) he had made himself a fool in the process he had in chapters x, xi, and xii argued that he was innocent of corrupt practices, and that in all respects he was at least the equal of his rivals. Yet it was not a defence, for a defence is a self-regarding composition, designed to further the writer's own interests and to commend him to the person who appears to be in a position to pass judgement (*before you*). And this was not at all Paul's intention. He was not standing in the dock in a Corinthian court (cf. 1 Cor. iv. 3). **You are wrong** (these words are not in the Greek, but the Greek implies them, and they help the flow and clarity of the English)**; it is before God, in Christ, that we are speaking.** The same words occur at ii. 17. Paul writes not as a man anxious to save his own reputation, but as a responsible theologian. It is *before God* (cf. v. 10; Rom. xiv. 10), not the Corinthians, that Paul stands for judgement, and it is God's standards, not the Corinthians', that he must satisfy. This he can do because he does not speak as an independent human being, standing upon and therefore defending his own integrity, but *in Christ*, his very existence being dependent on and determined by the fact of Christ (for the term *in Christ* see ii. 17, and the note). Moreover, Paul has not been acting for his own benefit: **all that we are doing** (literally, all things; Plummer supplies 'saying' rather than *doing*, but Paul has in mind his relation with Corinth as a whole)**, my dear friends** (as at vii. 1)**, is for the purpose of building you up**—not that Paul may be vindicated in their eyes, but that they may be better Christians. The metaphor of *building* is particularly characteristic of 1 Corinthians (iii. 9; viii. 1, 10; x. 23; xiv. 3, 4, 5, 12, 17, 26; see the notes on these passages). In the present epistle v. 1 is hardly a relevant parallel, but see x. 8; xiii. 10, which emphasise that Paul's authority, and thus his function, as an apostle is to build up the church. 'His aim in self-defence is to build up a Church, not merely to refute slander' (Strachan). It is thus correct to claim (Betz, p. 39) that Paul rejects the rhetorical form of apology, but the theological point is more important than the formal.

Paul has written as he has done not out of fear for himself, but
out of fear of what may become of the church in Corinth. **For I** 20
am afraid lest, when I come, I may find you not such men as I desire (θέλω; for this verb see *1 Corinthians*, p. 158), **and that you may find me** (the Greek has, I may be found by you, but the inversion, which does not change the sense, yields preferable English) **not the sort of man you desire.** The undesirable qualities Paul fears he may find in the Corinthians are listed, or at least illustrated, in the next sentence. Where he himself is concerned, his fear is presumably that he may have to visit Corinth not in love and a spirit of gentleness, but with a rod (cf. 1 Cor. iv. 21). He goes on to promise that on his next visit he will not spare them (xiii. 2); he will be in person at least as firm as he is by letter (x. 11). He has a positive authority to exercise in Corinth (x. 8; xiii. 10), and his behaviour will not conform to Corinthian requirements.

To be more specific: **I am afraid** (these words are not repeated in the Greek) **lest there should be** (supplying the necessary verb) **among you quarrelling** (on the text see note 2 on p. 326), **envying** (on the text see note 3 on p. 326), **outbursts of anger, intrigues, evil-speaking** (the word is in the plural, indicating a prevalent offence), **whisperings, inflated opinions** (φυσιώσεις; the noun occurs here only in the New Testament, but the verb is specially characteristic of 1 Corinthians (iv. 6, 18, 19; v. 2; viii. 1; xiii. 4—see the notes), and the fault was probably specially characteristic of the Corinthian church), **disorders.** *Intrigues* translates a word discussed in *Romans*, pp. 47 f.; it cannot here bear precisely the same meaning that it has in the different context of Rom. ii. 8, but suggests in the same way self-seeking and small-minded scheming. The sins in this list 'relate to the sort of situation that would be brought about by the incursion of rival apostles. Strife, anger, and evil-speaking are natural constituents of circumstances in which some sided with Paul, others with his rivals. The same is true of envy, whisperings, and disorders; and most circumstances, even the least promising, seem to have provided the Corinthians with a pretext for puffing themselves up with self-importance. Read in their context in 2 Cor. xii these sins suggest the effect of a rival mission, and though there can be no doubt that they were all to be found in the period of division referred to in 1 Cor. i. 11 the fact that Paul fears that he may find them present when he next visits Corinth shows that he thinks of them as belonging to the time of writing' ('Paul's Opponents', p. 247). It is important to note this in view of what is said in xii. 21; xiii. 2 (see the notes).

Paul fears, then, that he may on his third visit find Corinth divided by the presence there of a mission conducted in opposition to his own, with the Corinthians themselves angrily disputing about the relative authority of the two apostolates. The possibility
21 gives rise to further fear—**lest, when I come, my God should humiliate me again in your presence.** This sentence contains an insoluble grammatical problem. Should the word *again* (πάλιν) be attached to *come* or to *humiliate*? There is no doubt that each construction is possible. It is in favour of the former that the two words stand side by side in Greek (πάλιν ἐλθόντος), of the latter, that *coming* is incidental to the thought (the genitive—ἐλθόντος μου—should be read, and the use of the genitive absolute, though strictly incorrect, shows that the notion of coming is parenthetical), whereas *humiliate* is not only grammatically but substantially the main verb. Not only is each interpretation grammatically possible; each makes sense. Paul has just (verse 20) spoken of coming to Corinth; he had undoubtedly been there before; he might therefore speak of coming again. He had moreover had unpleasant experiences at Corinth; in particular, the Corinthians could speak of him (see x. 1, with the note) as 'going humbly' among them. This may well refer to an occasion (see vii. 12, with the note; also ii. 1) when he had received, with meekness, injury and insult from a rival apostle, while the Corinthians had stood by and failed to take his part—perhaps insufficiently Christian to recognize that meekness rather than retaliation was a Christian and apostolic attitude. *In your presence* suggests a similar situation; the Corinthians cast themselves for the role not so much of the aggressor as of the superior judge, likely to be more impressed by a tone of high-handed authority than by forbearance. In these circumstances Paul would be humiliated by opposition that talked louder than he, by his failure to convince his own converts of the authority and of the rightness of his Gospel, and by the consequent destruction of the work he had done, at the cost of sweat and tears, in Corinth. It must be noted however that the subject of the verb *humiliate* is God. Rival apostles and superior Corinthians might feel free to crow over a defeated Paul, but they could do nothing that was not

permitted and indeed willed by God. It might be God's will that this should happen, just as it had been God's will that the angel of Satan should beat Paul, and should not (even at his repeated prayer) be taken away (xii. 8 f.). It was God's will that Paul should carry about in his body the killing of Jesus (iv. 10). All this was in order that Paul the apostle should reflect in his person as well as in his preaching the word of the Cross (1 Cor. i. 18). That Paul *feared* this humiliation is in no way inconsistent with his recognition in it of the hand of God; Jesus feared death (Mark xiv. 33), and Paul prayed for the removal of the angel of Satan (xii. 8). Bultmann, *Probleme* pp. 30 f., argues that what Paul fears is that he will have to act forcefully against Corinthian disorder and disobedience. He continues: 'It is simply incredible that the possibility of carrying out a strict judgement in Corinth should for Paul appear as a possible humiliation by God in the presence of the Corinthians (*πρὸς ὑμᾶς*), and yet that this judgement should at the same time be a *δοκιμή* [proof] of the Christ who spoke within him, who will prove himself powerful over against the Corinthians (xiii. 3). So it may probably be supposed that an *οὐ* [not] has fallen out between *μου* [my] and *ταπεινώσῃ* [humiliate]: Paul fears that God will *not* (again) humiliate him in the presence of the church! That he *fears* and not *hopes* this shows that for him the *οἰκοδομή* [building up] of the church means everything. It agrees with this that with reference to his earlier appearance in Corinth he had described himself as *κατὰ πρόσωπον ταπεινὸς ἐν ὑμῖν* [going humbly among you] (x. 1). That is not how he will appear on his next visit' (p. 31). It is an interesting conjecture, but unnecessary, since the text makes (in the context) even better theological sense as it stands than with the addition of the conjectured negative. So also Kümmel.

Humiliation was failure; and this might go back beyond the present situation into the earlier history of the Corinthian church. A further possibility is that **I should mourn** (cf. 1 Cor. v. 2) **for many of those who sinned previously and did not repent of the uncleanness** (cf. Rom. i. 24; vi. 19), **fornication** (cf. 1 Cor. v. 1; vi. 13, 18; vii. 2), **and lasciviousness** (Rom. xiii. 13) **they had committed.** Paul will mourn simply that men should sin in this way, and not repent; there is nothing in the text to suggest that what he will mourn over will be their subsequent excommunication from the Christian society (though this might follow; cf.

1 Cor. v. 11). The sins in themselves excluded from the (future) kingdom of God (1 Cor. vi. 9 f.), an even more serious matter. For the two participles (*προημαρτηκότων*, perfect, and *μετανοησάντων*, aorist) see Robertson, p. 1117 (cf. p. 621); the sinning began earlier, and continued; the repentance that might have ended it did not take place. The participles are in the genitive case, wrongly; Paul does not mean (as his words strictly taken would imply) that there would be some unrepentant sinners over whom he would not mourn. The sins mentioned form a striking contrast with those of verse 20. This is noted by Georgi, *Gegner*, pp. 232 ff., but inadequately explained. Broadly speaking, those of verse 21 are all (unless they are to be violently allegorized) sexual sins of a physical kind, and bear little relation to the offences of verse 20. How is this unexpected continuation to be explained? 'We must reject the suggestion that *προαμαρτάνειν* [to sin beforehand] refers to sins committed before conversion; the very fact of conversion means that these sins had been repented of. We must reject also the view that there is no connection between the two verses—that verse 20 refers to sins connected with the intruding false apostles, and that in verse 21 Paul's mind reverts to completely different situations, such as that mentioned in 1 Cor. v. This view . . . may nevertheless point in the right direction. When Paul wrote 1 Corinthians one of the errors current in Corinth led in the direction of libertinism. The proposition was maintained that, as the belly was intended for food and food for the belly, so the body was made for fornication and fornication for the body (1 Cor. vi. 13). In this direction, and towards flirtation with idolatry, the Corinthian gnosis led. The theme of gnosis, and that of sexual immorality, have dropped out of 2 Corinthians; new troubles, doctrinal and moral, have taken their place. Yet not entirely; Paul fears that when he revisits Corinth he may find both new sinners, who in accepting the intruding false apostles have fallen into strife, envy, and so forth, and old sinners (*προημαρτηκότες*) of the gnostic, libertine kind, who have not repented of their fornication' ('Paul's Opponents', pp. 247 f.).

Paul feared a terrifying accumulation of evil in the Corinthian church; he may not have been wrong. Certainly he was preparing
1 for his pastoral task. **This is the third time I am coming to
you.** Compare xii. 14, and the note; also i. 23; ii. 1; and Introduction, pp. 5-11, 14-21. The first visit was the founding visit,

implied by the existence of the church (1 Cor. iv. 15; ix. 1; etc.) and described in Acts xviii. 1-18; the second was the visit to which Paul looked back with sorrow, because (it seems) he had been attacked by a rival missionary. He now contemplates a third visit—a fact which, as Windisch observes, shows that we cannot be dealing here with the 'sorrowful letter', since when he wrote that Paul was avoiding a visit, and sent Titus and a letter instead. The forthcoming visit Paul views in a legal, or judicial, light. **'At the mouth of two or three witnesses shall every matter be established.'** Paul quotes Deut. xix. 15, following quite closely the text of the LXX (which, with the Hebrew, has the word *witnesses* with each numeral), though in fact the wording is nearer to that of Matt. xviii. 16. On the use of this passage not only in the New Testament but in Judaism see H. van Vliet, *No Single Testimony: a study on the adopting of the law of Deut. xix. 15 par. into the New Testament* (1958). The author is probably right in saying of 2 Cor. xiii. 1 that the use of Deut. xix. 15 'in this way as a sort of proverb shows that this rule was a living one in the mind of Paul' (p. 88), and in the view that 'Paul means by his quotation that the warning by two or three witnesses, necessary for a valid complaint according to the oral law, was given by his repeated visits. See verse 2. The case is now matured for decision' (p. 96). The ordinals *third* and *second* in these two verses cannot fail to be connected with the cardinals *two* and *three* in the quotation. For the development of the idea of *witness* into that of warning see van Vliet, pp. 43-62; and note the use of *warning* in verse 2. Paul does not use his quotation as a proof (there is no 'as it stands written'—contrast iv. 13; viii. 15; ix. 9), but says, in effect: You have had due warning, as prescribed; I am now about to take action. This is a better interpretation than those that make Paul say, either 'I will hold a court in due form of law', or 'Three visits by one person will have the effect of three witnesses'.

Those who have sinned previously (see xii. 21; those whose 2
old errors led them into fornication and kindred sins), **and all the rest** (those who, in their reaction to the situation created by the coming of the false apostles, are now guilty of faction, envy, hatred, and the like), **I have warned and do now warn.** The verb Paul uses here (προλέγειν), though it may bear the simple meaning, 'to say beforehand', 'to tell in advance', is best taken to mean 'to warn' (see L.S., s.v., II 3); 'I have told you in advance and am

now telling you in advance' is not impossible but somewhat heavy-handed. The two tenses of the verb, perfect and present, correspond to the adverbial clauses that follow: **when I was present the second time** (see above) **and now that I am absent.** Paul has warned viva voce, he now warns by letter, **that if I come for another visit** (see Moule, *Idiom*, p. 69) **I shall not spare them** (no object is expressed in Greek; the verb may be used without object, but if any is implied it must be that given in the translation). In these words Paul may be quoting what he had actually said on the second visit (so e.g. Plummer, Allo). *To spare* (φείδεσθαι) is primarily to spare in battle—not to kill when the opportunity to do so exists; by a natural extension, and especially in the LXX (see L.S., s.v., V), it comes to mean 'to have mercy upon' (it is then usually employed with a preposition). It is natural to ask what Paul has hitherto forborne to do (i. 23) and will now do to recalcitrant Corinthians, and the only possible answer is to be found in terms of 1 Cor. v. 5—they would be handed over to Satan. See the discussion of this disciplinary act in *1 Corinthians*, pp. 125 ff. In 1 Corinthians it was an essential part of Paul's intention that the whole community should act with him in excluding the one offender; this would not be possible in the new situation—indeed, it is more likely that Paul would find himself excommunicated from the Corinthian society, since the context gives the impression that a majority were in rebellion against him, and a church meeting, if he had convoked one, might well have turned against him. Paul had in fact no weapon at all except the truth, the Gospel applied to the situation. As he had proclaimed in Corinth the good news constituted by the word of the Cross (1 Cor. i. 18; ii. 2), so he could now declare that those who by word and deed were denying the Gospel had thereby alienated themselves from the merciful God and fallen back into the realm of Satan. This is neither excommunication nor a curse, but an unrelenting faithfulness to the truth of the mercy in which alone God will deal with men (Rom. xi. 30 ff.). Paul must have known that his faithfulness might (humanly speaking) destroy him, and the church on which he had bestowed so much love and labour; there was however no alternative. And 'when Christ comes again, *He* will not spare'—so, with terrible but not un-Pauline directness, Denney.

3 But Paul must act in this way, **since you seek proof that it is Christ who speaks in me.** Schlatter compares Hab. ii. 1; Zech.

i. 10. This verse provides another way of saying that Paul's apostleship, his right to speak on behalf and in the name of Christ, had been called in question, and that by the Corinthians, who evidently felt free to lay down conditions of apostleship (see Introduction, p. 30, and 'Paul's Opponents', p. 251). They intended to be the arbiters. Betz, p. 133, is right in saying that Paul reacts to this situation by invoking theological fundamentals (*grundsätzlich-theologisch*). The Corinthians were right to raise the question (see the important discussion of this matter by Calvin), wrong only in the criteria they appear to have applied in answering it. The only test of the validity of any ministry is whether it conveys the word of Christ to his people; but it must not be supposed that the loudest and most impressive voice is the one that is most likely to bear the divine word, or that only the 'inspired' utterances of 'divine men' constitute the word of God (cf. Georgi, *Gegner*, pp. 293 ff.). Both these epistles (e.g. 1 Cor. ii. 2; 2 Cor. i. 5), and the other Pauline letters too, emphasise that Christ, the risen Christ, is present among his people as Christ crucified, and that his voice is heard in the word of the Cross, yet it is also true that the Christ who speaks in Paul is one **who is not weak towards you, but mighty in your midst** (or 'within you'; but Paul is thinking of the work of Christ in the church). Paul's own weakness, which was manifest enough, was the stage upon which the power of God in Christ was at work; this was why Paul delighted and boasted in his weakness, and dreaded the display of human power which could serve only to obscure God's (xi. 30; xii. 5). The power of Christ became visible in miracles (xii. 12; Rom. xv. 19; Gal. iii. 5), in Paul's preaching (1 Cor. ii. 4), and in the conversion of sinners, who were washed, sanctified, and justified (1 Cor. vi. 11). Christ had overcome the powers of evil, which were no longer in a position to separate from God those who were in him (Rom. viii. 35-9). The relation between weakness and strength, Christ and the apostle, needs further explanation. It is too simple to speak of the one as all-powerful, of the other as weak.

For indeed (*καὶ γάρ*; on the text see note 1 on p. 327) **he** 4
(Christ) **was crucified because of** (*ἐκ*) **his weakness, but he lives because of** (*ἐκ*) **God's power.** The preposition translated *because of* is thus given its causal sense (M. iii. 260), but the translation is nevertheless inadequate. Paul does not mean simply that Christ was crucified because he was weak—that is, not strong

enough to escape so unpleasant a fate—or that he now lives because God was strong enough to overcome death and raise him up. The crucifixion was the supreme expression of part of the truth about him; he was crucified because this part of the truth was true. It was of his grace, of his primary characteristic, that he became poor (viii. 9), and the weakness shown in his crucifixion, being a mark of his grace, is not an unfortunate lapse from strength but one aspect of the action God intended in his Son. Historically, he preferred crucifixion to the exercise of some kinds of power; he preferred crucifixion to the abandonment of the outcast groups of Palestinian society, with whose social and religious weakness he identified himself. Similarly, though it is true it is also inadequate to say that the resurrection was a signal manifestation of divine power. Since the resurrection Christ is alive, and at work in power. Power is as characteristic of him as weakness, wealth as characteristic as poverty (viii. 9). This is one basic form of New Testament Christology—Christ is both weak and strong. This pair of attributes is akin to, though not identical with, the other fundamental propositions of New Testament Christology—Christ belongs both to this age and to the age to come. Whether these two dynamic, functional propositions may be said to be adequately represented by the essential two-fold proposition of a 'two natures' Christology is a question of some difficulty and importance, not to be handled here. It is however impossible to understand Paul's argument at this point in this epistle (and elsewhere) without grasping its Christological foundation (cf. Wilckens, *Weisheit*, pp. 48 f., 217 ff. though more is meant here than 'spiritual' weakness; also Betz, pp. 56 f., 99 f.). This verse need not be regarded as Paul's correction of a 'gnostic theologumenon' (Güttgemans, p. 151), in which *weakness* was regarded as a 'power', responsible for the crucifixion. *Weakness* and *power* are both truths, at once moral and theological, about the one God who is known in his Son, Jesus Christ.

The corresponding proposition about Paul and his ministry follows. **For indeed** (καὶ γάρ; the new sentence begins in the same form as the last) **we** (perhaps 'we too'—like Christ) **are weak in** (on the text see note 2 on p. 327) **him, but we shall live with** (on the text see note 3 on p. 327) **him because of** (ἐκ; see above) **God's power—and that in relation to you** (the last phrase is wrongly omitted, probably because it seemed an awkward addendum, by B D^3). Since Christian existence is *in Christ* (on this phrase see ii. 17, and the note), and since apostleship means a specially sharply focused Christian existence, it is to be expected that Paul (the end of the sentence shows that *we* means here primarily the apostle himself) will reveal both the weakness and the power that are characteristic of Christ. This (as the epistle has already claimed—iv. 10) is in fact so. Since Paul, like all his fellow-Christians, lives in this age, on this side of death, it is to be expected that the main sign of Christian existence will be weakness—that is, the same kind of vulnerability that Christ himself chose to adopt. Paul too will serve rather than be served, and will give rather than receive (iv. 5; xii. 15; cf. Mark x. 45). Life *with him*, that is, with Christ, belongs primarily to the future (see J. Dupont, ΣΥΝ ΧΡΙΣΤΩΙ: *L'Union avec le Christ suivant S. Paul* (1952)); Christ himself has been raised from the dead as the first-fruits of those who sleep (1 Cor. xv. 20; see the note), and for the rest of mankind resurrection remains a future event. In some measure, however, it has been anticipated (iv. 10 ff.; also Rom. vi. 4 f.; Col. iii. 1), and here Paul says that it will be anticipated *in relation to you.* God will grant him such a measure of resurrection life as will suffice to deal with the situation in Corinth. In his weakness, God's power will be perfectly revealed (xii. 9).

It seems clear that the Corinthians have been testing Paul and other claimants to apostolic status, and that Paul is at least in some danger of being rejected, as a much less impressive missionary than others who have taken greater care to make their qualifications and merits known. He now replies that the Corinthians have been
testing the wrong persons; they should test themselves. **Examine** 5
not others but **yourselves** (the pronoun is in an emphatic position), **to see whether you are in the faith.** For *in the faith* (with the article—ἐν τῇ πίστει) see 1 Cor. xvi. 13 and the note. If *the faith* is used to mean something like 'the Christian religion' it means the religion which on the human side is marked by trust and obedience. Paul means, Consider whether you truly are Christians (see Kümmel, against Lietzmann, who thinks that *faith* refers specifically to experience of the Spirit; Kümmel also points out, rightly, that it is implied that one may cease to be a Christian—cf. Gal. v. 2 ff.; 1 Cor. ix. 27; see also Betz, p. 135). **Test** (δοκιμάζειν; the cognate adjectives, δόκιμος and ἀδόκιμος—tested and approved, tested and not approved—are used below, and an

attempt is made to indicate the verbal relationships) **yourselves** (see the note above on *Examine yourselves*). Betz, p. 89, compares Socrates' use of irony to bring his hearers to self-examination, citing Plato, *Charmides* 158D; *Alcibiades I* 124C. The next words at least are probably ironical, for Paul knew that the Corinthians would be in little doubt about the result of such a test. **Or do you not recognize that Jesus Christ is in you?** that is, that you are Christians. C. F. D. Moule, *The Phenomenon of the New Testament* (1967), p. 24, prefers 'among you' to *in you*, and this is certainly a possible translation (of ἐν ὑμῖν). But Paul's argument here seems to rest upon the actual existence as Christians of his readers, that is, on the relation between them and Christ, Christ's being in them and their being in Christ. Of course, then, you must recognize that Christ is in you, unless you are going to abdicate your position in the discussion—**unless indeed you fail to stand the test** (are ἀδόκιμοι—tested and found wanting). This result the Corinthians would be most unlikely to reach. 'Paul here uses the two expressions "to stand in the faith" and "Christ in you" as synonymous. Faith is the reality of the presence of Christ, is the life of Christ in the believer; in other words, faith means to be in Christ' (Wendland). But Calvin's negative inference ('He declares that those who doubt their possession of Christ and their membership in His Body are reprobates') can hardly be said to follow.

If however the Corinthians were convinced that they were Christians, that Christ was in them, they must draw the necessary
6 conclusion. **I hope you will recognize** (γινώσκειν in the sense of ἐπιγινώσκειν, used in verse 5; a compound verb is often repeated in the simple form—M. i. 115) **that we do not fail to stand the test** (are not ἀδόκιμοι; this word—see verse 5—belongs to the world of biblical theology; the analogy with the Hellenistic magician (γοητής; Betz, e.g., p. 132) is at best secondary). For if the Corinthians are Christians, it is through Paul's ministry. To throw doubt on his apostleship and apostolic message is to throw doubt on their own being as Christians; to affirm their own faith is to vindicate the preacher through whom they become believers. Compare 1 Cor. ix. 1 f.; *1 Corinthians*, p. 201. This is why Paul urges the Corinthians to test themselves.

Paul now returns to the point of xii. 19. The last two verses may have suggested once more that his object is to defend himself, to

prove that he at least will stand the test. But this is not so. He is
still concerned for his readers rather than for himself. **We pray** 7
to God that you may do no evil thing. An alternative translation
(adopted by Lietzmann) of the last words in this sentence (μὴ ποιῆσαι ὑμᾶς κακὸν μηδέν) is, that he (God) may do you no harm, that is, may not punish you, as men who do not stand the test. This is a very improbable rendering, as also is, 'that we may not (have to) harm you'. Paul might well pray that the Corinthians might not come under judgement, but the prayer 'that God may do you no harm' would be a very odd way of expressing this. More important, (a) as Kümmel (following Bauer) points out, in Greek 'to do harm' (κακὸν ποιεῖν) does not take a second accusative, and (b) later in the sentence the prayer becomes *that you may do what is good*, which is surely intended to balance *that you may do no evil thing*. Compare verse 9b; Paul is concerned for the restoration of his church to moral and spiritual health—and this not for his but simply for the church's sake: **not that we may appear when tested to be in the right** (that we may be δόκιμοι, may stand the test), **but that you may do what is good, though we should appear to be in the wrong** (ἀδόκιμοι). The last clause is loosely connected (literally, but that we may be as it were in the wrong), but the drift of Paul's thought is clear. He is not concerned for his own reputation; let him appear to be wrong, rejected, dismissed from his apostolic office, so long as his converts in Corinth are doing what is good. In fact he never appears more clearly as an apostle, an accredited representative, of Jesus Christ, than he does here, for he is prepared to take others' sins upon himself, and to be counted a transgressor for their justification. He might well say, 'Be imitators of me—as I am of Christ' (1 Cor. xi. 1).

What Paul has just said needs a certain amount of correction, or
at least of explanation, lest it be wrongly understood. That Paul
might himself prove to be in the wrong, and be rejected, is a real
possibility (1 Cor. ix. 27), but he is not affirming that this is
happening. **For** (γάρ; this clause explains the *appear*, the *as it* 8
were, of the preceding clause) **we can do nothing against the truth, but only** (this sense of ἀλλά is not necessarily due to Semitic influence, but see Beyer, p. 138) **for the truth.** *The truth* may be used here in a quite general sense: Paul is not out to get a verdict in his favour at any cost, but wishes the truth, whether it is favourable to him or not, to prevail. The word however is used

(by Paul and by other New Testament writers) for the Gospel (see e.g. iv. 2; vi. 7; xi. 10, with the notes), and Bultmann (*T.W.N.T.* i. 244; in *Exeg.*, p. 143, he seems to give a wider interpretation—'the very essence of what God wills and requires') is probably right in seeing in it here the true doctrine over against the 'different Gospel' of xi. 4. Paul's whole life is bound up with the Gospel committed to him (cf. i. 17-20). He could not preach a different Gospel without becoming a different person.

The service of the Gospel involves, as Paul has often said (e.g.
9 iv. 7-12), his weakness. **For we rejoice when we are weak, but you are strong.** Compare verse 4. The two properties are connected; it is by Paul's weakness in Christ, his unremitting service and self-abasement, that the Corinthians may become morally strong (to *do no evil thing* and to *do what is good*). This is the meaning of the next clause: **this is what we pray for, your restoration.** *Restoration* (κατάρτισις) is a noun derived from a verb (καταρτίζειν) used at xiii. 11, but also at, for example, Mark i. 19 of the mending of nets. It is used elsewhere of the setting of a dislocated limb (see L.S., s.v., I), and of the restoration of an erring brother (Gal. vi. 1). It may mean simply 'to prepare' (Rom. ix. 22), but more often suggests setting right something that has gone wrong. There was plenty in the Corinthian church that needed to be set right, and this is probably the meaning of the word as Paul uses it here. He prays that the Corinthians may be restored to a proper Christian life, as at 1 Cor. i. 10 he had prayed 'that you may be restored (κατηρτισμένοι) to unity of mind and opinion'.

This restoration is the purpose of the letter (or at least of chapters
10 x–xiii; see below). **The reason why, in my absence from you, I am writing these things** (*these things* will refer to the whole of x–xiii, but not to i–ix; as Windisch points out, this is a good reason for separating the two parts of the epistle) **is that** (taking διὰ τοῦτο at the beginning of the sentence to anticipate the ἵνα at this point) **I may not, when present, exercise severity.** Compare verse 2: *If I come again I shall not spare*—that is, on the assumption that my letter brings no improvement. Unsparing severity (for the word—here the adverb ἀποτόμως—cf. Rom. xi. 22) is no joy to Paul; if he can avoid using it by writing a sharp letter he will do so. Yet if he has to use it he will, **in accordance with the authority which the Lord gave me for building you up and not for**

pulling you down. 'Paulus infirmus has withdrawn and Paulus potens speaks again'—Windisch. Compare x. 8, where identical words are used. 'It is up to you to see that I do not have to use my authority for a purpose that does not lie within the Lord's intention' (Lietzmann; similarly Wendland). The Lord's intention, for which he has equipped his apostle with the paradoxical kind of authority in weakness that has been repeatedly noted in the epistle, is that there should be built up in Corinth a community of Christians, founded upon the Gospel and expressing their Christian existence in mutual love. If however those in Corinth who profess to be Christians turn to a different Gospel and practise not self-renouncing love but self-assertive arrogance, any amount of *severity* may become necessary in order to *restore* them to a right mind and to the Lord's intention.

F. CONCLUSION xiii.11–13

23. xiii. 11-13. LAST WORDS, AND GREETING

(11) Finally, brothers, goodbye. Pull yourselves together, exhort one another, be of the same mind, live at peace, and the God of love and peace shall be with you. (12) Greet one another with a holy kiss. All the saints greet you.

(13) The grace of the Lord Jesus Christ, and the love of God, and participation in the Holy Spirit, be with you all.

The epistle moves to a close. It is possible, perhaps probable, that the document as we now have it is composite (see Introduction, pp. 11-14). The greater part of chapters x–xiii form a unit, but we cannot be certain where this unit ended. Verse 11 seems to be linked with the immediately preceding paragraph. Verse 12 is so general that it could form the conclusion of any epistle; this however is no reason why it should not be the conclusion of x–xiii. Verse 13 might well have been added to round off the composition when the various pieces were put together. It is a more elaborate concluding formula than occurs in any other of the Pauline letters. See below, pp. 344 f.

11 **Finally** (on this word, λοιπόν, see Thrall, pp. 25-30; there can be little doubt of its meaning here in the last few lines of the letter), **brothers** (the word was used of Timothy at i. 1, and as an address to the readers at i. 8; viii. 1; see *1 Corinthians*, p. 31), **goodbye** (literally, Rejoice; but the word, χαίρετε, is a common Greek greeting, possibly so used by Paul at Phil. iv. 4; elsewhere in New Testament letters at Acts xv. 23; xxiii. 26; James i. 1 the corresponding infinitive, χαίρειν, is used; Windisch however thinks that, in view of the other imperatives in the verse this too should be understood as a simple imperative). So far the greeting contains nothing specially connected with the Corinthian situation. **Pull yourselves together.** The verb (καταρτίζειν in the middle or passive) is that cognate with *restoration* (xiii. 9; see the note). The passive would be, literally, Be restored; but Paul is thinking of something the Corinthians may (under God) do to and for themselves, and the translation attempts an idiomatic rendering of the middle. So also with the next word: **exhort one another** (cf. 1 Thess. v. 11). The Corinthians must engage in mutual ministry, in which each exhorts the rest. Alternatively, the verb may be passive, and mean 'Accept my exhortation'; compare Heb. xiii. 22. The word (παρακαλεῖν) should perhaps be 'encourage', or even 'comfort'. It has a wide range of meaning, from simply *ask* (ii. 8; viii. 6; ix. 5; xii. 18) to *beseech*, *exhort*, *encourage*, *comfort* (i. 4, 6; ii. 7; v. 20; vi. 1; vii. 6, 7, 13; x. 1; xii. 8). **Be of the same mind;** compare Rom. xii. 16; xv. 5; Phil. ii. 2; iv. 2. For the Jewish background of this see D. Daube, *The New Testament and Rabbinic Judaism* (1956), p. 344; but any society, and not least the Christian, may naturally hope for harmony among its members. **Live at peace** continues the same thought; it expresses the result of being of the same mind (Calvin). Compare Rom. xii. 18; 1 Thess. v. 13, in similar exhortations; also Mark ix. 50.

The imperatives are followed by **and** (καί) and the future indicative, **the God of love and peace shall be with you.** If this is a substitute for a conditional sentence ('If you pull yourselves together . . . then the God of love and peace . . .') it may rest upon a Semitic construction, but need not do so, since there are Greek parallels (Beyer, p. 253). But it is not certain that this form of conditional construction (plainly to be seen at vi. 17) is used here. In his final words Paul, it may be, simply puts separate propositions together. Do this; do that; God will be with you. Curiously, the term *the God of love* does not occur elsewhere in the New Testament. *The God of peace* occurs at Rom. xv. 33; xvi. 20; (1 Cor. xiv. 33); Phil. iv. 9; 1 Thess. v. 23; (2 Thess. iii. 16); Heb. xiii. 20. It was evidently a regular Pauline concluding formula. The meaning appears to be not only that God is himself characterized by love and peace, but that he supplies love (cf. Rom. v. 5) and peace (cf. Rom. v. 1; xiv. 17), thus making possible the fulfilment of the precepts Paul has just uttered.

Greet one another with a holy kiss. Compare Rom. xvi. 16; 12
1 Cor. xvi. 20; and see the notes. 'Paul's letters must have been communicated to the church members by being read aloud at a meeting of the church. Paul asks them to give one another the salutation he would have given them all had he been present. It is possible that the kiss was already a cult act' (*1 Corinthians*, p. 396); it had become so by the time of Justin, *1 Apology* lxv. 2 (though it is not referred to in the Apostolic Fathers—Windisch). See below; also Betz, *Lukian*, p. 115, for the background in mystery religions.

All the saints greet you. Compare 1 Cor. xvi. 20, 'All the brothers greet you'. There is no difference; *saints* and *brothers* are both terms that mean Christians. For *saints* see i. 1; also Rom. i. 7; 1 Cor. i. 2, and the notes. Probably Paul refers to the Christians gathered at the place of writing (see Introduction, pp. 9 f.); it is not impossible that he feels that he can speak to Corinth in the name of all the saints, that is, all the Christians there are. A sense of unity with all other Christian groups must have had on local communities an effect both encouraging and sobering.

On the connection between verse 12 and verse 13 Lietzmann writes, 'In the ancient liturgies the kiss of peace is always followed by the threefold greeting (verse 13), so that it is natural to suppose that the connection is old and originated in the rite of the Pauline churches. The letter is read out in the church meeting, then follows the kiss of peace and the Lord's Supper, introduced by the liturgical greeting of verse 13'. It may be so; it may also be, and this seems more probable, that the liturgical usage was secondary, being derived from the connection between the kiss of peace and the triadic formula in the epistle. It is further possible that the Trinitarian formulation was a post-Pauline formula, based on the earlier and simpler formulas and added to conclude the miscellaneous epistle which an editor had put together out of two or more fragments.

13 **The grace of the Lord Jesus Christ, and the love of God, and participation in the Holy Spirit, be with you all.** In 1 Cor. xvi. 23 (cf. Rom. xvi. 20) occurs the simpler greeting, The grace of the Lord Jesus be with you. 'In Paul's usage, *grace* is most characteristically action and gift . . . , and in these words Paul prays for a continuation and deepening of what has already been done and given in Corinth' (*1 Corinthians*, p. 398). Behind *the grace of the Lord Jesus Christ*, which is known as an observable event in history (cf. viii. 9), stands *the love of God*, which, though commended in time in the action and especially in the death of Jesus (Rom. v. 8) is an eternal fact. In the third clause *participation* translates the Greek word (κοινωνία) which is rendered 'common participation' at 1 Cor. x. 16; other translations have had to be used in this epistle at vi. 14; viii. 4; ix. 13, and the rendering here has been vigorously disputed. The various constructions of the word that occur in Greek are clearly set out by F. Hauck (*T.W.N.T.* iii. 798 f.); his own conclusion (p. 807) is that in the present passage we have an objective genitive (τοῦ ἁγίου πνεύματος) of that which is possessed in common; and this seems to be the most probable view. It is against this that the genitives in the first two clauses appear to be subjective—the grace manifested by the Lord Jesus Christ, the love exercised by God—and some commentators (e.g. Plummer, Schlatter, Wendland) argue that the third genitive also must be subjective, so that we should render, 'the fellowship created by, given by, the Holy Spirit'. Others however (e.g. Windisch, and Hauck in *T.W.N.T.*) argue that the third clause is not entirely parallel to the first two, 'in that the Spirit does not stand with God and Christ as a completely analogous factor (völlig gleichartige Grösse)' (Hauck). See also Lietzmann-Kümmel, and compare 1 Cor. x. 16 ('common participation in the blood . . . in the body of Christ'); Phil. iii. 10 ('participation in the sufferings of Christ'); also Rom. xv. 27; Phil. ii. 1; Philemon 6. This seems the most probable, though it is not a certain, view; it is moreover difficult to combine 'fellowship given by' with the concluding words *be with you all*, whereas if *participation* is accepted as a translation it is easy to understand these on the lines suggested above for the first and second clauses. Paul wishes for his readers a 'continuing and deepening' of their *participation in the Holy Spirit*. On the word *participation* (κοινωνία) see, in addition to lexica and commentaries, Reicke, *Diakonie*, pp. 25 f., where a

centripetal meaning (fellowship with or participation in something) is distinguished from a centrifugal meaning (sharing, giving, distribution; see viii. 4; ix. 13).

There is no convincing reason why we should see here a deliberately veiled reference to a baptismal formula (J. Jeremias, *Jerusalem zur Zeit Jesu* (1958), II B 109); liturgical blessings might be used for purposes other than baptism, and we do not know that the verse originated in a stereotyped liturgical form. Kümmel is right in describing it as 'a proper form of expression for the confession of faith in the historical and eschatological saving act of God: God sent his Son (Gal. iv. 4), God has given the Spirit (Gal. iii. 5), and therein God shows himself to be for the believer the final (*endzeitliche*) Deliverer'. It is not however clear why he denies that the verse is 'a first step on the way to a Trinitarian confession of faith'. If this means that Paul has not yet conceived the 'one *ousia*, three *hypostaseis*' of later Trinitarian orthodoxy it is true, and indeed obvious; but the kind of threefold formula that we have here (cf. 1 Peter i. 1 f.) provided a starting-point for such speculative thinking and for its credal formulation. Christ, God, the Spirit, appearing in balanced clauses in one sentence, must stand on one divine level (even if Paul himself did not yet see them in this way—see above); how then (the theologian must sooner or later ask) are they related to one another, and to the one supreme God of Old Testament theology and of Greek philosophical speculation? Paul deals (in an elementary way) with the relation of Jesus as the Son of God to the Father who sent him, and of the Spirit to the Son. He evolves no doctrine of the Trinity, but it is perhaps more important that he so expresses himself with regard to Father, Son, and Spirit as to make Trinitarian theology, given the setting of Christianity in the following four centuries, inevitable, yet does so unconsciously. For him, however, the final stress lies not upon three Persons, distinct yet consubstantial, but upon grace, love, and participation. Barth (*C.D.* IV ii. 766) speaks of a twofold epexegetical 'and', so that 'our translation ought really to be: "The grace of our Lord Jesus Christ, in which the love of God is exercised, and the communion of the Spirit disclosed and imparted, be with you all"'.

INDEX OF NAMES AND SUBJECTS

Abodah Zarah (Babylonian Talmud), 273
Aboth (Mishnah), 220
Achaea, 4, 9 ff., 25, 53, 55 f., 71, 232 f., 242, 283
Acts of Peter and Paul, 148
Acts of Philip, 224
Aelian, 102
Aeschylus, 191
Allo, E. B., 61, 64, 66, 73 f., 84, 93, 97 f., 111, 121, 123, 137, 150 f., 166 f., 173, 181, 188, 203, 212, 218, 225, 228, 266 f., 275, 314, 320, 324, 334
Amen, 77 f.
Anointing, 79
Anselm, 84
Apocalypse of Abraham, 273
Apocalypse of Moses, 286, 310
Apocalyptic, 37, 130 f., 150–7, 242
Apostle, 6–10, 16, 23, 28–33, 35, 41, 48 f., 53 f., 84, 135, 165 f., 178 f., 185–91, 230, 245, 248, 257 ff., 261–9, 273–87, 291 f., 295, 299 f., 312, 320 ff., 329 ff., 340 f.
Apuleius, 311
Aretas, 303 f.
Aristophanes, 265
Aristotle, 102 f., 236, 246, 255
Asia, 15, 63 f.
Augustine, 83 f.

Bachmann, P., 53, 58 f., 63, 66, 68, 87, 92, 112, 120, 123 f., 135, 138, 142, 147, 151, 161, 164, 167, 174 ff., 180, 212, 222 f., 238, 244, 248, 264 f., 311, 315 f.
Baptism, 37, 43, 80 f., 168 f., 345
Barth, K., 66, 78, 121, 132, 135, 140, 172, 175, 177, 210, 219, 253, 273, 317, 345
Bates, W. H., 14, 244
Bauer, W., 180, 203, 277, 283, 293, 339
Baur, F. C., 28, 245
Beare, F. W., 191, 293
Behm, J., 112
Beliar, 198
Bengel, J. A., 76, 93, 97, 130, 175 f., 179, 316
Benoit, P., 113, 176
Betz, H. D., 83, 98, 103, 125, 154, 183, 201, 222, 246 f., 251, 256, 260, 267, 269, 274, 278–81, 284, 291, 294 f., 302, 306 f., 310, 317, 320, 324, 328, 335–8, 343
Beyer, H. W., 265, 293
Beyer, K., 61, 201, 214, 322, 339, 342
Billerbeck, P., 121; *see also* Strack–Billerbeck
Black, M., 91
Blass, F., *see* Blass–Debrunner
Blass–Debrunner, 61 f., 64, 75, 87, 91, 94, 119, 130 f., 145 f., 148, 164, 176, 192, 195, 204, 207, 211, 214, 220, 222, 225, 227–30, 234 f., 239, 247 f., 255, 260, 263, 265 f., 271, 295, 299, 316
Boasting, 70, 165, 214 f., 263–9, 289 f., 302, 306 f., 311 f., 319 f.
Bonsirven, J., 116, 200 f.
Boobyer, G. H., 239
Bornkamm, G., 22 ff., 29, 120, 129, 150, 160, 218, 254
Bousset, W., 122, 125, 131, 133, 135, 269; *see also* Bousset–Gressmann
Bousset–Gressmann, 148, 180, 219, 273
Brandenberger, E., 150, 273
Braun, H., 78, 91, 113, 174, 194, 202
Bring, R., 120
Brother, 54
Brox, N., 131
Bruce, F. F., 297
Büchsel, F., 169, 172, 176

Bultmann, R., 83, 94, 96, 113, 129, 132, 135, 140, 142, 147, 149, 151 f., 163, 165, 167, 170 f., 173, 178–82, 192, 207, 211, 224, 245, 263, 267, 278, 283, 308, 331, 340
Burrows, M., 129

Cadbury, H. J., 297
Calendar, 225
Calvin, J., 60, 76, 84 f., 103, 113, 122, 127, 142, 147, 160 f., 168, 171, 180, 183, 194, 199, 212, 218, 225, 229, 250, 256, 275, 283, 310, 316, 324, 338
Cambridge Ancient History, 219
Cerfaux, L., 77, 79, 139, 164, 171, 224, 282
Chadwick, H., 36
Chavasse, C., 273
Chiasmus, 179
Christology, 41 f., 45–8, 247 f., 276 f., 282, 336
'Christ-party', 257
Chrysostom, 81, 125, 238, 252
Church, 49 f., 55, 84, 93, 230 f., 272 ff., 300 f., 328
Cicero, 137, 236, 297, 323
Clarke, W. K. L., 315
Clavier, H., 64, 314
Clementine Homilies and *Recognitions*, 315
Collange, J. F., 29, 114, 125, 138, 151, 162, 194
Collection, 6, 9 f., 12, 15, 20 f., 25–8, 217–42, 324 ff.
Colson, F. H., 146, 154
Conscience, 70 f., 129, 164
Conzelmann, H., 130, 132, 147, 159, 178, 184, 297, 301, 324
Corinth, 1 f., 36
Corpus Hermeticum, 146, 151, 239 f., 306
Cousin, A. R., 35
Covenant, 112 f.
Creation, new, 173 ff.
Cullmann, O., 180, 184
Cumont, F., 154
Cynics, 279 f., 295

Damascus, 16, 303 f., 306
Daube, D., 231, 342
Davies, W. D., 103, 109 f., 113, 123, 173, 273
Day of Atonement, 174
Death of Jesus, 168 ff., 175, 177
Debrunner, A., *see* Blass–Debrunner
Deissmann, G. A., 79, 106, 143, 202, 222, 235, 240, 298
Delcor, M., 91
Delling, G., 253
Denney, J., 67, 79, 84, 86, 92, 112, 125, 140, 148, 166, 170, 183, 223, 233, 244, 260, 282, 334
Deuteronomy Rabbah, 101 f.
Dibelius, M., 169, 300
Dinkler, E., 69, 80 f.
Dio Chrysostom, 185
Diodorus Siculus, 185
Dionysius of Halicarnassus, 64
Dittenberger, W., 64, 90, 316
'Divine man', 29, 54, 102 f., 321 f., 335
Dockx, S., 11
Dodd, C. H., 32 f., 70, 89, 105, 111, 141 f., 201
Driver, G. R., 198
Drug, 101
Duncan, G. S., 296
Dunn, J. G. D., 123
Dupont, J., 337

Ecstasy, 166 f., 250, 307–14
Eighteen Benedictions, 58, 65
Ellis, E. E., 152, 154, 201, 273
Epictetus, 145 f., 185, 191, 202, 211, 295, 320
Equality, 226 f.
Er, 309 f.
Eschatology, 45, 100, 105, 147 f., 150–7, 173 ff.
Ethics, 45
Ethnarch, 303 f.
Eucharist, 38, 44
Euripides, 197
Eve, 272 ff., 286
Exodus Rabbah, 115, 201

Faith, 158, 337 f.
Farmer, W. R., 172
Feuillet, A., 113
Firmicus Maternus, 79
Fitzmyer, J. A., 14, 115
Flesh, 72, 170, 202, 207, 249 ff.
Flogging, 296 f.
Förster, W., 198
Fraser, J. W., 172
Freedom, 118, 123 f., 204

Friedrich, G., 28 ff.
Furnish, V. P., 168

Galen, 128
Georgi, D., 26–9, 97, 102–5, 217 f., 226, 238 f., 241 f., 276, 285, 294 f., 322, 332, 335
Glory, 115–19, 124 f., 131 f.
Glossolalia, 38
Glover, T. R., 103
Gnilka, J., 14, 188, 196, 199 f., 202
Gnosis, gnosticism, 6, 10, 29, 36 f., 39 f., 104 f., 131 f., 135, 139, 155, 164, 224, 253, 294 f.
Goppelt, L., 122, 276, 278, 296
Grace, 56, 72, 144 f., 183, 218–28, 236 f., 241, 316, 344
Gressmann, H., *see* Bousset–Gressmann
Grundmann, W., 154, 173
Güttgemans, E., 247 f., 336
Gutbrod, W., 293

Hadrian, 154
Haenchen, E., 297
Hagigah (Babylonian Talmud), 309, (Mishnah), 309
Hamilton, N. Q., 80
Hatch, E., 90, 234
Hauck, F., 344
Heaven, 151 f., 155, 309 ff.
Heilsgeschichte, 184
Héring, J., 55, 57, 64 f., 68, 81, 97, 108, 120, 124, 135, 152, 160, 174 f., 203, 210, 219, 228, 240, 253, 263, 278, 315
Hermas, 68
Herodotus, 256, 274
Hesychius, 283
Historia Augusta, 154
Historical Jesus, 41, 171 f., 257
Holiness, 71
Holl, K., 26
Homer, 1
Hooker, M. D., 181
Horace, 204
Hort, F. J. A., 210
Hoskyns, E. C., 99
Hughes, P. E., 14, 81, 84, 91, 93, 97, 103, 113, 148, 164, 202, 220, 228, 265, 314

Idolatry, 199
Ignatius, 140
Image, 125 f., 132 f.
Immortality, 150–7
Irenaeus, 131

Jeremias, J., 32, 59, 124, 179, 311, 345
Jerome, 283
Jervell, J., 115, 125, 132 f., 135
Josephus, 83, 91, 220, 262, 296 f., 304, 308
Jowett, B., 145
Judaizers, 28 ff., 39 f., 172, 274, 287, 291, 300
Judgement, 143, 160 f., 163 f.
Jüngel, E., 161, 179
Justin, 68, 135, 343

Käsemann, E., 28, 30 f., 50, 100, 113, 116, 123, 166, 177, 181, 245, 257, 263 f., 266 f., 268, 274, 276, 278 f., 287, 312 f., 321
Kamlah, E., 314
Kasting, H., 177 f.
Kelly, J. N. D., 186
Ketuboth (Babylonian Talmud), 61
Kilaim (Mishnah), 195
Kiss, 343
Kittel, G., 158, 237
Knowledge, 98, 100, 135, 170 ff., 186, 252 f., 279 f.
Knox, W. L., 95, 98, 107, 111, 120, 126, 128, 150, 155, 158, 161, 174, 200, 239 f., 298, 308
Kümmel, W. G., 14, 17 f., 23, 28, 58, 66–9, 82, 89 f., 98, 100, 102, 107 f., 112, 122, 125, 132, 139, 141, 148, 154 f., 158 f., 168 ff., 184, 211 f., 229, 239, 246, 257, 264, 266, 293 f., 300, 307, 312, 331, 337, 339, 344 f.
Kuhn, K. G., 91, 293

Lampe, G. W. H., 81
Lattey, C., 291
Law, 112–22
Letter, 112 f., 258 ff.; *see also* Previous letter, Severe letter
Letter of commendation, 40, 106–10, 266
Leviticus Rabbah, 236
Liddell, H. G., *see* Liddell–Scott
Liddell–Scott, 90 f., 98, 108, 148 f., 158, 203, 235, 265, 283, 322, 333 f., 340

Lietzmann, H., 65, 68, 84, 89 f., 92, 98, 106, 108 f., 111, 119, 121, 123, 126, 130 f., 133, 142 f., 151, 167, 170, 172, 188 f., 191, 210 f., 218, 223–8, 238, 242, 244, 251 f., 259 f., 270 f., 293 f., 310 ff., 315, 325, 337, 339, 341, 343 f.
Life of Adam and Eve, 286
Lindars, B., 120
Livy, 219, 297
Lohse, E., 130
Love, 167 f., 176, 342 ff.
Lucian, 103, 124, 154, 322
Lütgert, W., 276
Luther, M., 62, 223

Macedonia, 7 f., 10 ff., 15–20, 24 f., 54, 75, 86, 95, 97, 206 f., 218–25, 228 f., 233 ff., 242, 268, 283, 322
Magician, 338
Makkoth (Mishnah), 296 f.
Man, inner, outward, 145 ff.
Manson, T. W., 97, 101 f., 138, 141
Marcion, 22
Marcus Aurelius Antoninus, 137
Marriage, 44 f.
Marshall, I. H., 184
Martyrdom of Peter, 236
Mastema, 315 f.
Maurer, C., 129
Megillah (Mishnah), 309
Menahoth (Mishnah), 226
Menoud, P. H., 314
Messianic suffering, 61 ff.
Michel, O., 135
Midrash Psalms, 173
Milligan, G., *see* Moulton-Milligan
Mixtures, 195
Moffatt, J., 210
Mommsen, T., 303
Moses, 42, 107, 114 ff., 118 f., 122, 308
Moule, C. F. D., 62 f., 67, 73, 76 ff., 83, 92, 94, 110, 114, 118, 130 f., 135, 141, 144, 148, 153, 157, 160, 165, 172, 185, 192, 214, 221 f., 224, 226, 234 ff., 251, 259 f., 263, 280 f., 283, 289, 308, 316, 324 f., 334, 338
Moulton, J. H. (and collaborators), 61, 64, 75, 80, 82, 91, 96, 100, 130 f., 138, 145, 153, 156, 160, 176 ff., 184, 192, 207, 210, 214, 218, 222, 227, 229, 251, 255, 260, 262, 265 f., 272, 275, 291, 295, 298 f., 325, 327, 335, 338; *see also* Moulton–Milligan
Moulton–Milligan, 64 f., 80, 106, 265
Munck, J., 26
Muratorian Canon, 21 f.
Murphy-O'Connor, J., 130
Mystery religions, 311

Nickle, K. F., 26 ff., 218
Niebuhr, R. R., 172
Noack, B., 144

Odour, 98–102
Orientis Graecae Inscriptiones Selectae, 64, 90
Oxyrhynchus Papyri, 106

Paradise, 310 f.
Parallelism, 179
Participle, imperatival, 230 f.
Paul as a man, 32–6, 64, 75 f., 134, 138–42, 191 f., 228, 261, 297, 301 f., 313–17, 324 ff.
Pausanias, 2
Peace, 56, 342
Philo, 80, 107, 111, 131, 135, 137, 146, 151, 154, 191, 197, 200, 226 f., 251, 272 f., 308, 310 f., 317
Philostratus, 103
Plato, 87, 103, 145, 151, 153, 167, 279, 290, 309, 320, 338
Plummer, A., 78, 81, 83, 121, 219, 328, 334, 344
Plutarch, 1, 138, 235, 246
Polycarp, 22
Power, 138, 181, 187, 317, 335 ff.
Predestination, 101
Previous letter, 3, 14, 194
Procksch, O., 133
Proclus, 310

Quell, G., 112
Qumran scriptures, 59, 78, 91, 117, 123, 129, 137, 176, 188, 200 ff., 294, 315
Qumran sect, 14, 24, 26, 110, 113, 117, 174, 194–200, 202

Rad, G. von, 293

Radermacher, L., 228, 235, 240, 255, 314
Rapture, 34, 308–12
Reconciliation, 175–9
Reicke, B., 121, 172, 220, 279, 291, 344
Rengstorf, K. H., 32, 313
Repentance, 211
Resurrection, 65 f., 150–7
Richardson, A., 177, 240
Righteousness, 116 f., 179 ff., 188, 197, 238 f.
Rissi, M., 29, 147, 161
Robertson, A. T., 58, 80, 82, 87, 94, 138, 142, 156, 167 f., 185, 192, 202, 207, 211, 221 f., 225, 227 ff., 259 f., 266, 271, 275, 289, 305, 307, 314, 316, 320, 324 f., 327, 332
Robinson, J. A. T., 147, 256
Rutherford, S., 35

Sanhedrin (Babylonian Talmud), 198, (Mishnah), 298
Satan, 272 ff., 277 f., 286 f., 313–16, 334
Schlatter, A., 36, 61, 64, 67, 71, 73, 83 f., 94, 99, 101, 103, 106, 118, 125, 141, 148, 151, 159, 164, 166 f., 197, 201 f., 211, 214, 219, 228, 240, 250, 262, 265, 275, 308, 315, 317, 325, 334, 344
Schlier, H., 118, 236
Schmithals, W., 29, 111, 133, 139 f., 150, 155, 164, 167, 185, 256, 261, 275, 278, 295
Schoeps, H. J., 106, 129, 131, 171, 173, 189, 273, 275, 289, 302, 307, 315
Schrenk, G., 253
Schürer, E., 296
Schulz, S., 114, 294
Schweitzer, A., 237
Schweizer, E., 83, 140, 154, 174, 179, 194, 265
Scott, R., *see* Liddell–Scott
Seal, 79
Selwyn, E. G., 231
Seneca, 139
Sevenster, J. N., 71, 151, 153, 237
Severe letter, 8 f., 13 f., 17, 19 f., 23, 25, 88 f., 96, 206, 208–15, 247, 259 f., 268
Shabbath (Babylonian Talmud), 101, 273
Shema', 59
Sherwin-White, A. N., 297
Shipwreck, 298 f.
Shorter Oxford English Dictionary, 265
Sifre Deuteronomy, 67, 138, 198, 317
Sifre Numbers, 114
Signs, 320 ff.
Silvanus, 76 ff., 230
Sin, 180, 329–32
Singer, S., 58, 65
Snake, 272 ff.
Sophists, 251, 274, 279, 281, 284
Sophocles, 131
Sotah (Mishnah), 273
Spicq, C., 167
Spirit, 80, 108, 112 f., 116 f., 122–6, 142, 157, 186 f., 202, 214, 326, 344
Spiritual gifts, 44, 312
Stählin, G., 226
Stauffer, E., 76, 173
Stoicism, 71, 139, 191, 237
Stoning, 297 f.
Strabo, 219
Strachan, R. H., 64, 103, 142, 328
Strack, H. L., *see* Strack–Billerbeck
Strack–Billerbeck, 7, 65, 99, 101, 106, 115, 143, 147, 173, 175, 238, 296, 303, 307, 310, 315, 317
Stuhlmacher, P., 113, 117, 161, 174, 177, 181
Stumpff, W., 102
Sufficiency, 102 f., 110 f., 237
Sylloge Inscriptionum Graecarum, 316
Symmachus, 79
Synagogue, 2, 36, 58 f., 120 f., 296 f.

Taanith (Babylonian Talmud), 65, 101
Tacitus, 220
Temple, 199
Temple tax, 26, 240
Tent, 150–5
Tertullian, 22, 89, 202
Theodoret, 65
Theodotion, 198
Theologia crucis, 250, 303, 321

Theologia gloriae, 49, 106, 139, 224, 304
Thierry, J. J., 314
Thorn in the flesh, 313 ff.
Thrall, M. E., 153, 156, 255, 342
Thucydides, 1
Timothy, 4, 17, 53, 55, 76 ff., 213 f., 230, 326
Titus, 8 f., 11 f., 15, 16–21, 25, 35, 94 f., 97, 187, 206–9, 213 ff., 220 f., 227–30, 234, 301, 325
Torah, 101 f., 115, 118, 120 ff.
Trinity, 343 ff.
Triumph, 97 f.
Troas, 8, 11, 15 ff., 19 f., 24, 93 ff., 97, 206
Truth, 129, 187, 339 f.
Turner, N., 122, 124, 140, 150, 152, 156, 222, 239

Unnik, W. C. van, 74, 76–9, 118 f., 124, 293

Veil, 114, 118–22, 130
Virgil, 61
Visions, 34, 250, 307
Vliet, H. van, 333

Weiss, J., 12, 14, 16–20
Wendland, H. D., 94, 99, 112, 115, 120, 143, 163, 171, 194, 200, 307 f., 311, 338, 341, 344
Westcott, B. F., 21, 210
Whitaker, G. H., 146, 154
Whyte, A., 35
Wilckens, U., 100, 125, 261, 321, 336
Wilson, R. McL., 36
Windisch, H., 28, 36, 55, 58 f., 61, 71 ff., 75, 80, 91 ff., 97 f., 102, 104, 106, 115, 118, 121, 125, 129, 137 ff., 142, 146, 151, 156, 158, 160, 167, 169, 171, 175, 178, 180, 184, 186, 202, 207 f., 210 f., 213, 225, 228, 232 f., 236, 238, 241, 246, 251, 256, 263, 273, 277, 283 f., 286, 300, 305, 308, 311, 314, 316, 323, 325, 333, 340–4
Wisdom, 72, 132 f.
Witness, 333

Xenophon, 207, 225, 229, 247, 282

Yebamoth (Babylonian Talmud), 273
Yoma (Babylonian Talmud), 102, 179

INDEX OF GREEK WORDS AND PHRASES

ἁγιότης 68, 71
ἀδικεῖν 213
ἀλλά 95, 104, 211, 265, 271, 339
ἄλλος 275
ἀνάγκη 185
ἀνοίγειν 191
ἁπλότης 68, 219 f., 239, 241, 273
ἀπόκριμα 64
ἀπολλύμενοι 100, 105
ἀπόστολος 30, 230, 295
ἀρραβών 80 f.
ἄρρητος 311
αὐγάζειν 127, 131
αὐτάρκεια 237

βάρος, κτλ. 148, 156
βέβαιος, κτλ. 63, 78–81

γνῶσις 37, 98, 131, 134 f., 186, 252, 280
γυμνός, κτλ. 153 ff.

διαθήκη 112, 114
διακονία, κτλ. 27, 108 f., 111, 114, 176, 182, 185, 220, 239 f., 294 f.
δικαιοσύνη, κτλ. 117, 180 f., 197, 227, 239
δοκιμάζειν, κτλ., ἀδόκιμος 92, 219, 229, 269, 331, 337 ff.

Ἑβραῖος 293
ἐθνάρχης 304
εἴ γε καί 153
εἶδος 158
ἐκ 87, 138, 225, 313, 335 f.
ἔλεος, κτλ. 59, 127
ἐλευθερία 124
ἐν 215, 250, 267, 299, 338
ἐξαπατᾶν 273
ἐξαπορεῖσθαι 64, 138
ἐξιστάναι 166
ἐπενδύεσθαι 152 f., 155, 157
ἐπίστασις, ἐπισύστασις 301
ἐπιτιμία 90
ἔσω ἄνθρωπος 145 f.
ἕτερος 275

εὐλογητός 58
εὐλογία 235
ἐφ' ᾧ 155 f.
ἕως τέλους 73

ἡμέρᾳ καὶ ἡμέρᾳ 145

θεός 251
θριαμβεύειν 97 f., 104

ἱκανός, κτλ. 102, 111
ἵνα 75, 222, 226, 234, 237
ἰσότης 27, 226

κακὸν ποιεῖν 339
κανών 264–8
καπηλεύειν 103
καταναρκᾶν 283, 323
καταρτίζειν, κτλ. 340, 342
κατοπτρίζεσθαι 124 f., 131
καυχᾶσθαι, κτλ. 70, 265, 290
κοινωνία 27, 197, 220, 241, 344
κομίζεσθαι 160
κύριος, κτλ. 59, 122 ff., 126, 134, 303

λαμβάνειν 291, 324
λειτουργία 239 f.

μετασχηματίζειν 285
μετρεῖν, κτλ. 262–8

νέκρωσις 139

οἰκτιρμοί 59
οὐδέν 320
ὀχύρωμα 251
ὀψώνιον 282

πανουργία, κτλ. 128, 274, 324
παράδεισος 311
παρακαλεῖν, κτλ. 60 f., 92, 163, 207, 221, 246, 316, 325, 342
παρρησία 118 f., 124, 204
περισσεύειν 144 f., 220, 222, 237
περισσότερόν τι 258
πιστός 199

INDEX

πλείων 91, 144
πλεονεκτεῖν, κτλ. 93, 203, 235, 282
πνεῦμα 124, 126, 157, 186 f., 250, 344
προλέγειν 204, 333
πρόσκαιρος 148
πρόσωπον 57, 67 f., 93, 135, 165, 247, 256, 331

σάρξ 72, 75, 141, 170 f., 249
σκῆνος 151
σκόλοψ 315
σοφία 37, 72
σπέρμα 294
συνείδησις 70, 129
σφραγίζειν, κτλ. 81
σῶμα 141, 308
σωφρονεῖν 166 f.

ταπεινός, κτλ. 207, 247, 282, 331
τέλος 120

ὑπέρ 62 f., 168, 178, 222, 230, 295, 316

φανεροῦν 108, 160, 164
φαῦλος 150, 161
φείδεσθαι 83, 312, 334
φησίν 260
φθάνειν 266

χαίρειν 342
χάρις 27, 69, 72, 74, 86, 144, 218, 220 ff., 227 f., 236 f., 241
χειροτονεῖν 228 f.
χρίειν 79
χωρεῖν 203

ψευδαπόστολος 30, 285

ὡς, ὡς ἄν, ὡς μή, ὡς ὅτι 45, 176, 178, 259, 290, 292

INDEX OF ANCIENT SOURCES

Old Testament

Genesis
1, 125, 135
1.3, 127n., 134
1.26f., 125
2.7, 169
3.13, 273, 274
8.21, 99
10.9, 251
30.22, 65

Exodus
16.18, 227
25.6, 102
25.8, 200
29.10, 177
29.18, 99
29.43ff., 200
30.7, 102
31.18, 107, 114
32.15f., 107
32.16, 114
32.32f., 117
34.28, 114
34.28–35, 113
34.29, 114
34.30, 114, 119
34.33, 114
34.34, 114, 122
34.35, 114

Leviticus
1.9, 99
6.28, 137
11.33, 137
14.50, 137
19.2, 203
19.19, 195
20.17, 160
26.12, 200

Numbers
11.29, 117
12.8, 158
15.3, 99
27.20, 114
33.55, 315

Deuteronomy
3.24, 67
6.5, 317
10.21, 73
11.22, 138
15.7ff., 198
19.15, 333
22.9ff., 195
22.10, 195
25.2f., 296
27.15–26, 78
28.12, 65
32.39, 65
34.7, 115

Joshua
2.15, 303
15.19, 235

Judges
19.22, 198
20.13[LXX], 198

1 Samuel
2.6, 65

2 Samuel
7.14, 200, 201
7.27, 200, 201

[2 Kingdoms
16.6, 298]

2 Kings
[4 Kingdoms]
5.15, 235

1 Chronicles
29, 241

Esther
3.4, 145

Job
28.28, 163

Psalms
31(32).11, 70
39(40).12, 59
39(40).14, 59
41.14, 78
68(69).17, 60
78(79).8. 60
111.4 [LXX], 134
111.9 [LXX], 238
112.9, 238
115.1 [LXX], 143
116.10, 143
119(118).32, 191

Proverbs
3.4 [LXX], 229
8.22, 133
8.30, 93, 133
9.10, 163
21.22, 251
22.8(9)a [LXX], 236

Ecclesiastes
12.14, 161

Isaiah
6.9f., 120
8.16, 311
25.8, 156
38.12, 150
40.1, 60
42.9, 173
43.6, 201
43.18f., 173
49.8, 183
49.13, 207
50.1, 273
51.3, 60
51.9ff., 173
51.12, 60
51.19, 60
52.4, 200
52.11, 200
53.6, 180
54.1–6, 273
54.9f., 173
55.10, 238
60.1, 132
61.1, 79
61.2, 184
64.8, 137

Jeremiah
1.10, 258
9.22f., 70, 269
11.5, 78
17.14, 73
19.11, 137
24.6, 258
31, 105, 113
31.9, 201
31.31ff., 201
31.31–34, 112
31.33, 107
51.45, 200

Lamentations
4.2, 137

Ezekiel
1, 133, 309
6.13, 99
9.4, 79
11.19, 107, 109
16, 273
16.63, 191
20.34, 200, 201
28.24, 315
29.21, 191
36.26, 107, 109
37.13, 65
37.27, 200

Daniel
4.34, 99
12.3, 91
12.4, 311

Hosea
1–3, 273
10.12, 239

Jonah
3.3, 251

Habakkuk
2.1, 334

Zechariah
1.10, 334–35

New Testament

Matthew
5.3, 190
5.34, 283
5.37, 76, 283
6.1, 238
8.20, 223
11.29, 246, 249
13.19, 262
13.23, 262
18.15, 89, 90
18.16, 333
18.20, 200
19.11f., 203
25.41, 315
26.28, 112

Mark
1.19, 340
3.5, 249
3.21, 166
4.11f., 130
7.9, 275
9.50, 342
10.45, 142, 168, 337
12.40, 290
13.31, 118
14.24, 112
14.33, 331
14.35–41, 316
14.58, 151
16.14, 131
16.17, 320
16.20, 320

Luke
4.19, 184
6.20, 190
9.45, 75
9.58, 223
12.47f., 226
17.3, 90, 92
18.1, 128
22.20, 112

John
1.1, 132
1.18, 132
5.39, 115
8.46, 179
16.30, 152
20.22, 257
20.25–29, 49

Acts
2.22, 321
4.8ff., 33
6, 29
6.1, 293
6.4–10, 33
7, 29
7.20, 251
7.57–60, 298
8.14, 32
9, 135
9.23, 299
9.24f., 304
9.29, 299
9.30, 298
11.22, 32
11.26, 298
11.27–30, 25
12.25, 25
13.4, 298
13.8, 299
13.11, 322
13.13, 298
13.45, 299
14.2, 299
14.5, 298
14.10, 322
14.12, 315
14.19, 298, 299
14.22, 66
14.26, 298
15.12, 322
15:20, 7
15.23, 342
15:29, 7
16, 297
16.8, 95
16.11, 298
16.18, 322
16.20, 299
16.22, 297
16.23–30, 296
16.37, 297
17.5, 299
17.10, 218
17.15, 298
17.32ff., 100
17.34, 56
18.1, 4
18.1–4, 76
18.1–18, 85, 333
18.2f., 4
18.3, 283
18.4, 2, 37
18.4f., 4
18.5, 54, 77
18.6, 299
18.6f., 4
18.7, 4
18.12, 56, 299
18.12–17, 4
18.18, 4, 298
18.19ff., 4
18.22f., 4
18.24–28, 4
18.27, 56
19.1, 4
19.1–20.1, 4
19.8, 4
19.11f., 322
19.21, 4, 56
19.22, 4, 54
19.23, 299
19.23–40, 64
19.37, 282
20.1f., 10
20.1ff., 75
20.2, 17
20.3, 10, 25, 299
20.4, 54, 229
20.10ff., 322
20.16, 4
20.19, 299
20.29f., 24
20.31, 4
21.28, 296
22, 135, 297
22.11, 132, 299
22.25, 297
22.27, 299
22.29, 297
23.2, 292
23.26, 342
24.17, 25, 217
25.10, 297
26.13, 135
26.19, 307
27, 298
27.14–44, 298
28.3–6, 322
28.8, 322

Romans
1.1, 33, 53, 59, 98, 134, 282
1.2ff., 78
1.3, 77
1.4, 71, 187
1.5, 133, 240, 316
1.7, 343
1.9, 76, 83, 187
1.11, 241
1.13, 63
1.16, 100, 138, 187
1.16f., 188
1.18, 100
1.18–23, 252
1.21, 252
1.24, 331
1.25, 58, 303
1.28, 252
1.29, 93, 235
2.5, 307
2.7, 185, 238
2.8, 329
2.15, 70, 107, 252
2.16, 160
2.17ff., 113
2.22, 282
3.5, 212
3.8, 35, 188, 287
3.19, 283
3.19f., 116
3.20, 238
3.25, 134
3.25f., 175
4, 177
4.3–8, 177
4.7, 197
4.11, 81
4.16, 63, 81
4.17, 65, 66
4.17–22, 158
4.18, 67
4.19, 139, 301
5.1, 56, 343
5.2ff., 316
5.3, 185
5.4, 219
5.5, 187, 343
5.8, 92, 134, 167, 176, 212, 344
5.9f., 176
5.10, 175
5.11, 165
5.12, 155
5.14, 77
5.17, 268
5.19, 253
5.20, 144, 145
5.21, 116
6, 44
6.3, 151, 158
6.3ff., 168
6.4f., 337
6.5, 143
6.6, 145, 146
6.10a, 169
6.10b, 169
6.11, 141
6.13, 188
6.18, 123, 124
6.19, 197, 331
6.19f., 116
6.20, 124
6.22, 123, 124
6.23, 169, 211
7, 147
7.1, 151
7.3, 124
7.4, 168
7.6, 168
7.7, 179
7.8, 284, 291
7.10, 115
7.11, 113, 273, 284, 291
7.12, 113, 115
7.13, 115, 147
7.14, 112, 113
7.22, 145
7.24, 66
8.1, 65
8.1–13, 80
8.2, 113, 123, 124
8.3, 179, 180, 240, 301
8.4–8, 249
8.5ff., 72
8.6, 113
8.9, 123, 250, 257
8.11, 143
8.15, 58
8.15f., 201
8.16, 187
8.17, 139
8.18, 147, 148
8.19, 307
8.21, 123, 124
8.23, 80, 152, 155
8.24, 100, 158
8.24f., 148
8.26, 311
8.27, 210
8.29, 59, 125
8.32, 140, 312
8.34, 101
8.35, 185
8.35–39, 335
8.38f., 155, 316
8.39, 252
9–11, 130
9.1, 83, 186, 189, 302
9.1ff., 27
9.1–5, 297
9.2, 190
9.4, 112, 113
9.5, 58, 77, 171, 303
9.6–13, 294
9.11, 150n.
9.15, 200
9.16, 122
9.22, 100, 340
9.25, 200

INDEX OF ANCIENT SOURCES

9.31, 267
10.1, 27, 297
10.3, 116
10.4, 77, 118, 120
10.6ff., 183
10.9, 59, 134, 143, 240, 274
10.10, 240
10.14ff., 143
11.8, 187
11.12, 322
11.14, 122
11.21, 312
11.22, 340
11.25, 63
11.26, 77, 122
11.27, 112
11.30f., 334
11.31, 27
11.36, 175
12.1, 59, 99, 246
12.1f., 105
12.2, 147, 229
12.3, 72, 133, 316
12.6, 316
12.7, 108
12.8, 219, 236
12.9, 187
12.12, 190
12.15, 190
12.16, 207, 252, 342
12.17, 229
12.18, 342
13.1–7, 246
13.5, 185
13.6, 240
13.8ff., 27, 92, 246
13.11, 100, 211
13.12, 188, 197
13.13, 331
14.1f., 301
14.1–15.6, 302
14.4, 290
14.7, 204
14.10, 143, 160, 328
14.13, 302
14.17, 85, 186, 190, 343
14.18, 269
15, 224
15(16), 25
15.3, 222
15.5, 342
15.8, 81, 134
15.13, 85, 187, 190
15.16, 99, 186, 240, 282
15.17–20, 265–66, 267
15.19, 187, 321, 335
15.20, 267
15.23f., 268
15.25, 108, 220
15.25–28, 25
15.25–32, 217
15.26, 10, 21, 25, 56, 218, 220, 241
15.27, 27, 226, 240, 344
15.28, 81
15.30f., 241
15.31, 25, 66, 220
15.32, 190
15.33, 343
16.1, 1, 233
16.1f., 106
16.4, 231, 301
16.6, 295
16.7, 98
16.10, 269
16.12, 295
16.16, 231, 301, 343
16.17f., 35
16.19, 190
16.20, 93, 343, 344
16.26, 240

1 Corinthians
1.1, 53, 54, 218, 228
1.1–9, 196
1.2, 43, 55, 99, 343
1.3, 56
1.4, 218, 316
1.5, 186, 190, 222, 223, 239, 282
1.6, 81
1.6ff., 79
1.7, 307
1.8, 74, 81
1.9, 76, 199
1.10, 340
1.11, 3, 19, 329
1.11f., 3
1.12, 172, 257, 279
1.13–17, 37
1.14, 4
1.14–17, 134
1.17, 3
1.18, 72, 99, 100, 130, 176, 178, 187, 282, 331, 334
1.20, 72
1.23, 184, 252, 282
1.23f., 43, 99
1.25, 222, 317
1.26, 27, 256
1.30, 78
1.31, 70, 269
2.1, 3
2.1–5, 261
2.2, 3, 46, 99, 334, 335
2.3, 2, 247
2.3f., 279
2.4, 54, 77, 123, 335
2.4f., 39, 187
2.5, 71, 72
2.6, 39, 72
2.8, 46, 130
2.11, 187
2.15f., 264
3.2, 211
3.3, 248
3.5, 185
3.6, 3, 319
3.9, 84, 183, 328
3.10, 319
3.10f., 3
3.10–15, 161
3.11, 46
3.16, 152, 193n., 199
3.17, 258, 287
3.18, 289
3.19, 72, 274
3.20, 252
3.22, 190
3.23, 191
4.2, 199
4.3, 3, 328
4.3f., 319
4.4, 72, 106, 129, 164, 203, 229
4.6, 285, 329
4.8, 37, 45, 223, 268, 271
4.8ff., 126
4.8–13, 73
4.9, 98, 189
4.9–13, 33, 39, 138, 185, 248, 300
4.10, 261, 290
4.10–13, 262
4.11ff., 126
4.12, 295
4.13, 45, 188
4.14f., 192
4.15, 3, 272, 319, 323, 333
4.16, 221
4.17, 17, 54, 199, 231, 301
4.18, 329
4.18–21, 85
4.19, 98, 329
4.19ff., 7, 247
4.21, 6, 187, 246, 329
5, 260, 332
5.1, 89, 209, 213, 331
5.1–5, 3
5.2, 329, 331
5.2–5, 213
5.4, 187
5.5, 74, 93, 187, 190, 334
5.9, 3, 194, 196
5.9f., 14, 195
5.10, 199, 235, 250
5.10f., 93
5.11, 199, 235, 332
6.1, 248
6.1–6, 195
6.1–8, 3
6.2f., 196
6.5, 203
6.7f., 203
6.9, 199
6.9f., 332
6.9ff., 196, 317
6.10, 93, 235
6.11, 335
6.12, 307
6.12f., 38, 186
6.12–20, 3
6.13, 331, 332
6.14, 143
6.16, 260
6.16ff., 152
6.18, 197, 199, 331
6.19, 187, 193n., 199
7.1, 3, 38, 39
7.1–40, 3
7.2, 331
7.5, 93
7.6, 222, 224
7.12, 290
7.12–16, 195
7.16, 45, 196
7.17, 231, 301
7.22, 45
7.25, 128, 199, 224
7.28, 312
7.29, 175, 235
7.29ff., 45, 196
7.30, 190
7.31, 147
7.32, 300
7.33, 300
7.34, 187, 202, 300
7.35, 224
7.36, 272
7.39, 195
7.40, 257
8, 199, 302
8.1, 186, 280, 328, 329
8.1–13, 3
8.4, 39
8.5f., 46
8.6, 37, 175
8.7, 202
8.9, 256
8.10, 328
8.10f., 195
8.11, 301
8.12, 301
8.13, 38
9, 285

9.1, 54, 123, 172, 189, 333
9.1f., 3, 48, 338
9.2, 73, 81, 107, 110, 262, 319
9.3, 328
9.4ff., 291
9.4–18, 281, 322
9.5, 3n.
9.5f., 285
9.5–14, 104
9.7, 282
9.12, 186, 190, 261
9.15, 186, 190, 234
9.15–23, 39
9.16, 142
9.16ff., 54, 281
9.18, 190, 261
9.19, 123, 124, 144
9.19–22, 323
9.20, 122
9.21f., 195
9.22, 302
9.23, 36
9.27, 161, 273, 291, 337, 339
10.1, 63
10.1–13, 38, 273
10.4, 123
10.5, 144
10.7, 199
10.13, 76, 199, 291
10.14, 38, 197, 199
10.14–11.1, 3
10.16, 39, 344
10.16f., 44
10.18, 256
10.19, 199
10.21, 195
10.23, 186, 258, 307, 328
10.25, 296
10.27, 196, 296
10.29, 123
10.32, 196, 229
10.32f., 184
11, 44, 133
11.1, 49, 221, 248, 263, 339
11.7, 125
11.11, 45
11.16, 231, 301
11.18, 37
11.18–22, 3
11.19, 269
11.23, 44
11.25, 112, 121
11.26, 158
11.32, 190
12.1, 63
12.2, 199
12.3, 38, 43, 46, 59, 104, 134, 186, 274, 277
12.5, 108
12.7, 44, 55–56, 123, 164, 307
12.8ff., 39
12.9, 222
12.10, 38
12.13, 43
12.23, 258
12.24, 258
12.25, 300
12.27, 43
12.28, 38, 178
12.28ff., 39
12.29, 55
12.30, 38
12.31, 147
13, 27, 44, 50
13.1ff., 34
13.2, 222
13.4, 329
13.5, 44
13.12, 159
13.13, 222
14.2, 166
14.2–5, 38
14.3, 328
14.3f., 166
14.4, 258, 328
14.4f., 50
14.5, 328
14.6, 307
14.12, 328
14.14, 187
14.16, 77, 279
14.17, 258, 328
14.18, 34, 38, 166
14.19, 38, 166, 312
14.22, 279
14.22f., 195
14.23, 279
14.23ff., 196
14.26, 307, 328
14.32, 187
14.33, 186, 231, 301, 343
14.34, 301
15, 37, 45, 150, 154, 157, 159
15.1, 218
15.3, 168
15.3f., 274
15.5–8, 189
15.6, 144
15.7, 286
15.8, 54, 172, 320
15.8f., 189
15.9, 98, 102, 278, 279, 320
15.9f., 128
15.10, 56, 98, 183, 258, 295, 316
15.11, 143, 151
15.12, 3
15.15, 189
15.20, 337
15.22, 77
15.25, 37
15.25f., 43, 45
15.26, 37
15.28, 46, 156
15.31, 139
15.32, 63, 296
15.34, 203
15.35ff., 155
15.35–49, 140
15.37, 155
15.42, 146
15.42–53, 39
15.44, 146, 155, 156
15.45, 123
15.45–49, 77
15.47, 146
15.49, 125
15.50, 146, 235
15.51, 151, 153, 156
15.51f., 140, 142
15.53, 146
15.53f., 153
15.54, 156
15.56, 37
15.58, 295
16.1, 220
16.1–4, 6, 7, 20, 25, 217, 221, 225
16.3, 106, 229
16.5, 4, 7
16.5ff., 75, 85, 86
16.5–9, 6, 25, 35
16.8, 4, 8
16.9, 94
16.10, 4, 17, 256, 285, 326
16.10f., 54, 106
16.13, 337
16.15, 56
16.16, 295
16.17, 190
16.17f., 3
16.18, 187, 214
16.19, 4
16.20, 343
16.21, 246
16.23, 344

2 Corinthians

1, 22
1–7, 9, 68, 243
1–8, 232
1–9, 9, 12, 13, 14, 21, 23, 70, 86, 203, 234, 242, 244, 245, 254, 268, 340
1.1, 51, 53–56, 63, 77, 84, 94, 220, 230, 233, 342, 343
1.1–2, 53–56
1.1–11, 51
1.1–2.13, 17, 19, 96
1.2, 51, 56, 83, 316
1.3, 58–60, 303
1.3–7, 63
1.3–11, 51, 56–68, 69
1.4, 60–61, 185, 207, 342
1.4–7, 204
1.5, 61–62, 139, 335
1.6, 60, 62–63, 64, 144, 185, 204, 342
1.6a, 63
1.6b, 57n.
1.7, 60, 63, 78, 81
1.7a, 57n.
1.8, 15, 33, 63–64, 66, 70, 88, 147, 148, 152, 156, 185, 218, 316, 342
1.8f., 60, 296
1.8ff., 59
1.9, 64–66, 80, 94, 110, 189, 207
1.9f., 296
1.10, 60, 61, 66–67, 139
1.11, 67–68, 144
1.12, 70–73, 74, 75, 104, 170, 258, 316
1.12–22, 51, 68–81
1.12–2.13, 51, 68–95
1.13, 73, 107
1.14, 73–74, 77, 165
1.15, 74, 83, 86
1.15f., 15, 35
1.15–24, 74, 76
1.16, 75, 218
1.17, 35, 75–76, 83, 170
1.17–20, 215, 340
1.17–22, 283
1.18, 69n., 76, 199
1.18f., 119
1.19, 47, 54, 69n., 71, 76–77, 78, 119
1.20, 46, 77–78, 79
1.20ff., 76
1.21, 63, 78–79, 157, 175
1.21f., 80, 81, 116
1.22, 78, 79–81, 126, 140, 157

INDEX OF ANCIENT SOURCES

1.23, 13, 15, 35, 74, 76, 78, 82n., 83–84, 86, 87, 93, 94, 208, 261, 312, 323, 324, 332, 334
1.23–2.13, 51, 82–95
1.24, 13, 82n., 84–85, 88, 92, 134, 178, 221, 258, 301
2.1, 73, 85–86, 87, 89, 94, 190, 208, 213, 261, 298, 323, 330, 332
2.1–4, 15
2.2, 86–87, 88
2.3, 13, 87–88, 190, 213
2.3ff., 23
2.3–5, 23
2.4, 12, 88–89, 94, 185, 209, 213, 247, 258
2.5, 89–90, 93, 213
2.5f., 88
2.5–8, 275
2.5–11, 15, 85
2.6, 90–91, 93, 144, 234, 249
2.7, 60, 91–92, 93, 190, 323, 342
2.8, 60, 92, 342
2.9, 13, 23, 92, 219
2.10, 92–93, 135, 323
2.11, 33, 92, 93–94, 97, 120, 130, 203, 235, 252, 273, 286, 325
2.12, 20, 94
2.12f., 11, 15, 19, 24, 96, 97
2.13, 11, 14, 23, 94–95, 97, 187, 202, 206, 207, 214, 218, 226, 234, 283, 298, 301
2.14, 11, 14, 23, 33, 49, 97–99, 101, 126, 135, 138, 175, 186, 199, 206
2.14ff., 111
2.14–17, 104
2.14–3.3, 51, 95–109
2.14–6.2, 195
2.14–6.13, 14, 16, 23, 96, 195, 206, 209
2.14–7.4, 11, 14, 23, 51, 95–204, 206, 243, 245
2.15, 24, 99–100, 197
2.15f., 130
2.16, 33, 100–3, 110, 111
2.16–3.3, 110
2.16a, 102
2.16b, 102
2.17, 15, 40, 102, 103–5, 106, 107, 128, 328, 337
3, 22, 40
3.1, 15, 49, 54, 73, 105–7, 133, 164, 184, 212, 262, 269, 319, 326n.
3.1f., 108, 128
3.2, 107–8, 164, 191, 204, 262
3.2a, 108
3.3, 108–9, 110, 111, 112, 114, 115, 116, 123, 125
3.4, 110
3.4–18, 51, 104, 107, 109–126
3.5, 33, 102, 104, 110–11
3.5a, 110, 111
3.5b, 110, 111
3.6, 102, 108, 110, 111–15, 123, 173, 185
3.7, 115–16, 118, 123, 135, 176
3.8, 108, 116, 118, 123, 125, 176
3.8f., 117
3.9, 116–17, 176
3.10, 64, 117–18, 119, 241
3.11, 116, 118, 119
3.12, 118, 124, 204
3.12–18, 118
3.13, 49, 116, 118–20, 131
3.14, 116, 120–21, 130, 252, 273
3.15, 121–22, 130
3.16, 121, 122
3.16f., 101
3.17, 40, 46, 108, 122–24, 126, 141
3.18, 96n., 108, 119, 124–26, 131, 132
3.18–4.6, 125
4, 22, 133
4.1, 108, 127–28, 136n., 145, 176
4.1–6, 51, 126–36, 145
4.2, 13, 40, 70, 103, 107, 128–30, 158, 164, 187, 212, 274, 324, 340
4.2b, 128
4.3, 47, 128, 130
4.3f., 120
4.4, 46, 125, 127, 130–33, 134, 252, 273
4.5, 33, 34, 48, 84, 133–34, 135, 136, 144, 166, 178, 221, 261, 276, 284, 291, 337
4.6, 47, 93, 98, 99, 125, 131, 133, 134–36, 138, 175, 186, 197, 200
4.7, 64, 137–38, 140, 187, 313
4.7–10, 248
4.7–12, 340
4.7–18, 41, 51, 136–48
4.8, 64, 138, 185, 192, 324
4.8f., 140, 147
4.8ff., 62, 185, 262, 300
4.8–12, 152
4.9, 138–39
4.10, 48, 54, 61, 100, 136n., 139–40, 141, 143, 158, 190, 204, 263, 269, 314, 331, 337
4.10f., 190
4.10ff., 317, 337
4.10b, 142
4.11, 139, 140–41, 170
4.11b, 142
4.12, 62, 139, 141–42, 143, 190, 204, 282
4.13, 142–43, 200, 333
4.14, 77, 140, 143
4.14f., 7
4.15, 142, 144–45, 236, 316
4.16, 137, 140, 141, 145–47, 155, 283
4.16–5.10, 147
4.17, 64, 143, 147–48, 156, 185
4.18, 34, 45, 77, 148, 151
5, 22, 137, 157, 168, 184, 223
5.1, 150–52, 155, 258, 328
5.1ff., 317
5.1–5, 157
5.1–10, 51, 77, 149–61
5.2, 152–53, 154, 155, 157, 241
5.3, 153–55
5.4, 140, 152, 155–56
5.5, 80, 81, 126, 140, 153, 157, 174, 175
5.6, 157–58, 159, 215, 247
5.6f., 150
5.7, 40, 49, 126, 148, 158–59, 175
5.8, 66, 142, 157, 159, 215, 247
5.9, 159–60, 161
5.9f., 150
5.10, 48, 74, 143, 160–61, 163, 164, 287, 328
5.11, 70, 83, 129, 161, 163–64, 167, 189, 203
5.11–21, 50, 51, 161–81
5.12, 49, 73, 133, 164–66, 167, 184, 207, 208, 212, 220, 228, 239, 262, 269, 280, 284, 326n.
5.13, 13, 62, 144, 164, 166–67, 290, 312
5.14, 167–69, 170, 172, 174, 175, 176, 177, 178, 183
5.14f., 173
5.15, 167, 169–70, 172, 178, 183
5.16, 34, 41, 47, 48, 165, 170–72, 173, 174, 175, 257, 275, 294
5.16a, 171
5.17, 135, 170, 173–75, 181, 211
5.18, 175–76, 177, 184
5.18f., 178

SECOND EPISTLE TO THE CORINTHIANS

5.18c, 178
5.19, 176–78, 187, 292
5.19f., 56
5.19ff., 134, 177, 183
5.19(18)–21, 177
5.19a, 176
5.19b, 177
5.20, 60, 176, 177, 178–79, 183, 342
5.21, 43, 116, 169, 175, 176, 177, 179–81, 194, 222, 223
6, 138
6.1, 60, 72, 163, 178, 183, 184, 194, 203, 316, 342
6.1–13, 51, 182–92, 194
6.2, 47, 183–84, 200, 211
6.3, 176, 184
6.3–10, 41, 138
6.3–13, 194
6.4, 185–86, 188, 212, 294, 317
6.4ff., 62
6.4–10, 73, 185, 248
6.5, 186, 188, 295, 300
6.6, 98, 186–87, 188, 326
6.7, 116, 187–88, 340
6.8, 118, 188–89
6.8ff., 49, 262, 300
6.9, 189–90, 211, 250
6.10, 190–91, 282
6.11, 191, 192, 204
6.11ff., 11, 119, 203, 324
6.11–7.1, 197
6.12, 191–92, 215
6.13, 11, 23, 192, 193, 194, 323
6.14, 11, 23, 193, 194, 195–97, 198, 238, 344
6.14–7.1, 3, 11, 14, 22n., 23, 24n., 96, 184, 192, 193, 194, 199, 206
6.14–7.4, 51, 192–204
6.15, 195, 197–99
6.16, 199–200
6.17, 200–1, 342
6.18, 201–2
7, 12, 22
7.1, 11, 13, 23, 71, 94, 187, 193, 201, 202–3, 214, 326, 328
7.2, 11, 23, 192, 193, 203, 235, 323, 325
7.2f., 11
7.2–4, 14, 23, 96, 206, 209
7.3, 33, 96n., 191, 203–4
7.4, 11, 14, 23, 24, 51, 60, 185, 190, 191, 204, 206
7.4–9.13, 96
7.5, 11, 14, 19, 23, 24, 94, 96, 97, 138, 165, 202, 206–7, 218, 226, 233, 283, 298, 301
7.5ff., 15
7.5–16, 17, 19, 51, 205–15
7.5–9.15, 51, 205–42
7.6, 20, 24, 60, 61, 94, 207, 247, 282, 342
7.7, 20, 60, 165, 190, 207–8, 211, 213, 217n., 228, 241, 342
7.7–11, 91
7.8, 88, 92, 97, 208–9, 247
7.8ff., 23
7.8–11, 210
7.8–12, 12, 15
7.8b, 208
7.9, 85, 88, 190, 210, 212
7.9f., 212
7.9ff., 88, 260
7.9b, 211
7.10, 190, 210–11
7.10a, 211
7.11, 186, 211–12, 214, 222, 241, 249, 319
7.11f., 210
7.12, 85, 89, 203, 209, 212–14, 275, 323, 330
7.13, 60, 90, 187, 190, 214, 258, 342
7.13–16, 15
7.14, 20, 95, 204, 207, 213, 214–15, 231, 234, 258
7.15, 19, 192, 215, 258
7.16, 13, 157, 208, 215, 218, 247
8, 12, 14, 19, 23, 218, 232, 233, 325
8.1, 27, 55, 63, 218, 221, 227, 228, 233, 236, 241, 283, 342
8.1–24, 15, 51, 216–31
8.2, 27, 185, 219–20, 222, 239, 240, 241, 268, 273
8.2ff., 16
8.3, 220, 228
8.4, 27, 60, 218, 220, 233, 239, 240, 241, 344, 345
8.5, 220–21, 222
8.5b, 221
8.6, 21, 27, 60, 74, 215, 218, 221, 224, 225, 227, 234, 246, 316, 325, 342
8.7, 12, 27, 98, 218, 221–22, 237
8.8, 222, 227, 233
8.9, 12, 27, 43, 47, 74, 144, 190, 218, 222–24, 241, 246, 282, 316, 336, 344
8.10, 19, 20, 221, 224–25, 233, 307
8.10ff., 233
8.11, 19, 225
8.12, 220, 225–26
8.13, 185, 226
8.13ff., 27
8.14, 226–27
8.15, 26, 227, 229, 333
8.16, 218, 227, 229
8.17, 60, 220, 221, 227–28, 234, 325
8.17–24, 234
8.18, 55, 228, 229, 231, 234, 301, 325
8.19, 27, 55, 108, 165, 218, 228–29, 230, 231, 301, 325
8.20, 108, 165, 229, 231
8.21, 26, 229
8.22, 13, 229, 231, 234
8.22f., 106, 325
8.23, 55, 63, 230, 301
8.24, 55, 165, 230–31, 232, 301
9, 12, 14, 17, 19, 218, 233, 242, 244, 324
9.1, 12, 27, 220, 232–33, 234
9.1–15, 15, 51, 231–42
9.2, 91, 144, 204, 222, 224, 233–34, 283
9.3, 231, 233, 234, 258
9.3f., 233
9.4, 234, 283, 290
9.5, 60, 234–35, 316, 342
9.6, 235–36
9.7, 12, 26, 190, 236
9.8, 144, 218, 236–38, 316
9.9, 26, 238, 239, 333
9.9f., 12
9.10, 26, 238–39
9.11, 165, 190, 208, 219, 239, 240, 251, 282
9.12, 27, 220, 233, 237, 239–40
9.12–15, 242
9.13, 27, 219, 220, 233, 239, 240–41, 344, 345
9.14, 27, 64, 218, 241, 316
9.15, 12, 23, 218, 241–42, 245
10, 12, 242, 306, 327, 328
10–13, 10, 12, 13, 14, 16, 19, 21, 23, 24, 25, 36, 70, 86, 96, 107, 164, 166, 189, 203, 204, 209, 214, 234, 242, 243, 244, 245, 247, 248, 250, 259, 261, 273, 281, 284, 324, 325, 340, 341
10.1, 23, 49n., 60, 157, 215, 245–48, 279, 282, 315, 319,

320, 330, 331, 342
10.1–6, 52, 243–54
10.1–11, 16
10.1–16, 73
10.1–13.10, 52, 243–341
10.1–13.13, 23
10.2, 13, 157, 215, 246, 247, 248–50, 252
10.2f., 256
10.3, 250–51
10.3b, 251
10.4, 188, 251, 258, 272
10.5, 98, 251, 252–53, 273, 280, 291
10.5b, 253
10.6, 13, 249, 253–54
10.7, 255–58, 259, 260, 261, 271, 275, 291, 295
10.7–11, 253
10.7–18, 52, 254–69
10.8, 49, 54, 93, 126, 221, 258–59, 306, 319, 328, 329, 341
10.9, 259–60, 315
10.9ff., 73
10.10, 41, 85, 256, 259, 260–61, 275, 279, 291, 315, 319, 320
10.11, 48, 256, 259, 260, 261–62, 271, 275, 291, 315, 329
10.12, 16, 49, 64, 184, 212, 255n., 262–63, 264
10.12f., 260
10.12ff., 267
10.12–16, 41, 306
10.12–18, 254, 271
10.13, 255n., 263–66, 267, 306
10.14, 266–67
10.14a, 267
10.15, 264, 267, 295, 306
10.15b, 267
10.16, 264, 265, 266, 267–69, 306
10.16f., 49
10.16a, 268
10.17, 70, 166, 268, 283, 306
10.18, 212, 269
11, 22, 30, 271, 306, 327, 328
11.1, 73, 271, 274, 277, 289
11.1–4, 16
11.1–15, 52, 270–87
11.2, 186, 212, 251, 270n., 271–73
11.2f., 35
11.3, 186, 219, 252, 272, 273–74, 285, 286, 324
11.4, 31, 40, 41, 47, 49, 95, 104, 183, 194, 260, 267, 269, 274–77, 291, 340
11.5, 16, 30, 31, 274, 277–79, 320
11.5f., 277
11.6, 41, 54, 98, 166, 186, 261, 278, 279–81, 294, 315, 319
11.7, 186, 207, 247, 281–82, 283, 284
11.7–10, 190
11.7–11, 16, 49, 261, 319, 322
11.8, 55, 71, 282
11.8f., 322
11.9, 186, 218, 282–83, 284, 323, 324
11.10, 186, 281, 283–84, 306, 340
11.11, 34, 89, 284, 324
11.12, 284–85, 306
11.12–15, 16, 260
11.13, 7, 30, 88, 94, 128, 130, 257, 274, 278, 285–86, 299, 306, 319, 320
11.13ff., 262, 272, 277, 278, 287, 294
11.14, 93, 197, 274, 286, 287
11.15, 30, 77, 257, 286–87
11.16, 33, 271, 289–90, 306, 319
11.16–30, 42
11.16–33, 52, 288–304
11.17, 234, 271, 290, 306, 319
11.18, 290, 306, 319
11.19, 271, 290–91
11.20, 16, 34, 41, 49, 54, 95, 134, 166, 249, 253, 282, 291–92, 320, 322, 324
11.20f., 184
11.21, 176, 271, 290, 292–93, 295, 301
11.22, 40, 293–94, 299
11.22f., 66, 166
11.22–27, 302
11.23, 41, 64, 185, 186, 254n., 257, 258, 287, 294–96, 300
11.23ff., 62, 64, 321
11.23–27, 60, 139, 152, 300
11.23–29, 185
11.23–30, 294
11.23–33, 16, 33, 188, 190, 237, 315
11.24, 296–97
11.25, 297–98
11.26, 191, 291, 298, 299–300
11.27, 186, 300
11.27–30, 217
11.28, 33, 55, 134, 231, 273, 300–1
11.29, 301–2
11.30, 302, 303, 306, 335
11.31, 76, 83, 189, 302–3
11.32, 303
11.32f., 303
11.33, 303–4
12, 22, 29, 271, 290, 306, 325, 327, 328, 329
12.1, 34, 41, 49, 166, 302, 306–7, 311, 319
12.1ff., 294
12.1–5, 13
12.1–7, 166
12.1–10, 52, 305–18
12.2, 34, 151, 250, 308–10
12.2ff., 34
12.2–4, 307, 317
12.2–10, 16
12.3, 310
12.4, 250, 310–11
12.5, 302, 306, 311–12, 319, 335
12.6, 129, 259, 268, 271, 306, 308, 312–14, 319
12.7, 33, 34, 64, 93, 140, 252, 261, 279, 286, 307, 314–16
12.8, 60, 63, 316, 331, 342
12.8f., 321, 331
12.9, 48, 283, 302, 306, 316–17, 319, 320, 337
12.9f., 292
12.10, 185, 301, 317–18
12.11, 30, 49, 73, 212, 271, 302, 306, 319–20
12.11f., 41, 278
12.11–18, 52, 318–26
12.12, 54, 223, 319, 320–22, 335
12.13, 16, 49, 55, 190, 261, 281, 283, 322–23, 324
12.13ff., 319
12.14, 16, 34, 85, 211, 234, 261, 272, 283, 323–24, 332
12.15, 134, 258, 322, 323, 324, 337
12.16, 13, 128, 274, 291, 324–25
12.16f., 243
12.16ff., 16, 73, 189, 229
12.17, 13, 235, 325
12.17f., 19, 21, 203
12.18, 60, 187, 221, 235, 325–26, 342
12.19, 49, 83, 104, 258, 327–28, 338
12.19–13.10, 52, 326–41
12.20, 18, 186, 329–30, 332
12.20f., 13, 16
12.21, 207, 211, 247, 330–32, 333
13, 22
13.1, 16, 85, 234, 261, 323, 332–33
13.2, 13, 18, 204, 312, 329, 330, 333–34, 340
13.3, 33, 73, 219, 280, 301, 321, 331, 334–35
13.4, 47, 48, 77, 139, 261, 269, 301, 335–37, 340
13.5, 13, 73, 107, 321, 337–38
13.6, 338–39

13.7, 150n., 268, 269, 320, 339
13.8, 339–40
13.9, 35, 190, 301, 320, 340, 342
13.9b, 339
13.10, 13, 48, 49, 54, 93, 126, 221, 258, 259, 328, 329, 340–41
13.11, 60, 63, 218, 340, 341, 342–43
13.11–13, 52, 341–45
13.12, 341, 343
13.13, 187, 341, 343, 344–45

Galatians
1, 172
1.1, 41, 107, 189, 230, 262, 319
1.4, 210
1.6, 275, 276
1.6f., 275
1.6ff., 40
1.8, 276
1.8f., 129, 269
1.10, 163
1.12, 189, 307
1.13, 98, 128, 147
1.14, 258
1.16, 122, 133, 135, 189, 307
1.20, 83, 189, 302
1.23, 98
1.24, 215
2, 172
2.2, 307
2.4, 31, 35, 123, 278, 291, 299
2.5, 187, 210
2.6, 31, 165, 166
2.7, 31, 133, 178, 189
2.9, 6, 27, 31, 40, 189, 254, 265
2.10, 25, 26, 217
2.11, 27, 30
2.14, 187
2.18, 212, 258
2.19, 115, 141
2.19f., 168
2.20, 48, 146, 167, 168, 250, 257, 263
3.1, 191
3.5, 321, 335, 345
3.9, 199
3.13, 168
3.13f., 180
3.15, 92, 112
3.16, 77, 200, 294
3.17, 112
3.19, 294
3.19–25, 118
3.21, 77, 115
3.26, 201
3.28, 201
3.29, 294
4.4, 59, 168, 223, 345
4.6, 58, 201
4.9, 286, 291
4.11, 295
4.12, 203
4.13ff., 315
4.14, 188
4.15, 315
4.19, 192
4.20, 215
4.22–31, 123
4.25, 123
5.1, 123
5.2, 246
5.2ff., 337
5.4, 286
5.6, 62
5.10, 275
5.12, 35, 271
5.13, 123
5.15, 256, 291
5.20, 199
5.22, 85, 190
5.22f., 44
5.23, 247
5.24, 315
5.24f., 168
6.1, 187, 247, 340
6.7, 236
6.9, 128
6.10, 241
6.11, 246
6.14, 283
6.14f., 168
6.15, 173, 174
6.16, 264
6.17, 140
6.18, 187

Ephesians
1.3, 59
1.13, 81
1.14, 81
2.12, 112
3.16, 146
4.22, 146
4.24, 146
4.30, 81
5.2, 99
5.15, 256
5.22–33, 273
6.8, 160
6.14–17, 251
6.19, 191
6.20, 178

Philippians
1.1, 33, 134
1.4, 190
1.6, 74
1.7, 81, 191
1.8, 76, 83
1.10, 71, 74
1.14, 144, 258
1.18, 190
1.20, 268
1.21, 146, 159
1.23, 155, 158, 168
1.25, 85
1.28, 100
1.29f., 219
1.30, 215
2, 224
2.1, 59, 344
2.2, 342
2.6, 247
2.6ff., 246
2.6–11, 132, 223, 224
2.7, 223
2.14, 252
2.16, 74, 295
2.17, 99, 239–40
2.20, 300
2.22, 219
2.25, 240
2.26f., 301
2.27, 190
2.30, 240
3.1, 233
3.2, 256, 285
3.2f., 35
3.4, 66
3.5, 293
3.10, 100, 139, 141, 269, 344
3.16, 267
3.17ff., 35
3.19, 287
3.21, 207, 285
4.2, 342
4.4, 342
4.5, 247
4.6, 300
4.7, 252
4.8, 186
4.9, 343
4.10–20, 219
4.11, 237
4.12, 237
4.15, 191, 218, 283
4.18, 99
4.19, 237
4.23, 187

Colossians
1.2, 199
1.5, 187
1.7, 199, 294
1.11, 85
1.13, 66
1.15, 47, 125, 133, 247
1.15–20, 132
1.19f., 177
1.23, 185
1.24, 62, 142, 240
1.25, 185
1.29, 295
2.7, 81
2.8, 256
2.15, 98
3.1, 337
3.4, 158
3.5, 199, 235
3.9, 146
3.12, 59, 247
3.13, 271
3.22, 219
3.25, 160
4.7, 199
4.7ff., 106
4.9, 199
4.10, 98
4.17, 256
4.18, 246

1 Thessalonians
1.1, 77
1.3, 295
1.5, 186, 187
1.6, 85, 187, 219
1.7, 56, 218
1.8, 56, 218
1.9, 199
1.10, 66
2.1–12, 248
2.2, 188, 282, 317
2.5, 76, 83, 235
2.8, 282
2.9, 282, 295, 300
2.10, 76, 83
2.13, 123
2.14, 219
2.16, 267
2.17, 165, 210, 258
2.18, 93, 246
3.3f., 219
3.5, 295
3.8, 301
3.12, 237
3.13, 71
4.8, 187
4.9, 233
4.9f., 219
4.10, 218
4.13, 63
4.15, 156, 267
4.17, 143, 309
5.1, 233
5.2, 74
5.5, 197
5.8, 251
5.9f., 159

INDEX OF ANCIENT SOURCES

5.11, 258, 342
5.12, 295
5.13, 342
5.23, 143, 187, 202, 343
5.24, 76, 199

2 Thessalonians
1.1, 77
1.4, 231, 301
1.4–10, 219
1.7, 307
2.2, 74, 176, 292
2.3, 197
2.7, 197
2.9, 93, 131, 321
2.10, 131
2.12, 187
3.2, 66
3.3, 76, 199
3.8, 295, 300
3.16, 343
3.17, 246

1 Timothy
1.12, 111
1.15f., 128
2.6, 168
2.7, 178
2.14, 273
3.16, 248
4.10, 199
4.12, 199
5.16, 199
6.12, 240
6.13, 240

2 Timothy
1.11, 178
2.20f., 137

Philemon
6, 344
7, 214
9, 178
10, 323
15, 210
18, 203
23, 98
25, 187

Hebrews
1.3, 132
3.1, 240
4.14, 240
6.4, 135
10.1, 132
10.23, 240
10.28, 59
11.1, 290
11.19, 66
13.20, 343
13.22, 342

James
1.1, 342
5.12, 76

1 Peter
1.1f., 345
1.3, 59
1.16, 203
3.7, 186
5.3, 84

2 Peter
1.13f., 151

1 John
2.20, 78
2.27, 78

Jude
9, 90
21, 193n.

Revelation
12.7, 315
12.9, 315
14.3, 311
19.7, 273
21.2, 273
21.4f., 174
21.9, 273
22.17, 273

Josephus

Antiquities
i.213, 83
iv.238, 296
iv.248, 296
vii.332, 220
xiii.214, 304
xiv.29, 303
xiv.151, 304
xiv.191, 304

Wars
i.127, 303
ii.138, 262
ii.146, 91
ii.308, 297
vii.349, 308

Philo

De Abr.
100, 272

De Cher.
46, 111

De Conf. Linguarum
129–31, 251

De Fuga et Inventione
150f., 80

De Gig.
25, 135

De Migr. Abr.
34f., 310
193, 137

De Mut. Nom.
27, 111
46, 111

De Somniis
i.26, 137
i.36, 308
i.148, 200
ii.248, 200

De Specialibus legibus
iii.1f., 310
iv.149, 107
iv.203–18, 197

De Virtutibus
76, 154

De Vita Mos.
i.69, 317
ii.139, 131

Legum Allegoriae
i.44, 111
ii.57, 154, 311
ii.59, 154
ii.67, 272
iii.59, 273

Quis Rer. Div. Her.
141–206, 226
191, 227

Quod Deterius Potiori Insidiari Solet
22f., 146
34, 191
170, 137
175, 311

Qumran

1QH
3.20f., 137
4.29, 137
6.19, 117
10.5, 137
10.14, 59
11.3, 137
17.14, 294

1QM
7.5f., 202
13.7, 294

1QpHab
12.7, 123

1QS
1.4f., 188
4.9, 117
8.5–10, 176
10.1–4, 78
11.22, 137

4Qflor.
i.11, 201

CD
2.12f., 129
6.13, 200
8.9, 200
13.7, 91
16.5, 315
19.22, 200

War Scroll
197

Apocrypha

Judith
8.25, 68
15.9, 73

Sirach
24.15, 99
35.11, 236
39.14, 99

Wisdom of Solomon
2.24, 274
3.5, 148
3.10, 90
7.21, 133
7.26, 125, 132
7.27, 133
9.1, 59
9.15, 151

Pseudepigrapha

Apocalypse of Abraham
23, 273

Apocalypse of Moses
xvii.1, 286
xxxvii.5, 310

Ascension of Isaiah
198
9.1, 150
9.2, 150
9.9–13, 150

2 Baruch
44.9, 148
44.12, 148
51.3, 125
51.7, 125
51.10, 125
67.6, 99
81.3, 148

3 Baruch
2.2, 309
15.2f., 236

1 Enoch
39.3f., 309
52.1, 309
69.6, 273

2 Enoch
7.1, 309
8, 309, 310
11, 309
17, 311
18, 309
22.8ff., 150
31.6, 273

4 Ezra
6.5, 79
8.57ff., 79
14.13f., 156

Life of Adam and Eve
ix.1, 286
xxxviii.1, 286

Psalms of Solomon
17.40f., 179

Testaments of the XII Patriarchs
14n.

Testament of Dan
6.10, 188

Testament of Issachar
4.1, 220
5.1, 220

Testament of Judah
24.1, 179

Testament of Levi
13.1, 220
18.9, 179

Testament of Reuben
4.1, 219

Testament of Simeon
4.5, 220

Talmud and Rabbinic Literature

B. Abodah Zarah
22b, 273

B. Hagigah
14b, 309

B. Ketuboth
8b, 61

B. Sanhedrin
111b, 198

B. Shabbath
88b, 101
146a, 273

B. Taanith
2a, 65
7a, 101

B. Yebamoth
103b, 273

B. Yoma
22b, 179
72b, 101, 102

Exodus Rabbah
xv.18, 201
xli.4(97c), 115

Leviticus Rabbah
xxxiv.9(131b), 236

Deuteronomy Rabbah
102
i.5, 101
i.6, 101

Merkabah
309

Midrash Psalms
18 [6] (69a), 173

M. Aboth
i.2, 220

M. Hagigah
2.1, 309

M. Kilaim
viii.2, 195

M. Makkoth
iii.1–9, 296
iii.2, 296
iii.10, 296
iii.12ff., 297

M. Megillah
4.10, 309

M. Menahoth
13.11, 226

M. Sanhedrin
6.1–6, 298

M. Sotah
3.3, 273

Sifre Numbers
140(52b), 114

Sifre Deuteronomy
27(71a), 67
32(73b), 317
48(84a), 138
117(96b), 198

Targum Onkelos
115

Greco-Roman Literature

Aelian
Hist. Animal.
III.7, 102

Aeschylus
Prometheus Vinctus
609ff., 191

Apuleius
Metamorphoses
xi.23, 311

Aristophanes
Birds
992–1021, 265

Aristotle
De Mirab. Auscult.
147(845b), 102
Nicomachean Ethics
IV.v.(11) 1125b, 246
Politics
i.9(1257AB 1258A), 103
i.9.2(1257B), 103
1318b.33, 255n.
Rhetoric
III.3.4, 236

Cicero
De Finibus
II.26, 323
II.85, 323
De Oratore
2.65(261), 236
In Verrem
5.62 (162), 297
5.66 (170), 297
Tusc. Disp.
I.22, 137
I.52, 137

Corpus Hermeticum
i.26, 154
x.18, 154
xi.30, 306
xiii.1, 240
xiii.5, 146
xiii.15, 151
xiii.22a, 239

Dio Chrysostom
8.15ff., 185

Diodorus Siculus
iv.43.5, 185

Dionysius of Halicarnassus
Ant. Rom.
vii.18.2, 64

Epictetus
II.vii.3, 145
II.viii.14, 145, 202
II.xix.24, 191
III.ix.10, 211
III.ix.14, 320
III.xxii.69, 295
III.xxiv.64ff., 295
III.xxiv.65, 185
IV.viii.25, 320
IV.xi.19, 211

Euripides
Iphigeneia in Tauris
254, 197

Firmicus Maternus
de Err. prof. Rel.
22, 79

Hadrian
Historia Augusta
xxv, 154

Herodotus
ii.114, 274
iii.71, 256

Homer
Iliad
ii.570, 1
xiii.664, 1

Horace
Carmina
III.ix.24, 204

Marcus Aurelius
viii.27, 137

Livy
x.9, 297
xlv.30, 219

INDEX OF ANCIENT SOURCES

Lucian
Hermotimus
7, 154
59, 103
Peregrinus
13, 103
Piscator
17, 124
Oxyrhynchus Papyri
I.32, 106
Pausanias
II.iii.7, 2
Philostratus
Life of Apollonius
i.13, 103
Plato
Alcibiades I
124C, 338
Charmides
158D, 338
Cratylus
403B, 153
Gorgias
523, 153
524, 153
Ion
532D, 279
Phaedo
67DE, 153
81C, 153
Phaedrus
234CDE, 320
244A, 167
Protagoras
310E, 87
313CD, 103
Republic
x(614–21), 309
ix.577B, 153
ix.589A, 145
Symposium
212, 290
Plutarch
Aemilius
32, 138
Alexander
25, 235
Aratus
XVI, XVII (1034), 1n.
Caesar
57, 246
Pericles
39, 246
Sertorius
25, 246
Seneca
Epistles
lxxi.25ff., 139
Sophocles
Philoctetes
218, 131
Strabo
ix.419, 219
Sylloge Inscriptionum Graecarum
804.30f., 316
1170.31f., 316
Tacitus
Hist.
iii.86, 220
Thucydides
viii.7, 1n.
Virgil
Aeneid
i.630, 61
Xenophon
Anabasis
IV.ii.23, 225
Cyropaedia
IV.i.6, 229
Hiero
vi.5, 207
Memorabilia
I.vi.12, 282
III.x.5, 247

Early Christian Literature

Acts of Peter and Paul
84, 148
Acts of Philip
141, 224
Augustine
Epistles
CCXI.2, 83–84
1 Clement
5, 185
5.6, 296
47.1, 22
Clementine Homilies
xx.19, 315
Ignatius
Romans
6.3, 140
Irenaeus
Against Heresies
III.7.1, 131
Jerome
Epistles
CXXI.x.4, 283
Justin
Apology
I.55.5, 68
I.56.2, 68
I.65.2, 343
Martyrdom of Peter
9, 236
Polycarp
ad Phil.
2.2, 22
3.2, 22
5.1, 22
6.2, 22
11.3, 22
Recognitions
x.61, 315
x.64, 315
Shepherd of Hermas
Similitudes
7.5, 68
Tertullian
Adversus Marcionem
V.1, 22
V.11, 22
V.12, 22, 202
De Pudicitia
13, 89